John Henry Walsh

The dog in health and disease;

Comprising the various modes of breaking and using him for hunting, coursing,

shooting, etc., and including the points or characteristics of all dogs, which are

entirely rewritten

John Henry Walsh

The dog in health and disease;
*Comprising the various modes of breaking and using him for hunting, coursing, shooting, etc.,
and including the points or characteristics of all dogs, which are entirely rewritten*

ISBN/EAN: 9783337814793

Printed in Europe, USA, Canada, Australia, Japan

Cover: Foto ©ninafisch / pixelio.de

More available books at **www.hansebooks.com**

IN HEALTH AND DISEASE.

COMPRISING THE VARIOUS MODES OF BREAKING AND USING HIM FOR
HUNTING, COURSING, SHOOTING, ETC., AND INCLUDING THE
POINTS OR CHARACTERISTICS OF ALL DOGS, WHICH
ARE ENTIRELY REWRITTEN.

By STONEHENGE,

EDITOR OF " THE FIELD,"
AUTHOR OF " THE GREYHOUND," ETC.

Fourth Edition.

LONDON:
LONGMANS, GREEN, AND CO.
1887.

PREFACE TO THE FOURTH EDITION.

———◇———

MORE than a quarter of a century has elapsed since I first attempted to describe the dog in his several varieties, together with the uses to which he is put in this country and the diseases which attack him. Until within the last ten years the societies formed in aid of this investigation have chiefly taken in hand the management of public shows of this animal, but recently special clubs have been formed which have undertaken to settle the points of the particular breeds which has been selected by them, and their descriptions have in each case been taken by me in lieu of those I had previously drawn up, even when I have not been able fully to agree with them.

I have also added descriptions of several breeds which have either come out from obscurity, as in the case of the Basset Hound, Welsh and Scotch Terriers, &c., or manufactured, as in that of the Irish Wolf-Hound. These additions are necessary to render complete any treatise on the dog in the present day.

The treatment of his diseases is also brought down to that of modern times.

STONEHENGE.

PREFACE.

———◇———

AMONG the various scientific and anecdotical writings in the English language on *The Dog*, it might be thought that the subject was exhausted, and that nothing remained to be done by the most careful observer of the habits and external forms of the varieties of this animal. But let any one seek for specific information upon several points connected with even well-marked and generally recognised kinds, and he will soon be brought to confess that he is lost in doubt and uncertainty. For instance, where shall we find a sufficient description of the spaniels and terriers, or of the various retrievers, for which such large sums are often given? Who will be able to discover, from any written account, the difference between the springer and the cocker, or between the Clumber and Sussex spaniels? Who, again, will tell us the colours and forms of the Skye and Dandie Dinmont terriers, or the characteristics of the English toy-terriers, pugs, and Maltese dogs? Yet there are thousands and tens of thousands who take a great interest in these animals, and who would spare neither money nor trouble to ascertain the exact properties of the variety to which each individual of their acquaintance belongs. Daniel, Youatt, and Richardson have all laboured hard to enlighten their readers upon the varieties of the canine species, and have no doubt done much towards the attainment of this end; but, as I before remarked, the deficiencies in their descriptions are patent to all.

It is true that the hound and the greyhound, the pointer and the setter, as well as many of the foreign varieties of the dog, have been favoured with special treatises, but beyond them the ground is almost untrodden, or else it is choked with weeds and rubbish which render it difficult to ascertain what is beneath them.

In the following pages I have been compelled to have recourse to the work of Mr. Youatt in the instances of some of the foreign dogs, both for the descriptions and also for the engravings which are contained in it.   At the time when he wrote, the Zoological Society of London possessed an extensive collection of dogs, which was made use of by him to great advantage ; and I can speak to the correctness of most of his illustrations, from having compared them with the originals soon after he first gave them to the public ; but unfortunately there is now no such collection in England. As far as possible, however, throughout the First Book the descriptions and illustrations are drawn from the life, the specimen selected being of the most perfect symmetry and of the purest breed within my reach.   For many of them I am indebted to gentlemen who have given up their best energies to improve the peculiar strain which has enlisted their attention, and for the facilities which they have afforded me I here beg to record my most sincere thanks.

BOOK I. contains the Natural History of the Dog, with a minute description of the varieties which are generally recognised.   The chief claims of this book rest upon its being a faithful transcript in writing of oral records which have been treasured up by the breeders of the dog in all its varieties, and which, being now made public, will render it comparatively easy in future to ascertain the position which any particular dog can claim, and how far it complies with the points which are attributed to it.

These records have been carefully collected; and I believe it will be found, that though some individuals may hold different views, yet that in each case that which I have presented is the one which is maintained by a large majority of those who have made the subject their particular study. It is impossible to attain a certainty of this in every instance; but should I be wrong, it can, at all events, be maintained that neither time, trouble, nor expense has been spared in arriving at it.

Book II. describes the best methods of breeding, rearing, breaking, and managing the dog, while in health, by means of appropriate food, exercise, and lodging. This division of the subject, therefore, embraces the entering and running of the greyhound; the breaking and working of shooting dogs; the entering and hunting of hounds; and the management of vermin terriers, toy, and house dogs.

Lastly, in the THIRD BOOK the most modern and successful treatment of the diseases to which the dog is subject is given at length, and in terms which will, it is hoped, be intelligible to all. My readers will, therefore, perceive that I have omitted no information at all likely to be interesting to the lover of *the dog* which a long experience and most extensive opportunities have enabled me to obtain.

STONEHENGE.

July 1st, 1859.

PREFACE TO THE THIRD EDITION.

—◇—

SINCE the First Edition of *The Dog* was published in 1859, his varieties have been studied, and their points minutely described, by a great number of breeders to an extent which was never contemplated before that time. As a consequence, I have been enabled to define them most minutely in the present edition, and I think no sufficiently known breed, either British or foreign, is omitted from the list. In the Second Book little or no change has been attempted, for the simple reason that there is no occasion for it, since the various uses to which the Dog is put in this country by the sportsman and the dog-fancier have not been altered during the interval which has elapsed.

The Third Book treats of his diseases, in which no great improvement has been effected since the publication of the Second Edition, and it is therefore printed as it then stood.

It is with some considerable satisfaction that I now present to my readers my original work on The Dog brought down to the level of the present day.

STONEHENGE.

June 10th, 1879.

CONTENTS.

———◇———

BOOK I.

THE NATURAL HISTORY, ZOOLOGICAL CLASSIFICATION, AND VARIETIES OF THE DOG.

———

INTRODUCTORY CHAPTER.

CHAPTER I.

WILD AND HALF-RECLAIMED DOGS, HUNTING IN PACKS.

CHAPTER II.

DOMESTICATED DOGS, HUNTING CHIEFLY BY THE EYE, AND KILLING THEIR GAME FOR THE USE OF THEIR MASTERS.

CHAPTER III.

DOMESTICATED DOGS, HUNTING BY THE NOSE, AND BOTH FINDING AND KILLING THEIR GAME ; COMMONLY KNOWN EITHER AS HOUNDS OR TERRIERS.

CHAPTER IV.

DOMESTICATED DOGS FINDING THEIR GAME BY SCENT, BUT NOT KILLING IT, BEING CHIEFLY USED IN AID OF THE GUN.

CHAPTER V.

PASTORAL DOGS AND THOSE USED FOR DRAUGHT.

CHAPTER VI.

WATCHDOGS AND HOUSE-DOGS.

CHAPTER VII.

TOY-DOGS.

CHAPTER VIII.

CROSSED BREEDS.

BOOK II.

THE BREEDING, REARING, BREAKING, AND MANAGEMENT OF THE DOG, IN-DOORS AND OUT.

———

CHAPTER I.

BREEDING.

CHAPTER II.

REARING.

CHAPTER III.

KENNELS AND KENNEL MANAGEMENT.

CHAPTER IV.

BREAKING AND ENTERING.

CHAPTER V.

THE EMPLOYMENT OF THE DOG IN COURSING, HUNTING, SHOOTING, ETC.

BOOK III.

THE DISEASES OF THE DOG AND THEIR TREATMENT.

CHAPTER I.

LIST OF ILLUSTRATIONS.

THE DOG.

BOOK I.

THE NATURAL HISTORY, ZOOLOGICAL CLASSIFICATION, AND VARIETIES OF THE DOG.

The Wolf, from a specimen in the Zoological Gardens.

INTRODUCTORY CHAPTER.

Origin—General Characteristics—Habitat—Varieties—F. Cuvier's Divisional Arrangement—Arrangement adopted by the Author.

FROM the earliest times we have reason to believe that the dog has been the faithful companion and assistant of man in all parts of the world, and his fidelity and attachment are so remarkable as to have become proverbial. Before the introduction of agriculture, it was by means of the hunting powers of this animal that man was enabled to support himself by pursuing the wild denizens of the forest; for though now, with the aid of gunpowder, he can in great measure dispense with the services of his assistant, yet, until the invention of that destructive agent, he was, in default of the dog, reduced to the bow and arrow, the snare, or the pitfall. The dog was also of incalculable service in guarding the flocks and herds from the depredations of the *Carnivora*, and even man himself was often glad to have recourse to his courage and strength in resisting the lion, the tiger, or the wolf.

Much has been written on the origin of the dog, and Pennant, Buffon, and other naturalists, have exhausted their powers of research and invention in attempting to discover the parent stock from which all are descended. The subject, however, is wrapped in so much obscurity as to baffle all their efforts, and it is still a disputed point whether the shepherd's dog, as supposed by Buffon and Daniel, or the wolf, as conjectured by Bell, is the progenitor of the various breeds now existing. Anyhow, it is a most unprofitable speculation, and, being unsupported by proof of any kind, it can never be settled upon any reliable basis. We shall not, therefore, waste any space in entering upon this discussion, but leave our readers to investigate the inquiry, if they think fit, in the pages of Buffon, Linnæus, Pennant, and Cuvier, and our most recent investigator, Professor Bell. It may, however, be observed that the old hypothesis of Pennant, that the dog is only a domesticated jackal, crossed with the wolf or fox, though resuscitated by Mr. Bell, is now almost entirely exploded; for while it accounts somewhat ingeniously for the varieties which are met with, yet it is contradicted by the stubborn fact that, in the present day, the cross of the dog with either of these animals, *if produced*, is incapable of continuing the species when paired with one of the same cross breed. Nevertheless, it may be desirable to give Mr. Bell's reasons for thinking that the dog is descended from the wolf, which are as follows:—

" In order to come to any rational conclusion on this head, it will be necessary to ascertain to what type the animal approaches most nearly, after having for many successive generations existed in a wild state, removed from the influence of domestication and of association with mankind. Now we find that there are several different instances of the existence in dogs of such a state of wildness as to have lost even that common character of domestication, variety of colour and marking. Of these, two very remarkable ones are the dhole of India and the dingo of Australia. There is, besides, a half-reclaimed race amongst the Indians of North America, and another also partially tamed in South America, which deserve attention. And it is found that these races, in different degrees, and in a greater degree as they are more wild, exhibit the lank and gaunt form, the lengthened limbs, the long and slender muzzle, and the great comparative strength which characterise the wolf; and that the tail of the Australian dog, which may be considered as the most remote from a state of domestication, assumes the slightly bushy form of that animal.

" We have here a remarkable approximation to a well-known wild animal of the same genus, in races which, though doubtless descended from domesticated ancestors, have gradually assumed the wild condition; and it is worthy of especial remark that the anatomy of the wolf, and its osteology in particular, does not differ from that of the dog in general, more than the different kinds of dogs do from each other. The cranium is absolutely similar, and so are all, or nearly all, the other essential parts; and, to strengthen still further the probability of their identity, the dog and wolf will readily breed together, and their progeny is fertile. The obliquity of the position of the eyes in the wolf is one of the characters in which it differs from the dog; and although it is very desirable not to rest too much upon the effects of habit on structure, it is not perhaps straining the point to attribute the forward direction of the eyes in the dog to the constant habit, for many successive generations, of looking forward to his master, and obeying his voice." *

Such is the state of the argument in favour of the original descent from the wolf, but, as far as it is founded upon the breeding together of the wolf and dog, it applies also to the fox, which is now ascertained occasionally to be impregnated by the dog; but in neither case, we believe, does the progeny continue to be fertile if put to one of the same cross, and as this is now ascertained to be the only reliable test, the existence of the first cross stands for nothing. Indeed, experience shows us more and more clearly every year, that no reliance can be placed upon the test depending upon fertile intercommunion, which, especially in birds, is shown to be liable to various exceptions. Still it has been supported by respectable authorities, and for this reason we have given insertion to the above extract.

* Bell's British Quadrupeds, pp. 196, 197.

GENERAL CHARACTERISTICS.

In every variety the dog is more or less endowed with a keen sight, strong powers of smell, sagacity almost amounting to reason, and considerable speed, so that he is admirably adapted for all purposes connected with the pursuit of game. He is also furnished with strong teeth, and courage enough to use them in defence of his master, and with muscular power sufficient to enable him to draw moderate weights, as we see in Kamtschatka and Newfoundland. Hence, among the old writers, dogs were divided into *Pugnaces, Sagaces,* and *Celeres;* but this arrangement is now superseded, various other systems having been adopted in modern times, though none perhaps much more satisfactory. Belonging to the division *Vertebrata,* class *Mammalia,* order *Feræ,* family *Felidæ,* and sub-family *Canina,* the species is known as *Canis familiaris,* the sub-family being distinguished by having two tubercular teeth behind the canines on the upper jaw, with non-retractile claws, while the dog itself differs from the fox with which he is grouped in having a round pupil in the eye instead of a perpendicular slit, as is seen in that animal.

The attempt made by Linnæus to distinguish the dog as having a tail curved to the left is evidently without any reliable foundation, as, though there are far more with the tail on that side than on the right, yet many exceptions are to be met with, and among the pugs almost all the bitches wear their tails curled to the left. The definition, therefore, of *Canis familiaris caudâ (sinistrorsum) recurvatâ,* will not serve to separate the species from the others of the genus *Canis,* as proposed by the Swedish naturalist.

HABITAT.

In almost every climate the dog is to be met with, from Kamtschatka to Cape Horn, the chief exception being some of the islands in the Pacific Ocean; but it is only in the temperate zone that he is to be found in perfection, the courage of the bulldog and the speed of the greyhound soon degenerating in tropical countries. In China and the Society Islands dogs are eaten, being considered great delicacies, and by the ancients the flesh of a young fat dog was highly prized, Hippocrates even describing that of an adult as wholesome and nourishing. In a state of nature the dog is compelled to live on flesh, which he obtains by hunting, and hence he is classed among the *Carnivora ;* but when domesticated he will live upon vegetable substances alone, such as oatmeal porridge, or bread made from any of the cereals, but thrives best upon a mixed diet of vegetable and animal substances ; and, indeed, the formation of his teeth is such as to lead us to suppose that by nature he is intended for it, as we shall hereafter find in discussing his anatomical structure.

VARIETIES OF THE DOG.

The varieties of the dog are extremely numerous, and, indeed, as they are apparently produced by crossing, which is still had recourse to, there is scarcely any limit to the numbers which may be described. It is a curious fact that large bitches frequently take a fancy to dogs so small as to be incapable of breeding with them ; and in any case, if left to themselves, the chances are very great against their selecting mates of the same breed as themselves. The result is, that innumerable nondescripts are yearly born, but as a certain number of breeds are described by writers on the dog or defined by "dog-fanciers," these "mongrels," as they are called from not belonging to them, are generally despised, and, however useful they may be, the breed is not continued. This, however, is not literally true, exceptions being made in favour of certain sorts which have been improved by admixture with others, such as the cross of the bulldog with the greyhound, the foxhound with the Spanish pointer, the bulldog with the terrier, &c., &c., all of which are now recognised and admitted into the list of valuable breeds, and not only are not considered mongrels, but, on the contrary, are prized above the original strains from which they are descended. An attempt has been made by M. F. Cuvier to arrange these varieties under three primary divisions, which are founded upon the shape of the head and the length of the jaws ; these being supposed by him to vary in accordance with the degree of cunning and scenting powers which the animal possessing them displays. The following is his classification, which in the main is correct, and I shall adhere to it with trifling alterations in the pages of this book.

F. Cuvier's Divisional Arrangement.

I.—MÂTINS.

Characterised by head more or less elongated; parietal bones insensibly approaching each other; condyles of the lower jaw placed in a horizontal line, with the upper molar teeth, exemplified by—

Skull of Dingo.

SECT. 1. *Half-reclaimed dogs*, hunting in packs; such as the dingo, the dhole, the pariah, &c.

SECT 2. *Domesticated dogs*, hunting in packs, or singly, but using the eye in preference to the nose; as, for instance, the Albanian dog, deerhound, &c.

SECT. 3. *Domesticated dogs*, which hunt singly, and almost entirely by the eye. Example: the greyhound.

II.—SPANIELS.

Characteristics.—Head moderately elongated; parietal bones do not approach each other above the temples, but diverge and swell out, so as to enlarge the forehead and cavity of the brain.

SECT. 4. *Pastoral dogs*, or such as are employed for domestic purposes. Example: shepherd's dog.

SECT. 5. *Water dogs*, which delight in swimming. Examples: Newfoundland dog, water-spaniel, &c.

SECT. 6. *Fowlers*, or such as have an inclination to chase or point birds by scenting only, and not killing. Examples: the setter, the pointer, the field-spaniel, &c.

Skull of Spaniel.

SECT. 7. *Hounds*, which hunt in packs by scent, and kill their game. Examples: the foxhound, the harrier, &c.

SECT. 8. *Crossed breeds*, for sporting purposes. Example: the retriever.

III.—HOUSE DOGS.

Characteristics.—Muzzle more or less shortened; skull high; frontal sinuses considerable; condyle of the lower jaw extending above the line of the upper cheek teeth. Cranium smaller in this group than in the first and second, in consequence of its peculiar formation.

Skull of Mastiff.

SECT. 9. *Watch dogs*, which have no propensity to hunt, but are solely employed in the defence of man or his property. Examples: the mastiff, the bulldog, the pug dog, &c.

As before remarked, this division is on the whole founded on natural laws, but there are some anomalies which we shall endeavour to remove. For instance, the greyhound is quite as ready to hunt in packs as any other hound, and is only prevented from doing so by the hand of his master. The same restraint keeps him from using his nose, or he could soon be nearly as good with that organ as with the eye. So also Cuvier defines his sixth section as "having an inclination to chase and point *birds*," whereas they have as great, and often a greater, desire for hares and rabits. Bearing, therefore, in mind these trifling defects, we shall consider the dog under the following heads :—

CHAP. I. Wild and half-reclaimed dogs, hunting in packs.

CHAP. II. Domesticated dogs, hunting chiefly by the eye, and killing their game for the use of man.

CHAP. III. Domesticated dogs, hunting chiefly by the nose, and both finding and killing their game.

CHAP. IV. Domesticated dogs, finding game by scent, but not killing it ; being chiefly used in aid of the gun.

CHAP. V. Pastoral dogs, and those used for the purposes of draught.

CHAP. VI. Watch dogs, house dogs, and toy dogs.

CHAP. VII. Crossed breeds, retrievers, &c.

The Dingo (Youatt).

CHAPTER I.

WILD AND HALF-RECLAIMED DOGS, HUNTING IN PACKS.

1. The Dingo—2. The Dhole—3. The Pariah—4. The Wild Dog of Africa—
5. The North and South American Dog—6. Other Wild Dogs.

I.—THE DINGO.

IT is upon the great similarity between these wild dogs and the
wolf or fox that the supposition is founded of the general descent
of the domesticated dog from either the one or the other. After
examining the portrait of the dingo, it will at once be seen that
it resembles the fox so closely in the shape of its body, that an
ordinary observer could readily mistake it for one of that species,
while the head is that of the wolf. The muzzle is long and

pointed, the ears short and erect.   Height about 24 inches, length
30 inches.   His coat is more like fur than hair, and is composed
of a mixture of silky and woolly hair, the former being of a deep
yellow, while the latter is grey.   The tail is long and bushy, and
resembles that of the fox, excepting in carriage, the dingo curling
it over the hip, while the fox trails it along the ground.*   While
in his unreclaimed state this dog is savage and unmanageable, but
is easily tamed, though even then he is not to be trusted, and
when set at liberty will endeavour to escape.   Many dingoes have
been brought to this country, and some of its crosses with the
terrier have been exhibited as hybrids between the dog and fox,
which latter animal they closely resemble, with the single exception of the pendulous tail.   Whenever, therefore, a specimen is
produced which is said to be this hybrid, every care must be taken
to ascertain the real parentage without relying upon the looks
alone.

II.—THE DHOLE.

The native wild dog of India, called the dhole, resembles the
dingo in all but the tail, which, though hairy, is not at all bushy.
The following is Captain Williamson's description, extracted from
his "Oriental Field Sports," which is admitted to be a very
accurate account by those who have been much in India:—"The
dholes are of the size of a small greyhound.   Their countenance
is enlivened by unusually brilliant eyes.   Their body, which is,
slender and deep-chested, is thinly covered by a coat of hair of a
reddish_brown or grey colour.   The tail is dark towards its extremity.   The limbs are light, compact, and strong, and equally
calculated for speed and power.   They resemble many of the
common pariah dogs in form, but the singularity of their colour
and marks at once demonstrate an evident distinction.   These
dogs are said to be perfectly harmless if unmolested.   They do
not willingly approach persons, but, if they chance to meet any
in their course, they do not show any particular anxiety to escape.
They view the human race rather as objects of curiosity than
either of apprehension or enmity.   The natives who reside near

* The engraving of the dingo was taken from an animal in confinement, in which
state the tail is seldom curled upwards.

the Ranochitty and Katcunsandy passes, in which vicinity the dholes may frequently be seen, describe them as confining their attacks entirely to wild animals, and assert that they will not prey on sheep, goats, &c.; but others, in the country extending southward from Jelinah and Mechungunge, maintain that cattle are frequently lost by their depredations. I am inclined to believe that the dhole is not particularly ceremonious, but will, when opportunity offers and a meal is wanting, obtain it at the expense of the neighbouring village. The peasants likewise state that the dhole is eager in proportion to the animal he hunts, preferring the elk to any other kind of deer, and particularly seeking the royal tiger. It is probable that the dhole is the principal check on the multiplication of the tiger; and although incapable individually, or perhaps in small numbers, to effect the destruction of so large and ferocious an animal, may, from their custom of hunting in packs, easily overcome any smaller beast found in the wilds of India."

Unlike most dogs which hunt in packs, the dholes run nearly mute, uttering only occasionally a slight whimper, which may serve to guide their companions equally well with the more sonorous tongues of other hounds. The speed and endurance of these dogs are so great as to enable them to run down most of the varieties of game which depend upon flight for safety, while the tiger, the elk, and the boar diminish the numbers of these animals by making an obstinate defence with their teeth, claws, or horns, so that the breed of dholes is not on the increase.

III.—THE PARIAH.

This is the general name in India for the half-reclaimed dogs which swarm in every village, owned by no one in particular, but ready to accompany any individual on a hunting excursion. They vary in appearance in different districts, and cannot be described very particularly; but the type of the pariah may be said to resemble the dhole in general characteristics, and the breed is most probably a cross with that dog and any accidental varieties of domesticated dogs which may have been introduced into the respective localities. They are almost always of a reddish brown colour, very thin and gaunt, with pricked ears, deep chest, and tucked-up belly. The native Indians hunt the tiger and wild boar, as well as every species of game, with these dogs, which have good noses and hunt well; and though they are not so high-couraged as our British hounds, yet they often display considerable avidity and determination in "going in" to their formidable opponents.

IV.—THE EKIA, OR WILD AFRICAN DOG.

The native dogs of Africa are of all colours, black, brown, and yellow, or red; and they hunt in packs, giving tongue with considerable force. Though not exactly wild, they are not owned by any individuals among the inhabitants, who, being mostly Mahometans, have an abhorrence of the dog, which by the Koran is declared to be unclean. Hence they are complete outcasts, and obtain a scanty living either by hunting wild animals where they abound, or, in those populous districts where game is scarce, by devouring the offal which is left in the streets and outskirts of the towns. The *Ekia*, also called the *Deab*, is of considerable size, with a large head, small pricked ears, and round muzzle. His aspect in general resembles that of the wolf, excepting in colour, which, as above remarked, varies greatly, and in the tail, which is almost always spotted or variegated. These dogs are extremely savage, probably from the constant abuse which they meet with, and they are always ready to attack a stranger on his entrance into any of the villages of the country. They are revolting animals, and unworthy of the species they belong to.

V.—THE NORTH AND SOUTH AMERICAN DOGS.

A great variety of the dog tribe is to be met with throughout the continent of America, resembling in type the dingo of Australia, but appearing to be crossed with some of the different kinds introduced by Europeans. One of the most remarkable of the South American dogs is the *Alco*, which has pendulous ears, with a short tail and hog-back, and is supposed to be descended from the native dog found by Columbus; but, even allowing this to be the case, it is of course much intermixed with foreign breeds. The North American dogs are very closely allied to the dingo in all respects, but are generally smaller in size, and are also much crossed with European breeds. In some districts they burrow in the ground, but the march of civilisation is yearly diminishing their numbers throughout the continent of America.

VI.—OTHER WILD DOGS.

Many other varieties of the wild dog are described by travellers, but they all resemble one or other of the above kinds, and are of little interest to the general reader.

CHAPTER II.

DOMESTICATED DOGS, HUNTING CHIEFLY BY THE EYE, AND KILLING THEIR GAME FOR THE USE OF THEIR MASTERS.

1. The Smooth English Greyhound—2. The Deerhound and Rough Greyhound—3. The Irish Greyhound or Wolf-Dog—4. The Gazehound—5. The French Mâtin—6. The Hare-Indian Dog—7. The Albanian Greyhound—8. The Grecian Greyhound—9. The Russian Greyhound—10. The Turkish Greyhound—11. The Persian Greyhound—12. The Italian Greyhound.

I.—THE SMOOTH ENGLISH GREYHOUND.

THIS beautiful animal is by many considered to be the original of all our domestic breeds, dividing that honour with the bulldog and mastiff. The authorities for these theories are chiefly founded on ancient statues and paintings, aided by written descriptions. At all events, the greyhound of these islands can be traced to the time of King Canute, who confined his use to the nobility by statute. Buffon considers him to be identical with the French mâtin, and very probably there was little difference between the two breeds; but we possess no reliable painting or statue of either of a very early date, and a written description will seldom serve to identify a species, while a definition of the variety is generally wholly beyond its powers. For these reasons, therefore, I shall not attempt to go into the history of the greyhound, nor shall I claim for it any greater antiquity than justly belongs to the bulldog, the mastiff, the terrier, or the turnspit.

Until the passing of the present game-laws, the use of the greyhound in coursing the hare was confined in England to the class who could qualify for that purpose by the possession of £100 a year in land; and meetings for that purpose were held only at Swaffham, Lowth, and Ashdown, where clubs were formed, consisting of a limited number of noblemen and county gentlemen. Between 1840 and 1850, however, the public at large began to think themselves entitled to share in the sport, many tenant farmers and professional men, without possessing the fee-simple of a single acre, beginning to keep and use the greyhound. Gradually coursing has become more and more general and popu-

Captain Daintree's " KING COB."

lar, and, in the present day, wherever there is an area of tolerably level country suited to the preservation and coursing of hares, meetings are instituted, either for the use of the public in general, or for clubs, which almost in all cases are open to all classes of good sportsmen. As a consequence, fully five thousand greyhounds are

B

now kept in the United Kingdom, independently of the rising generation of saplings, which is almost as numerous. This increase of the popularity of coursing is due—(1) to the small cost of keeping the greyhound in comparison with that of the racehorse; (2) to the love of competition which is inherent in the "Britisher;" (3) to the modern style of farming, which, by throwing numberless small fields into large ones, and abolishing high "ridge and furrows," has facilitated the pursuit of the hare in proportion to the retrogression in the elements necessary for partridge shooting. The result is, that in almost all districts even those tenant farmers who are forbidden to shoot are allowed to course, but generally they avail themselves of this permission not to kill the hares for direct "currant jelly" objects, but to afford practice in private for the greyhounds, which require it before being submitted to the eye of the public coursing judge. No one who enters keenly into the rivalry existing at Newmarket, Altcar, or Ashdown will condescend to attend a "private day," but will gladly kill a few hares when he is getting his dogs ready for either of these meetings or their less fashionable rivals; and hence, though there is some little difference between the public and the private greyhound, I shall mainly confine my description to the former.

The *Public Greyhound*, then, should combine a frame capable of giving the highest degree of speed which is consistent with the form to "stay a course," and with the capability of stopping this speed sufficiently quickly to follow the turns of the hare without too great a loss of ground. These three qualities must be combined in the dog to obtain success, for if any one is absolutely absent, or even proportionately so as compared with the best average, the chance of winning the series of courses necessary to get through a stake is extremely small. Beyond these qualities, to the possession of which the shape of each individual is to a great extent a reliable guide, there must also be an inherent nervous or mental power which shall give the desire to display them. These nervous qualities are, without doubt, to a limited extent dependent on the size of certain parts of the brain; but we are not, I think, in possession of sufficient data to lay down laws with reference to these organs, and in practice we must be content with apportioning a smaller value to the form and shape of the head than it deserves from theoretical principles. Undoubtedly a bad shape is more likely to succeed, in competition with an average dog, when combined with a highly organised brain and a determined will, than the very best form of propelling powers if there is no desire accompanying them to lay these powers out. But practically no one can with certainty foretell from the examination of the head whether or not, in any particular instance, its possession will develop a strong will or not; and consequently it is idle to lay too great a stress upon that which cannot be defined with exactitude. The following points are therefore laid down on the above basis:—

	VALUE		VALUE
Head,	10	Hind-quarters and legs,	20
Neck,	10	Feet,	15
Chest, shoulders, and forelegs,	20	Tail,	5
Loin, side, and back ribs,	15	Colour and coat,	5
		Total,	100

The *head* should be wide between the ears, measuring in a full-sized dog 14½ inches in circumference between the eyes and ears. It is generally described as snake-like, that is to say, it should be broad and flat, not arched or domed, as is the case with many other breeds. Many of the old-fashioned strains had very narrow heads, but either the cross with the bulldog or the selection of wide-headed sires and dams has led to the general possession of wide heads by the best strains of modern times. As a consequence, great determination and cleverness are displayed, and the puppy now is often at his best before the end of his first season, whereas in olden times it was often two or three years before the old-fashioned dog could be relied on either for working or killing powers. Those celebrated bitches " Mocking Bird " and " Cerito " were useless in their first seasons, but such an occurrence is now very rare, and at the end of half a dozen courses the young greyhound is as clever in turning and killing as he ever will be. This is especially the case with the bitch puppy, who is generally at her best some months before her brother of the same litter. The *jaws* should be long and lean, tapering to a point, and of even length, neither " pig-jawed " nor underhung. Good strong *teeth*, meeting level together, are also to be desired. As to the *eye*, it should be keen, bright, and of moderate size, the colour varying according to that of the coat. The *ears* are now always falling, small in size, thin and soft in texture. Formerly several good strains were noted for prick ears, but such a formation is now extremely rare, and as no fashionable strain exhibits it, breeders ignore it altogether. The last strain of note in which the prick ear was shown was that of Dr. Brown, the celebrated Scotch owner of "Heather Jock," "Rufus," &c.

The *neck*, like the head, has been compared to that of another animal, but here a bird was selected, the choice falling on the long, smooth, and rounded neck of the *drake*. The resemblance is not very striking, as the greyhound never displays anything approaching to such a formation; and, indeed, with the exception of the camelopard, there is no well-known quadruped whose neck is at all like that of the drake. Very little, therefore, is learnt by this simile; and all that can be said is, that in a well-formed greyhound the neck should be long, thin, and rounded towards its junction with the head, *as compared with its fellows;* but to expect in reality a drake's neck is out of the question. The length should be as nearly as may be the same as that of the head, but it is difficult to measure either to half an inch; two persons seldom agree as to the exact point of demarcation between the head and neck, and there is still greater difficulty in defining the point of junction of the neck with the shoulders.

The *chest*, *shoulders*, and *forelegs* must be considered together, as they are all dependent on one another for their respective actions. The chest must have a sufficient volume to contain the lungs and heart in full development, since these organs are required for staying power; but this volume must be obtained in depth rather than in width, because a very wide chest impedes the play of the shoulders on the thereby necessarily rounded ribs, and makes the gallop short, and the power of turning limited and slow. Hence the breeder selects his sires and dams with the chest of this formation, that is to say, moderately wide and deep, without being so keel-shaped as to strike any slightly prominent part of the ground, such as a large stone or heavy, rounded, and hard clod of earth. The *shoulder*, *arm*, and *leg* constitute what is called the *fore-*

quarter, and it will be found that these generally go together in shape. Thus, if the shoulder-blade is long and placed obliquely (or at an angle of 45 degrees with the ground), the true arm is also long and slanting, and the lower arm of average length. This is the desired shape, combined with the middle position of the elbow, that is to say, neither turned in nor out ; and with this shape it may be expected that the forelegs will be well thrust forward in the gallop, and the shoulder-blade will play freely on the ribs, not being confined by an inturned elbow, while an elbow turned out is almost as bad, by leading to a weak support during the time that the hind-legs are brought forward, and to a scrambling action in consequence of this defect. A greyhound " tied at the elbow," as the former malformation is technically named, is almost invariably useless, and is to be carefully avoided, as indeed is one with an out-turned elbow, but the latter is most frequently the result of muscular rheumatism, and is not often congenital, as is the case with the former. Let the courser, therefore, be careful to choose his greyhound with long oblique shoulder-blades, well clothed with muscle, but not too heavily so, and with long true or upper arms ; this combination ensuring that the joint of the shoulder shall be high and prominent, though not abnormally so. Then, again, let him see that the elbows are so set as to work in a plane parallel with that of the whole body, and that the lower (or fore) arm is long, strong in bone, and well clothed with muscle. The knee answers to the wrist of man, and should be wide and deep, that is to say, of full size, without being enlarged by disease, as is often seen in rickety puppies. Lastly, the pastern bones should be short and strong, not quite so large as the knees, but very nearly so. This is a point of the greatest importance, as the small and weak pastern very often gives way in a severe turn. Many coursers require this joint to be nearly or quite upright, but this is, I think, a mistake, for there is then a want of elasticity, which increases the risk of accident, and a slight departure forwards from the straight line of the arm is the desirable formation of the pastern, in my judgment.

The *loin, side, and back ribs* consist of the bony frame compounded of the vertebræ and the vertebral ends of the ribs, together with the muscles attached to them, constituting a more or less square mass, which has been compared to a *beam*, supported on sides very slightly rounded outwardly, or nearly flat like the *bream*. These two comparisons with other objects in nature are more correct than those to which I have already alluded, because the old-fashioned beam-like back, now very seldom seen, is really almost as if cut out of wood, so square and straight are the edges. Without doubt this beam-like back gives enormous strength, and when coursing was generally carried on in enclosed districts with high hedges, such a back was required for the enormous jumps which were often required to be cleared. Now-a-days, however, even when a fence does intervene, it is so low as almost to be taken in the dog's stride; and if the back is strong enough to give and maintain high speed on the flat, all the muscles beyond the amount necessary for that strength is so much dead weight, while experience tells the courser that the extra bulk interferes with rather than encourages great pace. With the solitary exception of "The Czar," son of "Foremost," and of a daughter of his owned by myself, I never saw great speed combined with a really beam-like back, but the combination in them was so marked as to show that the two may co-exist. Still the above cases must be regarded as exceptional, and the courser should in preference select a moderately wide and beam-like back, in which the muscles of the loin are strongly attached to the ribs above the shoulders, showing a prominent edge at the junction with the side. A very slight arch in the loin is, I think, to be desired, rather than a perfectly straight back, which again causes a departure from the type of the beam. As to the *side*, no comparison can be more true than that with the bream, which exactly resembles the amount of convexity required. The *back ribs* are only wanted to be deep for constitutional reasons, and regardless of locomotive purposes, for they are always deep enough for the attachment of muscles. It is, however, found by experience that a dog of any kind—and indeed a horse also—with short back ribs is almost always delicate in constitution, and hence deep back ribs are demanded in both of these animals, and with excellent reason.

The *hind-quarters* consist of the upper or true thigh, the lower thigh, connected together by the stifle-joint, the mass of muscle known as the quarter or buttock, the hock-joint, and the leg.

Between the hind-quarters and the loin are the hips or "couples," and these in fact constitute the posterior attachment of the muscles of the loins, whose volume is in great measure determined by the width of the hips. For this reason wide ragged hips are to be desired, and especially in the dog, whose body, being heavier alto- gether than that of the bitch, must have proportionately stronger propellers. A slight fall from the top of the hip to the haunch- bone on each side of the tail is, I think, the most desirable line of formation. Proceeding with our examination of the hind-quarters, we find that for high speed there must be an increase of length in the upper and lower thighs beyond the average, constituting what is called "well-bent hind-legs;" but not only must this shape exist, but the stifle-joints must also be set widely apart, or the hind-legs cannot be thrust forward in the gallop, which will be consequently weak and scrambling. "King Cob," whose portrait illustrates this breed, was remarkable for the possession of widely- spread stifles, and his grandson, "Bedlamite," possessed them in a still higher degree. To this probably was owing the extraordinary combination of working power and high speed possessed by "King Cob" and "Bedlamite," notably the latter, and most of their descendants; while "Figaro," son of "King Cob," and "Jacobite," son of "Bedlamite," in whom the stifles were not so widely set, both displayed even greater speed, but their working powers were so limited that they ran out many yards at every turn. After insisting on the length of the thighs, both upper (or true) and lower, the next thing is to see that they are well clothed with muscle; but in the upper thigh-bone, the mass covering the bone, and called the quarter or buttock, is often too bulky, leading to a dull, heavy style of gallop, and as a consequence to low compara- tive speed. This mass should naturally be wiry and firm rather than soft and spongy, though even this quality may be exaggerated by over-training; for a very hard, unyielding quarter is often an indication of the trained dog being "overworked." But the lower thigh can scarcely be too muscular, and this point should be care- fully examined by the connoisseur. The hocks, again, should be long and strong. They should be set and move in the same plane as the elbows, and should be nearly but not quite upright. Great length of hock is by no means conducive to a very high speed, but it enables its possessor to maintain a high rate for a longer time than a short hock will allow. The leg or part between the hock and foot, sometimes called the pastern, should be large in bone and sinew, and following the line of the back very slightly out of the perpendicular. I need scarcely remark that the hind-quarter is the chief propelling power, but it is greatly assisted by the loin in the stroke which it gives, the two together being really almost equally engaged in the thrust of the body forward, which is the essential feature in propulsion.

The *feet* are all equally important to propulsion, for if there are any of them defective, so as to give pain to their possessors, slight though it may be, during the gallop, the muscular powers are not duly exerted, even if that pain does not amount to the extent necessary to produce actual lameness. Before the time of training and actual coursing, the feet seldom are called on sufficiently to test their capabilities in this direction, but as soon as work begins and is carried to the required extent, the thin sole wears away and the dog becomes footsore. Hence the first desideratum is a hard horny covering to the pads and stopper, which latter should also be strongly connected to the back of the pastern, or it will be torn away during the turns, in which it greatly assists by grasping the earth. On this point, therefore, there is a full agreement among greyhound breeders, but on the exact shape of the foot most desirable there is a considerable difference of opinion. The question is, whether a cat-like foot with the toes well arched, and a set of pads arranged almost in a circle, as in the cat, is to be aimed at, or a more oval formation, with the toes less arched, such as exists in the hare. Most coursers prefer the former, but a long experi-ence leads me to think that they have often carried their desires in this direction too far, and that a foot supported almost entirely on the toes will break down sooner than one in which the central pad takes its due share of weight. Anything, however, is better than a flat, widely sprawling foot, such as generally is met with in puppies reared without a proper amount of liberty and its accom-panying exercise.

The *tail* in a well-bred greyhound is even more thin, taper, and bony than that of the *rat*, to which it is compared in the old rhyme. It should be large at the root, then suddenly tapering for an inch or two till it attains the size of a large thumb, after which it should gradually be reduced till it becomes as small as an average little finger.   In its whole length it should be covered with short hair, so as to show no fringe whatever.   It should fall close to the quarters for three-quarters of its length, after which it turns away from them and curves more or less upwards, sometimes forming a full circle, but generally less than three-fourths.   These points are only regarded as indications of a good breed.

The *colour and coat* are of so little importance as to be together only valued as equal to the tail, which is a higher indication of breeding than either of those points now under consideration. Whole colours are generally preferred, as being more pleasing to the eye, and not interfering with the apparent shape ; but the preference is seldom to such an extent as to cause the rejection of a well-made puppy because of its markings.   In the present day, white, more or less marked with black or blue, is very often met with on account of the successes of Mr. Campbell's " Scotland Yet," which celebrated bitch produced " Canaradzo," " Sea Foam," and " Sea Pink," and was grandam of " King Death," all white, or very nearly so, besides in a more remote degree scores of other winners of a similar colour.   For many years previously the prevailing colours were black, red, fawn, brindled or blue, with a small admixture of white, but since then the last-named colour has taken its full share of the honours of each year.   Brindle is, however, somewhat at a discount, in spite of the successes of " Patent " (a celebrated brindled sire) and his descendants; but still no one dreams of discarding a brindled puppy from his kennel simply for his colour. It has sometimes been alleged that the brindled greyhound owes his colour to a descent from the bulldog, but there is not the slightest reason for this opinion; indeed, the reverse is rather to be held, since in those cases where a bulldog cross is known to have been used, as in Sir James Boswell's " Jason," Mr. Loder's " Czar," and Mr. Hanley's dogs, which are fully described in Book II., Chapter I., under " Crossed Breeds," the brindled colour very rarely has appeared.   With regard to *coat*, a very high breed is evidenced by its shortness and silkiness of coat, and also by its total absence in the under parts; but these qualities are generally combined with softness and delicacy of constitution, and I regard with suspicion on that account their presence to any remarkable extent, preferring a moderately hard but short coat, generally diffused over the whole body except the belly, and protecting it from wet and cold.

Having now considered in detail the formation of every part of the body, it may impress their peculiar shapes upon the mind of the tyro if the old doggerel rhymes of the fifteenth century's date are once more quoted, subject to the modification which I have already suggested—

> " The head of a snake,
> The neck of a drake,
> A back like a beam,
> A side like a bream,
> The tail of a rat,
> And the foot of a cat."

Up to within the last thirty years each coursing district had its peculiar breed of greyhounds, best suited to the country over which it was used. Thus the Newmarket country required a fast and yet stout greyhound to run over its flats, great part of which was arable land, with coverts two or three miles apart. The undulating downs of Wiltshire and Berkshire, again, being almost entirely of grass, allowed a smaller and somewhat slower dog to succeed better than a larger and faster one over plough, which could not get up the severe slopes of Beacon Hill at Amesbury, or even the lower ones constantly met with at Ashdown, from Compton Bottom and other spots favoured in the memory of the courser. In Lancashire, again, the courses until lately were seldom severe, partly from the nature of the food of the hares, and partly from the short distance to covert. But now-a-days all this is altered, and a two or three mile course may be reckoned on at Altcar or Southport almost as certainly as at Ashdown or Newmarket, partly from the better feeding of the hares and partly from the introduction of fresh blood through the hares of the latter counties. As a consequence of these changes, and of the facilities afforded by the railways to the breeders of all parts of the country, such an interchange of these breeds has taken place that there is really no locality in which a strain peculiar to itself can be said to exist. Whether we take " Master M'Grath," as representing

Ireland, "Coomassie," as the best Newmarket winner, or "Cana-radzo" and "King Death," as the most successful from Scotland and the North of England, all are alike combinations of two or more different strains. The last-named are, it is true, only made up of two distinct strains, namely, the Lancashire in "Beacon" and the Scotch in "Scotland Yet," but the others are compounded of a much greater variety, chiefly, however, traceable to "King Cob," who was of true Newmarket and Bedfordshire blood. In making his choice, the young courser may, therefore, entirely dis-regard all but the individual greyhound from which his selections take their descent. Since the passing of the Ground Game Act hares have become so scarce in many of the old countries used for public coursing that a new plan has been adopted in order to keep these meetings up. This consists in enclosing by a hare-proof fence two or more hundred acres of grass, and supplying this area with hares bred in districts where coursing cannot be, or is not, carried on. This has encouraged the breeding of a very fast yet clever greyhound, generally descended in many lines from "King Cob," and in almost or quite as many from Scotch and Lancashire strains united in the late Mr. J. Campbell's kennel, by the union of Mr. Borron's "Bluelight" with his "Scotland Yet," of nearly pure Scotch blood. No modern dog has, however, pre-sented this union to a greater extent than "Master M'Grath," who had three lines of "King Cob" united with about equal pro-portions of the Scotch and Lancashire strains. Most of the win-ning dogs at these enclosed meetings are descended from "Cardinal York," a great grandson of "King Cob," combined with similar strains to those united to form "Master M'Grath." They have come chiefly through "Bab at the Bowster," descended from "Canaradzo," one of Mr. Campbell's best dogs—to produce "Bed-fellow," "Misterton," "Ptarmigan," "Marshal MacMahon," and "Bothel Park." Whether or no these dogs would have been able to compete with success in a more severe country cannot be settled, but there is no doubt that the fast Lancashire and Scotch strains of the members of the Altcar Club were able to hold their own at Amesbury and Ashdown twenty-five years ago, and there-fore it may be presumed that they would be able to do so now.

The further consideration of this variety of the dog, relating to its breeding, management, and use, will be considered under Part II.

II.—THE DEERHOUND AND ROUGH GREYHOUND.

The deerhound is a magnificent animal in size and symmetry of frame, the dog often standing 28 inches high at the shoulder; and though possessing almost as much lightness and elegance

L. WELLS

"CADER," a Deerhound of the pure Glengarry breed, 28 inches high, 34 inches in girth, bred by W. Meredith, Esq., Torrish, Sutherland.

of proportion as its congener the smooth greyhound, yet often weighing from 80 to 90 lbs., whereas the latter seldom exceeds 65 lbs. Until very recently the deerhound was invariably employed in aid of the deerstalker, but in modern days he is comparatively seldom so used, his place being taken by a collie or some nondescript, capable of being kept under such complete control as never to alarm the deer while being stalked. In most cases no dog whatever is taken out by the deerstalker, so that the deerhound has now become more ornamental than useful. But his magnificent shape and symmetry entitle him to be ranked among the dogs most suited to be *chiens de luxe*.

The deerhound follows the wounded deer, like all other dogs, by the eye in preference to the nose, but the moment he loses sight he drops his head and feels for the foot scent, which is generally aided by the blood which flows from the hit of the rifle-ball. Like the greyhound, he is silent in his pursuit, occasionally, like many of that variety, giving a low whimper, totally unlike the bell-like note of the true hound. When pure, he never attacks the head of his quarry, but lays hold of the hind-leg, or fastens on the flank, his instinct warning him that the horns of the deer are dangerous to him; but when crossed by the bull-dog, as was attempted by several breeders for the purpose of giving courage, the peculiar propensity of the latter "to go at the head" is displayed, and leads so frequently to the death of the dog that the cross has been abandoned. There is an unusual disparity in size between the sexes, amounting to nearly one-half in weight and to fully one-quarter in height. In general shape the deerhound closely resembles the greyhound, but there are a few points of difference which I shall proceed to describe.

The value of his points is as follows :—

	VALUE		VALUE
Head, nose, and jaw,	15	Quarters and legs,	7½
Ears and eyes,	5	Feet,	7½
Neck,	10	Colour and coat,	10
Chest and shoulders,	10	Symmetry,	5
Loin and back ribs,	10	Quality,	5
Elbows and stifles,	10	Tail,	5
		Total,	100

The *head* is slightly larger in proportion than that of the smooth greyhound, with larger and coarser jaws, but this latter part is rendered more striking by the coarser hair which covers the nose. The eyebrows also rise less than in the greyhound, the skull and nose in their upper outlines being nearly, though not quite, one straight line. The *jaws* are long and tapering, but not "snipey," the teeth being properly level, or very nearly so. The *nose* should be black at its tip, with open nostrils, but not widely so. There should be no fulness of the jaws below the eyes, and the muscles of the jaws must be well developed.

The *ears* of the deerhound should be like those of the greyhound, but they are usually carried a little higher than by that dog. As in him, pricked ears are sometimes seen, but they are to be considered as a defect. They are coated with fine, short, soft hair, except at the edges, which are fringed with longer hair. The *eyes* are fuller than those of the smooth greyhound. In the best strains they are hazel or blue.

The *neck* must be long enough to allow of the nose being carried low when the dog is at a fast pace, but not so "drake-like" as in the greyhound. It should be fine· and lean at the setting on of the head, but it soon widens to the depth of the shoulders.

The *chest* should be framed like that of the greyhound, the necessary capacity being obtained by depth rather than width. Still, as high speed is not so all-important, a little more width may be permitted. The girth is generally rather less in proportion to the height, a dog of 28 inches seldom girthing quite 32 inches, while a well-made greyhound of 26 inches will always measure 30 inches round the chest. The *shoulders* must be long, oblique, and muscular.

The *loin* is required to be of great strength, as the deerhound often has to hold a wounded stag by sheer force. Hence this is a most important point, and both width and depth should be regarded as all-important. Wide and somewhat ragged hips are necessitated for this development. The *back ribs* are seldom deep, and though, when present, they should be regarded with favour, their absence must not be penalised to the same extent as in those breeds where they may be expected as the rule rather than the exception. A straight back is often met with, but an arched loin is to be preferred.

The *elbows* should be set low down, so as to give a long true arm. They should neither be turned in nor out; but this extends to all breeds. The *stifles* should be set widely apart, and should be large both in width and depth. They should be set on high, so as to coincide with long upper thighs.

The *quarters* should be muscular, but not heavily so; in this part, however, the deerhound is seldom overdone. The lower *thighs* should be well clothed with muscle, exhibiting a large "calf." The *legs*, both before and behind, should be straight and bony, the pasterns being required to be large and strong.

The *feet* are generally rather long than cat-like, but the latter formation is generally desired by the deerstalker. My own opinion, as in the greyhound, is against the very round foot, with extremely arched toes. There should be plenty of hair on them, in any case.

The *colours* preferred by breeders are dark blue, fawn, grizzle, and brindled, especially the blue brindle in the order given above. There should be no white; but a small white star on the chest, or a white toe or two, should not be regarded as considerable defects. The fawn-coloured dog is preferred with dark brown tips to his ears, but many excellent strains are without this shade. The *coat* varies greatly in different strains, some having it as hard as in the wire-haired terrier, while in others it is intermediate between wool and silk, with a few hairs showing through. The body generally is clothed with this rough and almost shaggy coat, but there is no fringe on the legs and very little even on the tail. The jaws are furnished with a decided moustache, but the hair composing it should be so soft as to stand out in tufts, and not like a brush, as it is when the hair is hard, stiff, and wiry.

The *tail* should be long and tapering, slightly curved, but without any corkscrew twist.

III.—THE IRISH GREYHOUND OR WOLF-DOG.

This grand variety is now extinct, no one in the present day maintaining that he possesses a strain actually descended from the old stock. An attempt has, however, been made by several gentlemen to "resuscitate it," which appears to me a most absurd one; for whatever may be the result, the produce cannot be regarded as *Irish deerhounds*, but rather as a modern breed, to which any other name may be given except the one chosen for it. Of course the

Scotch deerhound is taken as the stock on which to graft greater size and power, and most probably this has been done, partly by the selection of very large specimens, and partly by crossing with the mastiff, or recently with the Great Dane. The result is, no doubt, the attainment of a small number of very fine animals, but there is great difficulty in keeping up the breed, even for the short time during which it has existed, as is generally the case with manufactured strains. Some of my readers may, however, like to see what is to be said by the most ardent of the breeders of this new strain, and I therefore insert a description published by Captain Graham in "The Country" of February 24, 1876, *in extenso*, as follows:—

THE IRISH WOLFHOUND, BY CAPT. GEORGE A. GRAHAM.

To do full justice to this subject is almost impossible, owing to the fact that there has been a generally received impression amongst modern writers that this noble breed of dog is entirely extinct. That the breed in its "original integrity" has apparently disappeared cannot be disputed, yet there can be equally little doubt that so much of the true breed is forthcoming, both in the race still known in Ireland as the "Irish wolfhound" (to be met with, however, in one or two places only) and in our modern deerhound, as to allow of the complete recovery of the breed in its pristine grandeur, with proper management, in judicious hands. It is a fact well known to all modern mastiff breeders who have thoroughly studied the history of their breed, that, until within the last thirty or forty years, mastiffs, as a pure race, had almost become extinct. Active measures were taken by various spirited individuals, which resulted in the complete recovery of the breed, in a form at least equal, if not superior, to what it was of yore.

Why should not, then, such measures be taken to recover the more ancient, and certainly equally noble, race of Irish wolfhounds? It may be argued that, the services of such a dog no longer being required for sport, his existence is no longer to be desired ; but such an argument is not worthy of consideration for a moment, for how many thousands of dogs are bred for which no work is provided, nor is any expected of them, added to which, the breed would be admirably suited to the requirements of our colonies. One after another the various breeds of dogs which had of late years more or less degenerated, as, for instance, mastiffs, fox-terriers, pugs, St. Bernards, collies, have become "the rage," and, in consequence, a vast improvement is observable in the numerous specimens shown from time to time. Let us, then, hope that steps may be taken to restore to us such a magnificent animal as the Irish wolfhound.

That we have in the deerhound the modern representative of the old Irish dog is patent; of less stature, less robust, and of slimmer form, the main characteristics of the original breed remain, and in very exceptional instances specimens "crop up" that throw back to and resemble in a marked manner the old stock from which they have sprung; for instance, the dog well known at all the leading shows (now for some years lost to sight) as champion Torrum. Beyond the facts that he required a somewhat lighter ear and still more massive proportions, combined with greater stature, he evidently approximated more nearly to his distant ancestors than to his immediate ones. The matter of ear here alluded to is probably only a requirement called for by modern and more refined tastes, as it is hardly likely that any very high standard as to quality or looks was ever aimed at or reached by our remote ancestors in any breed of dogs. Strength, stature, and fleetness were the points most carefully cultivated—at any rate, as regards those used in the pursuit and capture of large and fierce game.

It is somewhat remarkable that, whilst we have accounts of almost all the noticeable breeds, including the Irish wolfhound, there is no allusion to any such dog as the deerhound save in writings of a comparatively recent date.

The article or essay on the Irish wolfhound, written by Richardson in 1842, is, it is supposed, the only one on this subject in existence; and whilst it is evident to the reader that the subject has been most ably treated and thoroughly sifted by him, yet some of his conclusions, if not erroneous, are at least open to question. It is a matter of history that this dog is of very ancient origin, and was well known to and highly prized by the Romans, who frequently used him for their combats in the arena; and that he was retained in a certain degree of purity to within a comparatively recent period, when, owing to the extinction of wolves, and presumably to the indifference and carelessness of owners, this most superb and valuable breed of dog was unaccountably suffered to fall into a very neglected and degenerate state.

From the general tenor of the accounts we hear of this dog's dimensions and appearance, it is to be gathered that he was of considerably greater stature than any known race of dogs existing at present, and apparently more than equal to the destruction of a wolf.

It is an incontestable fact that the domestic dog, when used for the pursuit of ferocious animals, should be invariably larger and apparently more powerful than his quarry, as the fierce nature, roving habits, and food of the wild animal render him usually more than a match for his domesticated enemy, if only of equal size and stature. We know that the Russian wolfhounds, though equal in stature to the wolf, will not attack him single-handed; and wisely, for they would certainly be worsted in the combat.

The Irish wolfhound being used for both the capture and despatch of the wolf, it would necessarily have been of greyhound conformation, besides being of enormous power. When caught, a heavy dog such as a mastiff would be equal to the destruction of the wolf; but to obtain a dog with greyhound speed and the strength of the mastiff, it would stand to reason that his stature should considerably exceed that of the mastiff—one of our tallest as well as

c

most powerful breeds. The usual height of the mastiff does not exceed 30 inches; and, arguing as above, we may reasonably conclude that, to obtain the requisite combination of speed and power, a height of at least 33 inches would have been reached. Many writers, however, put his stature down as far exceeding that. Goldsmith states he stood 4 feet; Buffon states one sitting measured 5 feet in height; Bewick, that the Irish wolfhound was about 3 feet in height; Richardson, arguing from the measurements of the skulls of the Irish wolfhound preserved at the present time in the Royal Irish Academy, pronounced it his opinion that they must have stood 40 inches.

It is perfectly certain, from these and many other accounts, allusion to which want of space renders impossible, that the dog was of vast size and strength, and all agree in stating that, whilst his power was that of the mastiff, his form was that of the greyhound. The "Sportsman's Cabinet," a very valuable old book on dogs, published in 1803, which is illustrated with very good engravings after drawings from life by Renaigle, R.A., says—"The dogs of Greece, Denmark, Tartary, and Ireland are the largest and strongest of their species. The Irish greyhound is of very ancient race, and still to be found in some few remote parts of the kingdom, but they are said to be much reduced in size even in their original climate; they are much larger than the mastiff, and exceedingly ferocious when engaged." A very good and spirited drawing of this dog is given, which almost entirely coincides with the writer's conclusion as to what the Irish wolfhound was and should be, though a rougher coat and somewhat more lengthy frame are desirable. The dogs described in "Ossian" are evidently identical with the Irish wolfhound, being of much greater stature and power than the present deerhound. From these descriptions, and those given elsewhere, we may conclude that, in addition to the dog's being of great stature, strength, and speed, he was also clothed in rough hair. In support of this we find that in the present day all the larger breeds of greyhound are invariably rough and long as to coat.

Many writers have incorrectly confounded the Irish wolfhound with the Great Dane, though the two dogs vary entirely in appearance, if not so much in build. It seems more than probable, however, that the two breeds were frequently crossed, which may account for these statements. The late Marquis of Sligo possessed some of this breed, which he was in the habit (erroneously) of considering Irish wolfhounds.

Richardson was at very great trouble to get every information as to the probable height of this dog, but the conclusions arrived at by him (chiefly based on the lengths of the skulls measured by him) would seem to be decidedly wrong, for the following reasons:—He states "the skull is 11 inches in the bone;" to that he adds 3 inches for nose, skin, and hair, thus getting 14 inches as the length of the living animal's head. The head of a living deerhound, measured by him, is 10 inches, the dog standing 29 inches; he then calculates that the height of the Irish wolfhound would have been 40 inches, taking for his guide the fact that the 29 inches dog's head was 10 inches. This would appear to be correct enough, but the allowance of 3 inches for extras is absurd;

1½ inches are an ample allowance for the extras, and if the head is taken at 12½ inches the height of the dog will be reduced to 36 inches. Moreover, the measurement of 10 inches for the head of a 29 inches deerhound's head is manifestly insufficient, as the writer can testify from ample experience and frequent measurements. A deerhound of that height would have a head at least 11 inches; so, calculating on the same principles, the Irish skulls would have been from dogs that only stood 33½ inches. Richardson says that this skull is superior in size to the others, which would prove that the average must have been under 33½ inches, and we may safely conclude that the height of these dogs varied from 31 inches to 34 inches. In support of this view the writer would point to the German boarhound; this dog has retained his character from a very remote age, and as he is still used for the capture of fierce and large animals, the breed is not likely to have been allowed to degenerate. The height of this breed varies from 28 inches to 33 inches, the latter being probably the limit to which any race of dogs has been known to arrive. The writer has numerous extracts from various authors, and many engravings from pictures by artists, dating from the middle of the sixteenth century to the commencement of the present century; but want of space will not allow of their being introduced, though of much interest. From these sources it is gathered clearly that the dog was such as has been above stated; and from these varied accounts the following detailed conclusions as to the appearance and dimensions of the breed are arrived at, though perhaps they may not be considered as absolutely conclusive.

General Appearance and Form.—That of a very tall, heavy Scotch deerhound; much more massive and majestic looking; active, and tolerably fast, but somewhat less so than the present breed of deerhound; the neck thick in comparison to his form, very muscular and rather long.

Shape of Head.—Very long, but not too narrow, coming to a comparative point; nose not too small, and head gradually getting broader from the same evenly up to the back of the skull; much broader between the ears than that of present deerhound.

Coat.—Rough and hard all over body, tail, and legs, and of good length; hair on head long, and rather softer than that on body; that under the jaws to be long and wiry, also that over eyes.

Colour.—Black, grey, brindle, red, and fawn, though white and parti-coloured dogs were common, and even preferred in olden times.

Shape and Size of Ears.—Small in proportion to size of head, and half erect, resembling those of the best deerhounds; if the dog is of light colour a dark ear is to be preferred.

			Dogs.	Bitches.
Probable height at shoulder,	. . .	.	32 in. to 35 in.	28 in. to 30 in.
Girth of chest,	. . . .	.	38 ,, 44	32 ,, 34
Round fore-arm,	. . . .	.	10 ,, 12	8 ,, 9½
Length of head,	. . . .	.	12½ ,, 14	10½ ,, 11½
Total length,	. . . .	.	84 ,, 100	70 ,, 80
Weight in lbs.	. . . .	.	110 ,, 140	90 ,, 110

When Sir Walter Scott lost his celebrated dog Maida (which, by the way, was by a Pyrenean dog out of a Glengarry deerhound bitch), he was presented with a brace of dogs by Glengarry and Cluny Macpherson, both of gigantic size. He calls them "wolfhounds," and says, "There is no occupation for them, as there is only one wolf near, and that is confined in a menagerie." He was offered a fine Irish greyhound by Miss Edgeworth, who owned some of this breed, but declined, having the others. Richardson says—"Though I have separated the Irish wolf-dog from the Highland deerhound and the Scottish greyhound, I have only done so partly in conformity with general opinion, that I have yet to correct, and partly because these dogs, though originally identical, are now unquestionably distinct in many particulars."

As the rough Scotch greyhound is to the present deerhound, so is the deerhound to what the Irish wolfhound was!

It may be of interest to mention here that the last wolf is said to have been killed in 1710, but there is no accurate information as to the date. The height of the European wolf varies from 28 in. to 30 in., and he is, though of comparatively slight form, an animal of very great power and activity.

Richardson, being an enthusiast on the subject, and not content with simply writing, took measures to recover the breed. With much patience and trouble, he hunted up all the strains he could hear of, and bred dogs of gigantic size to which the strains now in existence can be distinctly traced. A gentleman of position and means in Ireland, deceased some six or eight years, possessed a kennel of these dogs, on the breeding of which he expended both time and fortune freely. They were, though not equal to the original dog, very fine animals. It has been ascertained beyond all question that there are a few specimens of the breed still in Ireland and England that have well-founded pretensions to be considered Irish wolfhounds, though falling far short of the requisite dimensions ; and, in concluding this paper, the writer would again earnestly urge that some decided action may be taken by gentlemen possessing both leisure and means to restore to us that most noble of the canine race —the Irish wolfhound.

Rednock, Dursley.

Since the year 1876 a club has been specially formed for the resuscitation of this breed, under the auspices of Captain Graham, and in the present year (1886) a class was made for their exhibition by the Kennel Club at their summer show—divided, as usual, between the two sexes. For these there were eighteen entries, but most of the male exhibits resembled the deerhound so closely, both in size and appearance, that they might just as well have appeared in that class. The bitches were generally of larger size than the corresponding sex of the deerhound, which is very much smaller than the dog, and this is probably due to the cross with the Great Dane, admittedly used for the purpose of increasing size. Thus Colonel Garnier's "Hecla" and Mr. Townsend's "Lufan of Ivanhoe" are by "Cedric the Saxon," a fine fawn-coloured Dane, both very large bitches; while Mr. Laloe's "M'Mahon," an own brother to them, is very little higher or heavier. With regard to their claim to be really descended from the old Irish wolf-dog, Captain Graham writes me that "the late Sir John Power of Kilfane had his breed in 1842, and that

The Irish Wolf-hound.

Mr. Mahony had the same strain about that time—that they were descended *closely* from Hamilton Rowan's celebrated 'Brian,' which he claimed to be *the last* of the old Irish wolf-dogs, descended, it is believed, from the O'Toole's dogs of 1815 or so. I knew Sir John Power well, and he remembered H. Rowan's dog, a great, rough, dark dog of the massive deerhound character. Of 'Kilfane Oscar' I now have a grandson, and there are one or two more in other parts of the country bred by me. 'Oscar' came to me from Sir Ralph Galway, who had him from Sir J. Power's son." It will thus be seen that Captain Graham claims to have in his possession lineal descendants of the genuine breed, but not pure, since they are of necessity crossed with the deerhound, or Great Dane, he not having possessed an example of each sex. If he could produce the breed in its purity, it would be extremely interesting from a natural history point of view; but as he cannot, it must be regarded as the nearest approach which he is able to make. Both the winners at the Kennel Club Show were bred by Captain Graham, and I have obtained an excellent portrait of the dog, from which my readers will be able to form their own opinions.

POINTS OF THE IRISH WOLFHOUND.

The following are the points of this breed as settled by the special club:—

1. *General Appearance.*—The Irish wolfhound should not be quite so heavy or massive as the Great Dane, but more so than the deerhound, which in general type he should otherwise resemble. Of great size and commanding appearance, very muscular, strongly though gracefully built, movements easy and active; head and neck carried high; the tail carried with an upward sweep, with a slight curve towards the extremity. The minimum height and weight of dog should be 31 inches and 120 lbs.; of bitches, 28 inches and 90 lbs. Anything below this should be debarred from competition. Great size, including height at shoulder and proportionate length of body, is the *desideratum* to be aimed at; and it is desired to firmly establish a race that shall average from 32 to 34 inches in dog, showing the requisite power, activity, courage, and symmetry.

2. *Head.*—Long, the frontal bones *very* slightly raised, and *very* little indentation between the eyes. Skull not too broad. Muzzle long and moderately pointed. Ears small, and greyhound-like in carriage.

3. *Neck.*—Rather long, very strong and muscular, well arched, with a dewlap or loose skin about the throat.

4. *Chest* very deep. Breast wide.

5. *Back.*—Rather long than short. Some arched.

6. *Tail.*—Long and slightly curved, of moderate thickness, and well covered with hair.

7. *Belly* well drawn up.

8. *Forequarters.*—Shoulders muscular, giving breadth of chest, set sloping. Elbows well under, neither turned inwards nor outwards. Leg forearm muscular, and the whole leg strong and quite straight.

9. *Hindquarters.*—Muscular thighs, and second thigh long and strong as in the greyhound, and hocks well let down and turning neither in nor out.

10. *Feet.*—Moderately large and round, neither turned in nor out. Toes well arched and closed. Nails very strong and curved.

11. *Hair.*—Rough and hard on body, legs, and head, especially wiry and long over eyes and under jaw.

12. *Colour and Markings.*—The recognised colours are grey, brindle, red, black, pure white, fawn, or any colour that approaches the deerhound.

13. *Faults.*—Too light or heavy a head, too highly arched frontal bone; large ears, and hanging flat to the face; short neck; full dewlap; too narrow or too broad a chest; sunken or hollow or quite straight back; bent forelegs, overbent fetlocks, twisted feet, spreading toes; too curly a tail, weak hindquarters, and general want of muscle; too short in body.

IV.—THE GAZEHOUND.

The gazehound of old writers is now extinct, and most probably has merged in the greyhound, if it ever differed from that breed of dogs. At all events, the accounts, both ancient and modern, of the gazehound are so indefinite as to be of little interest to any one. For myself, I confess that I am wholly ignorant of the subject.

V.—THE FRENCH MÂTIN.

In France, as well as in the neighbouring countries, a great variety of more or less greyhound-like dogs is kept for killing hares, in the most poaching way, as regarded from our point of view, coursing in English style not being carried on there, and also for aiding in killing the wolf. These dogs we should here regard as lurchers, but on the Continent they are called *mâtins*. It is admitted to be a very old breed, and is considered by F. Cuvier to be the originator of the greyhound and the deer-hound, but without affording the slightest proof. Pennant, on the contrary, regards it as a modern breed descended from the Irish wolf-dog.

VI.—THE INDIAN HARE-DOG.

This variety of the coursing division of dogs is thicker in shape than any of the others, and probably therefore not so fast, though from the quantity of hair covering the body it may be more greyhound-like when stripped than at first sight appears to be the

The Indian Hare-Dog (Youatt).

case. It is rarely found in the present day in a state of purity, and I believe no specimen has been imported into England for the last forty years. Its height is about that of the English greyhound, and in shape it closely resembles the collie, except in the ears, which are pricked like that of the spitz or Pomeranian dog ; the character of head is also fox-like as in that dog, but the coat is not so long, nor is the tail curved over the back. This dog was greatly used by the Indians of the Northern parts of America to hunt the moose and reindeer, and being required to do this in deep snow, those puppies were selected with spreading feet, which in other breeds would be rejected as unfitted for hard ground. The *colour* is peculiar, being composed of a light ground tipped with dark brown in irregular patches verging into black, so as to give an appearance of mottle.

VII.—THE GRECIAN GREYHOUND.

The Grecian Greyhound (Youatt).

This dog is probably as old as any breed in existence, and no doubt closely resembles the greyhound of Xenophon. In the present day he is met with throughout the islands of Greece, where he is extensively used for coursing hares, either by sight or nose, or both, at the discretion of the owner. The hair covering the body is moderately long and silky, while that of the tail resembles our English setters. With the exception of the ears, which are wholly pendant, this dog resembles the smooth greyhound of this country.

VIII.—THE ALBANIAN GREYHOUND.

A very large and magnificent animal of the greyhound or deerhound type is met with in Albania, coarser in shape and in the hair of his tail than the Grecian greyhound, but with a finer coat on the body. He is specially used as a guard against wolves, but also for hunting them. The varieties are too great to allow of any very definite description of this dog.

IX.—THE RUSSIAN OR SIBERIAN GREYHOUND.

Like all the dogs met with in Russia, this variety of the greyhound is covered with a coarse but silky coat. He is slightly larger than his English congener, but not nearly so fast. Though he is used for attacking bears and wolves, he is said to be so deficient in courage as only to hold them at bay till the hunter comes up with his gun or axe and despatches them. He hunts by nose as well as sight, and is said to have considerable power of scent. The coat on the body is very woolly, but not long; that on the tail is hairy and fan-like in form. Several of this breed have lately been introduced into England by Lady Peel and others.

X.—THE TURKISH GREYHOUND.

This little dog approaches the Italian greyhound in size, but is considerably stouter in his proportions. He is very thinly coated with hair, and is seldom met with in a state of purity, being generally crossed with some of the many varieties which are supposed to be the scavengers of all Turkish cities.

XI.—THE PERSIAN GREYHOUND.

In Persia, coursing the hare and antelope is a royal sport in high esteem, and the greyhound kept for the purpose is of very elegant proportions. He closely resembles the Grecian greyhound above described, but his ears and nose are hairy, as also is his tail. The body, on the contrary, is somewhat smoother, but still not so smooth as that of the English dog. This greyhound is fast, but not capable of pulling down an antelope single-handed, and in coursing it is so managed that relays may be slipped after those in possession are nearly exhausted.

XII.—THE ITALIAN GREYHOUND

Is so small and delicate as to be solely used in this country as a pet. I shall therefore postpone its description till I come to consider that division of the canine race.

CHAPTER III.

DOMESTICATED DOGS, HUNTING BY THE NOSE, AND BOTH FINDING AND KILLING THEIR GAME, COMMONLY KNOWN EITHER AS HOUNDS OR TERRIERS.

1. The Southern Hound—2. The Bloodhound—3. The Staghound—4. The Foxhound—5. The Harrier—6. The Beagle—7. The Otter-hound—8. The Great Dane—9. The Basset and other French Hounds—10. The Modern Basset Hound—11. The Dachshund—12. The Fox-Terrier (Rough and Smooth)—13. The Hard-Haired Scotch Terrier—14. The Irish Terrier—15. The Welsh Terrier—16. The Skye Terrier—17. The Dandie Dinmont Terrier—18. The Smooth English Terriers—19. The Bedlington Terrier—20. The Halifax Blue Fawn or Yorkshire Terrier —21. The Airdale Terrier.

I.—THE SOUTHERN HOUND.

THIS hound is now extinct in its purity, all now existing being more or less crossed with other breeds to increase the pace required by modern fashion. Until fox-hunting began to be regarded as a national sport, our hounds were divided into two kinds—the Southern hound and the Northern hound, of which the latter was the faster of the two, but still not approaching our modern foxhound in that respect. Hundreds of portraits exist of the several old-fashioned hounds under the name of talbots, bloodhounds, &c.; but they differ so much among themselves as to be clearly unreliable. It is currently believed that these hounds were possessed of noses more tender than those of the foxhound, and this opinion is supported by the accounts of chases lasting for many hours, and as having been maintained on colder scents than would be owned in the present day. It is, however, probable that the alterations in agriculture will account in great measure for this apparent change, for there is no doubt that drainage, now almost universal, diminishes scent very considerably.

Both the Northern and Southern hound were large, " throaty "

animals, with huge pendant ears like those of our modern bloodhound. The Southern hound had a dewlap almost like that of the
cow, as is shown in the portrait which Mr. Youatt gives of him,
and which is by permission transferred to these pages. In addition
to this heaviness of shape, and consequent slow pace, these hounds
had a habit of dwelling on a scent which is exhibited in a marked

The Southern Hound (Youatt).

manner by those descendants who resemble them the most closely,
namely, the modern otter-hound. If the scent is only moderate,
this hound tries on with steadiness and perseverance; but if he
suddenly comes upon a stronger one, he stops, throws his tongue
with his head in the air, and even sits on his haunches in the most
provoking manner. The bloodhound of the present day, when

quite pure, shows this same peculiarity. In Wales several packs
are still kept approaching the Southern hound in shape and other
peculiarities, but I believe they are all more or less crossed with
the foxhound, even though their masters deny the fact. Markman,
who lived three hundred years ago, describes the Northern hound
as follows :—"He has a head more slender, with a longer nose,
ears and flews more shallow, back broad, belly gaunt, joints long,
tail small, and his general form more slender and greyhound like;
but the virtues of these Northern hounds I can praise no further
than for scent and swiftness, for with respect to mouth, they have
only a little shrill sweetness, but no depth of tone or music." In
the present day, with the solitary exception of the Devon and
Somerset Staghounds, no hound is used but the foxhound, harrier,
beagle, and otter-hound. The bloodhound is kept almost entirely
for ornamental purposes, and the Southern hound, as I have already
mentioned, is altogether extinct in a pure shape. As the Southern
hound may be considered extinct, I cannot pretend to give his
points, as is done with all existing breeds.

II.—THE BLOODHOUND.

This breed is so named because it is supposed to possess peculiar
powers of scenting the blood flowing from the wounds made in its
quarry. Before the invention of the rifle, the arrow was used to
give the first wound, and this was sufficient to enable the forester
to make his pick from the herd, because though the arrow would
seldom cause immediate death, yet it would lead to a flow of blood
sufficient to induce the bloodhound to hunt that one deer in preference to the rest of the herd. He was also employed to track
the sheep-stealer, in which occupation his tendency to follow blood
was developed in a similar manner. At present the deadly rifle
has taken one occupation from him, and the law, by preventing
sheep-stealing, has deprived him of the other. Hence it has come
to pass that the bloodhound is now kept for ornamental purposes
only. Many breeders of this dog, however, still contend that he
might be made useful in tracking criminals if laid on the trail of
one shortly after a crime is committed. In Cuba, no doubt, a dog
of more or less pure breed was used to hunt slaves, and as the

African is well known to emit a strong scent, it is probable that this was taken advantage of by the white slave-owner. But it seems impossible that any dog can be taught to hunt a white man (supposing him to be a stranger) without exciting him to hunt all of the same colour. The matter was publicly tested at Warwick

Head of the Bloodhound (Youatt).

this year, but in a most imperfect manner, and it still remains unsettled. Having myself seen it tested several times, in private and public, I am altogether incredulous; but of course I do not pretend to say that the claim cannot possibly be supported. As a companionable dog he is not quite safe, since he does not readily bear control, and when his temper is roused he is apt to be dangerous even to his best friends. This character is disputed by Mr. Ray and other modern breeders, but from my own experience, and from confirmation received through reliable sources, I am strongly of opinion that it is founded on truth, and was certainly manifested in Mr. Grantly Berkeley's " Druid." Until the middle of the present century this dog was seldom in the possession of any of the middle classes, but about that time Mr. Jennings of Pickering managed to get hold of a very fine strain of blood from Lord Faversham and Baron Rothschild, and exhibiting his " Druid " and " Welcome " at the early dog shows, carried off all the first prizes for several years, finally selling the couple at what was then considered a high price to Prince Napoleon to cross with the French strains. Since then, Major Cowan and Mr. Pease, Mr. Holford and Mr. Ray, have divided the honours among them.

" DRUID," the Property of the Hon. Grantly Berkeley.

The points of the bloodhound are as follows :—

	VALUE		VALUE
Head, . .	. 15	Back and back ribs,	. 10
Ears and eyes, . .	. 10	Legs and feet, .	20
Flews, . .	5	Colour and coat, .	10
Neck, . . .	5	Stern, . .	5
Chest and shoulders,	10	Symmetry, .	10
		Total, . . 100	

In the *head* of this variety of the dog reside nearly all the peculiar features of his kind; nevertheless, as the dog under examination is useless unless he has an equally good frame, it is necessary to place a proper valuation upon other parts as well. It varies a good deal in the two sexes, that of the male being much the heavier and grander of the two. Its great peculiarity is, that while it is massive in all other directions, it is remarkably narrow between the ears, the whole of the upper surface being raised into a dome, finishing at the back with a great development of the occipital protuberance. The skin of the forehead is puckered into strong wrinkles, as also is that of the face around the eyes. The jaws are long, tapering, and deep, but not wide; very lean under the eyes, and cut off square at the end.

The *ears* are large and thin, hanging very close to the cheeks in folds, and should not spread out like a leaf, as they do when thick and gummy. They are clothed with short silky hair, and have no fringe on their edges. The *eyes* are usually of a hazel colour, small, and sunk so deeply as to give a peculiar character to them. In spite of their depth they show the third eyelid, or "haw," very plainly, and it is generally red from exposure to the air. So far as I know, this redness of the "haw" is only met with naturally in breeds crossed with the bloodhound, such as the Gordon setter, the St. Bernard, and the mastiff, but no doubt it occasionally occurs in other breeds after inflammation of the eyes.

The *flews* are long and pendant, falling considerably below the jaws, and they are inclined to "slaver" on the slightest provocation.

The *neck* is sufficiently long to allow of the nose reaching the ground, without any stoop of the body, but it is by no means remarkable in this direction. It is decidedly throaty, and there is more or less dewlap in addition.

The *chest* is round, giving a large girth; nevertheless the *shoulders* are fairly oblique. They are, or ought to be, very strong and muscular.

The *back* must be very powerful, and should be slightly arched. The *back ribs* should be very deep, and the couples should be ragged and wide.

The *legs* should be straight, strong in bone, and well clothed with muscle both before and behind. They should be set on so that the elbow and stifles shall play freely in the same plane. Partly from inbreeding and partly from confinement as puppies, bloodhounds very frequently are defective in their legs, which are then either crooked at the joints or actually "bowed" in the

D

long bones between them. The *feet* also are seldom perfect, but they ought to be cat-like, or at all events not spreading, as is often the case.

The *colour* is either tan or black and tan, the latter for choice. Indeed, many breeders reject the tan puppies, which will occur in all litters, even of the most carefully-selected strains. The black should extend to the whole of the upper parts, but it is seldom clearly defined, the tan running more or less on to it. No white is allowed, even on the toes, by those who are particular; but, as in all other varieties of the dog, however carefully bred, a little white will occasionally make its appearance. The *coat* should be short over the whole body, hard on the back and sides, but silky and soft on the ears and head.

The *stern* is carried gaily or in a " hound-like style," with a gentle scimitar-like curve, and it should not be raised above a right angle with the back. Its under side is slightly fringed with hair.

III.—THE STAGHOUND.

The staghound may now be considered to be almost an extinct breed, for even the Devon and Somerset pack, hunting wild deer, is crossed with the foxhound. Until recently it was alleged that this pack was entirely pure, and was descended from hounds kept exclusively to deer for many years. In the year 1877, however, nearly the whole pack was destroyed from the fear of having been bitten by a mad dog, and their place has been supplied by drafts from confessedly foxhounds kennels. Of the eight couples which were permitted to live, not having been submitted to the risk above mentioned, all are, I believe, more or less crossed, and there is no other source left for resuscitating the old breed.

The hounds used by Her Majesty and Baron Rothschild for hunting carted deer are pure foxhounds, drafted from other kennels for being over-sized or too fast for their respective Masters. In size the dog foxhounds used to hunt deer are about 25 inches high, while the bitch varies from 23 to 23½.

Beyond the above remarks I can give no description of this breed, for reasons which are apparent to the most casual reader.

IV.—THE FOXHOUND.

There is probably no animal in creation, and certainly no domestic animal, which possesses so high a combination of speed and stoutness as the foxhound. The mule is possibly as stout, but not nearly so fast; while the greyhound and racehorse are faster, but cannot stay with him, as has repeatedly been proved. It should, however, be remembered that, in comparing the horse's powers with that of the hound, we are apt to forget that the former is weighted with his rider, while the latter is turned loose.

" HERMIT," a High-bred Modern Foxhound.*

Still the difference is so great, that even this will not account for it. It is generally supposed that this extraordinary combination has been obtained by crossing the old-fashioned hound (whether Northern or Southern) with the greyhound; but of this cross there is no record in the kennel books of our earliest foxhound.

* Bred by J. J. Farquharson, Esq., by Lord Fitzhardinge's "Hermit," out of the Puckeridge "Venus."

packs, which trace back for nearly or quite two hundred years. Now, success in breeding generally leads to a confession of the method by which it has been attained, as is exemplified in the case of Lord Oxford with his bulldog and greyhound cross, and it is argued that if the greyhound had been used as alleged, some record of the fact would have been handed down to us. Hence this point in the history of the foxhound must be regarded as unsettled. At all events, it cannot be denied that great trouble and expense have been for a long time expended in arriving at the present high development of this breed, and that it is now existing in the highest state of perfection in those numerous hunting counties into which a great part of England and Scotland is divided, varying, of course, in proportion to the skill and care possessed for the time being by the several Masters of foxhounds and their huntsmen. The theory of breeding was carefully laid down a hundred years ago by Beckford, and has not been improved on since his time; but careful selection founded on his principles has, without doubt, produced a faster and at the same time stouter hound, capable not only of staying through a long run, when such a rare event occurs, but of getting away from a crowd of horsemen, which, in his day, was completely unheard of. In some fashionable countries this last-named faculty is cultivated and bred too in a most remarkable manner, and to such an extent that individual hounds belonging to the packs, when left behind in covert, thread through two or three hundred horsemen and get to the front without injury. This requires a high combination of speed, courage, and judgment, which ordinary hounds do not possess, and they would be sure either to be too slow, or too timid, or too stupid, to seize the right moment to overcome each successive obstacle. Speed is of course a *sine quâ non* for success in such a feat, but it likewise requires high courage to risk being ridden over, and with this must be combined judgment to make a push at the right moment, and to wait patiently till it occurs.

In looking at the modern foxhound, the uninitiated are apt to be misled by the "rounded" ears, which detract very much from his artistic appearance. Compared with the bloodhound's long sweeping appendages, the small semi-oval attached to the head of the foxhound looks mean, and detracts from his dignity and bearing. But in actual work it enables him to drive his way through gorse and thorns with much less injury to his ears, though without the advantage to the eyes which is supposed to accrue by some writers. How it can be imagined that an organ which hangs, when at rest, at some distance behind the eyes, should protect them from injury in driving the head forward through gorse or thorns, I am quite at a loss to know; but such is the extent to which certain theorists have gone. The fact really is, that experience teaches the huntsman to remove all superfluous parts which he finds liable to be torn in covert, at the same time taking care not to lose such as are advantageous. He knows that a most essential organ to keeping his pack together is that of hearing, by means of which every individual hound judges of the first whimper heard in "drawing" whether or not it is reliable, and owns it or not as he thinks right. Again, he requires it to ascertain the direction of the "cry," so as to get quickly to it, and, accordingly, enough of the flap of the ear is left on for good hearing, while the remainder, as being likely to be torn, is removed by the rounding-iron; and even from a humanitarian point of view the practice is entirely justified, as also is the removal of the dew claws, which, like the ear-flaps, are constantly liable to be torn. For these reasons the artist and the ardent lover of animals should forgive the practice of "rounding," *malgré* Mr. Colam, who has more than once run a tilt against it. In some packs rounding is now discontinued.

A third faculty in which this hound differs from his congeners is a mental one, leading him always, when he loses scent of his quarry, to cast forward rather than backward, and to do this with a "dash" altogether unlike the slow and careful quest of the bloodhound and others of that ilk. This, of course, may be overdone, like all good qualities, and in that case the hound constantly overruns the scent; but without it in these days few foxes would be killed, for unless they are hard pressed the scent soon fails and is altogether lost.

Beyond the formation of each individual in his pack, the M.F.H. also has to consider the "sortiness" and "suitiness," that is to say, he desires that all should be of the same "sort," or, in other words, should show themselves to be of the same breed, and should not resemble a " scratch " pack got together by chance, and that each should resemble each in every respect. Thus a pack may be " suity " although composed of very different strains, while it may be " sorty " though it may vary in size from 22 inches to 25. For absolute perfection in appearance, both these points must be attended to, while in the field it is also necessary that in their tongues there shall be the desired kind of music, and pretty nearly all alike. So also there must be an equality of pace and stoutness, without which "tailing" very soon begins, the long-drawn line from head to tail being developed, so much deprecated by every hunting man. Thus the task of the breeder of foxhounds is rendered more difficult than that of any other artist in a corresponding line, for he not only has to breed his hounds individually perfect, but also collectively so, and not only in externals, but in mental manifestations. Still these obstacles are to be overcome, and what man can do our modern M.F.H.'s actually accomplish, as is admitted to their honour by all their followers, the result being the modern foxhound.

His points are as follows :—

	VALUE		VALUE
Head,	15	Elbows,	5
Neck,	5	Legs and feet,	20
Shoulders,	10	Colour and coat,	5
Chest and back ribs,	10	Stern,	5
Loin,	10	Symmetry,	5
Hind-quarters,	10	Total,	100

The *head* should be of sufficient size to contain a brain capable of the mental manifestations required; but if absolutely heavy, there is sure to be the old-fashioned style of hunting to which allusion has already been made. Hence the breeder requires a fair size, measuring round the ears in the average dog hound 16 inches, and in the bitch 24½ inches. The top of the head is flat and not domed, as in the bloodhound. The *nose* should be 4½ inches long in the full-sized hound, wide and open in the nostrils, and cut off square at the end; *ears* set on low and lying close; *eyes* of moderate size, soft, yet full of expression.

The *neck* must be thin, round, and free from the slightest throatiness. This last point is one much insisted on in the present day, and indicates speed derived from the greyhound. It should very gradually deepen without widening as it is set on to the shoulders.

The *shoulder-blades* must be long and muscular, with their points lean and well raised from the bosom, but not heavy nor set widely apart. The *true arm*, between them and the elbow, should be long, and well clothed with muscle.

The *chest* in the average dog hound should girth 30 inches, and may be slightly more round than in the greyhound, but still should not be quite barrel-like. The *back ribs* must be deep, showing a good constitution, and also giving strong attachment to the muscles of the back.

The *hind-quarters* must in any case be strong, and most Masters prefer them rather straight than much bent at the stifles; but this will a good deal depend on the country to be hunted. Over stone walls the bent stifle is often injured from hitting the tops, and consequently in packs hunting where they abound there is no question that they are objectionable. On the other hand, over the Leicestershire pastures they undoubtedly give high speed and freedom in going at the greatest speed, so that what is best for one is worst for the other. Breadth of buttock and quarter is always a recommendation.

The *elbows* should be set on low, giving a long true arm, and neither turning in nor out.

As to the *legs* and *feet*, all are agreed that their formation should be regarded as highly important. Nearly every M.F.H. requires the fore pasterns to be quite perpendicular, and shaped as if cut out of a block of wood. This formation is, however, an exaggeration of what is wanted, in my opinion, and a slight bend at the knee-joint is to be preferred, as shown in the portrait of "Hermit" which illustrates this article. Fore-legs like his are much more likely to stand work than the model legs which constitute perfection in the eyes of most huntsmen, which soon become "groggy," and then knuckle over. In all cases the *feet* should be close, with the knuckles well up; and if so, it is not of much consequence whether they are quite round and cat-like, or rather inclined to be long.

The *colour* is not greatly to be regarded, but for choice the black, white, and tan colour is the best. This is commonly called the true hound colour; but many people prefer some one or other of the " pies," such as the red pie, blue pie, yellow pie, grey pie, lemon pie, hare pie, or badger pie, in which the respective shades are blended with white. Whole colours are not liked, and even black and tan without white is not generally popular. The "blue mottle" is supposed to indicate a descent from the Southern hound, and is often accompanied by a tender nose. I have myself known several good examples of this last combination, and in consequence have a leaning to it. Curiously enough, however, they all had squeaky tongues, which would by no means prove their descent from the old-fashioned hound. The *coat* should be short, hard, and dense, but glossy.

The *stern* is carried gaily over the back with a gentle curve, and should taper to a point. There should be a fringe of hair on the under side.

As to *symmetry*, it is considerable in good specimens; and what is called " quality " is highly regarded.

The most desirable average height is 24 inches for dog hounds and 22½ for bitches, but the height should vary according to the country. A big hound will not do for hills, while a little one is comparatively useless over deep arable flats.

V.—THE HARRIER.

A pure harrier, without the slightest mixture of foxhound blood, is extremely rare in the present day, the most notable exceptions being the rough strains kept in Wales, and said to be descended from the old Southern hound. These are known as Welsh harriers, and there is no doubt that they differ greatly from the modern hound used for hunting hares throughout England. In Lancashire, Shropshire, and Cheshire, the Masters of several packs claim a pure harrier descent for their packs, and notably Sir Vincent Corbett, whose beautiful strain certainly can be held to be pure, if there is such a state of things anywhere. Without doubt they are descended from the best harrier blood; but I should doubt whether such clean throats could be produced without recourse either to the foxhound or to the source from which his peculiar shape has in all probability been derived, namely, the greyhound. As a matter of course, all harriers are at first sight distinguished from the foxhound by their full ears, giving a different expression to the head; but, independently of this feature, they usually are longer and narrower in the face and head, and somewhat more hollow under the eye, which is also fuller and softer in expression. But the foxhound cross shows itself more in mental than in physical pro-

"GRASPER," * a Harrier, and "TRUEMAN," † a Foxhound-Harrier.

perties. There is a dash and tendency to cast forward for a failing scent rather than to return on it, that is peculiar to the foxhound cross,—how derived it is impossible to ascertain, as there is no other existing hound which possesses it. The bloodhound, otterhound, and Welsh harrier, which are probably the oldest breeds of

* "Grasper" by "Solomon" out of "Governess," from the late Mr. Furze's harrier pack in Devonshire. "Solomon" by Prince Albert's "Solomon."

† "Trueman" by Mr. Lisle Phillipps' harrier "Roman" out of "Damsel." "Damsel," a pure foxhound bitch, only 18 inches high, from the late Sir Richard Sutton's kennel, and of the famous "Trueman" blood, was by his "Dexter."

hounds now in England, all have a tendency to dwell on the scent, and to cast backward rather than forward. Even the Gordon setter, which is supposed to be crossed with the bloodhound, exhibits this peculiarity in a marked degree, and in him it is often extremely difficult to get him away from the scent of birds gone away. On the other hand, in the pointer crossed with the foxhound there is none of this pottering, but so much forward dash as to lead to unsteadiness on the point. The advocates of the two styles of hunt-

L.WELLS

"DAHLIA," * a pure Foxhound, used as Harrier.

ing exhibited by the modern foxhound and by the remnants of the old Southern hound, whether harrier, otter-hound, or bloodhound, are of course loud in praise of their own protégés, and as much opposed to those of their rivals; but the fashion of the day being all in favour of progress, the foxhound "has it" by a large majority. Nevertheless, my own experience leads me to put faith in the superior nose of the harrier or bloodhound; but then he wastes so

* "Dahlia" is by the Duke of Rutland's "Driver" out of the Bramhammoor "Dulcet." She is 21 inches in height.

much time in making out a scent, that at the end of a mile or two it would become cold as compared with its state if followed by a foxhound for the same distance, and practically there is not so much difference as at first sight would appear. Thus, with a pack composed of one-half of each breed, when first laid on the cold scent of a hare, the harriers could "speak to it" with much more certainty than the foxhound; but if left to themselves, they would not long keep the lead, and at the end of half an hour's hunting they would all be tailed off, their rivals having worked up to their hare and been able to drive her into straight running. Still it must be confessed, that for those who like to watch the hunting powers of a hound regardless of time, and of riding also, the careful manner of the harrier, and the way in which he follows every turn and double of the hare, are of high interest; but I regret to say, that in these modern days few followers either of the fox or hare care for these things, and the kind of hound which makes hare-hunting most like fox-hunting is preferred, and that kind is undoubtedly the foxhound. Besides this difference in style of hunting, the true harrier resembles the bloodhound in tongue much more nearly than the foxhound, and their "cry" is often melodious to a degree never reached by any foxhound cross.

The points of the harrier may be numerically similar to those of the foxhound, but it will be necessary to repeat the deviations in shape as they occur.

Points of the harrier:—

	VALUE		VALUE
Head,	15	Elbows,	5
Neck,	5	Legs and feet,	20
Shoulders,	10	Colour and coat,	5
Chest and back ribs,	10	Stern,	5
Loin,	10	Symmetry,	5
Hind-quarters,	10	Total,	100

The *head*, as before remarked, is rather wider between the ears, and the face is longer and hollower under the eyes, which are softer and slightly larger; ears unrounded, thin in leather, and soft in coat, falling slightly in folds, and nearly meeting on the nose, which is not quite so square as that of the foxhound. There are no absolute flews, but the lips are fuller than those of the foxhound.

The *neck* is thinner and less round than that of the foxhound, but except in the case of the Welsh harrier no "throatiness" is permitted. Still there is not the greyhound-like tightness so dear to the eye of the M.F.H.

In the *shoulders*, *chest*, *back*, *ribs*, and *loin* no variation is visible, but the quarters are seldom so full and wide as those of its rival.

The *elbows* are required to be straight, as indeed is the case with all animals kept for work.

The *legs* and *feet* should, as far as possible, resemble those of the foxhound, but it is seldom that they are exhibited so extremely straight as I have described the model pasterns of the M.F.H. I need scarcely remark that my opinions on this point are the same with regard to the legs of the two breeds. As to feet, there are no two opinions on these in either breed.

The *colours* most in demand for the harrier are black, white, and tan, commonly called "the true hound colours," but all the pies are met with nearly to the same extent. The coat is generally slightly softer than that of the foxhound, and on the stern a little more fringed.

The *stern* is carried, as in the foxhound, gaily over the back, and has a similar root and tip.

In *symmetry* the foxhound has a slight advantage, from the extra care and expense which have so long been devoted to breeding him.

The illustrations show the harrier as pure as it can be met with, and also the foxhound as used for hare-hunting.

In size most harrier packs are under 20 inches, and many are as low as 16 inches.

The rough Welsh harrier resembles the otter-hound (to be presently described) so closely, that I have only to refer my readers to the latter.

VI.—THE BEAGLE.

Any English hound less than 16 inches in height is in ordinary language called a beagle, but in reality there is as great a difference between a dwarf harrier or foxhound and a true beagle as between a bloodhound and a foxhound. The true beagle is a miniature specimen of the old Southern hound, except that, like almost all moderately-reduced dogs as to size, he possesses more symmetry than his prototype. Where, however, this reduction is carried to extremes, in order to produce a little hound capable of being carried in the pocket of a shooting-jacket, and slow enough to allow of his followers keeping up with him on foot, there is generally a loss of symmetry and of its ordinary accompaniment, a hardy constitution. In order to get a reduction of size in any

"BARMAID," a Dwarf Beagle, bred by Lord Gifford.*

breed, the smallest puppy in a litter is selected, and as this is also generally the most weakly, it is only to be expected that in course of time a constant repetition of such a selection will result in a loss of constitution. For this reason it has been found impossible to keep up a pack of beagles less than 9 or 10 inches in height; and Mr. Crane of Linthorn House, Dorset, who for some years maintained one, kept exclusively for hunting rabbits, never was

* This beautiful little bitch, presented to Mrs. Chapman of Cheltenham by Lord Gifford, is by Mr. Barker's "Ruler" out of his "Bluebell." Height, 12½ inches.

able to rear above one or two out of each litter, the remainder
either dying in the nest or being lost afterwards from fits or distemper.   Mr. J. Grimwood, of Stanton House, near Swindon, has
a very beautiful little pack of somewhat larger size, averaging
nearly 12 inches, and usually hunting hare; while Sir Thomas D.
Lloyd, of Bromroyd, Carmarthenshire, breeds to a still higher
standard.   For many years Lord Caledon was famous for his
beagles, with which he hunted hare in Tyrone, and they were said
to be of the purest old blood; but never having seen them, I
cannot speak from my own knowledge of their merits.   Mr.
Everett, of Abingdon, has been the most successful on the show
bench, and has attained a high reputation in the field, his little
hounds being able to account for sometimes a brace of hares in the
day, after showing a good run with each.   Some twenty years ago
Mr. Honeywood hunted over the Essex marshes on foot with
pocket-beagles very little above Mr. Crane's standard, but they
were often unable to get up the banks of the drains when the water
was low, and frequently required assistance to save them from
drowning.   The nose of the beagle when thus bred down to a very
low standard is apt to be lost, and, according to my experience,
no pack should, on this account, be less than 11 inches in height,
and for sport I should prefer even 12 inches.   Foot-beagles,
generally hunting "drag," sometimes hare, were kept by subscrip-
tion throughout the country in almost every populous parish, for
the purpose of giving exercise to the rising generation, but since
the coming in with a rush of lawn-tennis they have gone out of
fashion for this purpose, and very few packs are now kept, except
by those who love the chase pure and simple, irrespective of the
exercise it gives.   Like the harrier, the numerical value of the
beagle's points is identical with that of the foxhound, but I shall
repeat the scale for the sake of reference :—

	VALUE		VALUE
Head,	15	Elbows,	5
Neck,	5	Legs and feet,	20
Shoulders,	10	Colour and coat,	5
Chest and back ribs,	10	Stern,	5
Loin,	10	Symmetry,	5
Hind-quarters,	10		
		Total,	100

The *head* is wide and rather domed. *Nose* short and cut off square, but slightly tapering, as shown in the annexed engraving. Ears of full length and never rounded; they are thin in leather and hang in folds, but not so much so as in the bloodhound. In length across the head when spread out they should be from one-quarter to one-third more than the height at the shoulder. The *eye* is remarkably soft, rather full, and never weeping, which shows, when present, a spaniel cross.

The *neck* is rather short and chumpy, with a tendency to ruff in the old strains, but no absolute throatiness. There is also in them a suspicion of dewlap, but in the modern strains these points are altogether absent.

Shoulders rather wide apart, and not very sloping, but strong and muscular.

Chest girthing nearly double the height at the shoulder, that is to say, about 1½ to 1¾ times. Back ribs often defective, but this point should be insisted on.

Loin very muscular in both directions.

Hind-quarters thick and breech wide; but stifles generally straight.

Elbows apt to turn out or in, as in most dwarfed breeds. This should be carefully noticed in picking puppies.

Legs and *feet* not of quite so much importance as in the larger hounds, but still these points must not be neglected.

The *colours* are the same as with the previously described hounds.

Coat soft and shining.

Stern very thick at the root and tapering to a sharp point, carried, of course, "hound-like" over the back.

Symmetry very great, except as before remarked in the smallest strains.

The rough Welsh beagle is a reduced Welsh harrier in every respect.

VII.—THE OTTER-HOUND.

Between a large Welsh harrier and an otter-hound no one but an expert could detect any difference, which, after all, will be found only to exist in the coat and feet, and then in a very slight degree. From their constant exposure to the water it is necessary that they should have some further protection than the mere long open coat of the Welsh harrier, and no doubt, from selecting those hounds which stood the water best, it has come to pass that the otter-hound possesses a thick pily undercoat, which is, moreover, of a very oily nature. If, therefore, a specimen of each breed is immersed in water, the one will come out showing his shape like a half-drowned hare, while the coat of the other stands up and is only half wet. Again, in the feet there is a difference, owing also

L.WELLS.

"BELLMAN," an Otter-Hound; Pedigree unknown.

to the Master's selection of the best swimmers. A round cat-like foot is not here the desideratum, since the work is chiefly in the water, but an open one with plenty of web, spreading, when on the ground, in a way which would horrify the huntsman of the Quorn or the Pytchly. In all other respects the otter-hound is, like the Welsh harrier, a true descendant of the old Southern hound, and, like him, he dwells on a scent with the greatest gusto. In temper, also, he is very irritable, having so strong a tendency to fight in kennel, that, like the Kilkenny cats, there is sometimes only a tail or two left in the morning when the feeder enters the kennel. In sober truth, I have known six and a half couples found dead or dying after a night's fighting, and with wounds of a most savage description, evidently made with malice aforethought. The bloodhound, as I have observed in treating of his temper, is savage enough, but he has not this peculiarly cruel tendency, which, no doubt, is developed from the selection of those hounds who best and bravest tackle their hard-biting quarry.

As there are only these very trifling differences from the Welsh harrier and Southern hound, I shall not repeat the points which I have assigned to the former, the numerical value being the same, while the shape of feet and texture of coat are the only external differences, and these I have fully alluded to.

VIII.—THE GREAT DANE.

Within the last ten years the German boarhound has come into fashion in this country under the name of the Great Dane, having displaced the collie to a considerable extent from his position at the head of the larger class of companionable dogs. It is solely from this point of view that he is to be regarded here, as there are no boars to pursue, and he is not supposed to be used for any other purpose. In 1885 a club specially designed to promote the breeding of this dog was formed, and soon numbered thirty-eight members, under the presidency of the Earl of Lathom, and the vice-presidency of Mr. Adcock, who was the first advocate of the claims of the boarhound, or Great Dane, to distinction. Separate classes had for some time been allotted to the Great Dane at most of our large shows, but in 1885 a special show was instituted in the grounds of the Ranelagh Club at Putney, and attracted a large entry. In 1886 thirty-eight Great Danes, including puppies, were entered at the summer show of the Kennel Club, the German bred " Cedric the Saxon" gaining the first prize at each.

With regard to the antiquity of this breed, there is no doubt that it is very great, having been painted by Teniers in many of his boar-hunting pictures, and well known long before his time. He

E

unites the strength of the mastiff with much of the elegance of the greyhound, and a first cross between these two breeds closely resembles him, being formerly common in this country under the name of the "Keeper's dog." He hunts chiefly by sight, but, like the greyhound, can readily be trained to use his nose. Not having been crossed with the bulldog, he is more easily kept under restraint

The Great Dane.

when excited than the mastiff, and on that account he is said to be more suitable as a companionable dog.

The following has been drawn up by the Great Dane Club as

THE STANDARD OF POINTS.

1. *General Appearance.*—The Great Dane is not so heavy or massive as the mastiff, nor should he too nearly approach the grey-

hound in type. Remarkable in size and very muscular, strongly though elegantly built, movements easy and graceful; head and neck carried high, the tail carried horizontally with the back, or slightly upwards with a slight curl at the extremity. The minimum height and weight of dogs should be 30 inches and 120 lbs.; of bitches, 28 inches and 100 lbs. Anything below this should be debarred from competition.

2. *Head* long, the frontal bones very slightly raised, and very little indentation between the eyes. Skull not too broad. Muzzle broad and strong, and blunt at the point. Cheek muscles well developed. Nose large, bridge well arched. Lips in front perpendicularly blunted, not hanging too much over the sides, though with well-defined folds at the angle of the mouth. The lower jaw slightly projecting—about a sixteenth of an inch. Eyes small and round, with strong expression and deeply set. Ears very small, and greyhound-like in carriage when uncropped. They are, however, usually cropped.

3. *Neck* rather long, very strong and muscular, well arched, without dewlap or loose skin about the throat. The junction of head and neck strongly pronounced.

4. *Chest* not too broad, and very deep in brisket.

5. *Back* not too long or short, loins arched and falling in a beautiful line to the insertion of the tail.

6. *Tail* reaching to the hock, strong at the root, and ending fine with a slight curve. When excited it becomes more curved, but in no case should it curve over the back.

7. *Belly* well drawn up.

8. *Fore-quarters.*—Shoulders set sloping; elbows well under, neither turned in nor out. Leg forearm muscular, and with great development of bone, the whole leg strong and quite straight.

9. *Hind-quarters.*—Muscular thighs, and second thigh long and strong, as in the greyhound. Hocks well let down, and turning neither in nor out.

10. *Feet* large and round, neither turned in nor out. Toes well arched and closed. Nails very strong and curved.

11. *Hair* very short, hard, and dense, and not much longer than elsewhere on the under part of the tail.

12. *Colour and Markings.*—The recognised colours are the

various shades of grey (commonly termed "blue"), red, black, or pure white, with patches of the before-mentioned colours. These colours are sometimes accompanied with markings of a darker tint about the eyes and muzzle, and with a line of the same tint (called a "trace") along the course of the spine. The above ground colours also appear in the brindles, and in the mottled specimens. In the whole coloured specimens the china or wall eye but rarely appears, and the nose more or less approaches black, according to the prevailing tint of the dog, and the eyes vary in colour also. The mottled specimens have irregular patches or "colours" upon the above-named ground colours, in some instances the clouds or markings being of two or more tints. With the mottled specimens the wall or china eye is not uncommon, and the nose is often parti-coloured or wholly flesh-coloured.

13. *Faults.*—Too heavy a head, too highly-arched frontal bone and deep "step" or indentation between the eyes; large ears, and hanging flat to the face; short neck; full dewlap; too narrow or too broad a chest; sunken or hollow or quite straight back; bent fore-legs; overbent fetlocks; twisted feet; spreading toes; too heavy and much bent or too highly-curved tail, or with a brush underneath; weak hind-quarters, and a general want of muscle.

IX.—THE BASSET AND OTHER FRENCH HOUNDS.

In France about twelve distinct breeds of hounds are met with, including the St. Hubert, the smooth hounds of La Vendée, the Brittany Red Hound, the grey St. Louis, the Gascony, the Normandy, the Saintogne, the Poitou, the Bresse, the Vendée rough-coated hound, the Artois, and the little Basset, coupled with the Briguet. Of these, the grey St. Louis is almost extinct, and all the others, with the exception of the Basset, may be grouped with the St. Hubert and the Red Hound of Brittany. The former of these closely resembles the bloodhound, but some are white in colour, and of our old Talbot type. The La Vendée hounds, rough and smooth, approach very nearly to our English foxhound and otter-hound respectively. The Brittany is slightly rough, but not to the same extent as our Welsh foxhounds; while the Gascony approaches to our old mottled blues. The Normandy is of the Vendée type, and the Saintogne also follows in that direction, as well as the Poitou. The Bresse comes nearest to our old-fashioned harrier; and lastly, they have the Bassets and Briguets. The Briguets, which are used for hunting, have been so crossed and recrossed that they are no longer a distinct type, and are rarely capable of definition. The varieties of the Basset are innumerable, some being black and tan, and common throughout the Black Forest and the Vosges, while the others are either tricoloured or blue mottled. The tricolour has lately been introduced into England in large numbers, having been first shown to the English visitors at the French show of 1863. Since that time, Mr. E. Millais, Mr. Khrehl, and other Englishmen, have imported them largely, and at our large shows a good class of each sex is generally to be met with.

X.—THE MODERN BASSET-HOUND.

These hounds are used in France for hunting hares, and in this country have been tried for that purpose, and found to be superior to our modern beagles in point of nose. They are one of the oldest and purest breeds in France. The earliest French authority, Du Fouilloux, gives two illustrations of them in his "La Vènerie." In regard to these illustrations, I have noticed with some amusement that, although our ancient author describes them as "bassets d'Artois," yet a dachshund-fancier has claimed them to be representatives of his hobby-breed; whereas I should imagine that dachshunds (a later offshoot of the Flemish basset-hound) entered as little into the philosophy of Du Fouilloux as our own bull-terrier. Du Fouilloux explains the title "d'Artois," by telling us that the breed originally came from that province and near-lying Flanders. He divided them into two varieties—the Artesian, "with full-crooked fore-legs. smooth coats, brave, and having double rows of teeth like wolves;" the Flemish, "straight-legged, rough-coated, black, and sterns curled like a horn." This division was confirmed by two later old authors, Sélincourt and Leverrier de la Conterie. The last named expressed his preference for the Flemish, as being "faster; but they gave tongue badly, and were babblers;" he found the Artesians "courageous in going to earth (as shown in Du Fouilloux's engraving), long in the body, and with noble heads." The descendants of the Flemish type still exist in the Forêt Noire, in the Vosges, and, I believe, in the German dachshund, which, according to my theory, is descended from basset-hounds that found their way into South Germany (Würtemberg, the home of the dachshund) *viâ* Alsace, and were there crossed with the terrier, to give them that individual courage that is lacking in the hound. The Artesian type is that with which English dog-show *habitués* are now familiar. In the many political storms that have swept over France, carrying away her monarchical pageantry and the imposing ceremonies of the chase, many of that country's ancient breeds became almost extinct. Amongst them the basset-hound fared a little better than its blood neighbours—the hounds of Artois, Normandy, Gascony, and Saintogne. Thanks to the sporting and patriotic instincts of a descendant of the old noblesse, Count le Couteulx de Canteleu, who spared neither trouble nor expense in his purpose, the smooth tricolour basset-hound of Artois has been preserved in all its purity. The breed was not revived; it had never died out, but it was necessary to search all over the "basset" districts to find, in sportsmen's kennels, the few true and typical specimens, and to breed from them alone. In these efforts on behalf of the old breeds he was greatly benefited by the valuable assistance of M. Pierre Pichot, editor of the *Revue Britannique.*

It will be sufficient to divide the basset-hounds of to-day into two groups—the rough and smooth. The former are of Vendéan extraction, a branch of one of the original breeds. They have rough hard coats, with a woolly undergrowth, and are generally white, with lemon markings, or else iron-grey, like our otter-hounds, which they so closely resemble that, if one can imagine an otter-hound reduced in size and put on short legs, he will have the Basset-Griffon before him.

Their legs are very short, usually straight or demi-torse, bodies low, strongly built, and not very long. They are very hardy, and equal to any rough work. Mr. Macdona's "Romano," often exhibited in variety classes, is of this type.

It is, however, with the smooth and nobler race that I will now deal. These are inseparably connected with the famous kennel of Château St. Martin, and hounds of Count Couteulx's strain are now as highly prized and eagerly sought for in England as in France. They are very aptly described by the French writer De la Blanchère as "large hounds on short legs." It is the massiveness of these miniature hounds that first strikes a stranger's fancy.

The curious formation of their body and limbs, the grand head, and brilliant colouring combine to make a whole that is quaint and pic_

The Basset-Hound.

turesque, and in harmony with mediæval character. They are the dogs one expects to see on tapestries or roaming about castle-keeps.

There are few more useful all-round dogs to the sportsman than the basset-hound. In France this is well known and appreciated, and in a very short time people in this country will learn to value their marvellous powers of scent and peculiar manner of hunting. Deer and roebuck driving is their particular work, and no one can fail to see that a little low hound on crooked legs, with a nose never at fault, and a throat full of deep melodious music, is better than a lame or broken-legged terrier for the purpose. If the full-crooked be found slow, the demi-torse will prove to have plenty of pace.

They are capital to shoot any sort of fur to, hares, rabbits, deer, roebuck, &c. Two or three are sent into a covert, and the guns take their positions according to the runs, or where the music directs them. They are very clever at "ringing" out the game, and in small woods they drive the quarry about so slowly that one has plenty of time to get ahead and shoot it in a crossing. Deer and hares will actually play before the little hounds, stopping to listen to them coming. Though ground game is their special occupation, yet they are also employed to put up birds, pheasants, &c. They are chiefly used with the gun abroad, but there are several packs which hunt, like our beagles, rabbits, hares, &c. They usually kill a hare in two or three hours.

The extent of "crook" and the respective merits of "torse" and "demi-torse" have excited some attention amongst breeders. As the result of my inquiries made of French sportsmen on this subject, it can be taken that both are equally pure, both shapes of fore-legs occurring in the same litter, and buyers must choose whichever best suits their sport. In the show ring, with two dogs of equal merit in all other points, I should decide in favour of the full-crooked, as being harder to breed, more in keeping with the bizarre appearance of the dog, and because the bloodhound character is usually more conspicuous in the torse, though I have seen full-crooked specimens without bloodhound type, and half-crooked with it. The following is the value of the points :—

POINTS OF THE BASSET-HOUND.

	VALUE		VALUE
Head, skull, eyes, muzzle, and flews, . . .	15	Back, loins, and hind-quarters,	10
Ears, ...	15	Stern, ...	5
Neck, dewlap, chest, and shoulders, . . .	10	Coat and skin, . .	10
Forelegs and feet, . .	15	Colour and markings, . .	15
		"Basset character" and symmetry, ...	5
	55		45

Grand total   100

1. *Head.*—The head of the basset-hound is most perfect when it closest resembles a bloodhound's. It is long and narrow, with heavy flews, occiput prominent, *la bosse de la chasse,* and forehead wrinkled to the eyes, which should be kind, and show the haw. The general appearance of the head must present high breeding and reposeful dignity; the teeth are small, and the upper jaw sometimes protrudes. This is not a fault, and is called the *bec de lièvre.*

2. *Ears* very long, and when drawn forward folding well over the nose—so long that in hunting they will often actually tread on them; they are set on low, and hang loose in folds like drapery, the ends inward curling, in texture thin and velvety.

3. *Neck.*—Powerful, with heavy dewlaps. Elbows must not turn out. The chest is deep, full, and framed like a "man-of-war." Body long and low.

4. *Fore-legs.*—Short, about 4 in., and close-fitting to the chest till the crooked knee, from where the wrinkled ankle ends in a massive paw, each toe standing out distinctly.

5. *Stifles.*—Bent, and the quarters full of muscle, which stands out so that, when one looks at the dog from behind, it gives him a round, barrel-like effect. This, with their peculiar waddling gait, goes a long way towards basset character—a quality easily recognised by the judge, and as desirable as terrier character in a terrier.

6. *Stern.*—Coarse underneath, and carried hound fashion.

7. *Coat.*—Short, smooth, and fine, and has a gloss on it like that of a race-horse. To get this appearance they should be hound-gloved, never brushed. Skin loose and elastic.

8. *Colour.*—Black, white, and tan. The head, shoulders, and quarter a rich tan, and black patches on the back. They are also sometimes hare-pied.

XI.—THE DACHSHUND.

Owing to the termination of the name, this little dog is often considered in this country to be a hound, but the German word *hund* means simply *dog,* and not *hound,* as is supposed by many. He is merely a "badger-dog," as far as name goes, and though his

use on the Continent of Europe is not confined to the chase of the
badger, yet a very large proportion of the dogs used for that purpose are dachshunds.   In the vineyards of Germany and France
the badger abounds, and he is hunted partly for sport, and partly
to get rid of an intruder, who would, if left undisturbed, materially reduce the crop of grapes.   The dachshund is also used by

The Dachshund.

gamekeepers to drive game to the gun, and notably roedeer, which
are apt to head back if driven forcibly or with any amount of
noise.   For these two purposes two distinct strains are employed
—the one with crooked but very strong legs, for burrowing after
the badger; the other with straight ones, but still too short to give
any great pace, intended for driving game.   Both are terriers
rather than hounds, and have the squeaky tongue of the former.

so distinct from the bell-like note of the true hound. The temper of all the dachshund strains is short and crusty, little under control of the master, and leading the animal into constant fights, both in kennel and out of it. This little dog hunts the foot-scent with his nose low on the ground, and his natural love of hunting something is so great, that he often imagines a scent where none exists; and I have seen a young dog, which had never been introduced to any kind of game hunt a large garden for hours, with as much keenness as if half a dozen badgers were on foot, where he must of necessity have been imagining a scent all the time. In this feature he resembles the highly-bred setter, who is inclined to make imaginary points when no real ones can be made out. His worst point is, that he cannot be made to submit to control; and, slow as he is, he must be hunted in a leash if he is used for tracking wounded deer. Fortunately he does not care for feather, or it would be impossible to keep poultry where a dachshund is loose, for he would destroy every fowl within his reach, it being impossible to break him from the game which he fancies.

This little dog was, I believe, first introduced into England by the late Prince Consort, who, about thirty years ago, imported several from the kennels of Prince Edward of Saxe-Weimar, and used them in the Windsor Forest coverts for pheasant-shooting. His example was soon followed; and in 1869 we find Mr. J. F. Forbes winning a prize at Birmingham in the extra class for his "Satan," who, however, was a dachsdecker rather than a dachshund. In the following year Mr. Fisher obtained a similar distinction with his "Feldman," a very neat whole tan of the Saxe-Weimar breed, with which he laid the foundation of his celebrated kennel, winning with him individually between thirty and forty prizes, but succumbing in 1872 to the Earl of Onslow's "Waldmar."

In 1873 a special class for this breed was made both at the Crystal Palace and Birmingham shows, Mr. Hodge's "Erdman" winning at the former, and Mr. Fisher being again in front with "Feldman" at the latter. Since that time all our important exhibitions have had their dachshund class, and the breed became so fashionable that in 1876 a show dachshund was worth from £20 to £50. Of course, with this high market value, no time was lost in importing specimens by the score; and Mr. Schuller, I believe, brought over fully two hundred dogs in that and the following year. Latterly, however, either from the breed not being generally approved of, or from caprice, the market price has gone down, and a moderately good dog can be got for £5 or £10. He is now seldom seen in Rotten Row led by a lady, as was the fashion in 1875-76, for it would be idle to attempt to keep one at heel there or elsewhere, such is the uncontrollable nature of his temperament. The following is the numerical value of the points of the dachshund:—

	VALUE		VALUE
Head, .	10	Stern, . . .	10
Jaws, . .	10	Coat, . .	5
Ears, eyes, and lips,	10	Colour, . . .	10
Neck and body, . .	15	Size and symmetry,	5
Legs and feet, . .	20	Quality, . .	5
		Total, . .	100

The *head* is long and slightly arched. Occiput wide and skull narrowing rapidly to the eyes. Head and neck connected in a snake-like form, with a very obtuse angle, and little or no occipital protuberance. Eyebrows low, and scarcely raised above the general line of face.

The *jaws* are long and tapering to the nose, which is small and pointed, but cut off nearly square, not pig-jawed. The masseter muscles of the cheeks are very full, and being so, give the face an appearance of hollowness under the eyes which is not strictly present. Teeth level, strong, and even; skin covering the face tight and without wrinkle.

Ears, Eyes, and Lips.—The ears are set on farther back than in any English dog, and, though high, by no means pricked. This position of the ear is very remarkable, and distinguishes the dachshund from all his congeners. In the hound, pointer, and setter the front edge of the ear approaches the eye, but in the dachshund it is opposite the junction of the head and neck, or a very little in advance of that point. The ear itself is large, but not so large in proportion as that of the bloodhound, being generally about three-fourths of the length of the head and face; sometimes, however, considerably more. The leather is very thin, and the hair covering it fine, soft, and glossy. The eyes are of medium size, bright and intelligent, without any visible "haw;" rich brown in black and tan dogs, and pale brown in the tan variety. Lips short and without flew.

Neck and Body.—The main characteristics of these points is their length in proportion to height and bulk. The general appearance is weasel-like, and the whole length from tip of nose to tip of tail should be four times the height, in this proportion resembling the Skye terrier. The neck is rather long, but not in proportion to the body, and it should be free from throatiness, tapering gradually from the skull to the chest. The brisket projects considerably, and is only from 2½ to 3 inches from the ground. The chest is round and short in the back ribs, while the loin is arched and strong, the flanks being tucked up in a very peculiar manner, giving an elegant curve to the hinder parts. Shoulders strong and their points wide apart.

Legs and Feet.—A good deal of controversy exists on the proper formation of these parts. Many good judges contend for fore-legs so crooked as to be clearly rickety, while others prefer a leg of more useful formation. The excuse for the crooked leg is that it compels a slow pace, and that it allows the dog to scrape the soil back between the bowed fore-legs when digging in a badger-earth. My own belief is, that the bandy-leg has no such advantage; but it must be admitted that the German fanciers, as a rule, "go in" for this peculiar formation. In any case, the legs should be strong in bone, and so short as to lift the breast-bone only for the distance above mentioned from the ground. Even if bandy, the elbows should not turn out nor in, the latter point being a special defect, but they must stand well out from the body, so as to be, on the average, 6 inches apart, while the knees should not be more than 2½ inches; the closer the better. From the knees the feet turn outwards again, and are often 4 or 5 inches apart at the ground, but from pad to pad should not be more than 3½ inches. This formation is strongly commented on by German fanciers. In spite of their peculiar shape, the fore-legs must not be weak, and, in particular, the knees must be strong and the pasterns large in bone. The feet are rather large, but the pads should be firm, and should be covered with thick and hard horn. The claws should be dark. On the hind-legs there are often dew-claws, but they are not regarded as typical points. The hind-legs are longer in proportion than the fore-legs, being only slightly bent at the stifles. They are shaped with great elegance, and are by no means so muscular as the fore-legs. The second thigh is very short, and the calf well developed, but not clumsily so. Quarters wide rather than deep. Feet small and round, and inclining forward nearly on a straight line, the hocks being very slightly in and the feet out.

The *stern* is moderately long, strong at the root, and tapering to a fine point. It is carried gaily over the back in a hound-like manner, resembling the Dandie Dinmont terrier in this respect.

The *coat* is glossy and smooth, but hard and wiry, except on the ears, where it must be soft and silky.

Colour.—The experts are by no means agreed as to the comparative value of tan and black and tan, but between these two and any other colour there is no room for doubt. Sometimes, even in good strains, a whole black or chocolate puppy occurs, occasionally a liver and tan of varying shade, and even a hare or badger pie; but these colours are not fancied, and should, as far as possible, be bred out. If whole tan, the nose should be black, not flesh colour, and the nails also dark. The chocolate or liver colour is almost always attended by a flesh-coloured nose, which is supposed to indicate softness of constitution and want of courage. If black and tan, the black should be rich and unmixed with the tan, which should be confined to the spots over the eyes and on the cheeks, the lower parts of the body and tail, and the legs and feet. On the cheek the tan should not run to the eye, which must be set in black. A black line or two extend up the legs, resembling the pencilling of the English terrier, but not in so distinct a shape. No white is permitted on the toes, breast, or forehead in a perfect specimen, but a star on the breast generally occurs. Any large quantity of white in the shape of a "pie" indicates a cross with the French basset or German "dachsdecker."

Size and Symmetry.—In size the dog should measure, on the average, about 40 inches from tip to tip, and 10 inches in height. Weight from 11 to 18 lbs. The bitch is considerably less in all dimensions as well as weight. The symmetry of the dachshund is very great when the fore-legs are not too much twisted, but, in any case, the hind-quarters should be turned with elegant lines.

Quality.—Few dogs show more quality than the dachshund, owing to the careful way in which he has long been bred in Germany and the bordering countries.

XII.—THE FOX-TERRIER (ROUGH AND SMOOTH).

(A.) THE SMOOTH FOX-TERRIER.

For the last fifteen years this pretty little dog has been the favourite companion of " Young England," and has lately shared the favours of the other sex with the collie, the dachshund, and the black poodle. Probably not one per cent. of our existing fox-terriers have ever come across the scent of a fox, either in their own persons or in those of their immediate progenitors, but in most cases the strain is derived from some ancestor famous in his or her time for prowess against the reputed natural enemy of the race. Thus we find a large proportion of the modern winners at our shows going back to " Jock," " Trap," " Grove Pepper," " Grove Nettle," " Grove Tartar," the " Quorn Fussy," or some other well-known dog or bitch regularly entered to fox ; but, on the other hand, a much larger number cannot lay claim to a foxhound-kennel pedigree in the remotest degree, and are only set down in the stud-book as by " Fox " out of " Vic," or some similarly indefinite parentage. Of course there are " Foxes " and " Foxes," but the particular " Fox " is quite as likely to be some unknown animal as to be the son of old " Jock," belonging to Mr. Cropper, which would entitle him to be considered A-1 on the side of his sire. Such shape and colour as will entitle the possessor to a chance of a prize are considered as far more important than pedigree, and when they are sufficient, the dog is entered as by " nobody's Jack out of somebody's Jill," and all is done which is required by " the fancy." Of course a first-class pedigree enhances the value in the market ; but it is seldom that perfection in all respects can be attained, and as this kind of dog is now seldom used for entering a fox-earth, pedigree is not so necessary as in the case of a greyhound, foxhound, pointer, or setter, where performance goes even before good looks.

Until within the last thirty or forty years, terriers were attached in twos and threes to most foxhound-packs, and in some countries drew the coverts with them, keeping at the tail of the pack when running if the pace was not very good, and even if it was so,

The Fox-Terrier, Smooth and Rough.

generally managing to make up their leeway at each check. As the fields of horsemen became larger the poor little "follower" was constantly ridden over in his attempt to get to the front, and so it came to pass that he was usually left at home or sent to some farmhouse near the earths likely to be entered on the day in question. Many packs rely on chance for the nearest terrier, and, as a consequence, the veritable foxhound terrier entered to his game is rare indeed.

Most of the best modern strains trace back to the Wynnstay blood or that of Mr. Foljambe, and, as a natural consequence, Mr. John Walker, formerly huntsman to Sir Watkyns Wynn, was regarded as the oracle from whom we might expect the words of wisdom required to define the properties and points of the breed. But since the above strains were mostly white and tan, what is called "the true hound colour," viz., white marked with black and tan, was not at first so much *de rigeur* as it now is; for though many white and red and white and black fox-terriers get first prizes, yet the hound colour with most judges wipes out many trifling blots which would otherwise keep the individual in the H.C. division.

The origin of this colour is said by the admirers of the breed to have been a cross with the black and tan English terrier, but others allege that the beagle has been resorted to, adducing the close-falling ear as a proof of their theory. Certainly, with the exception of the Dandie Dinmont and the dog now under consideration, none of the terriers have ears falling close to the cheeks, and I see no reason to suppose that breeders would take the trouble in either case to obtain by selection a property entirely in opposition to that already displayed by the best examples of either. Without doubt it would be easy enough to do so in course of time, as we all know what can be done by careful selection; but my long experience teaches me that, when such changes have occurred, they have been accidental, and not the result of a plan laid down beforehand, unless some good purpose was to be answered, which is certainly not the case with the ears of fox-terriers. Formerly they were, like all other terriers, carefully cropped; and no doubt it was because the natural ear kept out the earth from the internal passages that the practice was discontinued; but the half-pricked ear of the English terrier answers this purpose equally well, as it is only the soil falling from the roof of the earth which can enter the passage, not that thrown back by the feet of the dog in his digging. Hence I can only account for this departure from the true terrier form of ear in both of these breeds by supposing a cross with some other dog,

F

and I believe the dachshund to be the source of the large falling ear in the one, and the beagle of the other. This theory is supported by the peculiar temper of the Dandie, to which I shall refer in treating of that breed, and by the thick, "cobby," and beagle-like frames which fox-terriers now often show, and specially those of the hound colour. As long as fox-terriers were only used for "marking" foxes at their earths, and aiding the digger in his operations, nose was not much required, for the scent of the fox is so strong as to be easily made out when in his earth; but when they became the fashionable companions of our rising generation, they were required to hunt hedgerows for rabbits, and then a cross with the beagle began to be of use. About thirty years ago I had several litters between the rough Scotch terrier of those days and the beagle, for retrieving purposes, and the produce exactly resembled the modern rough fox-terrier in ear and shape of body, so that the above theory on this point is not entirely unsupported by facts. As in the case of the Dandie, I do not expect a confession of this practice having been adopted, for, like the bulldog cross, it would be stigmatised as a derogation; but I confess I cannot in any other way account for the peculiar close-falling ear of the modern fox-terrier. At the same time, I do not attach much importance to this explanation, nor, indeed, to any other historically reputed fact in regard to dogs. All, as it seems to me, that is necessary, is to take each breed as it exists, and estimate its bodily and mental characteristics by the standard of utility, either in carrying out the intentions of man as far as regards the particular kind of work required, or in pleasing his eye by symmetry and colouring. It should be remembered that in the early dog shows from 1859 to 1863, the fox-terrier was ignored altogether, no class being assigned to him, owing to the fact that the breed, though existing in certain foxhound kennels, was not known beyond them. Even at the great London International Show of May 30, 1863, no class for this breed was made; and, as far as I recollect, no fox-terrier appeared among the " white smooth-haired terriers," as was the case at the Birmingham Show of 1862, when the afterwards celebrated " Jock " took the first prize in that class, though not, strictly speaking, conforming to its requirements either in colour or other points. In 1863 Mr.

John Walker of Wrexham, to whom I have already alluded, and Mr. Cornelius Tongue ("Cecil"), impressed upon the Birmingham Committee the importance of the breed, and ever since that time it has been growing into the notice both of the promoters of our shows and of the general public, so that it is by no means uncommon to find the fox-terrier classes making up a fifth or even a quarter of a whole show in point of numbers, and drawing to their benches fully one-half of the spectators.

As this breed thus crept into the favour of the public from a state of obscurity, it was to be expected that opinions on its size and shape should vary according to the point of view from which it was examined. Thus the hunting man said, "I must have a dog small enough to enter an earth; not too savage, because I want him to bark rather than to bite, for foxes are too precious in my eyes to be killed under ground. My limit in point of weight is therefore 16 lbs." "Oh!" says the young Oxonian in reply, "I don't want anything of the kind. What I require is a dog which will follow me on horseback, if I desire a companion in my rides, without being outpaced, and will hunt rabbits for me all day long. My dog should be 20 lbs. at least." Now, who is to decide between these two fox-terrier fancies? The hunting man says, "Well and good! I don't object to your dog, but he should not be called a *fox*-terrier;" and here I think he has his opponent hard and fast, for, as the controversy is always in reference to show prizes, the definition of the class in question is always for "fox-terriers." Still, irrespective of the question of prizes, it is clear that the fox-terrier of the present day is more frequently required as a companion than as a persecutor of foxes; and if he is to go beyond the duties of the companion, and is required to hunt, his game is far more frequently the rabbit than the fox; and a dog of 20 lbs. is not too large for that purpose, nor is the beagle cross objectionable, if it really exists. The fanciers of this dog should first agree as to his duties, and then it will be time to settle his size and other qualities; but till then, unless an absurd stress is placed on the prefix "fox," the promoters of our shows will do well to have two or even three classes, in which the weight is made to fix the limits of each.

Having adverted to this much-vexed question, it now only

remains to refer to another, which some years ago agitated fanciers quite as much, viz., the propriety or otherwise of the bulldog cross. Here again the distinct objects for which this terrier is kept are lost sight of; for admitting that the bull-cross spoils the fox-terrier *quâ* fox, it does not interfere with his rabbiting or attending on his master as a companion. For bolting foxes it often incapacitates the terrier, because it makes him savagely lay hold of the fox and keep hold, thereby not only interfering with his own proper vocation, but preventing the fox from bolting if he has an opportunity. All huntsmen are agreed on this question, and dislike any cross of the bulldog beyond a very remote one; so that as long as the fox-terrier is judged as a dog intended to go to ground after fox, so long must the bull-cross be condemned, if it is so near as to show itself in the decided form of a short full jaw and underhung teeth. But as every one who has possessed a bull-terrier admits his companionable qualities and his excellent hunting powers, so it must be admitted that the fox-terrier intended as a companion is none the worse for a cross of the bull.

From the strict M.F.H. point of view the following are the points of the fox-terrier :—

	VALUE		VALUE
Head, jaws, and ears,	15	Feet,	10
Neck,	5	Stern,	5
Shoulders and chest,	15	Coat,	5
Back and loin,	15	Colour,	5
Fore and hind quarters,	5	Symmetry and size,	10
Legs,	10		
		Total,	100

The *head* should be flat and narrow rather than wide, but not so narrow as to indicate weakness. It should taper from the ears to the nose, with a slight hollow in front of the brows, but no very marked stop. The *jaws* should be rather long and tapering, the bone strong and the muscle closing them prominent at the cheek, but not swelling out as in the bulldog, a cross of which breed is to be deprecated. The cheek-bones should be clearly cut with a very slight hollow. Teeth level and strong. An underhung mouth indicates the bull-cross, and is to be penalised. End of the *nose* black ; a cherry nose is very objectionable, and a white or spotted one almost worse. The *eyes* should be small and by no means prominent. Edges of the eyelids dark. *Ears* small and V-shaped, set close to the cheeks with the points looking forward and downward, not hanging hound-like. Pricked, tulip, or rose ears, as being indications of the bull-cross, should never be allowed.

The *neck* should be light yet muscular, with a pretty sweep in it upper lines. No throatiness is to be allowed.

Shoulders and chest.—Whether the dog should be 14 lbs. or 18 lbs. in weight, there can be no question that his chest must not be much larger than that of the animal whose earth he is required to enter; and this really should be the limitation as to size rather than the weight. Thus a 20-lb. dog, if made with a chest girthing 17 or 18 inches, can enter an earth which is beyond the power of another weighing only 16 lbs. but measuring 19 or 20 inches round, and especially if the chest of the former is round while that of the latter is as keel-shaped as the greyhound's. In a little dog of 15 or 16 lbs., I should, therefore, consider a moderately deep chest to be an advantage, giving room for the play of his lungs without that width which is detrimental to a free gallop. On the other hand, in a 20-lb. dog the chest *must* be round, or it is impossible for him to do his duty as a fox-terrier, and there must be no keel for the same reason. Of course, with the wide chest the *shoulders* cannot be very long and oblique, and this being the case, the dog of this formation may be excused for exhibiting them in a somewhat upright form. On the other hand, the little compact dog must be expected to possess them oblique and yet muscular, since he is required to dig, and if he is not so furnished he should suffer accordingly at the hands of the judge.

Back and loin.—The back of this dog is not required to be specially strong, but only sufficiently so to keep up his forequarters to their work underground, and to maintain a good pace when on the gallop. Deep back ribs are demanded, indicating a good constitution, and also as strengthening the back without increasing weight. The loin also should be of corresponding strength.

The *hind-quarters* should be foxhound-like, that is to say, straight in the stifles rather than much bent, as in the greyhound. A long maintenance of pace is required rather than a very fast one for a short distance in both breeds, and for this purpose short levers answer better than very long ones. The hocks should be straight over the backs of the hind-feet. The quarters should not droop, and they should be full of muscle. The fore-quarters, from the shoulder-joints to the arm, should be powerful; elbows placed quite straight and well let down.

The *legs* should be bony and straight, so as to play freely in parallel planes. Ankles strong, and showing no diminution of size below the knee. Lower thigh and fore-arm well clothed with muscle.

The *feet* are cat-like and of fair average size. The horn covering the pads should be thick and hard. There are usually no dew claws on the hind-legs, but nevertheless a great many well-bred dogs possess them, and as in most other breeds, I do not think this a point of any great importance.

The *stern* is carried gaily, but not quite hound-like. It is usually cropped to about one-third its natural length.

The *coat* is hard, thick, and glossy; skin tight without being "hide-bound."

The *colour* is always white, with more or less marking of black mixed with tan (hound colour), lemon, or black. Brindle spots are objected to as indicating the bull-cross, and liver as indicating mongrel blood.

Symmetry and size.—In the former point the fancier looks for proportions of the most elegant description consistent with the requisite power. Combined with these should appear a large amount of that indescribable feature called quality. As to size, I have already dilated upon it fully.

(B) THE ROUGH FOX-TERRIER.

The rough fox-terrier is still more modern than his smooth brother, as far as shows are concerned; no distinct class for the breed having been made until 1872, when the Glasgow officials offered a prize for "the best rough fox-terrier," and their example has since been followed at all the large exhibitions of dogs at Birmingham, London, &c. Nevertheless, though not called a *fox-*terrier, the breed has existed for the last fifty years to my certain knowledge, having myself possessed and seen many specimens of it fully as long ago. The Rev. John Russell in the West of England was long famous for his strain of rough terriers, so closely resembling the modern dogs exhibited by Mr. Sanderson, Mr. Carrick, and Mr. Lyndsay Hogg as to be inseparable by any ordinary test. It is true that the ears may not have complied with modern requirements, because they were invariably cropped, and I never saw one with full ears. Mr. Radcliffe's (Shropshire) breed of rough terriers certainly had tulip ears, and on that account were refused prizes at the London and Birmingham shows ten years ago, perfect as they were in every other point. For these reasons I cannot positively assert that the modern rough fox-terrier is identical with the old-fashioned dog known in England as the Scotch terrier, but in all other respects he closely resembles him.

The rough fox-terrier may be regarded in all respects as similar to his smooth brother, with the exception of his coat, which on the body and legs should be about twice the length of that on the smooth dog, with the addition of a thick under-pile of a woolly nature, and furnished, like that of the otter-hound, with a certain amount of oil, secreted by the glands of the skin, so as to resist the action of water. Mr. Carrick, the Master of the Carlisle Otter-hounds, purchased Mr. Sanderson's "Venture" from Mr. Wootton, who had bought the whole team in 1873, and has used him since that time with his hounds, and also as a stud-dog for improving his old breed of terriers, in which capacity he has been most useful. In the water his coat is said to stand exposure quite as well as the otter-hound's; and for those who want remarkably hardy dogs, without doubt the rough fox-terrier is better adapted than the smooth, who is often furnished with a soft silky coat which admits the rain to the skin almost in a worse manner than if it was bare. On the jaws a slight beard only is considered to be the correct thing, and in this point perhaps the modern dog is not exactly like the old-fashioned one, who had certainly a stronger and somewhat longer beard in most cases, but this difference is not enough to constitute a new and distinct breed. As far as my knowledge goes (and I have seen all the first-prize takers hitherto exhibited), the rough fox-terrier of the present day does not show quite so thick and "cobby" a body as the smooth, but his ear has the same size and shape, so that however this point has been obtained by the one, the same process must most probably have been adopted by the breeders of the other. The diminution of beard would lead to the supposition that Mr. Sanderson's dogs are a cross between the smooth fox-terrier (possibly already modified by the beagle cross) and the old-fashioned rough dog; and their possession of the under-pile in their coats, which I do not recollect to have existed in the latter, would lead me to believe that the Bedlington has been resorted to; but the body coat is too hard and wiry to induce the belief that this dog and the smooth fox-terrier are alone responsible for "Venture," "Turpin," and Co. The dog attains maturity so soon that several crosses may be carried out in a very few years, and a new breed can thus be manufactured to order by any single individual, certainly within ten years, and generally in half that time, always supposing that its elementary points are already in existence.

No dog is more available as a young man's companion than the subject of the present article, but he is not so well suited to the ladies' room, as his coat is apt to come off and disfigure her dress and carpet. With the single exception of the coat, the points of the rough fox-terrier resemble those of the smooth, and I need not therefore repeat them here. It is only necessary to substitute the above description of his coat for that given in the points of the smooth dog at page 86. The numerical value is the same.

XIII.—THE HARD-HAIRED SCOTCH TERRIER.

Until very recently no such breed as the above was recognised at our shows, where the only representatives of it were shown, first, when used for sporting purposes as rough fox-terriers, and, secondly, as toys which no doubt have been carefully bred from the original by selecting those possessed of the most lady-like coats and of the most beautiful blue and fawn colours. In Ireland a terrier closely resembling him is preserved and prized as he deserves, and may be considered to have, phœnix-like, risen from the ashes of the Scotch terrier. "Peto," the dog I selected twenty-five years ago to represent the breed, was absolutely bred in Scot-

land, and a better vermin-killing animal I never saw. I bred from
him and a beagle bitch several litters for retrieving purposes, which
they fulfilled extremely well; but as his ears were cropped, I have
no knowledge of what would have been their shape when entire,
nor, indeed, was the resultant cross left uncropped, as I preferred
preserving the terrier character as then known rather than that
of the beagle.

" PETO," a Scotch Terrier.

Up to the year 1875 an attempt was made to keep the breed
before the public by nominally allotting to it a class; but when
the prizes in it always fell to such dogs as Mrs. Foster's " Dundreary " and Miss Alderson's " Mozart," as was the case in 1873,
the class was abandoned and special ones constituted for wire-
haired terriers, to exclude the Halifax strain, which was defined
as " broken-haired." But alas for our poor Scottish friend! No
sooner was the nationality dropped than Mr. Sanderson's rough
breed of fox-terriers came to the front, and since that time they
kept there until about the year 1880.

It is admitted that the Scotch dog, as described below, with the sanction of nearly every well-known breeder of the present day, is of great antiquity, and it must not be confounded with the over-sized, long-backed dogs, with large and heavily feathered ears, whose traces of Skye ancestry are evident to those who understand the two breeds from which they spring. In fact, it is in the ears

The Hard-Haired Scotch Terrier.

that one of the chief characteristics of the Scotch terrier lies, for all unite in agreeing that they should be small, and covered with a velvety coat—not large, and fringed with hair like a prick-haired Skye terrier. As regards the carriage of the ear, the opinions of those best qualified to judge are a little divided between the merits of a perfectly erect and half-drop ear; but all unite in their condemnation of a perfectly drop, button, or fox-terrier ear. As to the half-drop ear, which stands erect, but falls over at the tip, half covering the orifice, a large, very large, majority of modern breeders agree in preferring the small, erect, sharp-pointed one; though all would probably hesitate to pass over a really good terrier who had half-prick ears. Another great feature in the Scotch terrier is his coat, which should be intensely hard and wiry, and not too long, and is well described in the appended scale of points, which bears the signatures of nearly all the leading breeders of the day.

As a dead-game animal, the Scotch terrier is not to be surpassed by any breed except bulls or bull-terriers, but the courage of the latter dogs is so exceptional that it is no disrespect to any other dog to place them for pluck in a class by themselves, and, pound for pound, there is no dog but a bull-terrier who can beat the hard-haired Scotchman by far. Still, he has a natural advantage over the bull-terrier, for his hard coat and thickly padded feet enable him to go through whins and over rocky places where the other would be useless, and he is far more easy to control, though naturally of a rather pugnacious disposition. His intelligence and love of home, his pluck, docility, and affection for his master, should make him a favourite with all who want a varmint dog; and nobody who once gets a good one, of the right style and stamp, will care to let him go.

Points of the Hard-Haired Scotch Terrier.

	VALUE		VALUE		VALUE
Skull,	5	Neck,	5	Coat,	20
Muzzle,	5	Chest,	5	Size,	10
Eyes,	5	Body,	10	Colour,	2½
Ears,	10	Legs and feet,	10	General appearance,	10
	—	Tail,	2½		—
	25		—		42½
			32½		

Total, 100.

Skull proportionately long, slightly domed, and covered with short hard hair about ¾ inch long or less. It should not be quite flat, as there should be a sort of stop or drop between the eyes.

Muzzle very powerful, and gradually tapering towards the nose, which should always be black and of a good size. The jaws should be perfectly level and the teeth square, though the nose projects somewhat over the mouth, which gives the impression of the upper jaw being longer than the under one.

Eyes set wide apart, of a dark brown or hazel colour; small, piercing, very bright, and rather sunken.

Ears very small, prick or half-prick (the former is preferable), but never drop. They should also be sharp-pointed, and the hair on them should not be long, but velvety, and they should not be cut. The ears should be free from any fringe at the top.

Neck short, thick, and muscular; strongly set on sloping shoulders.

Chest broad in comparison to the size of the dog, and proportionately deep.

Body of moderate length, not so long as a Skye's, and rather flat-sided; but well ribbed up, and exceedingly strong in hindquarters.

Legs and feet, both fore and hind legs, should be short, and very heavy in bone, the former being straight, or slightly bent, and well set on under the body, as the Scotch terrier should not be out at elbows. The hocks should be bent, and the thighs very muscular; and the feet strong, small, and thickly covered with short hair, the fore-feet being larger than the hind ones, and well let down on the ground.

The *tail*, which is never cut, should be about 7 inches long, carried with a slight bend, and often gaily.

The *coat* should be rather short (about 2 inches), intensely hard and wiry in texture, and very dense all over the body.

Size about 14 lbs. to 18 lbs. for a dog, 13 lbs. to 17 lbs. for a bitch.

Colours steel or iron grey, brindle, black, red, wheaten, and even yellow or mustard colour. It may be observed that mustard, black, and red are not usually so popular as the other colours. White markings are most objectionable.

General appearance.—The face should wear a very sharp, bright, and active expression, and the head should be carried up.

The dog (owing to the shortness of his coat) should appear to be higher on the leg than he really is; but, at the same time, he should look compact, and possessed of great muscle in his hind-quarters. In fact, a Scotch terrier, though essentially a terrier, cannot be too powerfully put together. He should be from about 9 inches to 12 inches in height, and should have the appearance of being higher on the hind-legs than on the fore.

FAULTS.

Muzzle either under or over-hung.

Eyes large or light-coloured.

Ears large, round at the points, or drop. It is also a fault if they are too heavily covered with hair.

Coat.—Any silkiness, wave, or tendency to curl is a serious blemish, as is also an open coat.

Size.—Specimens over 18 lbs. should not be encouraged.

XIV.—THE IRISH TERRIER.

For a long time I resisted the strong applications of several Irish friends to admit this dog as a breed distinct from the old Scotch terrier, to which I have just alluded. As, however, I find it, without doubt, highly valued in Ireland, and as it is really a well-shaped and useful-looking animal, I was at last induced to allow of his occupying a niche in the canine temple of fame, and to accept the scale of points, with their description, drawn up by a committee of Irish breeders of this dog, and signed by them. I do not quite agree with the numerical scale of points, as I see no reason for attaching more value to the head of this dog than to that of the fox-terrier; but as I hold the club responsible, and keep clear of all responsibility on the subject, I think it better to insert their scale and description as received from them.

Mr. R. G. Ridgway of Waterford has been most prominent in the above undertaking, and as he has been backed by two dozen Irish breeders and exhibitors, such unanimity may claim our adhesion, for I believe it would be almost impossible to get twenty-five

English signatures to any similar document. Mr. Ridgway states that the breed has been known in Ireland for fifty or sixty years; but so has a similar one in Scotland, and I certainly possessed a specimen more than fifty years ago. Nevertheless, there is no doubt that this breed now exists in Green Erin, and is prized there, as it certainly deserves; and as a consequence I introduce it here.

IRISH TERRIER CLUB'S CODE OF POINTS.

POSITIVE POINTS.	VALUE	NEGATIVE POINTS.	VALUE
Head, jaw, teeth, and eyes,	15	White nails, toes, and feet, *minus*	10
Ears,	5	Much white on chest,	10
Legs and feet,	10	Ears cropped,	·5
Neck,	5	Mouth undershot or cankered,	10
Shoulders and chest,	10	Coat shaggy, curly, or soft,	10
Back and loin,	10	Uneven in colour,	5
Hind-quarters and stern,	10		
Coat,	15		
Colour,	10		
Size and symmetry,	10		
Total	100	Total	50

Disqualifying points :—Nose, cherry or red. Brindle colour.

DESCRIPTIVE PARTICULARS.

Head long; skull flat, and rather narrow between ears, getting slightly narrower towards the eye; free from wrinkle; stop hardly visible, except in profile. The jaw must be strong and muscular, but not too full in the cheek, and of a good punishing length, but not so fine as a white English terrier's. There should be a slight falling away below the eye, so as not to have a greyhound appearance. Hair on face of same description as on body, but short (about a quarter of an inch long), in appearance almost smooth and straight; a slight beard is the only longish hair (and is only long in comparison with the rest) that is permissible, and that is characteristic.

Teeth should be strong and level.

Lips not so tight as a bull-terrier's, but well-fitting, showing through the hair their black lining.

Nose must be black.

Ears, when uncut, small and V-shaped, of moderate thickness, set well up on the head, and dropping forward closely to the cheek. The ears must be free of fringe, and the hair thereon shorter and generally darker in colour than the body.

The Irish Terrier.

Neck should be of a fair length, and gradually widening towards the shoulders, well carried, and free of throatiness. There is generally a slight sort of frill visible at each side of the neck, running nearly to the corner of the ear, which is looked on as very characteristic.

Shoulders and chest.—Shoulders must be fine, long, and sloping well into the back ; the chest deep and muscular, but neither full nor wide.

Back and loin.—Body moderately long; back should be strong and straight, with no appearance of slackness behind the shoulders; the loin broad and powerful and slightly arched ; ribs fairly sprung, rather deep than round, and well ribbed back.

Hind-quarters.—Well under the dog, should be strong and muscular, the thighs powerful, hocks near the ground, stifles not much bent.

Stern, generally docked, should be free of fringe or feather, set on pretty high, carried gaily, but not over the back or curled.

Feet and legs.—Feet should be strong, tolerably round, and moderately small; toes arched, and neither turned out nor in ; black toe-nails are preferable and most desirable. Legs moderately long, well set from the shoulders, perfectly straight, with plenty of bone and muscle; the elbows working freely clear of the sides, pasterns short and straight, hardly noticeable. Both fore and hind legs should be moved straight forward when travelling, the stifles not turned outwards, the legs free of feather and covered like the head, with as hard a texture of coat as body, but not so long.

Coat.—Hard and wiry, free of softness or silkiness, not so long as to hide the outlines of the body, particularly in the hind-quarters, straight and flat, no shagginess, and free of lock or curl.

Colour.—Should be "whole coloured," the most desirable being bright red ; next wheaten, yellow, and grey, brindle disqualifying. White sometimes appears on chest and feet; it is more objection-able on the latter than on the chest, as a speck of white on chest is frequently to be seen in all self-coloured breeds.

Size and symmetry.—Weight in show condition, from 16 lbs. to 24 lbs.—say 16 lbs. to 22 lbs. for bitches, and 18 lbs. to 24 lbs. for dogs. The most desirable weight is 22 lbs. or under, which is a nice stylish and useful size. The dog must present an active, lively, lithe, and wiry appearance ; lots of substance, at the same time free of clumsiness, as speed and endurance, as well as power, are very essential. They must be neither "cloddy" nor "cobby," but should be framed on the "lines of speed," showing a graceful "racing outline."

XV.—THE WELSH TERRIER.

A dog very closely resembling the Irish terrier except in size and colour has lately been paraded at our shows under the above name. In colour he is usually black, or grizzled, and tan, and in size about 15 or 16 inches. As to his points, they are so differently described that I shall not pretend to give them myself. But at a well-attended meeting of the special club for this breed, held at Carnarvon on the 4th August 1886, it was unanimously decided that the points of the Welsh terrier, as passed at the meeting at Hanley, be rescinded, and the present meeting decide upon the description to be adopted. To better enable the meeting to do this, the four winning dogs at the show then being held were brought into the meeting. So far as head was concerned, the type of Mr. Saunders's " Rattle," the winning bitch, was judged to be correct, and for body that of " General Contour," Mr. Colmore's successful dog, was decided to be the best. It was next suggested that either Mr. Whiskin or Mr. Yates, who had acted as judges of the variety, be requested to dictate to the meeting a description of the Welsh terrier, taking as their guide the two animals now before them. Mr. Yates consented to do this, and the following scale of points was approved and adopted :—

POINTS OF THE WELSH TERRIER.

Head.—The skull should be flat, and rather wider between the ears than the wire-haired fox-terrier. The jaw should be powerful, clean cut, rather deeper, and more punishing—giving the head a more masculine appearance than that usually seen on a fox-terrier. Stop not too defined, fair length from stop to end of nose, the latter being of a black colour.

Ears.—The ear should be V-shaped, small, not too thin, set on fairly high, carried forward and close to the cheek.

Eyes.—The eye should be small, not being too deeply set in or protruding out of skull, of a dark hazel colour, expressive and indicating abundant pluck.

Neck.—The neck should be of moderate length and thickness, slightly arched, and sloping gracefully into the shoulders.

G

Body.—The back should be short and well ribbed up, the loins strong, good depth, and moderate width of chest. The shoulders should be long, sloping, and well set back. The hind-quarters should be strong, thighs muscular, and of good length, with the hocks moderately straight, well let down, and fair amount of bone. The stern should be set on moderately high, but not too gaily carried.

Legs and Feet.—The legs should be straight and muscular, possessing fair amount of bone, with upright and powerful pasterns. The feet should be small, round, and cat-like.

Coat.—The coat should be wiry, hard, very close, and abundant.

Colour.—The colour should be black, or grizzle and tan, free from black pencilling on toes.

Size.—The height at shoulder should be 15 in. for dogs, bitches proportionately less. Twenty lbs. shall be considered a fair average weight in working condition, but this may vary a pound or so either way.

XVI.—THE SKYE TERRIER.

Few breeds have excited more controversy during the last twenty years than the Skye terrier. In the year 1860 I judged the terriers at Birmingham, and in a Scotch class, for which none of that breed were exhibited, I gave the first prize to a very beautiful white dog of the Hon. W. W. Vernon's, and the second to a dog imported by Major Irving, with a coat as curly and woolly as any Southdown sheep. Hereupon a controversy arose at the dinner-table, Major Irving alleging that his dog actually came from Skye, whereas Mr. Vernon did not claim more than a descent from the island several generations back. My decision was mainly founded on the woolly coat, which I believed then, and am since supported in that belief, to be by no means typical, but rather the contrary : while viewing the breed as toys, there can be no question that the straight and shining coat of the modern strain is far more beautiful than the woolly, matted coat of Major Irving's *protégé.* In the South of England, and notably in London, the former had long been considered to be the correct one, and I had seen many splendid specimens imported from Skye possessing it in a marked degree. Hence I acted on my previous opinions, and consider that I was quite justified in so doing; but I am not so sure about the colour (white), which I have never since that time met with in a purely-bred animal, and which I had previously tabooed in the first edition of this book, then just published. At the same time, I defined the coat as "long and straight, hard, and not silky, parted down the back, and nearly reaching the ground on each side, without the slightest curl or resemblance to wool." When, therefore, my definition of the proper colour was quoted, I was able to retort on the coat, and putting one against the other, I held my own pretty well. "Quilick," the original of my former illustration, was the son of imported parents, and when in full coat (which he was not at the time Mr. Wells drew his portrait) was a very handsome dog. I remember well his owner attempting to persuade Mr. Wells to draw on his imagination in this respect, but, like Mr. Baker, he would only copy what was before him, and the truthfulness of his work is quite as much to be relied on as that of the latter gentleman. Anyhow, the discussion waxed warm after the Birmingham Show, but it was mild in comparison with the subsequent terrific fights in relation to the same breed, as well as the Dandie, the fox-terrier, and the Bedlington.

For some years after Skyes were introduced in any number, the exhibits were confided to the drop-eared variety, which alone was prized in the South. At length, owing mainly to the exertions of Mr. H. Martin of Glasgow, a separate class was allotted to the two divisions, which cannot well be judged one against the other in the same class, and I shall, therefore, follow the precedent thus established.

During the year 1875, Mr. Gordon Murray attempted to force his own notions of the Skye on the doggy world, but without much success, in spite of the circumstantial way in which he supported his ideas. The portrait published by him as the real Simon Pure was so unfortunately ugly, that it certainly required a strong backer to induce the British public to take him up, and Mr. Gordon Murray's backbone was not stiff enough, if we may judge from the results. Anyhow, I shall ignore his definitions altogether, and describe the two breeds without any bias towards his "Mogstads," "Drynocks," or "Camusennaries," by which purely local names he distinguished his breeds.

During the present year (1886) the special Club formed for the purpose, have drawn up a code of points almost entirely in accordance with those I published in the last edition, the only alteration being the substitution of " height " for " length " and of " body " for " symmetry," which really amount to the same, for height can only be comparative with length, or length with height. I prefer, however, to substitute the whole of the description as accepted by the Club, which is as follows :—

THE SKYE TERRIER.

Introductory Remarks.—The " Skye Terrier " proper is a vermin dog, and is admirably adapted for his work, which, as is well known, is to enter vermin burrows, and make his way where larger dogs, or those of a different formation, would be unable to penetrate. He has necessarily very strong legs, short in proportion to the length of the body, which is long and measures well in girth. He possesses a keen scent, and in disposition is determined and courageous. Having a strong and muscular jaw, he is enabled to grip tenaciously. Dame Nature has provided this breed with an ample covering all over, and from the thickness and hard wet-resisting quality of his coat, the Skye can face with impunity almost any degree of cold to which he may be exposed in this country. The majority of Skyes are drop-eared, and the only distinction between the drop and prick-eared varieties consists in the muscular action of the ear. For sagacity, faithfulness, and attachment to their masters they are probably not excelled by any member of the canine species, and as house guards they are invaluable, their hearing being very acute.

In some districts of the Highlands of Scotland Skyes are bred, and used for the special purpose of following the fox and dislodging the wild cat from her den, generally among rocks and cairns of stone, at the foot of the hills, and when the fox, but for the assistance of the terriers, might bid the hounds defiance. Master Reynard when hard pressed either bolts or has to succumb to the terriers; and as to wild cats " no quarter " is the order of the dog. These remarks will tend to remove some misconception which unfortunately prevails in many quarters as to the characteristics of the Skye terrier, and also facilitate a right appreciation of the breed.

With such objects in view, and in order to place the Skye in a proper light with all admirers of the canine species, it is considered necessary to supplement the foregoing observations by a detailed description of the Skye terrier "points," and their relative value as indicative of the type to be desired in the breed.

Skyes —Prick-eared and Drop-eared.

POINTS AS DRAWN OUT BY THE SKYE TERRIER CLUB.

Head.—Long, with a powerful punishing jaw, a good set of teeth that should close square on the upper ones, just to look over the under ones. The skull between the ears should be narrow, and gradually expand towards the front of the brow, where it should be a good width, and then taper off gradually to the nose. There should be no, or very little, falling in of the skull at the eyes.

The eyes should be rather close set together and of a medium size and dark colour. In all cases the nose should be black.

Ears.—In the drop-eared variety the ears are a little larger than in the prick-eared, and should hang down at the side of the head, inclining a little to the front. In the prick-eared the ear should be carried nearly erect, projecting a very little outward at the top.

Body should be prominently long compared with the height; shoulders wide; chest deep and powerful. The ribs should be deep, so that the body will have a flat appearance. The back should have a small gradual slope down towards the shoulders.

Tail from the root should incline downwards to the centre, and then take a gradual turn upwards towards the point, but should never come above the level of the dog's back except when excited.

Legs very short and muscular, and the straighter they are the better; feet should be small, and claws are objectionable.

Coat.—Length on back should be from 3½ to 5½ inches, of a hard, wiry, water-resisting texture, lying straight and flat to the body, and should have no tendency to crimp or curl, equally dividing down the neck and back to the tail. Hair of the right texture will divide naturally, and will not require the brush to keep it in order. On the head the hair should be about 3 inches long and softer than that on the body, but straight and lying forward over the brow. The ears (in the drop-ear) should be sufficiently feathered to hang down and protect the inside of the ear, and mix away among the hair on the side of the head; the tail also should be well feathered, but not overdone.

Colours are numerous, but those recommended are dark and light blues, and dark and light greys, and fawn with black points. The head, legs, and body should be as near the one shade as possible; the ears should be much darker than the body.

Weight.—Dogs from 18 to 20 lbs., bitches 16 to 18 lbs. A pound or two over or under the above weight will not be objected to if the dog is possessed of good points otherwise.

MEASUREMENT.

Dogs.		INCHES	Bitches.		INCHES
Height, . . .	.	9	Height, . . .	.	8½
Length of head, .	.	8	Length of head, .		7
„ from head to root of tail, .	.	22	„ from head to root of tail, .		21
Length of tail without hair,	.	9	Length of tail without hair,	.	8
Total length from tip to tip,	.	39	Total length from tip to tip,	.	36

The foregoing description of points and measurements is required to complete a perfect specimen, and it should be the constant endeavour of every member of the club to breed up to or as near it as they possibly can.

POINTS.

	VALUE			VALUE
Coat, .	. 20	Ears, .	.	10
Height,	. 15	Tail, .	.	10
Head, .	15	Legs, .	.	10
Body, .	. 15	Colour,	.	5
				100

XVII.—THE DANDIE DINMONT TERRIER.

Almost all well-known breeds have altered in appearance more or less within the half-century during which I have been conversant with them, but in no one instance have I seen such fluctuations in shape as in the subject of the present article. From the evidence afforded by Landseer's well-known accuracy, the original possessed by Sir Walter Scott was a long, low, little dog, of a purely terrier type, and with small terrier ears, falling like those of the fox-terrier, though somewhat larger in leather. The chest is by no means wide, and there is very little to remark on as typical of the breed. There is certainly a slight top-knot, but there is no approach to the modern development, which now almost equals that of the Irish water-spaniel. An exact counterpart of Landseer's embodiment is familiar to my memory as belonging to a friend of mine forty-four years ago, and the dog was said by him. to have been brought from Scotland with the statement that he

was of the pure breed. In the early days of dog shows, such
different types of this variety were exhibited that Southern fanciers
were much puzzled ; and in 1867 Mr. Matthias Smith, who judges
the class at Birmingham, refused to give any prize, alleging that
the whole lot were mongrels. On this daring act ensued a paper
war, maintained with great boldness by Mr. Smith, who adduced
certain cogent facts in support of his opinions ; among others, the

The Dandie Dinmont Terrier.

existence of the Landseer picture, and also of a breed in his own
possession, which, however, he stated to have " prick ears." This
slip brought down on him the whole force of his opponents, and
he was silenced for a time, though with a little qualification he
might have held that he meant by the term to distinguish the
proper ear (according to his view) from the large falling, hound-

like ear of Mr. Mellor's " Bandy," which was among the disqualified class. Now I certainly could not entirely agree with Mr.
Smith's opinion when published in 1867–68, but he has lately
resuscitated the subject, after having examined into the evidence
in existence over the Border, and has published the following
letter in " The Field " of November 16 :—

THE DANDIE DINMONT.

SIR,—I must ask you kindly to allow me space in your next issue for a few
remarks, which cannot, I take it, fail to be of interest to those of your readers
who have an interest in, and care for, the dog called the Dandie Dinmont.
It is because of late there has been much division of opinion as to what is, or
what is not, the true and genuine breed of this particular dog, that I the more
readily venture to state my own opinion on the matter. It will be in the
recollection of most dog-fanciers that for two years in succession I had the
pleasure of being one of the judges at the Birmingham Show, and also that
I did, with my brother judges, disqualify and refuse to award prizes to certain
dogs entered as Dandies. It is not now my intention to put myself on the
defence because the course I took as a judge did not meet with the entire
approval of sundry exhibitors and others, nor is it my intention to attempt to
reply to the one-sided and palpably false argumentative reasoning which has
since appeared in public correspondence on the subject ; but my sole object
in addressing you is to give your readers the benefit of my experience and
opinion, at the same time adducing statements of facts which no dispassionate
dog-fancier can possibly gainsay or deny. I would beg, then, that members of
the Dandie Club, and Dandie fanciers generally, would either admit that my
opinion is entirely the correct one, or, if not correct, show in a truthful and
logical way that it is an erroneous one. The position, then, which I take is
this : That the so-called Dandies which are constantly receiving prizes at our
leading dog shows are not of the pure Dandie Dinmont breed, but are mongrels.
I admit that I have devoted much time, thought, and money to make myself
familiar with the numerous varieties called Dandies, and I generally allow that
those judges whose knowledge of the Dandie is not so matured as my own
ought not altogether to be blamed ; but if they persist in hugging ignorance, and pandering to that which ought to give way to an exact and true
knowledge of the matter which is really within their reach, then indeed
blame is their deserved portion. It is pitiable to note that from time to time
prizes have been awarded to dogs which differed from each other on points
which admit of no difference whatever in the case of dogs of a pure and
special breed ; and I am prepared to say that from time to time standards of
excellence for these " hybrid " Dandies have been made so as to suit the
particular animal owned by the fanciers ; and this, too, with the idea of
carrying out to a greater degree the determination of some that this so-called

Dandie shall be regarded as the true breed of Dandie. Further, I would say that certain gentlemen, in order to establish a breed peculiar to their own fanciful imaginations, have invented from time to time pedigrees worked out, as it would appear, from certain celebrated kennels; indeed, so far has this gone, that many now come to regard these prize hybrids as belonging to the true and original breed of Dandies as mentioned by Sir Walter Scott in his "Guy Mannering." Never was there a greater error, and I take it that the time has come when we should try once more to raise up amongst us the true breed of the Dandie Dinmont, and repudiate as unquestionable mongrels the bandy-legged, out-elbowed dogs which too often, alas! take off the prizes which should properly go to the genuine breed. Who does not remember the description given by Sir Walter Scott of old Davidson's dogs, which he prided himself so much on, especially the terriers Peppers and Mustards; and then, further on in the story, how it is stated that "the Deuke himself has sent as far as Charlie's Hope to get ane o' Dandy Dinmont's Pepper and Mustard terriers"? Now, it would seem to me that those dogs were not what the hybrid Dandies of the present day are; for, as he says, "I had them a' regularly entered, first wi' rottens (rats), then wi' stots (weasels), and then wi' the tods (foxes) and brocks (badgers); and now they fear nothing that ever cam' wi' a hairy skin on't." When in Scotland a few weeks since, I made a point of going to Abbotsford, where, as your readers are aware, is the portrait of a Dandie Dinmont painted by the late Sir Edwin Landseer, which dog, when alive, belonged to the late Sir Walter Scott. I affirm that this dog was never the same dog as the mongrel Dandie prize-dog of to-day. Some of your readers may also be aware that Mr. H. Bradshaw Smith, of Blackwood House, Ecclefechan, "the best authority, perhaps, in the world," had a pure Dandie Dinmont terrier from old Davidson, and, when this dog died, had it stuffed. I have seen this dog, and I say of it, as in the case of Sir Walter's dog painted by Sir E. Landseer, that it is totally different from the so-called Dandie of to-day.

It is further stated that this gentleman has in his kennels a great many dogs descended in a direct line from the Charlie's Hope kennels of Peppers and Mustards. These dogs I have seen and carefully examined, and my opinion respecting them is similar to that above expressed concerning Landseer's painting of Scott's Dandie and Mr. Bradshaw Smith's "stuffed" one. Further in support of my argument, I may say that I have seen a Dandie stuffed called "Old Pepper," which belonged to Mr. Pat. Lang, banker, at Selkirk. Dogs owned by Mr. Locke, of Selkirk; by Mr. Scott, of Jedburgh; by Mr. Miller, "a prize taker," of Moffat; numbers owned, of different strains, by small and limited fanciers—all, without one exception, differ entirely from the portrait at Abbotsford and the "stuffed" one at Blackwood House. Further in support of my argument, some of the oldest breeders of the so-called Dandies admit they are mongrels, and not "pure," because it is quite a chance if in a litter of their pups one will find two alike.

MATTHIAS SMITH.

125 HYDE PARK ROAD, LEEDS.

Entirely concurring as I do with the above opinions, and having previously stated almostly exactly similar ones in "The Field," I think it desirable to adduce Mr. Smith's testimony, though I confess I do not attach any great importance to the question of purity, nor to the Walter Scott type as the ideal of perfection. Still, if fanciers desire the original breed in all its pristine purity, I agree with Mr. Smith that it is not presented to them among the prize-takers at our modern shows.

But granting, as I think we must, that the modern Dandie is not purely descended from the old Teviot strain, it becomes a question what cross has been employed to produce the change. Now the variation is—(1) in ear; (2) in length of body; (3) in width of chest and bandiness of fore-legs; and (4) in temperament; and when we find all these points combined in the dachshund and in no other breed, it is a natural consequence that we should come to the conclusion, that recourse has been at some time had to the latter as a cross, possibly not intentionally, but from accident. But not being, like Mr. Smith, quixotic enough to expect breeders of the Dandie to set to work afresh with a view to resuscitate his original shape, I am content to take him as I find him in the kennels of Mr. Bradshaw Smith, Mr. James Locke, and other well-known breeders, and, excepting with his peculiar temperament, I have no quarrel whatever with the dog of the present day. But of this I certainly complain; for I have found the breed as utterly unmanageable as the dachshund when once on the scent of fur. While residing in Worcestershire in the year 1865, I reared "Rhoderick Dhu," given me when a puppy by Mr. Macdona, and attempted to break him as a rabbit dog, but could never get the slightest control over him when on bunny's scent. Whether in covert or hedgerow, he would persevere until actually restrained by force; and if he once got into a wood, it was hopeless to expect to recover him until he was compelled by hunger and exhaustion to leave off. No punishment had the slightest effect, and at length I gave up the task of breaking him as hopeless, parting with him as a show dog to Mr. Murchison, from whom I again obtained him in consequence of his bandy fore-legs forbidding his reaching premier honours. His end was that I lost him on Wimbledon Common, where he got on a rabbit scent, and worked it out in the scrub, regardless of voice, whistle, and every possible effort on my part to recall him. He had a mortal enmity to foxes also, and once killed five cubs in about as many minutes, to my great horror. Now such a temperament, however "varmint" it may be considered, is a bore and a nuisance, and for real use such a dog as "Rhoderick Dhu" would be quite out of the question. Mr. Bradshaw Smith's and Mr. Locke's pets are, however, not much employed in this way, and, as companionable dogs, if kept away from vermin, &c., they are unobjectionable in every way. It is, therefore, in the latter capacity that they are judged in the present day, and as such I shall consider them in the following description, commencing with their scale of points as originally laid down by the Club specially organised for the improvement of the breed.

The following is a description of the Dandie Dinmont terrier as settled by the special Club for that breed:—

Head, strongly made and large, not out of proportion to the dog's size, the muscles showing extraordinary development, more especially the maxillary.

Skull broad between the ears, getting gradually less towards the eyes, and measuring about the same from the inner corner of the eye to back of skull as it does from ear to ear, the forehead well domed; the head is covered with very soft silky hair, which should not be confined to a mere top-knot, and the lighter in colour and silkier it is the better; the cheeks, starting from the ears proportionately with the skull, have a gradual taper towards the *muzzle*, which is deep and strongly made, and measures about 3 inches in length, or in proportion to skull as 3 is to 5. The muzzle is covered with hair of a little darker shade than the top-knot, and of the same texture as the feather of the fore-legs. The top of the muzzle is generally bare for about an inch from the back part of the nose, the bareness coming to a point towards the eye, and being about $\frac{1}{2}$ inch broad at the nose. The nose and inside of mouth black or dark-coloured. The teeth very strong, especially the canines, which are of extraordinary size for such a small dog. The canines fit well into each other, so as to give the greatest available holding and punishing power, and the teeth are level in front, the upper ones very slightly overlapping the under ones.

(Many of the finest specimens have a " swine mouth," which is very objectionable, but it is not so great an objection as the protrusion of the under jaw.)

Eyes set wide apart, large, full, round, bright, expressive of great determination, intelligence, and dignity, set low and prominent in front of the head ; colour a rich dark hazel.

Ears large and pendulous, set well back, wide apart, and low on the skull, hanging close to the cheek, with a very slight projection at the base, broad at the junction of the head, and tapering almost to a point, the fore-part of the ear tapering very little—the taper being mostly on the back part, the fore-part of the ear coming almost straight down from its junction with the head to the tip. They are covered with a soft straight brown hair (in some cases almost black), and have a thin feather of light hair starting about two inches from the tip, and of nearly the same colour and texture as the top-knot, which gives the ear the appearance of a distinct point. The animal is often one or two years old before the feather is shown. The cartilage and skin of the ear should not be thick, but rather thin. Length of ear from 3 to 4 inches.

Neck very muscular, well developed and strong, showing great power of resistance, being well set into the shoulders.

Body long, strong, and flexible, ribs well sprung and round ; chest well developed, and let well down between the fore-legs ; the back rather low at the shoulders, having a slight downward curve, and a corresponding arch over the loins, with a very slight gradual drop from top of loins to root of tail ; both sides of backbone well supplied with muscle.

Tail rather short, say from 8 to 10 inches, and covered on the upper side with wiry hair of darker colour than that of the body, the hair on the under side being lighter in colour, and not so wiry, with a nice feather about 2 inches long, getting shorter as it nears the tip ; rather thick at the root, getting thicker for about 4 inches, then tapering off to a point. It should not be twisted or curled in any way, but should come up with a regular curve like a scimitar, the tip when excited being in a perpendicular line with the root of the tail. It should neither be set on too high nor too low. When not excited it is carried gaily, and a little above the level of the body.

Legs.—The fore-legs short, with immense muscular development and bone, set wide apart, the chest coming well down between them. The feet well formed *and not flat*, with very strong brown or dark-coloured claws. Bandy-legs and flat feet are objectionable, but may be avoided—the bandy-legs by the use of splints when first noticed, and the flat feet by exercise and a dry bed and floor to kennel. The hair on the fore-legs and feet of a blue dog should be tan, varying according to the body, colour from a rich tan to a pale fawn; of a mustard dog, they are of a darker shade than its head, which is a creamy white. In both colours there is a rich feather about 2 inches long, rather lighter in colour than the hair on the fore-part of the leg. The hind legs are a little longer than the fore ones, and are set rather wide apart, but not spread out in an unnatural manner, while the feet are much smaller; the thighs are well developed, and the hair of the same colour and texture as the fore ones, but having no feather or dew claws; the whole of the claws should be dark; but the claws of all vary in shade according to the colour of the dog's body.

Coat.—This is a very important point. The hair should be about two inches long; that from skull to foot of tail a mixture of hardish and soft hair, which gives a sort of crisp feel to the hand. The hair should not be wiry; the coat is what is termed pily or pencilled. The hair on the under part of the body is lighter in colour and softer than that on the top; the skin on the belly accords with the colour of the dog.

Colour.—The colour is pepper or mustard. The pepper colour ranges from a dark bluish black to a light silvery grey, the intermediate shades being preferred—the body colour coming well down the shoulders and back, gradually merging into the leg colour. The mustards vary from a reddish brown to a pale fawn, the head being a creamy white; the legs and feet of a shade darker than the head; the claws are dark, as in other colours. (Nearly all have some white up the chest, and some have also white claws.)

Size.—The length should be from 8 to 11 inches at the top of shoulder. Length from top of shoulder to root of tail should not be more than twice the dog's height, but preferably 1 or 2 inches less.

Weight from 14 lbs. to 24 lbs., the best weight as near 18 lbs. as possible; these weights are for dogs in good working order.

POINTS.

	VALUE		VALUE		VALUE
Head,	10	Body, . .	20	Colour, . . .	5
Eyes,	10	Tail, .	5	Size and weight, .	5
Ears,	10	Legs and feet,.	10	General appearance,.	5
Neck,	5	Coat, . .	15		
	35		50		15

Total, 100.

In December 1878 the war between Mr. Matthias Smith and the modern breeders was waging fiercely, and he had the best of it, being supported by the following letter in "The Field" of December 7, 1878, from a Mr. Davison, who was formerly a Border man, but has left the North more than forty years :—

SIR,—I, as rather more than a sexagenarian and a Border man, and one who in almost his childhood took up with Dandies, can, I think, throw some light on the origin of the Dandies by Mr. Davidson. The Border "muggers" were great breeders of terriers—the Andersons on the English side, and the Faas and Camells on the Scotch side. In their perambulations they generally met once or twice a year at Long Horsley, Rochester (the ancient Bremnium of the Romans), Alwinton, or some other Border village. If they could not get a badger, they got a foumart, wild cat, or hedgehog, at which to try their dogs. The trials generally ended in a general dog fight, which led to a battle royal amongst the tribes represented. This afterwards led to a big drink and exchange of dogs. Jack Anderson, the head of the tribe, had a red bitch, who for badger-drawing, cat, foumart, or hedgehog killing, beat all the dogs coming over the Border. Geordy Faa, of Yethom, had a wire-haired dog terrier, the terror not only of all the other terriers in the district, but good at badger, fox, or foumart. They met at Alwinton, where Willy and Adam Bell (noted terrier breeders) had brought a badger they had got hold of at Weaford, near the Cheviots. Both the red bitch and other black terriers drew the badger every time they were put in. "Jock Anderson," says Geordy, "the dogs should be mated; let us have a grand drink, the man first doon to lose his dog." "Done," says Jock. They sent for the whisky, which never paid the King's duty, to Nevison's at the little house, having agreed to pay two shillings a quart for it. Down they sat on the green, fair drinking; in eighteen hours Jock tumbled off the cart-shafts, and Geordy started off with the dogs. They were mated, and produced the first Pepper and Mustards, which were presented by Geordy to Mr. Davidson (Dandie Dinmont of "Guy Mannering"). Strange to say, the produce were equally the colour of pepper and mustard. The last pair I saw of what I considered perfect Dandies were Robert Donkin's, at Ingram, near Alnwick, just before I left the North in 1838. I have been at shows, but could never identify any Dandies shown as at all like the original breed belonging to the Telfords of Blind Burn, the Elliots of Cottonshope, the Donkins of Ingram, and other Border farmers. I am not a doggy man, but like to see all old breeds kept distinct.

J. DAVISON.

ANDOVER, *December* 2.

Thus we have the evidence of Mr. Matthias Smith, founded on a comparison of portraits and stuffed skins with modern dogs, my own opinion, depending on the portrait and a specimen sent south-wards to a friend of mine nearly fifty years ago, and the above letter from Mr. Davison, all tending to prove that the modern show Dandie is not identical with the original breed. I have thrown out a suggestion that the latter, supposing it to exist, is due to a cross with the dachshund, but this was indignantly denied by Mr. Bradshaw Smith, who maintained that it is quite impossible to have been effected without his knowledge, and that he was posi-tive no such cross has taken place. It is certainly very remark-able that the peculiarities of the dachshund (bodily and mental) should be so fully marked as they are in the Dandie of the present day, and that they should be exactly those points in which the latter differs, or is said to differ, from the old breed. Extra length of body, bandy fore-legs, a peculiar turn of the stifles, a high loin, and long ears, are all bodily characteristics of the two breeds, while the want of control over the hunting tendency is equally marked as a mental peculiarity. It is, however, treason to whisper such a suspicion among Dandie fanciers, and so I shall beg my readers to consider the above unwritten, and to accept the dicta of the Dandie Club, with Mr. Bradshaw Smith as their authority, as being incon-trovertible, in spite of all the proof that can be brought against them.

XVIII.—THE SMOOTH ENGLISH TERRIERS.

England has been noted for its terriers as long as we have any reliable record of our native breeds of dogs. Until the time of Daniel, who published his celebrated book on "Rural Sports" in

1801, no particular colour was attached to the breed, but he discribes "black and tan" as its peculiar attribute, and since his day 95 per cent. of the smooth terriers kept in this country were of that colour until the rage for fox-terriers came in. As in all breeds of this colour, occasionally one or two red puppies are met with, and even in the best strains more rarely a blue and fawn one will appear. White and parti-coloured English terriers other than fox are also not uncommon, but they are not prized, and the classes for "white English terriers" which were common twenty years ago are now abandoned.

THE BLACK AND TAN OR MANCHESTER TERRIER.

In the present day our English terrier, to be *en régle*, must be either black and tan, and is then called the Manchester terrier, or pure white. The latter is much admired by a select few, but the former prevails to a very much greater extent throughout the country, Manchester, however, being still the headquarters of the breed. Since the successive advent into fashion of the Dandie, the Skye, and the fox-terrier, and to a lesser extent of the Bedlington and the Halifax terriers, the old English dog has fallen into comparative insignificance; but this is purely a matter of fashion, for he was, without doubt, in former times fully the equal of each and all the above-mentioned varieties, in every point which goes to make up a companionable house-dog, as well as a dog useful out of doors for rabbit or vermin hunting. Unfortunately, in the early part of this century, in order to increase his elegance, recourse was had to the Italian greyhound; producing a cross intermediate between the two in shape, but retaining the delicacy of constitution and cowardice of the greyhound to such an extent as to make the dog unfit for the purposes to which young men generally put their pets. This little dog was then generally known as the spider-terrier, but he is now altogether out of fashion, the ladies, who greatly admired him at first, having discarded him in favour of the fox-terrier, which is certainly more in accordance with their Ulster coats than the poor little trembling animal who formerly shared their caresses with his foreign parent, the pug, or the Blenheim spaniel. Whether

H

or not show English terriers of the present time still go back to the Italian, it is admitted that they are not so hardy and courageous as the fox-terrier, the Bedlington, or the Dandie, and consequently there may be some reason for the neglect of the breed by the public at large. Still, as a house-dog pure and simple, he is not to be surpassed, being clean in his habits, free from skin smell (though he is apt to have foul breath if not carefully fed),

The Manchester Terrier and the Toy.

and easily taught tricks; but, on the other hand, he is apt to be jealous of all rivals, whether canine or human, and is not very particular in his attacks on his foes, whether he does injury with his teeth or not. His bark, also, is shrill and loud, and not very readily stopped, occasioning some considerable annoyance to visitors entering the room where he is. It may, therefore, be gathered that, in my opinion, the Manchester and white English terriers are not such desirable companions as several of the breeds which have supplanted them.

I am not now alluding to the toy black and tan terrier, which will be described in his proper place, though it cannot be disputed that he is only a Manchester terrier reduced in size. The subject of these remarks is a dog of about the same weight as the fox-terrier, ranging usually from 10 or 12 lbs. up to 18 lbs., or a trifle more. He is now much thicker in build than of yore, when he was of the type of the accompanying sketch of Lady.

"LADY," an English Terrier, the Property of the late Mr. C. Morrison of Walham Green.

The points of the black and tan terrier are as follows :—

	VALUE		VALUE
Head,	5	Legs,	5
Jaws and teeth,	5	Feet,	5
Eyes,	5	Coat,	5
Ears,	5	Colour,	25
Neck and shoulders,	10	Tail,	5
Chest,	10	Symmetry,	5
Loin,	10	Total,	100

The *head* has a narrow, long, and flat skull, with marked brows but no great rise at that part. It gradually tapers from the ears to the nose. The skin covering it is tightly drawn over the bones, and shows no tendency to wrinkle.

The *jaws* are long, tapering gradually from the cheeks, which should not be full and bulging, indicative of a bulldog cross. *Teeth* level, or, if anything, a trifle overhung. *Nose* perfectly black.

The *eyes* are small, sharp, and expressive, the iris being so dark a brown as to look black without a close examination. Though small, they should be set level with the edge of the orbit, and neither below nor above its surface.

The *ears* are almost invariably cropped, and that in a way to cause great pain to the dog, not only at the time, but for many weeks afterwards. In order to give a very sharp appearance, the "leather" is cut away almost level with the head, leaving a thin point standing up in a manner quite unnatural to the animal in any of his varieties. To do this requires a very good eye and some practice, but, however well the operation is done, the wound will contract and pucker the slip left if daily attention is not paid to it, by removing the scabs and stretching out the puckers; the thin and sharp point shrinks into an unsightly crumpled lump, and instead of an appearance being presented of greater sharpness than before, the reverse is exhibited. Hopes have been entertained of late years that this practice of cropping would be abandoned in the case of these terriers, as has been done with the pug, but I see no indications of such a happy result; and undoubtedly a Manchester terrier, however well made and marked, would be left out of the prize list by any of our judges if exhibited with his ears entire. The operation is not usually done till the puppy is six or seven months old, as until that time it is almost impossible to get the desired shape, and this makes it all the more painful, as by that time the cartilages have become hard, and a sharp pair of scissors must be used with considerable force to put through them. The natural ear is thin in well-bred dogs, and falls over outwards, but seldom lies quite close to the cheeks, often exhibiting a tendency to the rose or tulip form, and the two ears seldom matching exactly. It is a great deal on this account, I think, that the practice of cropping is kept up, for very few dogs would show neat ears if left entire; but when they are neat, they surely ought to be prized accordingly by the judges.

The *neck* should be light, round, and with a greyhound-like turn from the occiput to the setting on to the shoulders, tapering very slightly downwards. The under surface must be quite tight and concave, approaching the form of the cock's thropple. The *shoulders* must be sloping, but they are not required to be muscular, as in the fox-terrier, whose digging powers are regarded as of considerable importance.

The *chest* is deep, with an approach to the keel-shape of the greyhound, which it also resembles in its absence of width. The round barrel-like form of some strains arises from a bull cross, used to abrogate the evils of that attending on the cross of the Italian greyhound. The back ribs are often short, but good judges penalise this tendency.

The *loins* should be round and slightly arched, the muscle being developed in good specimens under the spine as well as above it. The flank should not be too much cut up.

The *legs* should be light of bone, set on quite straight, with elbows and hocks well let down, and stifles well bent. The forearms are muscular, but not excessively so, and the lower thighs are of the same character.

The *feet* are compact and round, but hare-like, with the toes well split up, and at the same time arched. The claws should be short and jet black. The dew-claws are generally removed.

The *coat* is fine, short, and glossy, but not soft.

The *colour* (including markings) is regarded as more important than any other point by the breeders and fanciers of this terrier, to such an extent as to justify the allotment of 25 out of the 100 in the scale of points. Of course, in any breed intended to be judged for its suitability to work, such an allotment would be absurd, but in a fancy article there can be no argument held on this principle, and we must be content to accept the *dicta* of those who have the command of the market. These gentlemen hold, first, that the black must be jet without admixture with the tan or a single white hair; secondly, the tan must be a rich mahogany, defined distinctly by a marked and clear line where it meets the black. But these colours encroach on each other in the following way. The black is shown over the whole of the upper surfaces and sides, except a spot of tan over each eye on the brow, and another on each cheek, in both cases being set in a circle of black; the tan also runs along the sides of the jaws backwards to the lower parts of the cheeks and ends in the throat. Examining the tan, we find it occupying all the lower parts of the body, the under sides of the ears, a spot on each side of the front of the chest, which it thereby shares with the black. The legs are tanned up to the knees and hocks outside and inside all the way up. The feet are entirely tan with the exception of a black line on each toe called " pencilling," while just above the foot and below the knee in front of the pastern a black mark called the " thumb-mark " is exhibited. These markings are regarded as of great importance, and, of course, puppies exhibiting them are carefully selected and bred from, but they are seldom shown till the second or third month. The clearer the black the higher the value accorded to them.

The *tail* is of the tobacco-pipe order, strong at the root and tapering to a fine point like the sting of a bee. It must be curved down, a curl over the back being specially disliked.

Symmetry in a dog regarded only for his beauty is of course valued accordingly.

THE WHITE ENGLISH TERRIER.

This breed until very recently has fallen into neglect, but within the last four or five years attempts have been made to resuscitate it with some success. In the early days of shows, and notably at Islington in 1862, Mr. White of Clapham carried all before him with his strain of pure white English terriers, but after that time few good specimens were shown until 1876, when Mr. G. Stables of Manchester came out with a strain superior in form to that of Mr. White, and indeed exactly resembling the Manchester terrier in shape, with more hair than Mr. White's terriers possessed. His kennel had evidently been too much inbred, and, probably owing to this cause, the strain seems to have died out.

This dog (when shown, which is now very rarely done) is judged by the same scale as the Manchester terrier, except that the thirty points unequally divided between coat and colour are here equally valued, each being allotted fifteen. A pure and opaque white is considered essential, without any tendency to pink or yellow, and the skin should be so well covered that no part is bare except the belly. The eyes, nose, and claws should be as dark as in the Manchester dog.

XIX.—THE BEDLINGTON TERRIER.

"TYNESIDE," Bedlington Terrier, the Property of T. J. Pickett, Newcastle-on-Tyne

Until within the last ten or twelve years this breed was unknown beyond the counties of Northumberland, Cumberland, and Westmoreland, and it was long before the general public would admit its existence as a separate one. Even its chief admirers do not profess that it is much older than the Dandie, and only date it eighty years back or thereabouts, when it is said to have been originated from the mating of a dog "Piper," belonging to Mr. Anderson, with "Phœbe," the property of a Mr. Coates, the produce of which was "Young Piper," bred by Mr. Ainsley of Bedlington, whence the breed was continued and derived its name. The pedigrees of "Piper" and "Phœbe" have been hunted up, and are given back for several generations; but all "doggy" men know what value to attach to such prehistoric testimonials. Excepting in the case of foxhounds, I confess I have little faith in them—even those of greyhounds, until the time of "Thacker," being in many instances unreliable. As Mr. Dalziel (himself a North-countryman) has remarked, if such a breed had existed in the time of Bewick, who was a native of Newcastle, surely he would have noticed its existence, and its absence from his "History of British Quadrupeds" is certainly an argument in favour of its modern creation.

No other terrier at all resembles the Bedlington, which is a leggy dog, with hound-like ears, and at the first glance seems to be a cross between a greyhound and an otter-hound. He is very quarrelsome, and is said to be extremely plucky. Of these qualities those who have seen a class exhibited on overcrowded benches must be convinced, for in many cases dogs allowed two or three inches too much chain have half killed each other during the first night of their being put together. Whether this kind of pugnacity could induce its possessor to face a badger in his earth, I do not pretend to say, but *primâ facie* it is an argument in favour of high pluck. My own experience of the breed is *nil*, never having had one in my possession; but the evidence in support of their courage is beyond dispute. Still I am not aware that there is any reason to suppose it higher in them than in the Dandie or fox-terrier of a good strain, and the Bedlington must be taken to be merely an average representative of the terrier tribe in point of courage, or perhaps a little above that level. In the South his "soft" appearance for a long time set every one against him, but at last it is generally admitted that in his case, at least, appearances are deceptive.

The numerical value of the points of this dog is as follows, according to the scale of the Bedlington Club:—

	VALUE		VALUE
Head,	10	Body (chest, ribs, and loin), .	20
Jaws,	5	Legs, . . .	5
Teeth,	5	Feet,	5
Ears,	5	Coat,	10
Eyes,	5	Colour,	5
Nose, . . .	5	Tail, . .	5
Neck and shoulders,	10	Size and weight, .	5
		Total, .	100

The *head* is long and wedge-shaped, resembling in this respect the English terrier, but with a greater proportion of jaw to skull than in that breed. There is a marked brow to the skull, and also a high occipital protuberance.

The *jaws* are long, but not so pointed as in the English terrier.

The *teeth* are large and regular, generally even, if not overshot. An undershot mouth is objected to.

The *ears* are longer than in any other terrier, filbert-shaped and lying close to the cheeks. They are set on low, and have a hound-like appearance, which has supported the theory of the otter-hound derivation. They are clothed with fine hair, slightly fringed at the edges.

The *eyes* are always of a light brown, varying in shade with the colour of the coat. In sandy and liver-coated dogs the brown is a light hazel, while in the blues it has a yellower shade. In shape and size they are small, deeply sunk, and placed close together, with the long axis of each in the same line.

The *nose* is large and fleshy. In colour it varies with that of the coat, being pink in the sandy and liver dogs, and black in the blues, whether whole blues or blue and tans.

Neck and shoulders.—There is nothing remarkable in these points, except that the neck should be of fair length, and not weak, as it is apt to be. Shoulders not loaded with wide blades.

Body (chest, ribs, and loin).—The chest is rather deep, long, and flat, with shallow back ribs in many otherwise good specimens. Loin arched and rising above the level of the tops of the shoulder-blades; very muscular, and with the greyhound-like continuation of the long dorsal muscles well formed, connecting powerfully the loin and chest. Hips wide, but not ragged.

The *legs* are small in bone and not very muscular, generally set on straight, with elbows rather high.   Hocks also high and stifles somewhat straight.

The *feet* are larger and rather flat, indicative of the otter-hound descent.   Claws strong and following the colour of the nose.

The *coat* is somewhat peculiar, resembling tangled flax in appearance and texture, and is hence called "linty." It is very open, and generally without much curl, but there is always a slight wave; and being always more or less tangled, there is an appear-of curl at first sight, which on closer examination is seen to be a deception.   Among the soft and fine hairs there are generally scattered a few coarse ones, but the fewer the better.

The *colours* are (1) blue or slate; (2) blue and tan; (3) liver; (4) liver and tan; (5) sandy in all shades, from dark fawn down to cream.

The *tail* is set on low, and is carried nearly straight on a level with the back.   It should be thick at the root, and end in a fine point with little hair on it.   •

Size and weight.—The size is from 14 inches to 18 inches, and the weight 15 lbs. to 25 lbs.

XX.—THE HALIFAX, BLUE FAWN, OR YORKSHIRE TERRIER.

This modern breed has sometimes been called the "blue fawn". terrier, but this is a misnomer, as there are many Bedlingtons of that colour, and it is now almost universal among the Dandie tribe. I do not at all know why the prefix "Halifax" was applied, as both Huddersfield and Bradford have a greater claim to be considered the headquarters of the breed.   According to my judgment, the whole tribe ought to be included among the "toys," since they are never used for any kind of terrier work; but the committees of our shows make two distinct classes for them, one being distinguished as for "Yorkshire terriers," and the other for "broken-haired toy terriers," in which latter small Yorkshire terriers always carry off the prizes.   Without doubt this little dog is a very beautiful animal, and in that respect has a great advantage over all nondescript broken-haired terriers.   Hence it is not surprising that, when exhibited in competition with them, it has always obtained the prize, reducing the old-fashioned Scotch terrier to the ranks, and excluding him from every show. The admirers of the breed allege that the Yorkshire dog is an improved Scotch terrier by careful selection; but in my opinion other breeds have been resorted to in order to obtain the long silky coat, which often is 3 or 4 inches long on the body, and on the face extends to 6 or 7. Now I set no bounds to the skill and art of the breeder, if only time is allowed him to carry out his wishes, but I scarcely think this change could be effected within the thirty years that have

"DUNDREARY," Blue Fawn Terrier, the Property of Mrs. Foster, Bradford.

been occupied in its production. Indeed, it is comparatively so easy to change externals by resorting to a cross, and so difficult to do this by selection alone, that I candidly confess the opinion that the Yorkshire terrier is not a Scotch dog improved by the latter process unassisted by a cross. As long as any distinct breed is left unmixed, every litter comes nearly true to the type; but cross it, and varieties in all directions crop up, sometimes in a direction quite opposite to that intended. From the texture of coat I should guess the Maltese dog has been selected, the colour points rather to the King Charles spaniel. Possibly both crosses have been used by Mrs. Foster and her allies, but I do not pretend to fathom these mysteries, about which great reticence is maintained.

The following are the points of this breed as settled by the Yorkshire Terrier Club :—

The general appearance should be that of a long-coated pet dog, the coat hanging quite straight and evenly down each side, a parting extending from the nose to the end of the tail ; the animal should be very compact and neat, the carriage being very sprightly, bearing an important air. Although the frame is hidden beneath a mantle of hair, the general outline should be such as to suggest the existence of a vigorous and well-proportioned body.

Head should be rather small and flat, not too prominent or round in the skull ; rather broad at the muzzle, with a perfectly black nose ; the hair on the muzzle very long, which should be a rich, deep tan, not sooty or grey. Under the chin long hair, and about the same colour as the centre of the head, which should be a bright, golden tan, and not on any account intermingled with dark or sooty hairs. Hair on the sides of the head should be very long, and a few shades deeper tan than the centre of the head, especially about the ear-roots.

Eyes.—Medium in size, dark in colour ; having a sharp, intelligent expression, and placed so as to look directly forward ; they should not be prominent ; the edges of the eyelids should also be of a dark colour.

Ears.—Cut or uncut ; if cut, quite erect ; if uncut, to be small, V-shaped, and carried semi-erect, covered with short hair ; colour to be a deep dark tan.

Mouth.—Good even mouth ; teeth as sound as possible. A dog having lost a tooth or two, through accident or otherwise, not the least objectionable, providing the jaws are even.

Body.—Very compact and a good loin, and level on the top of the back.

Coat.—The hair as long and straight as possible (not wavy), which should be glossy like silk (not woolly), extending from the back of the head to the root of the tail. Colour a bright steel blue, and on no account intermingled the least with fawn, light, or dark hairs.

Legs.—Quite straight, which should be of a bright golden tan, and well covered with hair, a few shades lighter at the ends than at the roots.

Feet as round as possible; toe-nails black.

Weight divided into two classes, viz., under 5 lbs. and over 5 lbs., but not to exceed 12 lbs.

POINTS IN JUDGING.

	VALUE		VALUE
Quantity and colour of hair on back,	25	Mouth,	5
		Ears,	5
Quality of coat,	15	Legs and feet,	5
Tan,	15	Body and general appearance,	10
Head,	10	Tail,	5
Eyes,	5		
		Total,	100

XXI.—THE AIRDALE TERRIER.

Like the Irish terrier, this breed has only been established a few years, and to an ordinary observer, the difference is chiefly in colour. He is a north country dog, and much fancied by the pitmen of that district. He is considered by his opponents to want heart in proportion to his size, and to throw back in breeding to other types, showing a want of purity of blood. Personally, I have no knowledge whatever of his characteristics.

The following points I have here drawn up by an influential body of devotees to the breed.

Head.—Flat, and of good width between the ears.

Muzzle.—Long, and of good strength; the nose being black, the nostrils large, and the lips free from "flews."

Mouth.—Level, teeth large and sound.

Eyes.—Small, bright, and dark.

Ears.—Thin, and somewhat larger in proportion to the size of the dog than a fox terrier's; carried forward like the latter's, but set on more towards the side of the head, and devoid of all long and silky hair.

Neck.—Strong, rather thin, neat; free from dewlap and throatiness.

Shoulders.—Well sloped.

Chest.—Moderately deep, but not too wide.

Hind-quarters.—Square, and showing a good development of muscle; thighs well bent.

Back.—Of moderate length, with short and muscular loins.

Ribs.—Well sprung and rounded, affording ample scope for the action of the lungs.

Legs.—Straight, and well furnished with bone.

Feet.—Round, and with no tendency to spread.

Tail.—Stout, and docked from 4in. to 7in.

The Airdale Terrier.

Coat.—Broken or rough, and close and hard in texture.

Colour—A bluish grey of various shades from the occiput to root of tail, showing a "saddle back" of same, also a slight indication on each cheek; rest of body a good tan, richer on feet, muzzle, and ears than elsewhere.

Weight.—From 40lb. to 55lb. for dogs, and 30lb. to 50lb. for bitches.

CHAPTER IV.

DOMESTICATED DOGS FINDING THEIR GAME BY SCENT, BUT NOT
KILLING IT, BEING CHIEFLY USED IN AID OF THE GUN.

I.—THE SPANISH POINTER.

As in most, and indeed all other breeds of the dog, the origin of
the Spanish pointer is lost in obscurity. As far as I know, there
is no proof that the pointer originated in Spain; but that he is
not in a state of nature is clear, and therefore some one people
must have first taught him to manifest his peculiar gift. No wild
dog is in existence in which the slightest tendency to point
instead of chasing his game is displayed, and that it can be taught
artificially is shown in the setting spaniel, now called the setter,
and even in the pig which a Hampshire gamekeeper once taught
this accomplishment. But though the spaniel, the Newfoundland,
and the terrier have often been taught to point, they none of
them show that rigid and cataleptic condition of the whole body
which is the peculiar characteristic of the pointer, and is so
strongly displayed in the Spanish and French pointers that it
is possible to throw them into "the point" by using the word
corresponding with "toho," in the language of the corresponding
countries. This was first made known to me at the Paris Dog
Show of 1865, when the exhibitor of a French braque, on my
asking if his dog was steady, threw him into a very perfect
state of catalepsy by a single word. Our modern dogs are seldom

so "full of point" as this, having, no doubt, lost the state of
nervous system in which it resides by crossing with the foxhound or greyhound.   In some breeds, however, it still exists;
but since the pointer has been used for grouse more than partridge, it has become very rare.   Upwards of forty years ago, I
saw six brace of pointers taken out by Lord Foley's keeper in
Worcestershire, all of which pointed and backed on the slightest
indication of a scent, showing the genuine catalepsy both "before"

The Spanish Pointer.

and "behind."   But this would have been a perfect nuisance on a
moor, and indeed was rather disappointing in the stubbles, for
more than half their points were false, and yet, with a full
knowledge of this defect, we were obliged to walk up to them,
or leave every dog behind, like so many Chinese idols.   These
dogs would remain on their point for an indefinite time, probably
till exhausted by want of food; but I question whether in these
days any breed could be found in which a single specimen of it

would be depended on to stand even for half an hour. At that time I have seen one pointer remain standing for upwards of six hours at least. I left him standing without his master, and found him there as I left him more than six hours afterwards on my return along the same road.

The old Spanish pointer, which is now quite extinct in this country, was remarkable for a large, heavy head, very long, wide, and square nose, pendant flews, large ears, slightly differing from those of the bloodhound in shape, width, and thinness, but quite as full, and with as much throatiness and dewlap as that dog. Behind the shoulders, however, the shapes of the two are quite different in character, though it would be difficult to point out the variations to an uninitiated amateur. It is, however, in the style of seeking their game that the two breeds differ most, and it is on this point entirely that the pointer must rest his claim to originality. The bloodhound (and indeed all hounds) depends on the foot-scent primarily, though he will own the body scent in the air when so strong as to prevail over that adhering to the soil. On the other hand, the pointer, if pure, disregards the foot-scent, and seeks for that of the body with his head in the air. Every experienced shooting man expects this peculiar style of hunting in his pointers and setters, and knows that if it is not displayed by a dog exhibited to him for sale he must expect him to "potter" (which is a dwelling on the foot-scent) in a very short time. Even in "roading" a grouse, a well-bred pointer does not drop his nose like a hound, but winds the foot-scent with it held about breast-high. Probably from neglect in rearing, and afterwards during the summer season, the Spanish pointer in this country becomes slack in his loins, spreading in his feet, and very slow in his gallop, which pace indeed is seldom displayed, a steady trot being the usual one, even when first turned off in a large stubble field. Still a brace of these dogs when well broken would quarter a field almost while their master was walking across it, *and they would never leave a head of game behind*, even on the worst scenting day. I fear this cannot be said of any of our modern breeds, who, it is true, will beat twice as much ground as the Spanish pointer in half the time, but in so doing will probably flush a covey or two, or possibly leave a few single birds to get up as soon as the guns are over the gate. The engraving heading this article is from a well-known portrait of the old-fashioned dog, and exhibits him in his best form, with a strong loin and plenty of propelling power; but though I have seen some scores of the breed in my early sporting days, I never met with such a frame among them. The head, however, is quite correct, and I have little doubt that the original of the portrait was an exceptional animal in respect of body and legs. He is represented with his tail docked, as was invariably the practice in the early part of this century, owing to the constant lashing of it frequently causing it to bleed, to the great annoyance of the shooter and the loss of strength by the dog.

II.—THE MODERN ENGLISH POINTER.

It is possible that this comparatively light and elegant animal has been produced by careful selection from the original Spanish pointer above described, but it is more probable that in all cases a cross directly with the greyhound, or indirectly with that breed through the foxhound, has been resorted to. In any case, the result is a dog still pointing steadily, and, in many cases, with true cataleptic rigidity, but showing the pace and endurance of the foxhound, and indeed being almost as fast as a slow greyhound. Instead of the loose heavy frame of the Spanish dog, we have a beautiful compact shape, with sloping shoulders, straight muscular limbs, and a dash which is quite distinct from the inertness of the imported animal. The head is still square and heavy as compared with the greyhound, and slightly more so than that of the foxhound, but flews, dewlap, and throatiness have disappeared, and the aspect is now light and sprightly, instead of being heavy and somnolent. In good strains the high style of hunting for the body-scent is retained, but too often it is replaced by the hound-like gallop, with head down and stern trailing quietly behind, which indicates that the breeder, after resorting to the hound for pace and endurance, has not been careful to reject those puppies in whom the hound's partiality for the foot-scent has been retained. There is no excuse for this stupidity, because every breeder ought to be aware that when he puts two different animals together, though the offspring will, as a rule, partake of the qualities of both, he can at will in the next and subsequent crosses either keep or get rid of any of them which he may like or dislike. Whether, therefore, Mr. Edge and his contemporaries, who produced the modern pointer, crossed the Spanish dog with the foxhound or not, they ought carefully to have got rid of low-hunting; and this Mr. Edge undoubtedly did, but there are other kennels of nearly equal celebrity in which a low style of hunting and a trailing stern, with a tendency to work in circles rather than in straight lines, indicate unmistakably that the hound's faults (*quoad* shooting) have been retained. Such

"SANCHO," a Modern English Pointer.

dogs I have seen receive prizes at field trials, though I would hang every one of them if I had my will; for though some useful animals will sometimes be met with retaining a disposition to hunt for a few years, yet the great majority of them at the end of their first season do nothing but potter at the hedgerows, and are thereby rendered utterly useless.

Within the last thirty years the change in farming has completely upset the vocation of the pointer as a partridge-dog, except in a few counties, such as Devonshire and Cornwall, where the warm and damp climate encourages the growth of covert for birds in the autumn, and at the same time permits dogs to scent their game. As a rule, however, not a tithe of the dogs formerly kept in the south for partridge-shooting are now in existence, in spite of the large increase of certificated sportsmen, who, however, rely on walking turnips with a retriever or on "driving" for the sport they anticipate. A moderately fast and steady dog who can find birds in turnips is now a rarity, and pace is regarded as the *sine quâ non*, because that quality really is essential to the grouse-dog. But for partridges it is better to have no dog than one which will flush every other covey and drive it off the manor without a shot. Nose, and steadiness "before" and "behind," are the essentials in him, united with as much pace as is consistent with their display. So rare is this combination, that, in all the field trials I have ever seen, I have only twice seen birds found in turnips; once by that very fast dog Mr. Macdona's "Ranger," and once by a bitch of Mr. Llewellyn's; but, in the latter case, she was made to range within forty yards of the gentleman who hunted her, and as an aid to the gun would be useless. Even "Ranger" has only on one day shown this power, within my knowledge of him, and on five or six other occasions has flushed his game from not moderating his pace. Mr. Price's celebrated "Drake" I never saw in turnips but once, and then he was upset by his companion refusing to back him, so that I cannot speak as to his powers in that respect; but the noise made by such a flyer in the turnips must always cause him to flush birds, unless he moderates his pace on his own accord, as "Ranger" did on the occasion in question, and as Mr. Llewellyn's bitch was made to do.

For the last thirty years the shooting world has been in doubt as to the respective merits of the two strains of the pointer, distinguished by their respective colours as the "liver and white" and the "lemon and white." These two colours compose 95 per cent. of the pointers kept in Great Britain, the remainder being whole liver (very rare from not being admired) and whole blacks. a celebrated kind of which has long been highly valued in the North of England. Mr. Edge, Mr. Moore of Appleby, Lord Sefton, Lord Derby, Lord H. Bentinck, Mr. Antrobus, Sir Dudley Marjoribanks, Sir R. Garth, Mr. R. J. Ll. Price of Bala, and Mr. S. Price of Devonshire, have been the most prominent breeders of the liver and whites, and until about twenty years ago that colour was the favourite one; but in 1865 Mr. Whitehouse exhibited a beautiful lemon and white at the first field trial, which did his work so well as to command the admiration of the judges and spectators; and the late Mr. Lang of Cockspur Street, well known as a thorough sportsman, also extolling the breed, the fashion changed, and "Hamlet," "Bob," "Major," and others "of that ilk," had a good time of it. Sir R. Garth, however, stuck to his colours, and producing his wonderful dog "Drake" year after year at the field trials, where he was able to beat all comers, a return has recently been effected towards the old direction, partly caused by this marvellous and exceptional animal, but aided greatly by Mr. R. J. Ll. Price's "Belle" and by Mr. S. Price's "Bang," who, though not so fast as those two flyers, is fast enough for real work. With the exception of Mr. Whitehouse, no other breeder has of late shown any prominent lemon and whites, and he has not produced anything approaching to either of the above three dogs. "Hamlet" was in his day a very good performer, but not quite first class; and the same may be said of his descendants, a good many of whom have at various times appeared in public. Hence it is not wonderful that the fashion should have again changed, and that the liver and white strains should now be regarded as the best, and especially as Mr. Whitehouse himself has crossed his bitches with it, and produced his very useful dog "Macgregor," from which he has himself bred.

The points of the pointer are as follows:—

	VALUE		VALUE
Skull,	10	Legs, elbows, and hocks,	12
Nose,	10	Feet,	8
Ears, eyes, and lips,	4	Stern,	5
Neck,	6	Texture of coat,	3
Shoulders and chest,	15	Colour,	5
Back, quarters, and stifles,	15	Symmetry and quality,	7
		Total,	100

The *skull*, as containing that organ in which resides the pecu-

liar features of the breed, is of great importance as to size and
shape, and I confess that if the body is only of a satisfactory shape
as to form and speed, I can hardly think the brain can be overdone. Size, therefore, without heaviness, is to be regarded as
without limit, but a heavy head, as indicated by expression, is
almost sure to be attended by a bad temper and a slow pace. If,
however, a large head is accompanied by a cheerful, lively countenance, I should value it highly, but unfortunately this combination
is by no means common. By all means, however, prize a large
head *per se*, but attend to the expression of the countenance the
more carefully in proportion. There should be a marked brow and
occipital protuberance, but the latter should not be so raised as
in the bloodhound, and the top of the skull should on no account
be domed, as in that breed, but, on the contrary, flat, excepting
a slight furrow down the middle, separating it into two slightly
rounded halves. The skull of the pointer is somewhat wider than
that of the setter.

The *nose* is the organ on the lining membrane of which the
nerves of smelling are spread out, and consequently it is of equal
importance with the skull. Neither of the two is of any use
without the other, for a clever dog of the best temper *cannot* find
game if he has a bad nose, while a keen sense of smell is useless
if he will not display his powers from obstinacy or laziness. It
should be of full size to allow of nerve surface, long and broad,
with nostrils large and open to allow of the air entering readily.
For health's sake, the end should feel cold and moist, and, as
indicating hardness, it is better dark in colour, a pink nose being
a mark of softness, except in the lemon and whites, who generally
have it. The end should be square and not pointed (known as
" snipey " or "pig jawed ") or underhung.

Ears, eyes, and lips.—The ears should be moderately long in
leather, but flat and filbert-shaped, not folding like those of the
hound. They should be set on low, and any tendency to prick
them is an abomination. The leather should be thin and flexible,
and the coat covering them very soft. Eyes of middle size and
depth, soft in expression, and of the various shades of brown,
according to colour of coat. Lips full, but not showing any flew
frothing when at work.

The *neck* should be an elegant arch in its upper outline, and should be round, firm, and tapering to the shoulders, without any tendency to throatiness. A dewlap is out of the question.

Shoulders and chest.—Many of the old breeds had very round barrels and upright shoulders in consequence. A moderately flat side is now approved of, and deep back ribs are regarded as all important, marking not only a strong connection with the loins, but also a strong constitution. With this formation, long, powerful, and sloping blades may be demanded and expected.

Back, quarters and stifles.—A pointer with a weak back soon tires, though of course he may be fast and flashy. A slightly arched loin is a mark of strength, and if there is a trifling droop to the root of the tail, that strength is not likely to be less. Wide ragged hips are preferred by most pointer judges. Usually the stifles are straight, but if well bent the dog can command himself much better and stop to a scent more rapidly.

Legs, elbows, and hocks.—Without good legs the best nose is comparatively useless, because the dog either cannot go at all or soon tires. Hence they should be straight and strong in bone, especially below the knees, in order to enable the animal to stop himself suddenly when on the point. They must also be well clothed with muscle on the fore-arm and lower thigh. The elbows and hocks should be well developed and set straight, neither turning in nor out, but especially the former, as the turned-in elbow cramps the action most unmistakably.

The *feet* are generally expected to be round and cat-like, but the quality of the horn covering the pads is of the most importance, for if thin the dog soon becomes footsore. When the pointer is wanted for grouse-hunting, he should be selected with as much hair between the toes as possible. It is in this point especially that the setter has the advantage over him, as a bare foot soon becomes sore on heather. *Cæteris paribus*, a cat-foot is better than a bare foot in this dog.

The *stern* should come out of the back of full size, immediately after which it begins to taper, and ends in a decided point like the sting of a bee. The straighter it is the better, but there is generally a very slight curve. It should be carried low, and when at work should lash the sides merrily.

The *coat* should be soft in texture, but not silky.

As to *colour*, I have dilated on it above to a full extent. In the present fashion I should range them as—(1.) liver and white, (2.) lemon and white, (3.) black and white without tan, (4.) whole black, (5.) whole liver, (6.) black, white, and tan (too hound-like for modern taste).

The *symmetry* of the pointer is considerable, and a judge penalises its absence highly. The same may be said of that indispensable point *quality*.

III.—THE PORTUGUESE POINTER.

Never having seen this variety, I can only allude to it as resembling the Spanish dog, with the exception of the stern, which is bushy.

IV.—THE FRENCH POINTER.

This dog varies greatly throughout the several provinces of France, and is seldom of any pure breed, being crossed with the poodle, the dachshund, the basset, or some one or other of the French hounds. When he is most pure he resembles the Spanish pointer, but is seldom so large and heavy as that dog. For these reasons, it is impossible to describe even the typical French pointer, since I have shown that no such animal exists. Most of the prominent French sportsmen import English dogs, either setters or pointers, and as this has now been done for many years, no doubt these breeds are to a certain extent established in France.

V.—THE DALMATIAN DOG.

Though this peculiarly marked variety of the species is only used in Great Britain as a carriage dog, in his native country he is made to stand very steadily at game, and is employed in aid of the gun exactly as are our "Pontos" and "Dons." Until very recently, his ears were invariably closely cropped, like those of the pug, which altered his appearance completely, and deprived him of his resemblance to the pointer. I am not aware that he has ever been tried in the field in England, where he has contracted a fondness for horses and carriages which is a very prominent feature in his character. Most other dogs soon tire of hard road-work, and refuse to accompany a carriage day after day for the fifteen or twenty miles which is probably the average distance travelled by private conveyances; but the Dalmatian is always pleased to be so employed, and if he is allowed the run of the stables and enough food, has all that he cares for. Of his own accord he places himself close behind the heels of the horses, where

The Dalmatian Dog.

he is safe from the control of all external circumstances, and rarely leaves his berth for any temptation, except when the carriage is stopped, when he looks about him and assumes the air of any other of his kind. The English pointer also follows a carriage well, but seems to do so from his associating it with the gun, for he prefers riding in it to running behind it, and jumps into a dog-

cart the moment the door is opened. Not so the Dalmatian, who
perhaps is wise enough to know that exercise is healthy; but anyhow there is this difference between them. A reference to my
engraving will show that the Dalmatian differs only very slightly
from the pointer, his ears being somewhat smaller, and his colour
being the chief point of difference. Formerly, as appears from
Youatt's engraving, the spots differed very slightly from the ticks
of the pointer, but now by careful breeding they are converted into
distinct circular spots, averaging about an inch in diameter, and
the more distinct they are from one another the more highly they
are prized.

Points of the Dalmatian dog :—

	VALUE		VALUE
Head, .	. 10	Coat, .	. 5
Neck, .	. 5	Colour, .	. 10
Body, . .	5	Markings, .	. 40
Legs and feet,	10	Symmetry, .	10
Tail, . .	5		
		Total, .	. 100 .

The *head* may be described in the same terms as that of the
pointer, having a similar central furrow and flat upper surface,
with marked brow. A square nose, cleanly cut under the eyes,
accompanies this formation; but fanciers do not insist on length
and width, nor on open nostrils. The dog is, in fact, judged for
beauty and not utility, as far as this part goes. Eyes small, sharp,
and dark. Ears vine-shaped, set on rather far back, somewhat
smaller than the pointer's, with thin leather, and quite free from
folds.

The *neck* is an exact reproduction of the pointer's.

The *body* must be strong and compact, with a slightly arched
loin, and sloping muscular shoulders.

The *legs* and *feet* are the only points in which utility is considered; for as the dog is required to do a great deal of road work,
the legs must be strong, straight, and working freely on the elbows
and stifles. The feet, again, are imperatively demanded without
spread of the toes, and possessing hard, horny pads. If thin-soled
or with spreading toes, a single journey knocks this dog up; but,

as usually met with, his soles are so hard as to stand a daily road journey for an indefinite term. Great substance of bone is, however, not regarded as of any importance.

The *tail* closely resembles the correct type of the pointer's, but is usually carried higher than is approved of in that dog.

The *coat* is short and moderately fine, but not silky.

The *colour* is by preference black spotted on a white ground, but liver and dark blue are also permitted. A slight stain of tan about the face and legs is also allowed. A rich jet black counts first; then black and tan; thirdly, liver; and fourthly, blue; but there is not much difference in value between the two last.

The *marking*, however, makes the dog in the eye of the fancier, many good judges going for it alone. When perfect, the spots on the body are evenly distributed, but quite clear of one another, and should not exceed the size of a half-crown piece, nor be less than a shilling. Such absolute perfection is, however, yet in *nubibus.* On the tail there should be several spots without coalescing.

Symmetry in this dog is regarded as a *sine quâ non.*

VI.—SETTERS (ENGLISH, IRISH, SCOTCH, WELSH, AND RUSSIAN).

That the setter is a spaniel taught by art to point his game is universally admitted, and Daniel in his " Rural Sports " gives a copy of a bond signed by John Harris, on October 7, 1485, in which he covenants to keep for six months and break a certain spaniel to " set partridges, pheasants, and other game, in consideration of ten shillings of lawful English money." Thus it is certain that four hundred years ago the setting spaniel existed in this country, and most probably he was nearly identical with our modern setter, though probably not so fast. There is reason to believe that, until the gun was used to shoot game flying, the setting spaniel was preferred to the pointer, because from his crouching attitude the net could be drawn over him more easily. On the invention, however, of the flint lock, it was found that the attitude of the pointer rendered him more visible to his master, and as the net was no longer used by sportsmen, the Spanish pointer was imported, and used in preference to the native setting spaniel. In course of time, either by crossing or careful breeding, the setter assumed the pointer's standing position, and this has now become as common with the one breed as with the other.

There is a much greater variety among setters than among pointers, and not only has each division of the United Kingdom its peculiar breed of them, but there is also a Russian strain in this country, celebrated for nose and steadiness, but too woolly coated for our early autumn work. As a rule, the setter is faster than the pointer, but not so steady, frequently requiring a day or two's work before he can be relied on. Usually he will not work long without water, and many breeds are quite useless on land where water is out of reach. From his hairy feet he stands the friction of the heather on moorland shootings better than the pointer, and he also bears exposure to wet and cold with more impunity. Hence the setter was always considered *the* grouse-dog and the pointer *the* partridge-dog; but, as I have elsewhere remarked, the retriever has now superseded the latter in his proper vocation, and he must either work on the moors or not at all.

I shall now proceed to describe the four varieties of the setter, beginning with—

(A) THE ENGLISH SETTER.

In my young days the use of the setter was almost confined to the moors of Scotland, Wales, the North of England, and Ireland. Almost every grouse-shooter had his own particular breed or strain, but the five I have alluded to in process of time absorbed all the rest. Gradually the setter was spread over England, but in most cases preference was given to dogs resembling those which are now *par excellence* called English, that is to say, setters with no marked difference from the type of their kind, either in colour or shape. About sixty years ago the late Mr. Laverack of Manchester began to be noted for his breed, which was derived from a single pair, and he alleged that ever since that time he bred "in and in" to them without outcross of any kind. These two were named "Ponto" and "Old Moll," bred by the Rev. A. Harrison, near Carlisle, and he had kept the breed pure for thirty-four years, so that, if Mr. Laverack's account is true, the Laverack setter has been bred "in and in" for a hundred years.

Fearing a bad result, he said that he had at various times crossed his bitches with external blood, but always finding a falling off in the produce, had gone back to his old stock. Probably, however, he occasionally made a slip in his memory, and certainly there was a curious admixture of colour in his kennel, if we are to believe his account. In other cases of inbreeding, even of much less stringency and duration than his, I have always remarked

The English Setter.

that the colour and markings were almost repeated throughout the strain, but Mr. Laverack's dogs were of all colours with a white ground, some being white and red, some white and blue, some white and black, and others again white, black, and tan. Latterly the blue Belton (a thickly ticked white and black) was the prevailing colour, but even with these a whole litter never appeared alike. His celebrated "Countess" was of this colour, but her brother and sister were black and white in large patches. It is not, however, denied that his strain were very much inbred, and by carefully selecting dogs with a strong tendency to natural point, his breed showed the same condition of the nervous system, and would, like the Frenchman's pointer, fall into attitude at the "toho." Unfortunately this close breeding produced a great many idiots and delicate constitutions, and if only a Laverack puppy had his senses, his limbs of good formation, and escaped the ills of teething, distemper, &c., he was sure to be a good dog in the field *when well broken*, but he required a deal of this, being naturally wild and headstrong.

Soon after the introduction of field trials the Laverack setter attained a very high reputation. chiefly founded on the performances of "Countess" and her sister "Nellie," aided to some extent by the result of the cross between the Laverack blood and the strains of Mr. Paul Hackett of Newcastle, Mr. W. Lort (the well-known judge), Mr. Wittington, Sir Bellingham Graham, and Mr. Statter. Mr. Purcell Llewellyn has spent a great deal of time and money in carrying on the "selection of the fittest" for breeding purposes, and has produced a strain which he calls the "field trial" breed, composed of lines from all the above sources, and which has been fairly successful in this country as well as in America. Commencing with Laverack bitches purchased at various times, he crossed them with Mr. Statter's "Dan," which dog he purchased at the Shrewsbury field trials of 1871, together with his brother "Dick," after performing there marvellously well in the stake for the best brace. On the whole, it may be said that the Laverack setter has attained a higher reputation during the last fifteen years than any other English setter; but I very much question whether it was equal to some other breeds, such as Sir Bellingham Graham's, Sir Vincent Corbett's, Mr. Wittington's, Mr. Paul Hackett's, Mr. W. Lort's, and some others whose names escape my memory. I have myself possessed one or two setters superior even to "Countess," and one bitch quite as fast, with a better nose; while out of a litter I bred from her, two dogs turned out A–1 in all but pace, which certainly was not equal to that of their mother. But Mr. Laverack was lucky in getting "Countess"

and "Nellie" into the hands of a gentleman who spared nothing
in obtaining success in public, for with their exception and that
of Mr. Brewiss's "Dash II." (who was not a pure Laverack, being
crossed with Armstrong's "Kate.)" nothing else has appeared
from his kennel approaching perfection. His dogs were heavy
and spaniel-like, as far as I have seen; "Dash II.," however,
though showing a spaniel-form, displaying good pace, and standing in grand style.

Points of the English setter :—

	VALUE		VALUE
Skull,	10	Legs, elbows, and hocks,	12
Nose,	10	Feet,	8
Ears, lips, and eyes,	4	Flag,	5
Neck,	6	Texture and feather of coat,	5
Shoulders and chest,	15	Colour,	5
Back, quarters, and stifles,	15	Symmetry and quality,	5
		Total,	100

The *skull* of this dog differs from all others, being intermediate
between that of the field-spaniel and the pointer's, indicating
almost with certainty that the breed was established by a cross
between the two, but, when tried nowadays, producing what is
called "the dropper." Though this dog is useful enough in the
first generation, and often exactly like one or the other of his
parents; yet, if the cross is persevered with, the result is always
a failure. The occipital protuberance of the pointer is absent, and
the brows are more distinct, the skull itself being narrower across
the ears.

The *nose* should, on the average, be at least 4 inches long from
the corner of the eye to the tip, and as wide as possible, without
the slightest approach to "snipiness," but not quite so square as
the pointer's. In the best breeds the upper outline is slightly
hollow, and the brows should be raised at a sharp and decided
angle from it, with a leanness in front of the eyes which is very
characteristic. As in the pointer, and for the same reason, the
nostrils should be wide apart and patulous, and the end of the nose
moist and cool. Excepting in white setters or very pale lemon
and whites, the end should be always black or dark liver, and

even in them it is preferred of that colour; but a pink nose may be pardoned in a whole white dog. The teeth should be quite level.

Ears, lips, and eyes.—The ears should be shorter than the pointer's in leather, but the hair fringing them brings them in appearance nearly to the same length. The leather must be thin and soft, and must hang close to the cheeks, without the slightest tendency to "prick." The hair is very silky on the ears of good breeds, and is usually about two inches in length. The *lips* are, perhaps, not quite so full as the pointer's, but there is a decided pouch at the angle, which when on game is usually full of slaver. The *eyes* are of medium size, more animated than the pointer's, and of all shades of brown, the darker the better. They should be set straight across, and not at any angle.

The *neck* has a different contour from the pointer's, not showing the decided convexity in either direction peculiar to that dog, and feeling thin and soft to the touch, with a slight hollow on each side. The skin is loose, but no throatiness or dewlap is allowed.

Shoulders and chest.—In Mr. Laverack's breed, the chest of the dogs is usually very round and barrel-like, making their elbows stand wide apart, and tending to produce a slow pace. In the bitches no such conformation exists, and hence, perhaps, the latter have generally come out better in public than the former. I have not remarked this difference in any other breed, but certainly I have seen no exception in his, nor have I ever known any other strain of setters so thick and "cobby" in the body, and so like the Clumber spaniel in outline; of course, not to the same extent as in that dog. Mr. Laverack was so prejudiced in favour of his own breed, that in his book he even went so far as to recommend a wide chest. I very much prefer, in common with all other setter fanciers, a somewhat narrow chest, moderately deep in front, *but with the back ribs well let down.* This formation gives the light airy gallop of the Irish setter, and yet allows sufficient room for lungs and heart. The shoulders should be very sloping, and the blades wide at the top from before backwards, so as to give plenty of room for the muscles moving the arm.

Back, quarters, and stifles.—A strong back is a great point in this dog, who is apt to be narrow in this part, and especially at

the junction with the ribs. Ragged hips are often met with
in the best strains, and, with a proper allowance of muscle,
should be valued instead of the reverse. A slight arch falling
to the root of the tail is a beauty in my eyes, but not set as
in the "wheel-back." Wide stifles, well bent, should be looked
for; and, in fact, the propellers must be attended to in every
respect.

Legs, elbows, and hocks.—Setters are almost always straight
on their legs, with elbows well let down and strong hocks. The
absence of these points is, therefore, to be regarded as unpardon-
able. Strong lower thighs are very important.

The *feet* are the strong points of the setter, and without hard
soles and plenty of hair between the toes he loses half of his
recommendations. The toes are often hare-like, instead of resembling those of the cat; and I am by no means sure that when so
formed there is not an advantage.

The *flag* differs from that of all other dogs, being fringed with
long hair falling like the teeth of a comb, and without the bushi-
ness of other hairy tales. The bones themselves should taper from
the root, and should be curved like a scimitar when at rest, rising
a little above the level of the back when "on the point," and then
displaying the comb-like appearance to which I have alluded, with
a very slight curve only. The *feather* should be free from curl,
silky in texture, and about 6 or 7 inches long in the middle,
tapering to half an inch at the extreme point.

Texture and feather of coat.—The texture is an indication of
breed, and should be silky, with a slight wave, but no curl. In
the best breeds the coat looks and feels greasy without being really
so; at least no grease is left on the hand when patting it. The
feather should fringe the fore and hind legs thinly but regularly,
and also the flag, as above remarked.

The *colour* varies greatly, and is valued according to the following scale:—(1) Black and white ticked with large splashes,
known as the "blue Belton;" (2) orange and white freckled,
known as "orange Belton;" (3) orange or lemon and white without ticks; (4) liver and white ticked; (5) black and white, with
slight tan markings, which, though the colour of the Gordons,
is met with in many pure-bred English strains; (6) black and

K

white; (7) liver and white without ticks; (8) pure white; (9) black; (10) liver; (11) red or yellow.

Symmetry and quality are displayed by the setter as much as or more than any other breed. There is a very elegant outline, with artistic proportions; and even when no longer used as an aid to the gun, this dog delights the eye as much as the greyhound. He has also a most affectionate disposition, and makes an excellent companion to either sex.

(B) THE IRISH SETTER.

In the list of colours given above it will be seen that I have placed red last, though it is the special colour of the Irish setter, and without the slightest intention of undervaluing that elegant dog. But though it is considered highly beautiful in him, and really is so when of the proper golden shade, yet it is not appreciated in the English breeds, and indeed is very rarely met with among them. Until very recently, Irish setters were not often seen out of their own country, a prejudice existing against them in England, where they were supposed to be difficult to break, and always inclined to be unsteady. Since the institution of shows, however, and the exhibition of the splendid specimens which we have seen in them, the Irish setter has been more highly valued, and now takes his share of the work on Scotch and Welsh moors as well as on his native mountains. I have seen several at work, and certainly have no reason to think them more unsteady than their English rivals, but neither will compare with the pointer in that respect. They are slashing goers, with heads and flags well up, and the latter lashed merrily in most cases, though, like the English dog, not invariably so. In endurance they are quite up to the best English form, but not above it, as far as I know, though I confess I have not had sufficient experience of them to settle this vexed question. The differences in shape from the English breed are not great, but sufficient to distinguish the one from the other.

The most famous old strains are the La Touche, Lord Clancarty's, Lord Dillon's, Lord de Fresne's, Lord Lismore's, the Mont Hedges, the Marquis of Waterford's, and Lord Rossmore's.

The value of the points is nearly the same as in the English dog, the following being the variations, as laid down by the Irish Terrier Club:—

POINTS OF THE IRISH SETTER (AS LAID DOWN BY THE IRISH SETTER CLUB).

Head should be long and lean, the skull oval (from ear to ear), having plenty of brain-room, and with well-defined occipital protuberance; brow raised, showing stop; the muzzle moderately deep, and fairly square at end. From the stop to the point of the nose should be long, the nostrils wide, and the jaws of nearly equal length; flews not to be pendulous. The colour of the *nose* dark mahogany or dark walnut, and that of the *eyes* (which ought not to be too large) rich hazel or brown. The *ears* to be of moderate size, fine in texture, set on low, well back, and hanging in a neat fold close to the head.

Neck should be moderately long, very muscular, but not too thick, slightly arched, and free from all tendency to throatiness.

Body should be long—shoulders fine at the points, deep, and sloping well back; the chest as deep as possible, rather narrow in front—the ribs well sprung, leaving plenty of lung-room. Loins muscular and slightly arched. The hind-quarters wide and powerful.

Legs and feet.—The hind-legs from hip to hock should be long and muscular, from hock to heel short and strong, the stifle and hock-joints well bent, and not inclined either in or out; the feet small, very firm; toes strong, close together, and arched.

Tail should be of moderate length, set on rather low, strong at root, and tapering to a fine point; to be carried in a scimitar-like curve on a level with, or below, the back.

Coat on the hind part of legs and tips of ears should be short and fine, but on all other parts of the body and legs it ought to be of moderate length, flat, and as free as possible from curl or wave.

Feathering on the upper portion of the ears should be long and silky; on the back of fore and hind legs long and fine; a fair amount of hair on the belly, forming a nice fringe, which may extend on chest and throat. Feet to be well feathered between the toes. Tail to have a nice fringe of moderately long hair, decreasing in length as it approaches the point. All feathering to be as straight and flat as possible.

Colour and markings.—The colour should be a rich golden chestnut, with no trace whatever of black; white on chest, throat, or toes, or a small star on the forehead, or a narrow streak or blaze on the nose or face, not to disqualify.

Standard of points :—

	VALUE			VALUE			VALUE
Head,	10		Body,	20		Coat and feather,	10
Eyes,	6		Hind legs and feet,	10		Colour,	8
Ears,	4		Fore legs and feet,	10		Size, style, and gen-	
Neck,	4		Tail,	4		eral appearance,	14
	24			44			32

Total, 100.

(C) THE BLACK-AND-TAN OR GORDON SETTER.

After a lengthened controversy, it is now generally admitted that the Gordon setter was originally white, black, and tan, and that many black-and-tan setters are not descended from the Gordon Castle kennels. The classes for this breed are, therefore, not now defined as for *Gordon setters*, but for *black-and-tan setters*, whether Gordons or not, and certainly this appears to be the most sensible plan.

The Black-and-Tan Setter.

Without attempting to sift the history of this handsome strain, I shall simply describe it as it exists in the present day, whatever may be its origin or pedigree. Although most black and tans are heavier than either the English or Irish breeds, yet they have no spaniel-like appearance, and resemble the bloodhound more than they do either the pointer or the spaniel. By many people it is supposed that this dog has been used as a cross for the purpose of getting the colour which is similar to his, but there are plenty of black-and-tan spaniels without going outside the pale of the shooting dogs, and there can have been no necessity for adopting this expedient for colour alone. Nevertheless, I cannot help thinking that this cross has been used, and for the following reasons :—(1.) A great number of black-and-tan setters show the red "haw" in the corner of the eye, which is almost in itself a proof. (2.) The nose of this dog is remarkably good, but there is a tendency to seek for the foot-scent, and to potter over it at a comparatively early age. (3.) There is nothing like the endurance of the English and Irish breeds, and the style of gallop is heavy and hound-like, rather than clever and active, as in the best strains of the setter. With these defects, whether due to bloodhound parentage or not, it is by no means surprising that the black-and-tan setter does not sustain the reputation which he achieved by means of dog-shows and field trials ten or twelve years ago. At the field trials he has been very lucky in getting rewards for nose alone, for certainly my dog "Rex," who won several prizes at Stafford, was not first-rate in any other respect. Like most of the Kents, his powers of scenting were wonderful, but he must do his work his own way or not at all, and after five or six hours he was completely knocked up. I have tried a good many of the strain, and seen more in other hands, but I have not yet seen one which could be shot over with pleasure. They all work "to their own hook," and are never seen to cast an eye at their masters, which I hold to be the essential feature in a dog working in aid of the gun ; but still with their fine noses they may be made very useful by those who do not mind working to their dogs, instead of making their dogs work to them.

The deviations in points from the English type are as follows :—

The *skull* is heavier than that of either the English or Irish setter, with the occipital protuberance much developed, and a slight dome on the top, resembling at a humble distance that of the bloodhound. *Ears* rather longer also, and *eyes* very often furnished with "sealing-wax," like that dog.

The *nose* is of full width, and seldom has the concave upper line of the English dog.

The *flag* is rather short, and is apt to be "teapotty."

The *coat* is in many strains hard and open, and in others curly, but the best breeds are provided with coats nearly as silky as a Laverack's.

In *colour*, the black should be jet, and the tan a deep mahogany. The tan is shown in the same places as in the Manchester terrier, already described.

(D) THE WELSH SETTER.

Throughout Wales a very curly-coated setter is met with, which is said to resist the wet and cold of the mountains in a marvellous manner. I have seen several of them at various times, but, excepting this thick curly coat, I could never make out any peculiar type, and their colours are as various as Mr. Laverack's. They possess good pace, but hunt with their heads and tails down on the ground, and on this account they have never taken my fancy. Not knowing more of them than the above, I cannot go into further detail.

(E) THE RUSSIAN SETTER.

Having had no further experience of this dog since I wrote the first edition of this book, I cannot do better than transcribe the description I then gave :—

This dog was at one time—that is, about twenty years ago—considered to be superior to our English breed, and many of them were then introduced into the kennels of our best sportsmen, but they are now almost lost sight of again. In the year 1841 the late Mr. Lang, well known as a first-rate shot both at game and pigeons, and as a breeder of pointers and setters, wrote to the editor of the "Sporting Review" a letter warmly in praise of them, from which the following is an extract :—

"In the season of 1839 I was asked for a week's shooting into Somersetshire by an old friend, whose science in everything connected with sporting is first-rate. Then, for the first time for many years, I had my dogs, English setters, beaten hollow. His breed was from pure Russian setters, crossed by an English setter dog which some years ago made a sensation in the sporting world from his extraordinary performances ; he belonged to the late Joseph Manton, and had been sold for a hundred guineas.

Although I could not but remark the excellence of my friend's dogs, yet it struck me, as I had shot over my own old favourite setter (who had himself beat many good ones, and had never before been beaten) for eight years, that his nose could not have been right, for the Russians got three points to his one. I therefore resolved to try some others against them the next season; and having heard a gentleman well known as an excellent judge speak of a brace of extraordinary young dogs he had seen in the neighbourhood of his Yorkshire moors, with his recommendation I purchased

'A ELLS.

A Russian Setter slightly crossed with English blood.

them. I shot to them in August last, and their beauty and style of performance were spoken of in terms of praise by a correspondent to a sporting paper. In September I took them into Somersetshire, fully anticipating that I should give the Russians the go-by; but I was again disappointed. I found, from the wide ranging of my dogs, and the noise consequent upon their going so fast through stubbles and turnips (particularly in the middle of the day, when the sun was powerful and there was but little scent), that they constantly put up their birds out of distance, or, if they did get a point, that the game would rarely lie till we could get to it. The Russians, on the contrary, being much closer rangers, quartering their ground steadily—heads and tails up—and possessing perfection of nose, in extreme heat, wet, or cold, enabled us to bag double the head of game that mine did. Nor did they lose one solitary wounded bird; whereas, with my own dogs, I lost six brace the first two days of partridge-shooting, most of them in standing corn.

"My old friend and patron having met with a severe accident while hunting last season, determined to go to Scotland for the next three years. Seeing that my dogs were well calculated for grouse-shooting, as they had been broken and shot to on the moors, and being aware of my anxiety to possess the breed of his Russians, he very kindly offered to exchange them for mine, with a promise that I would reserve a brace of Russian puppies for him. Although I had refused fifty guineas for my brace, I most gladly closed with this offer. Since then I have hunted them in company with several dogs of high character, but nothing that I have yet seen could equal them. If not taken out for six months, they are perfectly steady, which is a quality rarely to be met with. Every sportsman must know that the fewer dogs he can do his work with properly the better; for if they are in condition they cannot be too frequently hunted, and their tempers, style of working, &c., become more familiar to him. On this the whole comfort of shooting depends. Upon these grounds I contend that, for all kinds of shooting, there is nothing equal to the Russian or half-bred Russian setter in nose, sagacity, and every other necessary qualification that a dog ought to possess."

Since then, however, Mr. Lang lost the breed, and, I believe, for some reason or other, had also lost confidence in them. They are now very scarce in this country of pure blood, and even the cross with the English setter is seldom seen.

The actual form of the Russian setter is almost entirely concealed by a long woolly coat, which is matted together in the most extraordinary manner, and which would lead to the supposition that he would be unable to stand heat as well as our curly setters; but, on the contrary, he bears it almost like a pointer. He has the bearded muzzle of the deerhound and Scotch terrier, but the hair is of a more woolly nature, and appears to be between that of the poodle and the water-spaniel, or perhaps the ordinary setter, but far thinner than either, which may account for the sustenance of heat. The legs are straight and strong, and the form of the body well adapted for the pace which the setter has to keep up ; but this dog is not very fast, though quite sufficiently so for all sporting purposes. The feet are generally rather flat, but the soles are stout, and stand work well, while the quantity of hair on them fits them to bear the friction of heather or other rough work. I have never tried one of these dogs myself, but I have always heard the highest character of their nose and sagacity, as well as of their powers of endurance.

VII.—THE FIELD SPANIEL.

A great variety of these dogs exists throughout Great Britain, and until lately they were divided into large spaniels (springers) and small (cockers). Nowadays, however, only four distinct varieties are acknowledged, viz.—(a) the Clumber, (b) the Sussex, (c) the Norfolk, and (d) the modern cocker. All these strains are employed to find game without pointing it, giving notice (with the exception of the Clumber, who is mute) of their being "on it" by their tongues, which vary so as to enable the shooter to act accordingly.

(A) THE CLUMBER SPANIEL.

This variety has been established for a long time at the seat of the Duke of Newcastle, from which its name is derived, but it is only within the last fifty years that it has been generally known and appreciated. It is not, however, a poor man's dog, as it soon tires, and less than two or three couple would be quite useless in any covert of average size. Being mute, the Clumber spaniel is taught never to range more than from 25 to 40 yards from his master, who thus never loses sight of his team for more than a few minutes at a time, and whatever game is stirred rises within gunshot. Since the general use of human beaters instead of canine in the *battués* which are now the fashion, the spaniel has been at a discount, except for rabbit-shooting and for beating small spinneys for pheasants before the commencement of the regular season. Still there is work to be done by the keepers preparatory to *battués* in which dogs are required, and in large establishments Clumbers are still kept for that purpose, in which their mute, steady, and quiet style of hunting make them eminently useful.

The Clumber Spaniel.

The points of this breed are as follows :—

	VALUE		VALUE
Head,	20	Legs,	$7\frac{1}{2}$
Ears,	10	Feet,	$7\frac{1}{2}$
Neck,	5	Colour,	5
Length of body,	15	Coat,	5
Shoulders and chest,	10	Stern,	5
Back,	10	Total,	100

The *head* is heavy as compared with that of the setter or pointer, but otherwise resembles the former, having a flat top divided by a furrow down the middle, high brows, and an occipital protuberance of a marked character. *Nose* very long, broad, and deep; the nostrils being more patulous than those of any other spaniel. The end is of a dark flesh-colour, sometimes apparently that of liver. Eyes large and soft, generally hazel.

The *ears* are vine-shaped, like the setter's, not lobular as in other spaniels. The leather is very long, but as there is not much feather, the whole ear does not look so large as in most other spaniels.

The *neck* is very strong and long for so thickly-made a dog. As, however, the vertebræ generally are elongated, those of the neck partake of the same character. There is no dewlap in the skin of the neck, but there is a slight "ruff" in the hair.

The *length* is considered a very important point, and should be at least 2½ times the height.

Shoulders and chest.—In such a heavy animal good shoulders are imperative, or he will tumble over every tussock of grass in his work and tire himself in half an hour. A large *chest* is also looked for to give bellows-room; but here I confess I do not see the force of the demand, as the pace is too slow to call on the wind.

The *back*, for the same reason, should be muscular, but breeders go for a straight one—why, I am at a loss to know. At all events, an arched loin in a Clumber spaniel is reprobated strongly. Deep back ribs are, of course, necessary in so heavy a frame.

The *legs* must be straight and strong both in bone and muscle, with elbows well let down and set straight; the hocks also and stifles should be bony, and neither turned in nor out. From his great width of chest the Clumber is often out at the elbows and crooked in the fore-legs, but this is a great defect.

The *feet* are large as compared with those of the setter, but then the extra weight to be carried must be taken into consideration. Strong horny soles are a great desideratum.

The *colour* is always a white ground with yellow or orange spots. A decided lemon is, however, the correct thing, and if possible freckled; but this is more rare than with orange.

. The *coat* should be like that of the English setter, with a very slight wave, but no curl; abundant, but not long, except in the feather of the legs and stern.

' The *stern* should be set on high, but carried low, especially when at work. It is not docked.

(B) THE SUSSEX SPANIEL.

This dog was almost unknown out of his own county until I drew attention to him in the first edition of this book in the year 1859.

L. WELLS.

"GEORGE" and "ROMP,"* Sussex Spaniels, the Property of E. Soames, Esq., of London.

In the early dog-shows no notice whatever was taken of him, and until 1872, if shown, he was relegated to the miscellaneous classes. Since then, however, he has taken precedence of the Clumber, and has a special class at all the principal shows. Mr. Soames' "George," selected by me twenty years ago, still continues to be

* Bred by the late A. E. Fuller, Esq., of Rose Hill, Brightling, Sussex, and descended from the celebrated stock of Mr. Moneypenny, of Rolvendon.

the type of the breed, and the only difficulty is to breed up to him. A great many spaniels exhibited as Sussex, and even possessing the correct golden liver colour, are no doubt more or less impure, but the same may be said of most breeds. This spaniel is much faster in his work than the Clumber, and more lasting, by which qualities he recommends himself to the general shooter. A couple or a leash will suffice for most people, and even a single dog will beat a great extent of covert, if he is a good one. He is gifted with a full bell-like tongue, which he varies according to the game before him; and by this means an experienced shooter can tell whether to expect "fur" or "feather," and can also distinguish a hot scent from a stale one, by which he is considerably benefited. There is no better "all-round" spaniel than this, and I am not surprised at the rise in fashion shown in his case of late years.

Points of the Sussex spaniel :—

	VALUE		VALUE
Head, .	15	Legs, .	5
Eyes,	5	Feet, .	5
Nose,	10	Colour, .	10
Ears, . .	5	Coat, .	5
Neck, . . .	5	Tail, .	10
Shoulders and chest,	10	Symmetry, .	5
Back, ...	10		
		Total, . . .	100

The *head* should be wide and long, showing the central furrow very clearly, and the side arches also. The brows are high, and there is a slight occipital protuberance, but not nearly so marked as in the Clumber. The whole head is still heavy, but not so massive as the latter's.

The *eyes* are very full and soft, but there must be no weeping at the corners.

The *nose* is long and wide, end liver-coloured. Nostrils open, but not remarkably so.

The *ears* are long in leather and lobe-shaped, not vine-shaped. They have more feather than the Clumber, but are still not heavily clothed.

The *neck* is somewhat short, with a well-marked frill. It is not raised much above the level of the back. There is no throatiness or dewlap.

Shoulders and chest.—The shoulders are generally more sloping than those of the Clumber, owing to the chest narrowing in front. The latter is very full towards the back ribs, which are very deep, and in front is not nearly so wide and round. This makes the dog very active for his weight.

The *back* is more arched than the Clumber's, and very strong in its coupling with the loin and hips. The proportion of length to height is about $2\frac{1}{4}$ times.

The *legs* in front are, like those of all wide-chested dogs, apt to be broad, but this defect is not so common as in the Clumber. Still it should be carefully attended to.

The *feet* are generally very good in this breed, neither spreading nor with soft pads. The toes are well arched, and there is plenty of hair between them.

The *colour* is a golden liver without white, and after the first year there is generally a faded look about the coat.

The *coat* is decidedly wavy, and not the slightest approach to curl should be seen.

The *tail* is carried low; it is usually cropped.

The *symmetry* of this dog is by no means a prominent feature, but still it is worthy of the points allotted to it.

(c) THE NORFOLK SPANIEL.

A spaniel of full size, of a liver-and-white or black-and-white colour, is met with very generally in the eastern counties, but it varies too much to admit of any definite description. The chief points of difference from the Clumber and Sussex are, that the length is not so great, and that the ears are furnished with more feather, often almost reaching the ground.

(d) THE MODERN COCKER.

Although in Wales and Devonshire a small liver-coloured cocker is still used, yet the fashion of the day in other parts of the country is to use a somewhat larger spaniel, generally of a black colour, and known as the modern cocker. This dog is now expected to be the servant-of-all-work to the shooter, and takes

his turn at rabbits, pheasants, or even partridges, when he is
called on, with the greatest zest. He is bred from a cross of
the Sussex with the old-fashioned cocker of Devon or Wales,
selecting the blacks, so as now to become almost invariably of
that colour.

English and Welsh Cockers.

Points of the modern cocker :—

	VALUE		VALUE
Head,	15	Feet,	10
Ears,	5	Colour,	5
Neck,	5	Coat,	10
Body,	20	Tail,	10
Length,	5	Symmetry,	5
Legs,	10		
		Total,	100

The *head* is long, and not so heavy as either that of the Clumber
or Sussex. The brow is also more sloping, and the occipital protuberance well defined. Nose long, broad, and square. Eyes soft
and gentle, but not very full; and by no means watering.

The *ears* are set low, and lobular as in the Sussex, which dog he resembles in this point.

The *neck* is moderately long, and rises from well-formed shoulders.

Body.—The chest must be deep rather than wide, girthing well, nevertheless. Back and loin strong and well coupled.

The *length* should be slightly more than twice the height.

The *legs* should be long and muscular. Elbows, stifles, and hocks all in one plane.

The *feet* are round and cat-like; hairy between the toes, and with hard horny pads.

The *colour*, by preference, is a jet black without white. In almost every litter, however, there are one or two true liver-coloured puppies.

The *coat* is flat and wavy, soft and silky in texture. There is a good deal of feather, but no top-knot should be permitted.

The *tail* is always cropped, but it *must* be carried below the back.

In *symmetry* this spaniel excels those already described.

VIII.—THE WATER-SPANIEL.

In England what is called the water-spaniel is of a very indefinite character; nearly all that can be said of him being, that he is a large, curly, liver-and-white spaniel, used for wild-fowl shooting. In Ireland, however, there are two varieties of this kind of dog, one chiefly known in the north and the other in the south. I shall begin by describing the Irish spaniel *par excellence*, viz., that used in the south.

(A) THE IRISH WATER-SPANIEL.

This breed attracted great notice in England about fifteen years ago, and several splendid litters were reared by Mr. Skidmore, Mr. Lindoe, Captain O'Grady, Mr. Willett, Mr. Robson, and others; but of late, either from delicacy of constitution or some other cause, great difficulty has been experienced in rearing puppies, so that it is seldom that a specimen is exhibited at all coming up to the 1865–70 standard. Nor do the Irish themselves

L

seem to have had better luck ; indeed, from all accounts, the falling off in the Emerald Isle has been even greater than in England.
Those who have possessed a dog of this breed speak very highly of
them, so that it does not seem that the decay is to be attributed to
carelessness or neglect.

According to trustworthy evidence, Mr. M'Carthy alone seems
to have the credit of originating this strain, which is very remarkable, as there is no breed of dogs in existence closely resembling
it ; and how he created it I am quite at a loss to know.   The bare

The Southern Irish Water-Spaniel.

face and tail, the marked top-knot, the long curls all round the
legs, and the heavily curled coat on the body and ears, are all
peculiarities which must have been derived from some source, but,
alas ! I confess my ignorance as to its *habitat*.   The only objection
I know of is, that the breed is very quarrelsome ; but still this
cannot be carried to the extent of extermination, which is what

seems to threaten it. Mr. Lindoe and others who have possessed good specimens tell me that a more useful spaniel does not exist, either for land or water, and that he possesses a good nose, retrieves well, with a tender mouth, if not spoiled by bad management. Added to these good qualities is an untiring disposition to hunt, while as a companionable dog he is A-1.

Points of the southern Irish water-spaniel :—

	VALUE		VALUE
Head,	10	Feet,	5
Face and eyes,	10	Coat,	10
Ears,	10	Colour,	10
Top-knot,	10	Tail,	10
Chest and shoulders,	7½	Symmetry,	5
Back and quarters,	7½		
Legs,	5	Total,	100

The *head* is remarkable for the absence of brow, the nose being quite of the Grecian order, and making nearly a straight line with the top of the head. It is covered with long fine curls to within an inch of the eyes, when the hair becomes quite short. This is quite distinct from the wig of the poodle, in which the curls are short and crisp.

Eyes small, and set almost level with the skin. The *face* is long, with open nostrils and level teeth. It is covered with very short hair, *not glossy*.

The *ears* are long, both in leather and feather. The former extends beyond the nose when drawn forward, and the latter several inches beyond it.

The *top-knot* is a long wisp of hair falling forward between the eyes, and rising from the skin in a decided peak.

Chest and shoulders.—The chest does not girth so much as in any other spaniel, a full-sized dog not measuring more than 22 inches. In the shoulders there is nothing to be noticed; from the thick coat it is difficult to ascertain their formation.

Back and quarters.—The back is straight and not remarkably strong. The quarters also are not very muscular. As the dog is leggy the stifles are nearly straight.

The *legs* are straight, but the fore-pasterns generally bend a good deal below the knee, giving an appearance of weakness.

They are clothed with short curls all round, but no feather, as in other spaniels.

The *feet* are large, and inclined to spread, improving the swimming powers considerably, but not tending to bear road-work.

The *coat* is composed of short curls of hair, without any approach to the wooliness of the poodle or to the silkiness of the land spaniel and setter.

As to *colour*, there is only one which belongs to the pure breed, viz., a deep puce liver colour, without a white hair, except an occasional white toe.

With regard to *symmetry*, I do not think the dog has any high claims to consideration.

(B) THE NORTHERN IRISH WATER-SPANIEL.

This dog has short ears with little or no feather. The body is covered with short crisp curls. His colour is an ordinary liver or liver and white. The type is not settled clearly enough to enable me to give any more definite description.

(C) THE ENGLISH WATER-SPANIEL.

Since 1859 I confess that I have gained no further knowledge of this breed, and I must content myself with reprinting what I then wrote, as follows :—

Water-spaniels are commonly said to have web-feet, and this point is often made a ground of distinction from other dogs; but the fact is, that all dogs have their toes united by membranes in the same way, the only distinction between the water and land dogs being that the former have larger feet, and that the membrane between the toes being more lax, they spread more in swimming, and are thus more useful in the water. Most people would understand, from the stress laid on web-feet in the water-dogs, that the toes of the land-dogs were nearly as much divided as those of man, but there are none so formed, and, as I before remarked, the toes of all are united throughout by a strong membrane. The coat in all the water-dogs is woolly and thickly matted, often curly, and in all more or less oily, so as to resist the action of the water. This oil is rank in smell, and hence they are all unfit to be inmates of our houses, which is a strong objection even to the poodle as a toy-dog. As, therefore, we have no ground for separating the land from the water dogs by this strong line, I have not attempted to do so, but have grouped them according to the divisions under which they naturally fall.

The Old English water-spaniel is particularly fond of the water, and will enter it in almost all weathers by choice, while it never is too cold for him when any game is on it. His powers of swimming and diving are immense, and he will continue in it for hours together, after which he gives his coat a shake and is soon dry. Indeed, when he first comes out he does not seem thoroughly wet, his oiled and woolly coat appearing to set at defiance the approach of water. His nose is pretty good, and he is capable of an excellent education; but it takes some time to break him thoroughly, as he is required to be completely under command, and is a very restless dog by nature, whereas his duties demand perfect silence. There are generally said to be two distinct breeds, one larger than the other, but in other respects alike.

His points are as follows :—Head long and narrow, eyes small, and ears of medium length, covered with thick curly hair. Body stout, but elegantly formed, with strong loins and round barrel-like chest, which is broad across the shoulders. The legs are rather long, but very strong, the bone being of great size and well clothed with muscle. Feet large and spreading, tail covered thickly with long curly hair, and slightly curved upwards, but not carried above the level of the back.

IX.—THE POODLE.

In this country the poodle is chiefly kept as a companion, but in France and Germany he is the main dependence of the small proprietors and farmers who indulge in *la chasse* as *the* sport *par excellence* of these two nations, and there he is the only water-dog known. Within the last few years a good many have been imported into England for wildfowl shooting, but a still greater number have been introduced as ladies' pets, the fashion of the

day being in favour of a poodle with a black satin jacket trimmed
with Astrakan.

In Russia the poodle is chiefly used as a house-dog, and is
taught many tricks there, for the amusement of the families
during the long winters, when no one goes out of doors without
necessity.   In France and Germany there are a great many slight
variations in size, colour, and general appearance, but all exhibit

Lady Di Huddleston's " Mossoo."

a neatly rounded symmetrical body, covered naturally with short
crisp curls, in some cases woolly and in others silky, and exhibiting a decided wig of crisp curls over the eyes.

Dr. Fitzinger, the chief German authority on the dog, enume-
rates six distinct varieties, but I shall not follow him through the
whole.   His chief points of difference seem, however, to reside in
the size, beyond which he is rather indefinite.   Both for sporting

and companionable purposes, the poodle is always clipped in France and Germany during the summer, but his coat is allowed to grow during the cold season—a much more humane plan than that adopted by our English ladies, who exhibit them in satin even at Christmas, considering, I suppose, a few tufts of Astrakan enough to keep them warm.

No dog is possessed of more intelligence than the poodle, and the best tricks exhibited in circuses and elsewhere are almost always performed by this breed. As a retriever he is indefatigable, but on land he uses his brains more than his nose, and hunts in circles rather than by following the trail. He dives well, and rarely fails to find his bird in the water, while his coat is so impenetrable that he can remain immersed for an almost indefinite time.

The very handsome specimen of the breed from which my illustration of it is drawn is a black poodle belonging to Lady Di Huddleston, and when he has been just clipped by Mr. Rotherham, he exhibits the satin and Astrakan coat in perfection. Less woolly than most of his brethren, he has almost a silky sheen in his ringlets, but they are not soft like the setter's. Nevertheless, with a very fine frame he unites good legs and feet, and altogether is as perfectly shaped a dog as can be imagined.

"Mossoo" took the first prize at the Crystal Palace Show of 1878, beating Mrs. Compton's equally celebrated dog, who had previously taken two first prizes in Germany. He is full of tricks, like most of his breed, and is of a remarkably affectionate disposition.

No points have ever been assigned to the poodle, and I confess that I have not sufficient knowledge of him to assign them.

CHAPTER V.

PASTORAL DOGS AND THOSE USED FOR DRAUGHT.

1. The English Sheep-Dog—2. The Collie : (A) Rough ; (B) Smooth—3. The Drover's Dog—4. The German Sheep-Dog—5. The Pomeranian : (A) The Large Wolf-Dog ; (B) The Small or Spitz—6. The Newfoundland and Labrador : (A) The True Newfoundland ; (B) The Landseer Newfoundland ; (c) The St. John's or Labrador—7. The Esquimaux Dog—8. Iceland and Lapland Dogs—9. Chinese Dogs—10. The Chinese Pug.

1.—THE ENGLISH SHEEP-DOG.

I CANNOT do better than transcribe the description of this dog which I wrote in 1859, as follows :—

The English sheep-dog is tolerably represented in the annexed engraving, but there are so many different breeds that it is difficult to describe him very exactly. He has a sharp muzzle, medium-sized head, with small and piercing eyes; a well-shaped body, formed after the model of a strong low greyhound, but clothed in thick and somewhat woolly hair, which is particularly strong about the neck and bosom. The tail is naturally long and bushy, but, as it has almost invariably been cut off until of late years, its variations can hardly be known. Under the old excise laws, the shepherd's dog was only exempt from tax when without a tail, and for this reason it was always removed; from which at last it happened that many puppies of the breed were born without any tails, and to this day some particular breeds are tailless. In almost all sheep-dogs there is a double dew-claw on each hind-leg, and very often without any bony attachment. The legs and feet are strong and well formed, and stand road-work well, and the untiring nature of the dog is very remarkable. The colour varies greatly, but most are grey, or black, or brown, with more or less white.

Such is the true old English sheep-dog, but a great proportion of those in actual use are crossed with the various sporting dogs, such as the setter, which is very common, or the pointer, or even the hound; and hence we so often find the sheep-dog as good in

The English Sheep-Dog.

hunting game as in his more regular duties, while a great many are used as regular poaching dogs by night, and in retired districts by day also.

II.—THE COLLIE (ROUGH AND SMOOTH).

(A) THE ROUGH COLLIE.

One of the most beautiful and useful of all our dogs is the Scotch sheep-dog or collie, an excellent engraving of which is shown on next page. With a fine muzzle he combines an intelligent-looking and rather broad head, a clear but mild eye, and a pricked and small ear slightly falling at the tip. His body is elegantly formed, and clothed with a thick coat of woolly hair, which stands out evenly from his sides, and protects him from the rain and snow to which he is exposed in his work, clothing him round the neck with

a " ruff," which is more marked in him than in any other breed of
dogs with which I am acquainted.

Of late years the collie has descended into the South, and fairly
taken us by storm, being used, however, chiefly as a companionable dog, though on many farms his proper vocation is allotted to
him.   An attempt has been made to meet the fashionable demand
for a pretty colour by crossing with him the black-and-tan setter, and

The Collie (Youatt).

this cross has taken the fancy of those who require an ornamental
rather than a useful dog, but it has completely destroyed the
main features of the breed for which he was prized.   Instead of a
thick woolly coat with a very close undergrowth, it has given the
shining but open hair of the setter, letting in the wet, so that the
dog would be utterly useless on a Scotch hill.   Instead of the bare
legs of the true breed, which, even if wet, do not hold water in any
quantity, the legs are feathered like a setter's, and would speedily

be fringed with icicles if folding sheep in a white frost. The cross, however, answers the purpose for which it was intended by filling the pockets of the breeders with Southern gold, and is perfectly suited to Rotten Row or an undergraduate's room at Oxford or Cambridge. My purpose, however, is to describe the collie as a sheep-dog, and, regarded from this point of view, there must be neither a setter's coat nor setter's feather.

Points of the rough collie :—

	VALUE		VALUE
Head, .	. . 10	Feet, . .	10
Muzzle, . .	5	Coat, .	. 15
Ears and eyes.	5	Colour,	. 10
Shoulders, .	7½	Tail, .	. 5
Chest, . .	7½	Symmetry, . .	. 5
Loin, .	10		
Legs, . .	. 10	Total, .	. 100

The *head* should be fox-like in shape, that is to say, widest at the ears and tapering rapidly to the nose. This causes the eyes to be nearer together than in most dogs, the formation being seen also in the dingo, Esquimaux, spitz, and Chinese sheep-dog, which last closely resembles the spitz. The top of the head is quite flat, without any furrow, and very little brow, nor is there any occipital protuberance. The skull looks small when there is much frill, but it is not really so, its great width between the ears lodging a considerable amount of brain.

The *muzzle* tapers to a very sharp point, and the nostrils are small, leading to the belief that the powers of scent are low ; but this is not really the case, many collies being most successful and determined poachers, even when quite free from the Gordon setter cross. The *teeth* are strong and even, and the masseter muscles of the jaw highly developed, causing the bite of this dog to be very sharp and punishing. The hair on the face in front of the eyebrows is very short.

Ears and eyes.—The proper type of the collie's ear is a small, semi-erect, and pointed one, the tip turning outwards and forwards. With the setter cross every gradation occurs, nearly up to the full Gordon allowance of leather and feather. This change of shape may or may not be considered as important, according to the taste of the inspector, but it indicates without doubt a departure from the true breed, and on that account is to be deprecated. The eyes are set more closely together than usual, as above remarked, and the axes of the openings are oblique, in this also resembling the dingo and fox. In size they are not remarkable either way, but they are sharp and cunning in expression, at the same time being altogether without fierceness. The colour is generally brown in its various shades of hazel.

The *shoulders* are required to be of the most useful formation, that is to say, sloping and muscular. If heavy, the dog cannot be quick over rough ground, as he is required to be, and notably down-hill, nor can he stop himself suddenly in correspondence with the flock he is guarding.

The *chest* is required to be of sufficient volume for the play of lungs and heart, but to secure the shoulders of the requisite form it must not be barrel-like, nor should it be keel-shaped to the full extent, or it will strike against inequalities of the ground.

The *loin* must be muscular for the hill-work it has to do, and a slightly arched one is particularly suited to it. Deep back ribs are not required for this kind of strength, but they also indicate the hardy constitution absolutely necessary for the sheep-dog.

The *legs* must have no weak point anywhere. *Elbows* should be strong, well let down, and set on straight. *Stifles* and *hocks* large, powerful, and clean. *Arms* muscular as well as long, and *knees* wide, and not with too much bend backwards, though, as in the foxhound, I object to a very upright pastern. This last must be of large bone and tendon. The hind-legs often have a double dew-claw, but this is sometimes entirely absent.

The *feet* are hare-like, with strongly arched toes and horny pads.

The *coat* in the true breed is very characteristic, somewhat shaggy, and very thick in its long hair, and with a woolly undercoat, which becomes visible on separating the outer one. Round the neck is a remarkable frill or ruff, which seems to have been recently copied by the ladies by means of the fur capes which have come into fashion with the collie. On the upper side there is not nearly so long a development of this frill, which is, however, nearly as long at the sides as below. The fore-legs have a little feather on them—the less the better; but the hind ones are quite bare.

The *colour* is black and tan, or either of these colours alone, more or less mixed with white. When black and tan, the two colours occupy their usual positions on the face as well as the legs and body. The black, except in the Gordon cross, is seldom deep, and the tan is full, and altogether unlike the mahogany-red tan of the setter.

The *tail* is bushy, not comb-like, as in the setter, and is carried gaily when the dog is excited.

The *symmetry* of this dog is above the average.

The illustration of this dog, which I copied from Youatt, is exactly in accordance with my ideas of the true type, and is so considered by the best North-country breeders.

(B) THE SMOOTH COLLIE.

The Smooth Collie.

In the North of England and in some districts of the Highlands of Scotland a collie of smaller size and lighter make is preferred, which is also smooth in coat. He is said to resemble his rough brother in all other respects, but certainly the numerous specimens I have seen are without the foxy characteristics in any marked degree. You cannot say where the difference is, for it is so slight as to elude all measurements but those of the eye. Under this delicate organ, however, the experienced judge of animals detects a difference in appearance which the ordinary observer would probably pass over. The head is not so wedge-shaped. The nose is not so straight, and the eyes, if not set in a straight line, are very slightly oblique.

The *coat* differs in being short, hard, and quite smooth.

The *colour* is generally a mottled grey mixed with white, but some celebrated breeds are black and tan ; occasionally it is tan and white.

The numerical value of the points is the same as in the rough collie.

III.—THE DROVER'S DOG.

In the different grazing counties of England dogs of all sizes and types are employed to drive cattle, most of which are tailless either by nature or art. There is no doubt that in certain strains of the pointer, as well as the sheep and drover's dog, the tail is absent beyond one or two vertebræ. Such a malformation is now very rare in the pointer, and nearly as much so in the sheep-dog, and has become so *pari passu* with the cessation of the custom of artificial docking. In my young days a pointer with a full tail was never seen, the reason given for the mutilation being that, if left entire, the dog would lash it to pieces, and, moreover, would disturb his game by the noise he made with it in the high stubbles of those days. So with the sheep-dog : the tax was formerly levied on all but bob-tails, it being supposed that no one would keep a mutilated dog for anything but real service. Since the tax was altered so as to include all dogs in its meshes, sheep-dogs have not been docked, and, as I said before, concomitantly with the cessation of the operation has been the disappearance of the natural " bob." But other breeds have been docked for generations without a similar result, such as the spaniel and certain breeds of terriers, among whom a natural " bob " is unheard of. On the other hand, the bulldog loses his tail, or nearly the whole of it, under the name of the " screw tail," yet he has never been submitted to the scissors as far as I know, and certainly not for the last half-century. The subject is a very curious one, which I confess I am altogether unable to explain.

IV.—THE GERMAN SHEEP-DOG.

This is a small and very variable breed, resembling greatly the spitz in appearance, but without any definite points.

V.—THE POMERANIAN (LARGE AND SMALL).

(A) THE POMERANIAN WOLF-DOG.

The larger Pomeranian is kept for guarding the sheep from wolves, hence called the Pomeranian wolf-dog. He resembles the St. Bernard in shape, but has not so large a head, and his colour is almost invariably a beautiful stone-fawn, without white, and with black points. He is by no means common in this country, but I have seen a few specimens of late years, which have been shown me as of pure breed, and from the high position of those who possessed them I have no doubt of the fact.

(B) THE SMALLER POMERANIAN OR SPITZ, ALSO CALLED LOUP-LOUP.

This pretty little dog is now very common in this country as a ladies' pet, his pretty white coat and lively manners rendering him a general favourite, except with young children, among whom he is seldom to be trusted. In his native country he is the ordinary sheep-dog, and is there preferred of a black colour, which from its rarity here is also greatly prized. I am not aware of his having ever been put to his natural occupation in this country, where he has been introduced as a pet dog altogether. He has one advantage, which is, that his coat, though long and rough, seldom becomes offensive.

The points of the spitz dog :—

	VALUE		VALUE
Head, . .	. 10	Feet,	10
Muzzle, . .	5	Coat, .	15
Ears and eyes,	. 5	Colour, .	15
Shoulders, .	5	Tail, .	5
Chest, .	. 5	Symmetry,	5
Loin, .	. 10		
Legs, .	. 10	Total, .	100

The *head* resembles greatly that of the collie, being even more

Pomeranian or Spitz Dog.

taper and fox-like. There is, however, a slight furrow down the middle of the forehead, and more brow than in that dog. There is also a prominent occiput beyond the average.

The *muzzle* is also collie-like, or rather fox-like in its formation, and the nose ought always to be black at the tip even in perfectly white specimens. There is generally a slight tendency in the upper teeth to be overshot.

Ears and eyes.—The ears are perfectly pricked, without any falling over at the tip, as in the collie, and are, indeed, exactly like those of the fox and dingo. They should be small and neat in shape. The eyes are larger than the average of the species, dark brown in colour, and set obliquely close together.

The *shoulders* ought to be oblique; but for a house-dog this is of little consequence.

The *chest* is generally round and the back ribs shallow, but, of course, these points ought to be valued accordingly when their shape is perfect.

The *loin* is frequently defective from shallow back ribs, but the hips are generally wide enough to give sufficient attachment to the muscles moving the back.

The *legs* are almost always straight and muscular, with elbows well let down, good strong stifles, and clean hocks.

As to the *feet*, they are usually small, round, and cat-like, but the soles are often thin and unfit for road-work, which may account for this dog following badly behind a horse or carriage.

The *coat* is very remarkable, being more like fur than hair, but very coarse fur. There is an under-coat, but it also is furry rather than woolly. There is as marked a frill as in the collie, and there is nearly more feather on the fore-legs. The face is bare of all but very short hair.

The *colour* most esteemed is a jet black without white. The only other allowable colour is a pure flake white, without any shade or spot of yellow. A red strain is met with in Germany, but it is unknown in this country.

The *tail* is curled over the back and carried on the side, usually the left. It is heavily feathered, and rather short in dock.

The *symmetry* of the spitz is quite up to the average of the canine race.

VI.—THE NEWFOUNDLAND AND LABRADOR.

Several varieties of this dog are met with, which I shall proceed to describe, beginning with—

(A) THE TRUE NEWFOUNDLAND.

Until Sir Edwin Landseer painted his celebrated " Distinguished Member of the Humane Society," the Newfoundland was always

M

considered a black dog, with no more white than in Lord Byron's
"Boatswain," or than is given in the beautiful engraving by Orrin
Smith published in Youatt's book on the dog, which I admire
so much that I should be sorry to replace it even by a life-
like portrait of Mr. Maplebeck's "Leo." Landseer's authority

The Larger Newfoundland Dog (Youatt).

was, however, so high, that black-and-white dogs came into
fashion, and continued so until a few years ago, when a correspondent of "The Field" started the subject, and ultimately succeeded
in silencing the Landseer party. In many shows, however, the

Landseer type is allotted a class to itself, but the authorities who live on the island declare that there is no native breed with a groundwork of white. I shall, therefore, follow suit, and describe each as a distinct strain; for there can be no dispute that a large number of dogs resembling the Newfoundland are of the Landseer colour.

There is another point on which great diversity of opinion exists, namely, as to size. Most people in this country like a very large and majestic animal, if they go in for size at all, and accordingly prize a Newfoundland if 30 or 31 inches in height. But it is alleged that the true island breed is never more than 25 inches at the shoulder, and if so, they say a 30-inch dog is not pure-bred. From all that I have gathered, however, I can only conclude that the descendants of these 25-inch dogs grow in this country to the height of 30 or even 32 inches. I shall, therefore, take it for granted that the particular breed I am now describing must be black without any great quantity of white, and that he may be of any size not less than 25 inches in height.

The Newfoundland is a remarkably sagacious dog, and hundreds of stories are told of his nobility of disposition, courage, and affection for the human race. In his native land he is chiefly employed as a beast of draught, but in England he is a companion only, and is seldom used for any other purpose. His natural love of water, and his great power of bearing immersion in it, render him an excellent water-dog; but for wildfowl shooting and retrieving on land this variety is not so useful as the smaller or St. John's Newfoundland, which is large enough without being cumbersome in a punt or dogcart. All have good noses, but not equal to that of the setter, and even the best retriever of pure Newfoundland breed I have ever seen trusted more to his brains than to his nose to find the game he was seeking. Still, a clever brain, even with a moderate nose, makes a better retriever than the best nose in the possession of a fool.

The following are the points as laid down by the special club of the breed. They are, however, differently arranged.

No value is given by the club, but I should fix it as follows :—

	VALUE		VALUE		VALUE
Symmetry,	. 10	Body, .	. 10	Tail, .	5
Head, .	. 20	Chest,	5	Coat, .	. 5
Ears, }		Fore-legs,	10	Colour, . .	5
Eyes, }	. 5	Hind-quarters } and bone, }	. 10	Height and weight,	10
	35	Feet, . .	. 5		25
			40		

Total, 100.

Points of the Newfoundland Dog.

Symmetry and general appearance.—The dog should impress the eye with strength and great activity. He should move freely on his legs, with the body swung loosely between them, so that a slight roll in gait should not be objectionable, but, at the same time, a weak or hollow back, slackness of the loins, or cow-hocks should be a decided fault.

Head should be broad and massive, flat on the skull, the occipital bone well developed ; there should be no decided stop, and the muzzle should be short, clean cut, and rather square in shape, and covered with short fine hair.

Ears should be small, set well back, square with the skull, lie close to the head, and covered with short hair, but no fringe.

Eyes should be small, of a dark brown colour, rather deeply set, but not showing any haw, and they should be rather widely apart.

Body should be well ribbed up, with a broad back, a neck strong, well set into the shoulders and back, and strong muscular loins. Slackness of loins is a great defect.

Chest should be deep and fairly broad, and well covered with hair, but not to such an extent as to form a frill.

Fore-legs should be perfectly straight, well covered with muscle, elbows in, but well let down, and feathered all over.

Hind-quarters and *legs* should be very strong ; the legs should have great freedom of action and a little feather ; cow-hocks are a great defect. Dew-claws are objectionable, and should be removed.

Bone massive throughout, but not to give a heavy, inactive appearance.

Feet should be large and well shaped. Splayed or turned out feet are objectionable.

Tail should be of moderate length, reaching down a little below the hocks. It should be of fair thickness, and well covered with long hair, but not to form a flag. When the dog is standing still and not excited it should hang downward, with a slight curve at the end. Tails with a kink in them or curled over the back are very objectionable.

Coat should be flat and dense, of a coarsish texture and oily nature, capable of resisting the water. If brushed the wrong way it should fall back into its place naturally.

Colour jet black. A slight tinge of bronze or a splash of white on chest or toes is not objectionable.

Height and *weight*.—Size and high weight are very desirable, so long as symmetry is maintained. A fair average height at the shoulder is 27 inches for a dog, and 25 for a bitch. A fair average weight is 100 lbs. and 85 lbs. respectively.

(B) THE LANDSEER TYPE OF NEWFOUNDLAND.

This variety differs from the above, being usually more loosely made, and possessing a less majestic appearance; the colour also is a white ground with black spots, and the coat is more woolly. Most dogs of this breed are also more "on the leg" than the black type.

The club state that it should in all respects follow the black, except in colour, which may be any, so long as it disqualifies for the black class; but the colours most to be encouraged are bronze and black and white, beauty in marking to be taken greatly into consideration.

(C) THE ST. JOHN'S NEWFOUNDLAND OR LABRADOR DOG.

In Great Britain the small variety of the Newfoundland is seldom kept as a mere companion, being chiefly used as a retriever, either pure or more or less crossed with the setter or spaniel. He is then commonly known as "a retriever" of the wavy-coated kind, to distinguish him from the curly-coated cross with the water-spaniel. Many of these retrievers are imported direct from Newfoundland to Hull and other ports trading with that island; others are bred in this country from imported parents, but most breeders prefer to cross them for the sake of improving the nose. There is not the same grand size and nobility of deportment as in the large breed, very few standing more than 22 or 23 inches high; nor is there the same mental development, as

The St. John's or Labrador.

indicated by the head, which is not so massive in proportion to the body. The colour is always black without white, and Mr. Bond Moore, who is considered to be the highest authority on the breed, would disqualify a dog for a white toe or white spot of the smallest kind on the breast or forehead. This is very absurd in a dog intended for use. Fancy dogs may be measured by any rule, however artificial, but a shooting dog should only be judged by points which are relevant to his work.

The following are the points of the Labrador dog :—

	VALUE			VALUE
Skull, . .	. 15	Feet, :		. 5
Nose and jaws,	. 5	Tail, .		. 5
Ears and eyes,	5	Coat, .		5
Neck, . . .	5	Colour, . .		5
Shoulders and chest,	10	Symmetry		5
Loins and back, .	10	Temperament,	.	. 5
Quarters and stifles,	. 10			
Legs, knees, and hocks, .	10		Total,	. 100

The *skull* is wide, but not so much so as in the larger variety; flat at the top, but with a slight furrow down the middle; moderately long, with a brow only just rising from the straight line; a very slight occipital protuberance.

Nose and jaws.—These must be long enough to carry a hare, and wide enough for the development of the nasal organ of scent, with open nostrils. Teeth level.

Ears and eyes.—The ears are small and pendant close to the head; the hair short, with a very slight fringe at the edge. Eyes of medium size, intelligent and soft.

Neck moderately long, that is to say, as long as it can be got, imported and pure Labradors being very often too short to stoop for a scent without difficulty.

Shoulders and chest.—The chest is apt to be barrel-like, but it is better somewhat narrow and deep, giving lodgment for more oblique shoulders, and rendering the dog better able to stoop.

The *back and loins* should be strong and well coupled, with deep back ribs.

Quarters and stifles.—Bent stifles are seldom met with in this breed, but they should not be confined in width. The quarters are generally straight, but a slight slope is by no means a disadvantage.

Legs, knees, and hocks.—These ought always to be straight, muscular, and strong in bone.

The *feet* are large, and should be specially attended to, as they are apt to be flat and thin-soled.

The *tail* is bushy without setter feather. It is carried high during excitement, but should not be curled over the back.

The *coat* is moderately short, but wavy, from its length being too great for absolute smoothness. It is glossy and close, admitting wet with difficulty to the skin, owing to its oiliness, but possessing no under-coat.

The *colour* is a rich jet black without rustiness. No quantity of white is admissible, but the best-bred puppies often have a white toe or star.

Symmetry is of some importance, as indicating adaptation to the work this dog has to do. It is often considerable.

Temperament.—Without a good disposition and temper, no dog can be made into a good retriever, and therefore this point should be carefully examined in it.

VII.—THE ESQUIMAUX DOG.

The Esquimaux Dog (Youatt).

This dog is the only beast of burden in the northern parts of the continent of America and adjacent islands, being sometimes

employed to carry materials for hunting or the produce of the
chase on his back, and at others he is harnessed to sledges in
teams varying from seven to eleven, each being capable of drawing
a hundredweight for his share. The team are harnessed to a single
yoke-line by a breast-strap, and being without any guide-reins,
they are entirely at liberty to do what they like, being only restrained by the voice of their master and urged forward by his
whip. A single dog of tried intelligence and fidelity is placed as
leader, and upon him the driver depends for his orders being
obeyed. In the summer they are most of them turned off to get
their own subsistence by hunting, some few being retained to
carry weights on their backs; sledges are then rendered useless
by the absence of snow; and as there is a good subsistence for
them from the offal of the seal and the walrus which are taken
by the men, the dogs become fat at this season of the year. The
Siberian and Greenland dogs are nearly similar to those of
Kamtschatka, but somewhat larger, and also more manageable,
all being used in the same way. The Esquimaux dog is about
22 or 23 inches high, with a pointed, fox-like muzzle, wide head,
pricked ears, and wolf-like aspect; the body is low and strong,
and clothed with long hair, having an under-coat of thick wool;
tail long, gently curved, and hairy; feet and legs strong and well
formed; the colour is almost always a dark dun, with slight disposition to brindle, and black muzzle.

VIII.—ICELAND AND LAPLAND DOGS.

These are nearly similar to the Esquimaux, but rather larger,
more wolf-like, and far less manageable.

IX.—CHINESE DOGS.

The dog most commonly met with in China is the Chow Chow,
or edible dog. This variety closely resembles the Pomeranian in
shape, but is almost always of a rich red colour—the exceptions
being black—and the coat is also more furry. The inside of the
mouth is always of a deep black. In other respects this dog is

scarcely distinguishable from the Pomeranian, as will be seen from the annexed engraving.

The Chow Chow or Chinese Edible Dog—The Crested Chinese Dog.

Next in numbers is the hairless dog of China, which somewhat resembles the English toy-terrier of thirty years ago. The skin is generally mottled either blue or red. The head is very round and comparatively large; the ears bat-like, standing out from the head; and the weight about 8 or 10 lbs.

A third breed, though rarely met with, is the crested dog, several of which have been imported into this country within the last thirty years. The shape is greyhound-like, the size being intermediate between the English and Italian breeds. There is a long crest of silky hair on the forehead, and the tail ends in a similar tuft. I give an engraving of this remarkable animal, the colour of which is usually like that of the hairless dog.

X.—THE CHINESE PUG.

This dog closely resembles the King Charles Spaniel in size and general appearance, but has shorter ears and less coat generally. He is always of a black-and-white colour.

CHAPTER VI.

WATCHDOGS AND HOUSE-DOGS.

1. The Bulldog—2. The Mastiff: (A) English; (B) Cuban—3. The Mount
St. Bernard: (A) Rough; (B) Smooth—4. The Lion-Dog—5. The Shock-
Dog—6. The Thibet Dog.

THE peculiarity of this division is, that the dogs composing it are
solely useful as the companions or guards of their owners, not being
capable of being employed with advantage for hunting, in consequence of their defective noses, and their sizes being either too
large and unwieldy or too small for that purpose. For the same
reason they are not serviceable as pastoral dogs or for draught,
their legs and feet, as well as their powers of maintaining long-
continued exertion, being comparatively deficient. These dogs
nearly all show a great disposition to bark at intruders, and
thereby give warning of their approach; but some, as the bulldog,
are nearly silent, and then their bite is far worse than their
bark. Others, as, for instance, the little house-dogs, generally
with more or less of the terrier in them, are only to be used for
the purpose of warning by their bark, as their bite would
scarcely deter the most timid. The varieties are as follows:—

I.—THE BULLDOG.

F. Cuvier has asserted that this dog has a brain smaller in
proportion than any other of his congeners, and in this way
accounts for his assumed want of sagacity. But though his
authority is deservedly high, I must beg leave to doubt the fact
as well as the inference; for if the brain is weighed with the body
of the dog from which it was taken, it will be found to be rela-
tively above the average, the mistake arising from the evident

disproportion between the brain and the skull. The whole head, including the zygomatic arches and cheek-bones, is so much larger than that of the spaniel of the same total weight of body, that the brain may well look small, as it lies in the middle of the various processes intended for the attachment of the strong muscles of the jaw and neck. I was able to obtain the fresh brain of

The Bulldog.

a pure bulldog for the purpose of comparison in 1879, and from an examination I have no doubt of the fact being as above stated. The mental qualities of the bulldog may be highly cultivated, and in brute courage and unyielding tenacity of purpose he stands un-rivalled among quadrupeds, and, with the single exception of the game-cock, he has perhaps no parallel in these respects in the brute

creation. Two remarkable features are met with in this breed:
First, they always make their attack at the head; and, secondly,
they do not bite and let go their hold, but retain it in the most
tenacious manner, so that they can with difficulty be removed by
any force which can be applied. Instances are recorded in which
bulldogs have hung on to the lip of the bull (in the old days of
baiting that animal) after their entrails had been torn out, and
while they were in the last agonies of death. In this they are
assisted by the shortness of the face, which allows the nostrils to
remain potent, even when the nose and mouth are imbedded in any
soft substance. Indeed, when they do lay hold of an object, it is
always necessary to choke them off, without which resource they
would scarcely ever be persuaded to let go. From confinement to
their kennels they are often deficient in intelligence, and they
can rarely be brought under *good* control by education; and,
from the same circumstance, they show little personal attachment,
so that they are almost as likely to attack their friends as their
enemies in their fury when their blood is put up. Many a bulldog has pinned his master's leg in revenge for a tread on his foot,
and it is very seldom that liberties can be taken with him by any
one. There is an old story strongly characteristic of this tendency,
which will illustrate this passion for pinning, and also the fondness
of the lower orders in some districts for the fighting and baiting
propensities of their dogs. A Staffordshire coal-miner was one day
playing with his bulldog, an unentered puppy, when the animal
became angry and pinned his master by the nose. On this the
bystanders became alarmed, and were going to treat the dog
roughly, but the owner interfered with, "Don't touch un, Bill; let
un teaste blood, an' it'll be the meaking on him." And so the
puppy was allowed to hang on and worry his master's nose to his
heart's content.

Most writers, whether political or otherwise, are fond of dilat-
ing on the "bulldog courage" of Englishmen, yet, in the same
breath, they vilely asperse the noble animal from whom they draw
their simile. The bulldog has been described as stupidly ferocious,
and showing little preference for his master over strangers; but this
is untrue, he being an excellent watch, and as a guard unequalled,
except perhaps by the bull-mastiff—a direct cross from him.

Indeed, he is far from being quarrelsome by nature, though the bull-terrier in many cases undoubtedly is so, and I fancy that some writers have taken their description from this dog rather than from the pure bulldog, which has been at all times rather a scarce animal. If once the pure breed is allowed to drop, the best means of infusing fresh courage into degenerate strains will be finally lost, except with the addition of extraneous blood which may not suit them; for I believe that every kind of dog possessed of very high courage owes it to a cross with the bulldog; and thus the most plucky greyhounds, foxhounds, mastiffs, pointers, &c., may all be traced to this source. Though bull and badger baiting may not be capable of extenuation, to them we owe the keeping up of this breed in all its purity; and though we may agree to discontinue these old-fashioned sports, yet I am sure my brother sportsmen will see the bad taste of running down a dog who, with all his faults, is not only the most courageous *dog*, but the *most courageous animal in the world.*

An attempt has recently been made by Mr. Adcock, who is a most enthusiastic lover and breeder of the bulldog, to show that he was originally much larger than the English bulldog of the first half of the present century. My own opinion is, that he has altogether failed, and that, instead of 70 or 80 lbs., which is the weight he insists on, 45 to 50 lbs. should be considered correct. The Bulldog Club have arrived at the same conclusion, and have recorded their opinion in their scale of points, which is as follows, with very slight literal corrections made by myself.

STANDARD DESCRIPTION OF THE CORRECT APPEARANCE AND THE SEVERAL POINTS IN DETAIL OF A PERFECTLY-FORMED BULL-DOG (CORRECTED IN 1885).

In forming a judgment on any specimen of the breed, the general appearance—which is the first impression the dog makes as a whole on the eye of the judge—should be first considered. Secondly should be noticed its size, shape, and make, or rather its proportions, or the relation they bear to each other. (No point should be so much in excess of the others as to destroy the general symmetry, or make the dog appear deformed, or interfere with its powers of motion, &c.) Thirdly, his style, carriage, gait, temper, and his several points should be considered separately in detail, as follows, due allowance being made for the bitch, which is not so grand or as well developed as the dog :—

(1.) The *general appearance* of the bulldog is that of a smooth-coated, thick-set dog, rather low in stature, but broad, powerful, and compact ; its head strikingly massive, and long in proportion to the dog's size ; its face extremely stout ; its muzzle very broad, blunt, and inclined upwards ; its body short and well-knit ; the limbs stout and muscular ; its hind-quarters very high and strong, but rather lightly made in comparison with its heavily-made fore-parts. The dog conveys an impression of determination, strength, and activity, similar to that suggested by the appearance of a thick-set Ayrshire or Highland bull.

(2.) The *skull* should be very large—the larger the better—and in circumference should measure (on front of the ears) at least the height of the dog at the shoulder. Viewed from the front it should appear very high from the corner of the lower jaw to the apex of the skull, and also very broad and square. The cheeks should be well rounded, and extend sideways beyond the eyes. Viewed at the side the head should appear very high and very short from its back to the point of the nose. The forehead should be very flat, neither prominent, rounded, nor overhanging the face, and the skin upon it and about the head very loose, hanging in large wrinkles.

(3.) The *frontal bone* should be very prominent, broad, square, and high, causing a deep and wide groove between the eyes. This indention is termed the "stop," and should be both broad and deep, and extend up the middle of the forehead, dividing the head vertically, being traceable at the top of the skull.

(4.) The *eyes*, seen from the front, should be situated low down on the skull, as far from the ears as possible. Their corners should be in a straight line at right angles with the "stop," and quite in front with the head. They should be as wide apart as possible, provided their outer corners are within the outline of the cheeks. They should be quite round in shape, of moderate size, neither sunken nor prominent, and in colour should be very dark, almost, if not quite, black, showing no white when looking directly forward.

(5.) The *ears* should be set high on the head, *i.e.*, the front inner edge of each ear should (as viewed from the front) join the outline of the skull at the top corner of such outline, so as to place them as wide apart and as high and far from the eyes as possible. In size they should be small and thin. The shape termed "rose ear" is the most correct. The "rose ear" folds inwards at its back, the upper or front edge curving over outwards and backwards, showing part of the inside of the burr.

(6.) The *face*, measured from the point of the cheek-bone to the nose, should be as short as possible, and its skin should be closely and deeply wrinkled. The muzzle should be short, broad, turned upward, and very deep. The nose should be large, broad, and black; its top should be deeply set back almost between the eyes. The distance from the inner corner of the eye (or from the centre of the stop between the eyes) to the extreme tip of the nose should not exceed the length from the tip of the nose to the edge of the under lip. The nostrils should be large, wide, and black, with a well-defined straight line between them.

(7.) The *flews*, called the "chop," should be thick, broad, pendant, and very deep, hanging completely over the lower jaw at the sides (not in front). They should join the under lip in front, and quite cover the teeth, which should not be seen when the mouth is closed.

(8.) The *jaw* should be broad, massive, and square; the canine teeth or tusks wide apart. The lower jaw should project considerably in front of the upper, and turn up. It should be broad and square, and have the six small front teeth between the canines in an even row. The teeth should be large and strong.

(9.) The *neck* should be moderate in length (rather short than long), very thick, deep, and strong. It should be well arched at the back, with much loose thick and wrinkled skin about the throat, forming a darker dewlap on each side from the lower jaw to the chest. The chest should be very wide, round, prominent, and deep, making the dog appear very broad and short-legged in front.

(10.) The *shoulders* should be broad, slanting, and deep, very powerful and muscular.

(11.) The *brisket* should be capacious, round, and very deep, from the top of the shoulders to its lowest part where it joins the chest, and be well let down between the forelegs.

N

(12.) The *back* should be short and strong, very broad forward, and comparatively narrow at the loins. There should be a slight fall close behind the shoulders, whence the spine should rise to the loin, thence curving again more suddenly to the tail, forming an arch, termed the roach-back, or more correctly "wheel-back," which is a distinct characteristic of the breed.

(13.) The *tail*, termed the "stern," should be set on low, jut out rather straight, and then turn downwards, the end pointing horizontally. It should be quite round in its whole length, smooth, and devoid of fringe or coarse hair. It should be moderate in length, rather short than long, thick at the root, and then tapering to a fine point. It should not have a decided upward curve at the end or be screwed or deformed, and the dog should, from its shape, not be able to raise it over its back.

(14.) The *fore-legs* should be very stout and strong, set wide apart, thick, muscular, and straight, with well-developed calves, presenting a rather bowed outline; but the bones should be large and straight, not bandy or curved. They should be rather short in proportion to the hind-legs, but not so short as to make the back appear long or detract from the dog's activity. The elbows should be low and stand well away from the ribs. The ankles or pasterns should be short, straight, and strong. The fore-part should be straight, and turn very slightly outward, of medium size, and moderately round; the toes compact and thick, being well split up, making the knuckles prominent and high.

(15.) The *hind-legs* should be large and muscular, and longer in proportion than the fore-legs, so as to elevate the loins. The hocks should be slightly bent and well let down, the thighs long and muscular from the loins to the point of the hock. The lower part of the leg should be short, straight, and strong. The stifles should be round, and turned slightly outwards away from the body. The hocks are thereby made to approach each other, and the hind-feet to turn outwards. The latter, like the fore-feet, should be round and compact, with the toes well split up and the knuckles prominent.

(16.) The most desirable size is about 50 lbs. in weight.

(17.) The *coat* should be fine in texture, short, close, and smooth; hard, but not wiry.

(18.) The *colour* should be whole or smut, that is, a whole colour with black mash or muzzle. The colour should be brilliant and pure of its sort. The colours, in their order of merit, if bright and pure, are (1) whole colours and smuts—viz., brindles, reds, white, with their varieties, as whole fawns, fallows, &c.; (2) pied and mixed colours. ◆

Gait.—From his formation, the dog has a peculiar heavy and constrained gait, appearing to walk with short quick steps, on the tips of his toes, his hind-feet not being lifted high, but appearing to skim the ground, and running with the right shoulder rather advanced, similar to the manner of a horse in cantering. Amongst the dogs of the present day (1886), though not each faultless, the following are considered to approach and fairly represent the true type described and sought to be preserved and perfected:—Mr. J. E. Shirley's "Cervantes;" Mr. H. Layton's "Monarch;" Mrs. Sprague's "Gather;" Mr. Pybus Dillon's "Diogenes;" and Mr. A. Benjamin's "Britomartis."

The following are the respective points as originally drawn up by the club, but these are now abandoned by them:—

	VALUE		VALUE
Skull, .	20	Back, .	5
Stop, .	5	Tail, . .	5
Eyes,	5	Fore-legs and feet,	5
Ears, . .	5	Hind-legs and feet, .	5
Face, upper jaw, and nostrils,	5	Size, . .	5
Chop, ...	5	Coat and colour, .	5
Mouth and lower jaw,	5	Symmetry and action, .	5
Neck, . . .	5		
Shoulders and chest,	5	Total, .	100

II.—THE MASTIFF.

Admirers of the mastiff consider him to be indigenous to Great Britain, but I confess I see no reliable grounds for such an opinion. There are two distinct varieties—the English and the Cuban.

(A) THE ENGLISH MASTIFF.

This dog is a very handsome and noble-looking animal as now bred, having lost the weak formation of back which formerly

attached to him, by careful breeding in the hands of Mr. Lukey,
Mr. Edgar Hanbury, Captain Garnier, and others.   Mr. Lukey was,
no doubt, the first in this undertaking, and though, perhaps, his
dog " Wallace," which I selected twenty years ago as the type of

I.WELLS.

" WALLACE," an English Mastiff, the Property of T. Lukey, Esq.

the breed, has since been slightly surpassed by his own " Governor," still I think it desirable to retain him as my illustration,
showing, as he does, how little has been done since his time.   Mr.
Lukey's account to me of the origin of his breed is as follows :—
" In 1835 I bought of the late George White of Knightsbridge a

brindled mastiff bitch, at a high price (£40), from the Duke of Devonshire's stud. I bred from her with a fawn black-muzzled dog, 'Turk,' the property of the late Lord Waldegrave, a splendid high-couraged dog. I kept two brindled bitch pups; and with great interest and considerable cost I obtained the use of 'Pluto,' the Marquis of Hertford's well-known mastiff dog, considered by judges the finest and best-bred dog of his day, and valued immensely by the Marquis. I have not had any other cross but the 'Turk' and 'Pluto' breed, having kept bitches from the one and dogs from the other. 'Wallace,' the grandsire of the dog engraved, was an immense animal, standing 33 inches at the shoulder, 50 inches round the body, and weighed 172 lbs. The Nepaulese Princes bought his brother and sister at eight months old, and gave £105 for them. The late Pasha of Egypt for five successive years had two pair of whelps (brindled) sent spring and autumn from Southampton.—T. L."

The mastiff, like the bulldog, has had his would-be improvers in the wrong direction, among whom may be reckoned Mr. Kingdon, who, in his attempt to go back to what he calls the "pure breed," has produced a miserable substitute for such a shape as that of "Wallace," "Governor," "Prince," and their like. I shall not, however, go further into this question, which has lately been settled in favour of the Lukey type, mainly by the aid of Captain Garnier, Mr. E. Hanbury, and Mr. Lukey himself. Captain Garnier thus writes of his own strain :—

"I bought of Bill George a pair of mastiffs, whose produce, by good luck, afterwards turned out some of the finest specimens of the breed I ever saw. The dog 'Adam' was one of a pair of Lyme Hall mastiffs, bought by Bill George at Tattersall's. He was a different stamp of dog to the present Lyme breed. He stood 30½ inches at the shoulder, with length of body and good muscular shoulders and loins, but was just slightly deficient in depth of body and breadth of forehead ; and from the peculiar forward lay of his small ears, and from his produce, I have since suspected a remote dash of boarhound in him. The bitch was obtained by Bill George from a dealer in Leadenhall Market. Nothing was known of her pedigree, but I am as convinced of its purity as I am doubtful of that of the dog. There was nothing striking about her. She was old, her shoulders a trifle flat, and she had a grey muzzle; but withal stood 29 inches at the shoulder, had a broad round head, good loin, and deep, lengthy frame. From crossing these dogs with various strains, I was easily able to analyse their produce, and I found in them two distinct types—one due to the dog, very tall, but a little short in the body and high on the leg, while their heads were slightly deficient in breadth ; the other due to the bitch, equally tall, but deep, lengthy, and muscular, with broad massive heads and muzzles. Some of these latter stood 33 inches at the shoulder, and by the time they were two years old weighed upwards of 190 lbs. They had invariably a fifth toe on each hind-leg, which toe was quite distinct from a dew-claw, and formed an integral portion of their feet. By bad management, I was only able to bring a somewhat indifferent specimen with me on my return to England from America, a badly reared animal, who nevertheless stood 32 inches at the shoulder, and weighed 170 lbs. This dog, 'Lion,' was the sire of 'Governor' and 'Harold,' by Mr. Lukey's bitch 'Countess,' and so certain was I of the vast size of the breed in him, that I stated beforehand, much to Mr. Lukey's incredulity, that the produce would be dogs standing 33 inches at the shoulder—the result being that both 'Governor' and his brother 'Harold' were fully that height. In choosing the whelps, Mr. Lukey retained for himself the best-marked one, an animal that took after the lighter of the two strains that existed in the sire ; for 'Governor,' grand dog and perfect mastiff as he was compared to most others of the breed, was nevertheless shorter in the body, higher on the leg, and with less muscular development than 'Harold,' while his head, large as it was, barely measured as much round as did his brother's. I, who went by the development of the fifth toe (in this case only a dew-claw), chose 'Harold,' a dog which combined all the best points except colour of both strains, and was a very perfect reproduction on a larger scale of his dam, 'Countess.' This dog was the finest male specimen of the breed I have met with. His breast at ten months old, standing up, measured 13 inches across, with a girth of 41 inches, and he weighed in moderate condition 140 lbs., and at twelve months old 160 lbs. ; while at 13½ months old 'Governor' only weighed, in excellent condition, 150 lbs., with a girth of 40 inches ; and inasmuch as 'Governor' eventually weighed 180 lbs. or even more, the size to which 'Harold' probably attained must have been very great. His head also in size and shape promised to be perfect.

"I will mention three other dogs. The first, Lord Waldegrave's 'Turk,' better known as 'Couchez,' was the foundation of Mr. Lukey's breed. This dog has frequently been described to me by Bill George and Mr. Lukey, and I have a painting of his head at the present moment. He stood about 29½ inches or 30 inches at the shoulder, with great length and muscular development, and, although he was never anything but thin, weighed about 130 lbs. Muzzle broad and heavy, with deep flews ; skin over the eyes and about the neck very loose ; colour red, with very black muzzle. He was a most savage animal ; was fought several times with other animals, and was invariably victorious. The second was a tailless brindled bitch, bought by Mr. Lukey from George White of Knightsbridge. She was a very large, massively built animal, standing 30 inches at the shoulder. Her produce with 'Couchez' were remarkably fine. 'Long-bodied, big-limbed, heavy-headed bitches. They *were* mastiffs Mr. Lukey had in those days!' is Bill George's eulogium of them. This bitch was bred by the Duke of Devonshire, and must therefore have been one of the Chatsworth breed. The third animal, 'L'Ami,' was a brindled dog of such vast size and weight that he was taken about and shown in England in the year 1829, the price of admission being one shilling. Of the head of this dog also I have a drawing, and it shows him to be very full and round above the eyes, with a broad, heavy muzzle and remarkably deep flews, the ears being cropped close. This dog, with the exception of rather heavier flews, answered exactly to the type of Vandyke's mastiff."

The mastiff has been crossed with the bulldog in many cases, some modern strains being largely imbued with that blood, which is shown in the small semi-erect ear, in the turned-up nose, and in general shape. There is no objection to a slight infusion of this blood, which amalgamates remarkably well with that of the mastiff, but a bloodhound cross is to be strongly deprecated, on account of the savage temper transmitted with it. Hence a long, narrow, domed head, with a large ear and a red "haw," which are all bloodhound points, are to be carefully eschewed. As I shall presently state, the Cuban mastiff, being crossed with the bloodhound, is for that reason to be avoided in breeding English mastiffs.

The points of the English mastiff are :—

	VALUE		VALUE
Head,	20	Size,	5
Eyes,	5	Colour, .	5
Ears, .	5	Coat, .	5
Muzzle,	5	Tail, .	5
Neck, .	5	Symmetry, .	5
Shoulders and chest,	10	Temperament,	5
Legs and feet, .	10		
Loins, . . .	10	Total, . 100	

The *head* is massive in all directions, but should be specially flat, and free from bloodhound dome or occipital protuberance. There is, however, a slight furrow down the middle, as will be seen in the head of " Wallace." Brows sharp but low.

Eyes.—These are small, and not at all prominent, but they must not show the sunken setting of the bloodhound type, and on no account " the sealing-wax " or red " haw." The expression, though grand, is mild, and without sourness. In colour they are brown of various shades.

The *ears* must be small and pendant, tolerably close to the cheeks, but not so much so as if of larger dimensions. There must be no folds in them, but one even vine-shaped flap of cartilage, covered with smooth skin and short, soft hair.

The *muzzle* is of average length, cut square at the end, with level teeth; but many good dogs have a slight protuberance of the lower ones, and this should not be considered a defect. There should be a full lip above and below, but no absolute flew.

The *neck* is very muscular, and turned with elegance, considering its massive proportions. At its junction with the head there is a prominence as in the pointer, but no large occipital protuberance as in the bloodhound. No throatiness or dewlap is permissible.

Shoulders and chest.—Massive proportions, which are essential in this breed, necessitate a full chest, and with this the shoulders cannot be very oblique; but they must be full of muscle, to make up for this deficiency.

Legs and feet.—This dog being generally chained up, his feet and legs suffer accordingly, and in most cases there is a deficiency in them. A great many otherwise fine mastiffs are complete cripples in their hind-quarters, and not much better before. Flat splay feet accompany these defects, which should be penalised highly. I need scarcely say that, instead of weak understandings, so large a dog requires them specially strong in all directions. Straight, muscular legs, with elbows and hocks neither in nor out, are desired, and also round, cat-like feet, *when you can get them.* Dew-claws may or may not be present.

The *loin* also should be wide and deep, with back ribs proportionately long; but such a formation is exceptional.

Size is of the highest importance, and in the dog should not be less than 29 inches, in the bitch 27.

The *colour* is either stone-fawn with black points or brindled. Occasionally a red puppy is met with, but it is not considered the correct thing. No white should be permitted as a rule, but a white toe will occur occasionally.

The *coat* is fine and short, except on the tail, where a slight roughness is permissible.

The *tail* is long, strong at the root, and tapering, with a slight bend, but no curl or twist. It is pendant, except under excitement.

The *symmetry* of the mastiff, considering his size, is of a high order.

Temperament should be specially attended to. In a show it can only be judged by the expression of the countenance, unless the dog is absolutely savage.

The Cuban Mastiff (Youatt).

(B) THE CUBAN MASTIFF.

The Cuban mastiff closely resembles the English breed, but is to all appearance crossed with the bloodhound. (See cut.)

III.—THE MOUNT ST. BERNARD DOG.

Closely allied to the mastiff, but resembling the Newfoundland in temper and in his disposition to fetch and carry, is the Mount St. Bernard breed, until lately confined to the Alps and the adjacent countries, where he is used to recover persons who are

The Mount St. Bernard Dog (Youatt).

lost in the snowstorms of that inclement region. Wonderful stories are told of the intelligence of these dogs, and of the recovery of travellers by their means, which are said to extend almost to the act of pouring spirits down the throats of their patients; but, however, there is no doubt that they have been, and still are, exceedingly useful, and the breed is kept up at the monastery of Mount St. Bernard. The coat varies a good deal in length, there being in England two distinct varieties founded upon this point, viz., the rough and the smooth. Mr. Macdona, who has been at great trouble and expense to import both of the best Swiss strains, leans to the rough, but there are many who still adhere to the smooth variety. I shall now describe each in order.

(A) THE ROUGH ST. BERNARD.
(See Frontispiece.)

I shall not attempt to settle the vexed question whether the rough or smooth variety is the genuine one, believing that both, as now existing, are completely modern creations. From the engraving given by Youatt, which is reproduced on the opposite page, we should be led to believe that the old breed was certainly not smooth, but, as I said before, no existing strain can be traced back more than thirty or forty years, and as it has always been limited until lately to a very small district, there is no reason to consider it as anything more than a strain of mastiff crossed at the discretion of the monks of St. Bernard. It is not even pretended that they have kept up their breed without out-cross, but having lost it for a time, they obtained a dog of the old strain which had been kept in another kennel, and used him in their stud, but the bitches from which they bred to him were not pure-bred. Mr. Macdona began by importing "Tell" and his sister "Hedwig," both rough; he then obtained his smooth "Monarque," after which Mr. Murchison obtained his rough dog "Thor," and Miss Hales her "Jura." From these sources the various strains now occupying the show-benches of the chief shows have been obtained. "Thor," though of a bad colour (red and white), has been more successful as a sire than "Tell," and most of the best dogs of the present day are descended from him. Both the rough and smooth greatly resemble the mastiff, but specially the latter, the former showing a cross with the Newfoundland, and both being, from their narrow head, sunken eyes, and frequent exhibition or "sealing-wax," most probably crossed with the bloodhound, whose fine nose was no doubt the temptation.

Points of the rough St. Bernard :—

	VALUE		VALUE
Head, .	20	Size, .	10
Ears and eyes,	10	Symmetry,	10
Line of poll,	10	Temperamen ,	5
Neck, .	5	Colour, .	5
Body, .	5	Coat, .	5
Legs and feet.	10		
Dew-claws, .	5	Total,	100

The *head* is as large as that of the mastiff, except in width, which is considerably less. There is a marked occiput and also a higher brow than in the mastiff or Newfoundland. The muzzle is long and cut square, with lips slightly pendulous. Teeth level.

Ears and eyes.—The ears are slightly larger than the mastiff's, but should have no folds. They are pendant, and very slightly rougher than the rest of the body. Eyes full, but set deeply, and showing the "haw," which is sometimes red, but not by preference.

Line of poll.—This line, which is supposed to resemble the white band of the Benedictine monk, is of course wholly arbitrary, but it is strongly insisted on by the monks; it is not often met with in the English-bred strains.

The *neck* is of ordinary shape, with a slight tendency to throatiness, no doubt due to the bloodhound cross.

The *body* is large and massive, with a somewhat deeper chest and better shoulders than in the mastiff.

Legs and feet.—These are generally good, owing to the exercise given to the dog in his native country. The feet are very large, but not spreading, and are said to be bred of this size to keep the dog from sinking into the snow.

Double *dew-claws* on the hind-legs are considered by many good judges to be absolute indications of true breeding, and their absence, they think, should condemn a dog to exclusion from the class awarded to this breed in a show. My own opinion is, that dew-claws are not to be relied on in any breed, and that when present in the St. Bernard, they only indicate a cross with the Newfoundland, who certainly possesses the double dew-claw in many instances of dogs imported from the island.

Size is as important as in the mastiff, and is about the same.

In *symmetry* the rough St. Bernard is quite up to the average, and he is far more active and graceful than any large English dog.

The *temperament* is mild and gentle, but not so much so as in our English mastiff.

In *colour* there is a considerable variety. Most people prefer the rich orange-tawny mixed with brown, but not brindled, as exhibited by "Tell," "Hedwig," "Alp," "Gessler," and many of their descendants. "Thor" and his family are, most of them, red and white. Others, again, are brindled or fawn, or these colours more or less mixed with white, sometimes almost entirely of the latter colour.

The *coat* is wavy upon the body, and very bushy on the tail, with a little feather on the legs.

(B) THE SMOOTH ST. BERNARD.

(See Frontispiece.)

This variety differs from the rough chiefly in coat, which is quite smooth. There is, perhaps, less of the bloodhound and more of the mastiff than in the rough strain, with an equal proportion of the Newfoundland, sinking his rough coat. The points are the same in value as in the rough variety.

IV.—THE LION-DOG.

This little dog appears to be a cross between the poodle and the Maltese dog, being curly like the former, but without his long ears and square visage. He is now very seldom seen in this country, and is not prized among fanciers of the canine species. Like the poodle, he is generally shaved, to make him resemble the lion.

V.—THE SHOCK-DOG.

This dog also is now almost unknown, but formerly he was very generally kept as a toy-dog. He is said to have been a cross between the poodle and small spaniel, both of which varieties he resembled in part.

VI.—THE THIBET DOG.

The Thibet Dog (Youatt).

This animal to some extent resembles the English mastiff in general appearance, and, being also put to the same use, the two may be said to be nearly allied. According to Mr. Bennet, he is bred on the Himalaya Mountains, on the borders of Thibet, for the purpose of guarding the flocks and the women who attend them. The portrait annexed sufficiently describes the shape of this dog, whose colour is a dark black, and his coat is somewhat rough.

CHAPTER VII.

TOY-DOGS.

1. The King Charles and Blenheim Spaniels—2. The Maltese Dog—3. Toy-Terriers—4. The Italian Greyhound—5. The Pug-Dog.

I.—TOY-SPANIELS.

Two breeds are known and recognised under this head, namely, the King Charles and the Blenheim spaniels, the former being slightly the larger of the two, and by most people considered the more handsome. To an ordinary observer, the chief points of distinction in the King Charles are the colour, which is black and tan more or less mixed with white—the less the better—and the length of the ears, which is greater than in the Blenheims, the latter being also lighter in frame, and always yellow or red and white. Both are small, delicate dogs; and though they have pretty good noses, and will hunt game readily, yet they so soon tire that they are rarely used for the purpose, and are solely kept for their ornamental properties. They make good watchdogs indoors, barking at the slightest noise, and thus giving notice of the approach of improper persons; nor, though they are somewhat timid, are they readily silenced, as their small size allows of their retreating beneath chairs and sofas, from which asylum they keep up their sharp and shrill note of defiance. The great objection to these handsome little creatures as pets is, that they follow badly out of doors, and as they are always ready to be fondled by a stranger, they are very liable to be stolen. Hence many people prefer the toy-terrier or the Skye, which is now introduced very extensively as a toy-dog, and might with equal propriety be inserted in this chapter as in that which he occupies. The King. Charles and Blenheim spaniels are often crossed, and then you may have good specimens of each from the same litter; but if true, their colours never vary.

Points of the King Charles and Blenheim:—

	VALUE		VALUE
Head,	10	Colour, .	. 10
Stop, .	10	Coat, .	10
Nose, .	10	Feather,	10
Lower jaw,	5	Size, .	. 5
Ears,	10	Symmetry, .	. 5
Eyes, .	5		
Compactness,	10	Total,	. 100

King Charles and Blenheim Spaniels.

The head.—In this breed, probably from crossing with the bull-dog and Chinese pug, or from inter-breeding, the head has within my memory become almost a perfect hemisphere. It was always inclined to be rounded in its upper surface, but it is now raised to a dome far beyond that of the bloodhound, and only equalled by the small, stunted smooth terrier of the apple-headed variety.

Occasionally this dome is more than a half-circle, and projects over the brows.

The *stop* is also lately introduced, probably from the bulldog, and is as pronounced as in that breed, or even more so.

The *nose*, again, is shortened from the same cause, and turned up in true bulldog style. There is no remnant of the true spaniel type in anything about the head but the eye and ear. The colour of the end must be black, and it should be deep and wide, with open nostrils, the mouths of which face forwards and upwards as in the bulldog, without the same excuse for this formation, as the King Charles is certainly not used for bull-baiting.

The *lower jaw* has also changed its shape, and is now required to be wide and turned up, again imitating the bull type. This formation is said to give room for the lodgment of the tongue, which would otherwise protrude—why, I am at a loss to know; but the fancy wills it, and we must follow suit in a fancy article.

The *ears* should be almost long enough to touch the ground with the head in position. They are set low, and are carried very close by virtue of their weight. The King Charles slightly exceeds the Blenheim in length of ear, the average in his case being 24 inches across, and that of the Blenheim 22.

The *eyes* are set square and wide apart. They are large, languishing, dark brown in colour, with very large pupils, and always inclined to weep at the inner angles.

Compactness in shape is a very important point, a "cobby" dog being the *ne plus ultra* in this respect. Short, strong legs and a great girth of chest and loin are, of course, the chief features in this formation.

The *colour* in the King Charles must be a rich jet black, with deep tan markings in the usual places, as described in the article on the black-and-tan setter. No white is permitted, and the old-fashioned black, tan, and white in equal proportions is now quite out of fashion. In the Blenheim the colour must have a ground-work of white, which must be pearly, not dead. On this rich chestnut markings must be evenly distributed in large patches. The ears and cheeks should be wholly red, with a white blaze down the forehead, in the centre of which there should be a spot of red about the size of a sixpence.

o

The *coat* should be long, soft, silky, and wavy, but without decided curl. The Blenheim has a profuse mane flowing down in front of the brisket.

The *feather* is profuse on the ears, backs of the legs, and toes, in which last it projects far in front of the nails. The feather on the ears of the King Charles is considerably longer than on that of the Blenheim, as already mentioned.

The *size* of the two breeds is the same, namely, from 5 lbs. to 10 lbs.; *cæteris paribus,* the smaller the better.

The *symmetry* is above the average in these dogs, which do not seem to suffer from defective rearing, &c., as is the case with the toy-terrier.

Fanciers now (1886) recognise four varieties of the toy-spaniel —(1) the King Charles or black-tan; (2) the Prince Charles or tricolour (black-tan and white); (3) the Blenheim or red and white; and (4) the Ruby or all red spaniel. Except in colour, there is little difference between them.

THE JAPANESE PUG.

A spaniel-like breed is known in Japan, generally white and black, but called a pug—why I know not. The King Charles was some years ago crossed with this breed in order to shorten the face, but while obtaining this assorted beauty, it lost the much-admired length of ear, and on this account the cross was soon bred out.

II.—THE MALTESE DOG.

This beautiful little dog is a Skye terrier in miniature, with, however, a far more silky coat, a considerably shorter back, and a tail stiffly curved over the hip; actions lively and playful, and altogether rendering it a pleasing pet. The breed was so scarce some time ago as to induce Sir E. Landseer to paint one as the last of his race, since which several have been imported from Malta, and, though still scarce, they are now to be obtained with comparative ease. Of late years, Mr. Mandeville and Mrs. Monk have been the most successful on the show-bench, but I have seen none superior to Miss Gibbs' "Psyche." The little bitch from which the annexed portrait was sketched was the property of Miss

Gibbs of Morden, and was descended from parents imported by Mr. Lukey direct from Manilla.

"Psyche," * a Maltese Bitch, the Property of Miss Gibbs of Morden.

Points of the Maltese dog :—

	VALUE		VALUE
Eyes,	5	Size,	15
Ears, .	. 5	Tail, .	. 15
Nose, .	5	Symmetry, .	. 5
Coat, .	. 30		
Colour, .	. 20	Total, .	. 100

* "Psyche," the original of the engraving, was bred by Mr. Lukey of Morden, direct from the parent stock, being by "Cupid" out of "Psyche," who were both brought from Manilla in 1841, and bought there at a high price by Captain Lukey of the East India Company's Service. They were intended as a present for the Queen, but, after being nine months on board ship, were found on their arrival in England not presentable, from their coats having been entirely neglected during the voyage. "Psyche" is now (1859) twenty months old, pure white, weighs 3¼ lbs., measures in length of hair across the shoulders 15 inches, and when in her gambols presents in appearance a ball of animated floss silk, her tail falling on her back like spun glass. Of all the canine pets this breed is the most lovable, being extremely animated and sagacious, full of natural tricks, and perfectly free from the defects of the spaniel, viz., snoring and an offensive breath, being naturally cleanly and capable of instruction.

The *eyes* are black, full, but without weeping.

The *ears* are moderately long, but not spaniel-like, the hair on them mixing with that of the neck, as in the Skye terrier.

The *nose* is short and the end black, as also is the roof of the mouth.

The *coat* is long and silky, no wooliness being permitted. No curl is allowed.

The *colour* should be pure white, semi-transparent. Fawn patches are often met with, but must be penalised.

The *size* should not exceed 5 or 6 lbs.

The *tail* is short, and curled tightly over the back, as in the pug. It is heavily feathered.

The *symmetry* is not easily discernible, but the dog should be well formed, and as "cobby" as the King Charles.

III.—TOY-TERRIERS.

Toy-terriers are of the various kinds known as black-tan, smooth, blue-fawn or Yorkshire, and broken-haired. Skyes are also considered as toys, and even Dandies and fox-terriers, which last are now frequently made such by young ladies of the present day. All these breeds, when toys, have the same points as their larger brethren, and differ only in weight, which should not exceed 5 or 6 lbs. at most. The most beautiful of all is, perhaps, the Yorkshire when his coat is in full condition, but this cannot be preserved for any length of time. The smooth English terrier, not exceeding 6 lbs. in weight, is much prized; and when he can be obtained of 3½ or 4 lbs. weight, with perfect symmetry and a good rich black-and-tan colour without a white hair, he is certainly a very perfect little dog. The black lines ("pencilling") of the toes and the richness of the tan on the cheeks and legs are points much insisted on. Most of the toy-terriers now sold are either crossed with the Italian greyhound or the King Charles spaniel. If the former, the shape is preserved, and there is the greatest possible difficulty in distinguishing this cross from the pure English terrier; indeed, I am much inclined to believe that all our best modern toy-terriers are thus bred. They have the beautiful long sharp nose, the narrow forehead, and the small sharp eye which characterise the pure breed; but they are seldom good at vermin, though some which I have known to be half Italian have been bold enough to attack a good strong rat as well as most dogs. Many of these half-bred Italians are used for rabbit-coursing, in which there is a limit to weight, but it is chiefly for toy purposes that long prices are obtained for them. When the cross with the spaniel has been resorted to, the forehead is high, the nose short, and the eye large, full, and often weeping, while the general form is not so symmetrical and compact; the chest being full enough, but the brisket not so deep as in the true terrier or in the Italian cross.

At page 115 will be found an engraving of the black-and-tan toy-terrier contrasted with the larger Manchester.

IV.—THE ITALIAN GREYHOUND.

This little dog is one of the most beautifully proportioned animals in creation, being a smooth English greyhound in miniature, and resembling it in all respects but size. It is bred in Spain and Italy in great perfection, the warmth of the climate agreeing well with its habits and constitution. In England, as in its native country, it is only used as a pet or toy-dog, for, though its speed is considerable for its size, it is incapable of holding even a rabbit. The attempt, therefore, to course rabbits with this little dog has always failed, and in those instances where the sport (if such it can be called) has been carried out at all, recourse has been had to a cross between the Italian greyhound and the terrier, which results in a strong, quick, little dog, quite capable of doing all that is required.

The chief points characteristic of the Italian greyhound are shape, colour, and size, and the scale must, therefore, be altered from the English dog as follows:—

Scale of points of the Italian greyhound:—

	VALUE			VALUE
Head,	5	Tail,		5
Neck,	5	Coat,		5
Ears and eyes,	5	Colour,		15
Legs and feet,	10	Symmetry,		15
Fore-quarters,	10	Size,		15
Hind-quarters,	10			——
			Total,	100

In *shape* he should as nearly as possible resemble the English greyhound, as described at page 16, *et seq.* The nose is not usually so long in proportion, and the head is fuller both in width and depth. The eyes, also, are somewhat larger, being soft and full. The tail should be small in bone and free from hair. It is scarcely so long as that of the English greyhound, bearing in mind the

Italian Greyhounds, "BILLY" and "MINNIE."

difference of size. It usually bends with a gentle sweep upwards, but should never turn round in a corkscrew form.

The *colour* most prized is a golden fawn. The dove-coloured fawn comes next; then the cream-colour and the blue fawn or fawn with blue muzzle; the black-muzzled fawn, the black-muzzled red, the plain red, the yellow, the cream-coloured, and the black; the white, the blue, the white and fawn, and the white and red. Whenever the dog is of a whole colour, there should be no white whatever on the toes, legs, or tail; and even a star on the breast is considered a defect, though not so great as on the feet.

The *size* most prized is when the specified weight is about 6 or
8 lbs. ; but dogs of this weight have seldom perfect symmetry, and
one with good shape and colour of 8 lbs. is to be preferred to a
smaller dog of less perfect symmetry. Beyond 12 lbs. the dog is
scarcely to be considered a pure Italian, though sometimes exceptions occur, and a puppy of pure blood with a sire and dam of
small size may grow to such a weight as 16 lbs.

The *black dog* from which the engraving at the head of this
article was taken was remarkable for a degree of inbreeding rarely
seen, as will be evident from the annexed pedigree. He was of a
black colour, was very handsome, and was considered by " fanciers "
to be perfect in all his points. The engraving gives his proportions most exactly, but represents him as altogether too large,
he being in reality only $14\frac{1}{4}$ inches high, and $8\frac{3}{4}$ lbs. in weight.

Pedigrees of Mr. Gowan's " Billy " and Mr. Hanley's " Minnie."

BILLY †
(*Gowan's*,
22 Dean
Street,
Fetter
Lane).

PRINCE *
(*Gowan's*).

BILL
(*Anderson's*),
came from
Italy.

VIOLA
(*Gowan's*).

FLY
(*Barker*),
came from
Italy.

BILL
(as above).

CHUM
(*Stebbin's*).

BILL
(as above).

MYRTLE
(*Thorn's*).

BILL
(as above).

BILL
(as above).

ZIDO
(*Thorn's*).

BILL
(as above).

A bitch
from Italy.

MINNIE

BILL, whose pedigree is already furnished.

JENNY.

CHARLEY.

JENNY.

PRINCE.

MYRTLE.

---

* Took a prize of a silver collar in 1851.   † Took a silver collar in 1856.

V.—THE PUG.

This curly-tailed and pretty little toy-dog was out of fashion in
England for some years, but came again into vogue twenty years
ago, though only for a short time. The British breed, however,
which is one of those known to have existed from the earliest times,
was never entirely lost, having been carefully preserved in a few
families. The Dutch have always had a fondness for the pug-dog,

L.WELLS

"Punch" and "Tetty," * Pugs, the Property of Mr. C. Morrison of Walham Green.

and in Holland the breed is common enough, but the same attention has not been paid to it as in England, and yellow masks, low
foreheads, and pointed noses are constantly making their appearance in them, from the impure blood creeping out, and showing
evidences of the crosses which have taken place. For the sketch
of the very beautiful pair of these dogs which is engraved on
this page, I am indebted to one of the first toy-dog breeders of

* "Punch," out of Mr. Morrison's "Minnie;" "Tetty," out of his "Mouse;"
both by his "Charlie."

modern days, the late Mr. Morrison of Walham Green, who was long engaged in bringing his stock to their present state of perfection, and whose admirable management was shown in the healthy appearance of all of them. These dogs are not remarkable for sagacity displayed in any shape, but they are very affectionate and playful, and, like the Dutch and Flemish cows, they bear the confinement of the house better than many other breeds, racing over the carpets in their play as freely as others do over the turf. For this reason, as well as the sweetness of their skins and their short and soft coat, they are much liked by the ladies as pets.

In opposition to this Morrison strain is that of Lord Willoughby D'Eresby, which was obtained from a totally different source, and varies in colour, being a light stone-fawn, while that of Mr. Morrison is a yellow fawn. Both strains are now (1886) somewhat out of fashion, and instead of being worth £30 or £40 a piece, the average price has fallen to £5, or a trifle more.

The points are as follows :—

	VALUE			VALUE
Head,	10		Mask and vent,	7½
Ears,	5		Trace, . .	5
Eyes,	5		Wrinkles, .	2½
Neck,	5		Coat, . .	10
Moles,	5		Tail, . .	10
Body, .	10		Symmetry and size,	5
Legs and feet,	10			
Colour. .	10		Total, . .	100

The *head* is round and of great size, second only in proportion to that of the bulldog. Face short, but not retreating, the end being square. Teeth level. Tongue large and often hanging out. Cheeks full and muscular.

The *ears* are small and vine-shaped, formerly cropped close, but now always entire; black in colour at all but the roots.

The *eyes* are full and soft in expression; in colour dark brown. No weeping permitted.

The *neck* is full and strong, but clean cut.

A *mole* of a black colour must be present on each cheek, with several strong black hairs growing from it. These are usually reduced to three by pulling.

The *body* is thick, square, and strong, of the kind called "cobby," or punchy in a very high degree.

Legs and feet.—The legs are straight and small in bone. *Feet* narrow, with toes well split up. Those of the Willoughby strain are cat-like, of the Morrison hare-like. The nails must in all cases be dark, and there should be no white on the toes or any other part.

The *colour* is fawn with black points, to be presently described. The difference in shade of fawn has already been noticed.

Mask and vent.—These must be black, with well-defined edges. In the Willoughby strain the black extends above the brows, and is not so well defined as in the Morrison.

Wrinkles across the forehead.—There should be distinct wrinkles in the skin, deepened by black lines.

A *trace* or black line along the back should always be shown, the clearer the better. If this spreads over the back, it is called a "saddle-mark," which is considered a beauty in the Willoughby pug and a defect in the Morrison.

The *coat* is short, soft, and glossy, except in the tail, where it is longer and rougher. A small tail is objected to.

The *tail* must curve tightly, so as to lie flat on the side of the loin, with a little more than one turn.

Symmetry and size.—The symmetry is of a high order; size, 10 to 12 inches; weight, 10 to 14 lbs.

CHAPTER VIII.

CROSSED BREEDS.

1. Retriever : (A) The Curly-Coated ; (B) The Wavy-Coated—2. Bull-Terrier —3. Lurcher—4. Dropper—5. Dog and Fox Cross.

ALTHOUGH many of the breeds which have been enumerated in the preceding chapters were most probably originally the produce of crosses between distinct varieties, yet at present they are continued by breeding from a sire and dam of the same kind, whereas, with those which we are now considering, there is constantly a necessity for having recourse to the original breeds. For instance, some breeds of the greyhound are known to be crossed with the bull, and the identical animal with which the cross first commenced is well ascertained, as in the case of Sir James Boswell's "Jason," Mr. Etwell's "Eurus," &c. ; so also with the foxhound, though here the particular cross is not so well ascertained, but it is admitted to have taken place within the last century. Yet these are not called mongrels, and the breed, instead of being despised as such, is more highly prized than those of the pure strain which formed one side of the parent stock. The term *mongrel* may more properly be applied to those chance crosses which occur from accident or neglect, the bitch selecting her own mate, and being guided by caprice, without reference to the fitness of the match in regard to the progeny resulting. Hence we see the monstrosities which disgrace our streets—animals which might puzzle the most learned in dog-lore to say in what proportions they are allied to recognised varieties of the species *Canis*, but which are sometimes highly valuable in point of utility, and are often broken by the poacher to perform the most difficult feats. Indeed, it often happens that a poaching labourer—who is the worst kind of poacher—selects some mongrel in preference to a better-bred dog, in order to escape notice ;

but the gamekeeper should never despise the most wretched-looking animal on his beat, if the cur has size and strength to do what is required.

I.—THE RETRIEVER.

In speaking of the retriever, it is generally understood that the dog for recovering game *on land* is meant, the distinct kind known as the water-spaniel being already alluded to at page 161. With regard to the propriety of using a separate dog for retrieving in open or covert shooting, there is great difference of opinion, but this subject will be better considered under the next division of this book, and I shall now confine myself to a description of the crosses used solely as retrievers, including the Newfoundland, alluded to at page 177, and the ordinary cross between that dog and the setter, and that between the terrier and the water-spaniel, which is recommended by Mr. Colquhoun, and which I have found especially serviceable.

The *qualities* which are required in the regular retriever are: great delicacy of nose and power of stooping (which latter is often not possessed by the pointer); cleverness to follow out the windings of the wounded bird, which are frequently most intricate, and puzzle the intelligence as well as the nose to unravel them; love of approbation, to induce the dog to attend to the instructions of the master; and an amount of obedience which will be required to prevent his venturing to break out when game is before him. All these are doubtless found in the retriever, but they are coupled with a large heavy frame, requiring a considerable amount of food to keep it, and space in the dogcart when he is to be conveyed from place to place. Hence, if a smaller dog can be found to do the work equally well, he should be preferred; and as I think he can, I shall describe both.

The *large black retriever*, if crossed, is known by his resemblance to the small Newfoundland and the Irish water-spaniel or setter, between two of which he is bred, and the forms of which he partakes of in nearly equal proportions, according to the cross. Hence the modern retriever is distinguished as either the curly-coated or wavy-coated, separate classes being made for them at most of our shows, and sometimes a third depending on colour alone.

(A) THE CURLY-COATED RETRIEVER.

This variety of the retriever is always a cross between the St. John's Newfoundland and a water-spaniel, which is generally Irish. Hence it has become a necessary point that his face shall be bare and his tail free from feather and sting-like, as in the Irish breed. We cannot trace with certainty the foundation of the curly retriever, but, from his appearance and the prominence of the

The Curly-Coated Retriever.

above points, no doubt can be entertained that his origin is as I have described. A cross with the poodle has been probably attempted, but it is said to spoil the coat, though I should fancy it would improve the utility of the dog as a retriever. At present the wavy-coated variety is in fashion, the prevailing opinion being that he is more under control and has a softer mouth. Almost all shooters now depend on a retriever for fetching their game, and as sometimes there are more than half a dozen out, their qualities are of considerable importance, especially as time is never allowed for retrievers, and if it is not done at once, the task is given over to the keepers, for otherwise a whole line of shooters would be kept idle, which in the present day would be thought a nuisance. Formerly we used to consider the retrieving of a wounded bird or hare quite as important and interesting as the shooting of others, but all this is changed, and of course we must take the shooting world as we find it. Anyhow, the curly-coated retriever is rare, both on the show-bench and in the field, as compared with his numbers fifteen years ago.

Points of the curly-coated retriever :—

	VALUE		VALUE
Skull, . .	10	Feet, .	5
Nose and jaws,	10	Tail,	5
Ears and eyes,	5	Coat,	15
Neck, . .	5	Colour, .	5
Shoulders and chest,	10	Symmetry,	5
Loins and back, .	10	Temperament,	5
Quarters and stifles,	5		
Legs, knees, and hocks,	5	Total,	100

The *skull* is long and wide, with scarcely any brow, the slightest possible rise being only visible at that point.

Nose and jaws.—These must be long for carrying purposes and wide for scenting powers, with open moist nostrils and level teeth.

The *ears* must be of moderate length, without much hair on them, and neither vine-shaped nor lobular, but intermediate. The eyes are of medium size, soft, and intelligent in expression.

The *neck* should be long enough to allow stooping for a scent without difficulty : a chumpy-necked retriever is not admired.

Shoulders and chest.—The chest is round and not very deep. Shoulders rather short but muscular.

The *back and loin* are usually strong and well knit, with fairly deep back ribs.

Quarters and stifles.—The former are strong, and the latter should be set wide apart, to allow the dog to command himself in his work.

Legs, knees, and hocks.—All these parts must be bony and strong, the legs well clothed with muscle.

The *feet* are apt to be spreading from the Irish cross, but they should have the toes well up, and strong horny pads.

The *tail* is free from feather, but covered up to within six inches of the point with short crisp curls, which gradually disappear towards the tip. A stiff (and not a limp) tail is a *sine quâ non,* without any great curl upwards, and it should be quite free from any side bend.

The *coat* is not woolly, but of crisply curled hair, each curl being distinct, as in the Astrakan sheep, but even more regularly so. It is frequently oiled or glycerined for show purposes, which the hand readily detects. The whole face and forehead, up to the setting on of the ears, is covered with very short hair, which should shine in a way to show that it is not clipped. With this exception the whole of the upper part of the body is covered with the above-described curls. Sometimes the back is "saddle-marked" by the absence of them, and this is considered a grave defect.

The *colour* is either jet black or liver, the latter being considered inferior in value, though both are admitted to be true to the breed. The former is derived from the Newfoundland, the latter from the water-spaniel.

The *symmetry* is not very remarkable.

As to *temperament,* great attention should be paid to it, as the breed is apt to be deficient in this respect.

(B) THE WAVY-COATED RETRIEVER.

This fashionable breed, now considered a necessary adjunct to every shooter, even if he only attends a *battue* or a "drive," is often pure St. John's or Labrador; at other times he is more or less crossed with the setter. The former has already been fully described at page 181, and the latter only differs from him in

length and feather of ears, which are more or less setter-like. It
is, therefore, needless to describe the breed further.

Retriever (crossed with Setter).

II.—THE BULL-TERRIER.

Many of our smooth terriers are slightly crossed with the bulldog, in order to give courage to bear the bites of the vermin which
they are meant to attack. When thus bred, the terrier shows no
evidence of pain, even though half a dozen rats are hanging on to
his lips, which are extremely tender parts of the body, and where
the bite of a mouse even will make a badly-bred dog yell with
pain. In fact, for all the purposes to which a terrier can be
applied, the half or quarter cross with the bull, commonly known
as the "bull-terrier" or "half-bred dog," is of more value than

either of his purely-bred progenitors. Such a dog, however, to
be useful, must be more than half terrier, or he will be too heavy
and slow, too much under-jawed to hold well with his teeth, and
too little under command to obey the orders of his master. Sometimes the result of the second cross, which is only one-quarter bull,
shows a great deal of the shape peculiar to that side; and it is
not till the third or fourth cross that the terrier shape comes out
predominant; but this is all a matter of chance, and the exact

"Madman," Bull-Terrier.

reverse may just as probably happen, if the terrier was *quite free
from the strain of the bull*, which is seldom the case; and this may
account for the great predominance of that side in most cases, as
we shall see in investigating the subject of breeding for the kennel
in the next book.

This was the fighting dog of former days, possessing the courage

P

of the bulldog added to the quickness of the terrier, and being
without the tenacity of grasp of the former, which prevented his
doing the mischief to his antagonist that was required. The bull-
terrier, barring his tendency to quarrel, is a very excellent companion, but this makes him a nuisance out of doors, and few
gentlemen will now keep him for that purpose. He is still, however, largely patronised for some purpose or other, as he is shown
in considerable numbers both at Birmingham and in London.

Points of the bull-terrier :—

	VALUE		VALUE
Skull,	15	Feet,	5
Face and teeth,	10	Coat,	5
Ears,	5	Colour,	5
Neck,	5	Tail,	5
Shoulders and chest,	15	Symmetry,	10
Back,	10		
Legs,	10	Total,	100

The *skull* must be flat, and should taper regularly from its
greatest width between the ears to the nose, giving a peculiar
shape to the jaws, which is characteristic of the breed. There
is scarcely a vestige of brow; no stop, and no hollow down
the middle, except between the eyes, where the skull is slightly
" broken up." The eyes are small, dark, and sparkling.

Face and teeth.—The jaws must be long and powerful, without
any hollow under the eyes. The teeth should be level and very
strong. It is equally objectionable whether they are over or
under hung. The end of the nose should be black, but it is
often mottled in good breeds. The upper lip should be as tight
as possible, free from any approach to chop; the under lip must
be also small.

The *ears* are always cropped, and if so, they must be cut to a
fine point, which should stand well up, and they should match
exactly. If uncropped, they are often very large and unsightly.

The *neck* is long but strong, with a nice curve above, and no
throatiness below.

Shoulders and chest.—There is nothing remarkable here, except
that the back ribs are generally short.

The *back*, in spite of the short back ribs, is generally well let into the chest and coupled to the hips. The long dorsal muscles run in full bundles right up to the space between the shoulder-blades.

The *legs* before and behind are straight, bony, and muscular.

The *feet* are generally hare-like, from the terrier descent. The toes, however, are well arched, and do not spread.

The *coat* is short, close, and hard.

The *colour* must be a pure white, without mark of any kind. Of course spots will occur in this as in all white breeds, but they are severely penalised by show judges.

The *tail* is set on low. It is small in bone, and should be curved straight out horizontally.

The *symmetry* of the bull-terrier is of a high order.

III.—THE LURCHER.

Although this dog is not used by the fair sportsman in this country, yet he must be recognised as a distinct and well-known cross. From his great speed, combined with his good nose and his silence, he is *par excellence* the poacher's dog ; but he is very little better than the pure-bred greyhound accustomed to the same kind of work and with the same amount of practice. I have known a great many greyhounds which would never miss a hare if once sighted, or even put on the fresh scent, dropping their noses, and hunting out all the turns of the hare nearly as well as the beagle. Hence it is not to be supposed that the nose of the lurcher is derived from the sheep-dog's side only, for, both being good, he may be readily said to owe it to each in due proportions. When the lurcher is bred from the rough Scotch greyhound and the collie, or even the English sheep-dog, he is a very handsome dog, and even more so than either of his progenitors when pure. He is also a most destructive animal, showing speed, sagacity, and nose in an extraordinary degree, from which causes the breed is discouraged, as he would exterminate all the furred game in a very short time. A poacher possessing such an animal seldom keeps him long, every keeper being on the look-out, and putting a charge of shot into him on the first opportunity ; and as these *must* occur of necessity, the poacher does not often attempt to rear

the dog which would suit him best, but contents himself with one
which will not so much attract the notice of those who watch him.

It is needless to describe the *points* of the lurcher, further than
to remark that he partakes of those of the greyhound in shape,
combined with the stouter frame, larger ears, and rougher coat of
the sheep-dog, but varying according to the breed of each employed
in producing the cross. Formerly these lurchers were invariably
deprived of their tails, in order to pass muster as sheep-dogs, and
some are still thus cropped; but as hundreds of these farmers'
friends are now suffered to enjoy their full proportions, the lurcher,
when he does exist, is also full-tailed. The colour varies greatly,
and may be any one of those belonging to either of the breeds
from which he springs.

IV.—THE DROPPER.

This is a cross of the pointer with the setter, which at one time
was supposed to be superior to either, but is now seldom met with;
for, though the individual is useful enough, he is not ornamental,
and has the inconvenience of being unfitted for breeding purposes,
the second cross being invariably a failure.

V.—THE DOG AND FOX CROSS.

It is now generally admitted that the dog and fox will breed
together, but so little is known with certainty of the resulting produce that it is scarcely desirable to attempt a minute description.
Still it will be perhaps interesting to allude to the best authenti-
cated specimen within my knowledge, which is now the property
of Mr. Hewer of Reading. She is a daughter of the first cross,
which was described by Mr. Tomlin in *Bell's Life* in the year
1855, and is by an ordinary terrier dog.

Letter by R. Tomlin, Esq., on the subject of the Dog and Fox Cross.

"MR. EDITOR,—As your *Life* is the only 'Old Curiosity Shop' for the
reception of 'fancy articles,' I venture to forward you one respecting the fox
and dog cross, and although somewhat out of season, it may perhaps prove
interesting to the sportsman and the naturalist. In 1853 various accounts
appeared in *Bell's Life in London* of the fox and dog cross, the fact being

established by a gentleman of Kent, who then possessed a vulpo-canine bitch which had produce by a dog (vide *Bell's Life*, Dec. 1853 and Feb. 1854). This bitch (half fox, half dog), now in my possession, had produce in the month of February last by a terrier dog. The produce are two dog whelps and three bitches, some of which were (to ease the dam) suckled by a cur bitch. Two of the litter prove in nature shy as a fox ; three of them dog-like in appearance, colour, and perfectly quiet, and follow well at heel. Still they have the real fox-muzzle and 'fox-action,' about which (to those who have well studied it in the hunting-field) there exists but little mistake. Many there are who doubt the existence of any such animal as that between fox and dog. I am, however, in perfect condition to prove (by the living articles themselves) that the fox is merely a separate species of the *genus* dog, and intercopulates with the bitch, producing not a hybrid or mule animal, but one which will propagate its species to the very end of the chapter.—Yours, &c.　　　　ROBERT TOMLIN.

" PETERBOROUGH, *June* 1855."

The following letter, sent by Mr. Tomlin to the above paper in 1857, refers to this particular bitch, which formed one of the litter therein mentioned :—

Second Letter on the above subject.

" MR. EDITOR,—In 1855 you were good enough to describe in *Bell's Life* some history of a vulpo-canine bitch in my possession at Peterborough which had bred whelps, and as you are at this period of the year 'for the fox, and nothing but the fox,' perhaps you can spare a niche in your 'fancy columns' for a subject that may not be considered out of season. The vulpo-canine vixen is now, like all the fox *genus*, in full coat, and a beautiful-looking animal, higher on the leg than our common foxes, with more frame and size, and looks like going a slapping pace, and carries that unmistakable odour which accompanies 'the beast of stinking flight.' She bred a litter of whelps in the spring of the years 1855 and 1856 (got by a 'lion-tawny' coloured terrier dog), and goes ' on heat' only at one regular period. Her produce are endued more or less with the natural shyness and timidity of the vulpine species, and which it appears somewhat difficult to remove. The formation of their heads is faultless—long and punishing ; in fact, the appearance of these animals resembles terrier dogs, with the perfect head and countenance, back, body, and feet of the fox. The vulpo-canine bitch is now suckling four whelps (got by a good white terrier dog), and as their colours are likewise good—white ' with black and pied ear-patches '—it is likely to prove a better cross of its sort than the two former litter of whelps which the bitch reared, they being all of foxy, wild, dark-looking colours ; and as the terrier dog which got them was somewhat wicked and crafty in nature, I am now inclined to think that, ' as like begets like,' he was not altogether a suitable partner for the vulpo-canine bitch—an animal but one remove from the ' veritable fox itself,' as wild, too, as the wildest fox which ever broke away in a state of nature from any 'ever-green gorse covert,' with a pack of hounds in pursuit, all eager for the fray.— Yours, &c.   ROBERT TOMLIN.

"DANE COURT, ISLE OF THANET, *January* 1857."

The original of the engraving which illustrates this article has all the crouching look of the fox, with many of the wild habits of that animal. Mr. Hewer tells me that up to six or eight months old

L. WELLS.

A Dog and Fox Crossed Bitch, the property of ——- Hewer, Esq., of Reading.

she would hiss and spit like a kitten, but has quite lost that pecu-liarity now. She still often disappears into the adjacent coverts for a day or two, after which hunger compels her return. She has bred a litter by a terrier, but has not been put to one of her own cross, which is necessary to be done before Mr. Tomlin's assertion is to be accepted, that the individuals of the dog and fox cross will breed *inter se*. And this being the only proof of a distinction of species which is now recognised, until the experiment is carried out successfully we are not in a position to admit that the dog and fox belong to the same species.

BOOK II.

THE BREEDING, REARING, BREAKING, AND MANAGEMENT
OF THE DOG, IN-DOORS AND OUT.

CHAPTER I.

BREEDING.

Principles of Breeding—Axioms for the Breeder's Use—Crossing and Crossed
Breeds—Importance of Health in both Sire and Dam—Best Age to Breed
from—In-and-in Breeding—Best Time of Year—Duration of Heat—
Management of the Bitch in Season—The Bitch in Whelp—Preparation
for Whelping—Healthy Parturition—Destruction or Choice of Whelps
at Birth.

GENERAL PRINCIPLES OF BREEDING.

THE principles upon which the breeding of the dog should be conducted are generally in accordance with those necessary for the
production of other domestic animals of the class *Mammalia*,
remembering always that it is not reliable to argue from one class
of animals to another, because their habits and modes of propa-
gation vary so much as to interfere with the analogy. Thus, as
the pigeon, in common with other birds, does not rear her young
with the produce of her own body to the same comparative size as
most of the individuals of the class *Mammalia*, the mother has
not so much more to do with the process than the father as is the
case with the bitch, mare, and cow, &c., where the quantity and
quality of the milk are to be taken into the calculation. Hence,
in selecting a sire and dam for breeding purposes among dogs, the
bitch is most to be considered, for many reasons; one being that
she usually continues the property of the breeder, while the sire
can be changed each time she breeds; but the chief argument
in her favour being founded upon the supposition that she really
impresses her formation upon her progeny more than the dog.
This, however, is a vexed question in natural history as well as in
practical breeding, but from my own experience I am strongly of
opinion that it is true. Many horses and dogs may be instanced

which have got good stock from all sorts of mares and bitches;
but in opposition to this may be instanced the numbers which
have had enormous opportunities of showing their good qualities,
but while they have succeeded with one or two, they have failed
with the larger proportion of their harems. So with mares and
bitches; some have produced, every year of their breeding lives,
one or more splendid examples of their respective kinds, altogether independent of the horse or dog which may be the parent,
so long as he is of the proper strain likely to hit with hers. It is
usually supposed that the sire impresses his external formation
upon his stock, while the bitch's nervous temperament is handed
down; and very probably there is some truth in the hypothesis.
Yet it is clearer that not only do the sire and dam affect the progeny, but also the grandsires and granddams on both sides, and
still further than this up to the sixth and perhaps even the seventh
generations, but more especially on the dam's side, through the
granddam, great-granddam, &c. There is a remarkable fact connected with breeding which should be generally known, which is
that there is a tendency in the produce to a separation between
the different strains of which it is composed; so that a puppy composed in four equal proportions of breeds represented by A, B, C, and
D, will not represent all in equal proportions, but will resemble one
much more than the others, and this is still more clear in relation
to the next step backwards, when there are eight progenitors;
and the litter, which, for argument's sake, we will suppose to be
eight in number, may consist of animals each "going back" to one
or other of the above eight. This accounts for the fact that a smooth
terrier bitch put to a smooth terrier dog will often "throw" one or
more rough puppies, though the breed may be traced as purely
smooth for two or three generations, beyond which, however, there
must have been a cross of the rough dog. In the same way colour
and particular marks will be changed or obliterated for one, two, or
even three generations, and will then reappear. In most breeds of
the dog this is not easily proved, because a record of the various
crosses is not kept with any great care; but in the greyhound the
breed, with the colours, &c., for twenty generations, is generally
known, and then the evidence of the truth of these facts is patent
to all. Among these dogs there was a well-known strain descended

from a greyhound with a peculiar nose, known as the "Parrot-nosed bitch." About the year 1825 she was put to a celebrated dog called "Streamer," and bred a bitch called "Ruby," none of the litter showing this peculiar nose; nor did "Ruby" herself breed any in her first two litters; but in her third, by a dog called "Blackbird," belonging to Mr. Hodgkinson, two puppies showed the nose ("Blackbird" and "Starling"). In the same litter was a most celebrated bitch, known as "Old Linnet," from which are descended a great number of first-rate greyhounds. In these, however, this peculiarity has never appeared, with two exceptions, namely, once in the third generation and once in the fifth, in a dog called "Lollypop," bred by Mr. Thomas of Macclesfield, the possessor of the whole strain. One of the bitches of this breed is also remarkable for having always one blue puppy in each litter, though the colour is otherwise absent, never having been seen since the time of the above-mentioned "Ruby," who was a blue bitch. These facts are very remarkable, as showing the tendency to "throw back" for generations; but, as they are well known and fully recognised by all breeders, it is unnecessary to dilate upon them, and the above instances are only introduced as absolutely proving to the uninitiated what would otherwise depend upon dogmatic assertion.

AXIOMS FOR THE BREEDER'S USE.

But it may be asked, What, then, are the principles upon which breeding is to be conducted? To this, in many of the details, no answer can be given which can be relied on with certainty. Nevertheless, there are certain broad landmarks established which afford some assistance, and these shall be given, taking care to avoid all rules which are not clearly established by general consent.

1. The male and female each furnish their quota towards the original germ of the offspring; but the female, over and above this, nourishes it till it is born, and, consequently, may be supposed to have more influence upon its formation than the male.

2. Natural conformation is transmitted by both parents as a general law, and likewise any acquired or accidental variation.

It may therefore be said that, on both sides, "*like produces like.*"

3. In proportion to the purity of the breed will it be transmitted unchanged to the offspring. Thus a greyhound bitch of pure blood put to a mongrel will produce puppies more nearly resembling her shape than that of the father.

4. Breeding in-and-in is not injurious to the dog, as may be proved both from theory and practice; indeed it appears, on the contrary, to be very advantageous in many well-marked instances of the greyhound which have of late years appeared in public.

5. As every dog is a compound animal, made up of a sire and dam, and also their sires and dams, &c., so, unless there is much breeding in-and-in, it may be said that it is impossible to foretell with absolute certainty what particular result will be elicited.

6. The first impregnation appears to produce some effect upon the next and subsequent ones. It is therefore necessary to take care that the effect of the cross in question is not neutralised by a prior and bad impregnation. This fact has been so fully established by Sir John Sebright and others that it is needless to go into its proofs.

By these general laws on the subject of breeding we must be guided in the selection of the dog and bitch from which a litter is to be obtained, always taking care that both are as far as possible remarkable, not only for the bodily shape, but for the qualities of the brain and nervous system which are desired. Thus, in breeding the pointer, select a good-looking sire and dam by all means, but also take care that they were good in the field; that is, that they possessed good noses, worked well, were stout, and if they were also perfectly broken so much the better. So, again, in breeding hounds, care must be taken that the animals chosen are shaped as a hound should be; but they should also have as many of the good hunting qualities and as few of the vices of that kind of dog; and if these points are not attended to the result is not often good.

To secure these several results *the pedigrees* of the dog and bitch are carefully scanned by those who are particular in these matters, because then assurance is given that the ancestors, as far as they can be traced, possessed all those qualifications without which their owners would not in all human probability retain them. Hence a pointer, if proved to be descended from a dog and bitch belonging to any well-known breeder of this dog in the present day, or from Sir H. Goodrich, Mr. Moore, or Mr. Edge, so celebrated for their breeds some years ago, would be valued more highly than another without any pedigree at all, although the latter might be superior in shape, and might perform equally well in the field. The importance of pedigree is becoming more fully recognised every year, and experienced breeders generally refuse to have anything to do with either dog or bitch for this particular purpose, unless they can trace the pedigree to ancestors belonging to parties *who were known to be themselves careful in their selections.* In most cases this is all that is attempted, especially in pointers, setters, spaniels, &c., but in greyhounds and foxhounds of first-class blood the genealogy may generally be traced through half a dozen kennels of known and established reputation ; and this same attention to breed ought to prevail in all the varieties of the dog whose performances are of importance, and indeed without it the reproduction of a particular shape and make cannot with anything like certainty be depended on. Hence the breeders of valuable toy-dogs, such as King Charles spaniels, Italian greyhounds, &c., are as careful as they need be, having found out by experience that without this attention they are constantly disappointed.

CROSSING AND CROSSED BREEDS.

Crossing is practised with two distinct objects in view :—1st, To prevent degeneration in consequence of keeping to the same blood, or what is called "in-and-in" breeding ; and 2dly, With the view of improving particular breeds when they are deficient in any desirable quality, by crossing with others which have it in perfection, or often in excess. The first of these will be better understood after alluding to the practice of "in-and-in" breeding, but the second may now be considered with advantage.

Among dogs, as among horses, certain varieties are remarkable for particular qualities, and as the latter are more numerous in the species *Canis familiaris* than in the horse, so there is a greater opportunity for alteration. Thus in the horse there are speed,

stoutness, courage, temper, and shape (which includes action) to
be considered; but in the dog there are also, over and above these,
nose and sagacity, the presence or absence of which in some breeds
is of the greatest importance. Now, it happens that there are
certain old strains which have some of these qualities developed in
a very high degree, but are deficient in others, and therefore they
are only adapted to those breeds in which the qualities they are
deficient in are in excess. It is by a knowledge of these properties,
and by taking advantage of them, that our modern breeds have
been brought to the perfection at which they have arrived; carefully combining the plan with the principle of selection, which is
the great secret in all kinds of breeding. In this way the foxhound
has been produced by introducing the speed of the greyhound, and
in like manner the courage of the bulldog has been added to the
speed of the greyhound, to establish the present high form of that
animal. So also the terrier, though ardent enough in pursuit of
vermin, is too great a coward to bear their bites without flinching
unless he is crossed with the bulldog; and hence the bull-terrier
is the most useful dog for that purpose. Although many breeds of
terrier so crossed are not admitted to contain the bull strain, still
it is notorious that a vast proportion, if not all, have been crossed
in this way some generations back, and I firmly believe that
without this blood in their veins they are utterly useless.

It might naturally be supposed by any person who has not been
convinced to the contrary, that it would take several crosses to get
rid of the heavy form of the bulldog when united with the light
and graceful shape of the greyhound. But on actually trying the
experiment it will readily be seen that in the third generation very
little trace remains of the bulldog, while in the fourth there is
none whatever apparent in external form. My friend the late Mr.
Hanley, of the 1st Life Guards, was the last who tried the experiment, and having kept a daguerreotype of every individual used in
it, which he kindly placed at my service, I have been enabled to
present to my readers perfectly trustworthy proofs of the correctness of this assertion. The bulldog "Chicken" used was a very
high-bred animal, and of him also Mr. Hanley has preserved a
daguerreotype; but as his breeding is admittedly high, I have not
thought it necessary to engrave him. The bitch "Fly," put to

"Chicken," was also highly bred; but the most satisfactory proceeding will be to insert the whole pedigree at length, as shown on next page.

That the illustrative engravings are literal copies of the abovementioned daguerreotypes is a fact which should be plainly stated; in the first place, because, without a knowledge of it, the strangely uncouth forms of the first two would hardly be accepted; and in the second, to account for the attitudes in which the whole four are represented.

L.WELLS

" HALF-AND-HALF," * First Cross from the Bulldog.

From "Chicken" and "Fly" came the above thick and clumsy-looking animal, which was named "Half-and-Half," being the first cross.

The next step was to put this "Half-and-Half" to a well-bred dog belonging to Mr. Hanley, called "Blunder," whose descent is shown in the extended pedigree. From these came the second

* From a daguerreotype in the possession of Hugh Hanley, Esq., 1st Life Guards.

Pedigree of Mr. Hanley's "Hecuba," "Hecate," and "Half-and-Half."

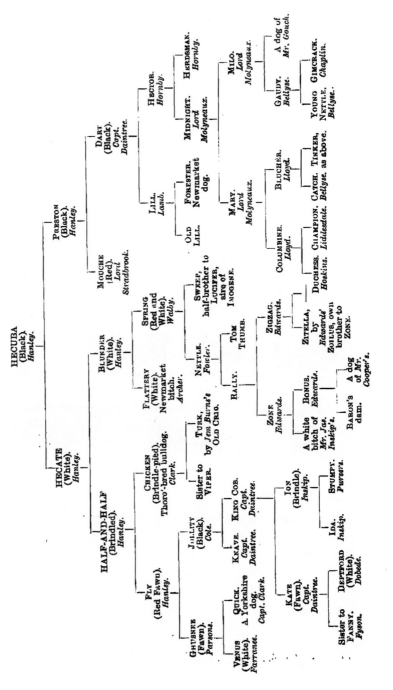

cross, " Hecate," a white bitch still presenting some slight characteristics of the bulldog breed, but by an ordinary observer this
would be scarcely noticed. There is, however, a remarkable want
of symmetry and true proportion in this bitch, which the portrait
conveys exactly.

She was again put to " Preston," a very fast dog belonging to
her owner, and from them the produce was " Hecuba," a large
black bitch of good shape, and, as I before remarked, scarcely dis-

L.WELLS.

" HEOATE," * Second Cross from the Bulldog.

tinguishable from the pure greyhound. She was very fast, but
could not work very cleverly, and her staying powers were very
limited indeed.

Mr. Hanley sent her to the celebrated dog " Bedlamite," expecting in this fourth cross to have some good runners, but they were
all remarkably deficient in stoutness, though fast as well as clever.
One of them is represented at page 243, having run in public as
" Hysterics."

* From a daguerreotype in the possession of Hugh Hanley, Esq., 1st Life Guards.

Q

This bitch has been put to " Ranter," a son of " Bedlamite ; " but the result of this, the fifth cross, is not as yet, I believe, more satisfactory than the fourth.

Before resorting to any particular strains, with a view of improving upon defects, it is necessary to consider what breeds are remarkable for each quality which is likely to be desired— namely, speed, courage, nose, and sagacity. Of these, the first is so remarkably prominent in the greyhound that there is no neces-

" HECUBA," Third Cross from the Bulldog.

sity for going further ; and whenever it is desired to increase the pace of any kind of dog, no discussion would arise as to the best means of effecting the object, this breed being immediately selected. So also the bulldog is proverbial for courage, and fortunately he is so formed as to be readily made to amalgamate with other breeds. Even the greyhound recovers his peculiar shape completely in the fourth generation, and in the third it would be difficult to discover any certain proof of the existence of the cross.

With regard to nose, there may be a difference of opinion depending upon the purpose to which it is devoted; but as it is seldom that this quality is wanted to be engrafted on speed or courage, the reverse being the usual course, it is scarcely necessary to dilate upon it. Thus it may be desirable to alter or improve the nose of the hound, the pointer, the setter, the spaniel, or the terrier, and in that case it would only be necessary to have recourse to the best specimens, as regards nose, in each breed, because

" Hysterics, ' Fourth Cross from the Bulldog.

there is a peculiarity attending on each mode of using the nose, which renders it more adapted to the work to be done than any other. Hence the pointer, when crossed with the foxhound, is apt to hunt too low, besides other faults which interfere with the usefulness of the cross; and the same may be said of the cross with the setter and spaniel. So that it may be laid down as a rule, that in the article nose it is not safe to look beyond the particular breed for improvement in this important quality.

Sagacity may be looked for in several breeds, but it is most highly developed perhaps in the poodle, the Newfoundland, and the terrier; chiefly, I imagine, because these dogs are more frequently the companions of man than the sporting dogs, which are kept in kennels. No dog is more capable of being taught than the half-bred bull-terrier, although the bulldog is by no means so, and as he is almost always tied up, the reason is obvious enough. Solitary confinement makes all animals, and even man himself, more or less idiotic, and if any dog is to be rendered as sagacious as possible, he must be constantly associated with his master. Hence it is that the poacher's dog is so much more clever than the fair sportman's, for, being the constant companion and friend of his master, he understands every word he says, and is ready also to communicate his own ideas in return.

To sum up, it may be assumed that the following breeds may be taken as types of the qualities so remarkable in each, and may be resorted to when any other kind is deficient in them. Thus, speed is typified in the greyhound, courage in the bulldog, and nose or scenting power in the bloodhound; for hunting purposes, the pointer or setter, when required in conjunction with setting; and the spaniel or terrier, for finding or "questing" both fur and feather. Lastly, sagacity is displayed in the poodle, Newfoundland, and terrier, chiefly because they are the constant associates of man.

IMPORTANCE OF HEALTH IN BOTH SIRE AND DAM.

Health in both parents should be especially insisted upon, and in the bitch in particular there should be a sufficiently strong constitution to enable her to sustain the growth of her puppies before birth, and to produce milk enough for them afterwards, though in this last particular she may, of course, be assisted by a foster-nurse.

BEST AGE TO BREED FROM.

The best age to breed from, in almost all breeds, is soon after the sire and dam have each reached maturity. When, however, the produce is desired to be very small, the older both animals are, the more likely this result is—excepting in the last litter which the bitch has, for, this being often composed of only one or two puppies, they are not smaller than the average, and sometimes even larger. All bitches should be allowed to reach full maturity before they are allowed to breed, and this period varies according to size, small dogs being adult at one year, whereas large ones are still in their puppyhood at that time, and take fully twice as long to develop their proportions. The mastiff is barely full-grown at two years; large hounds at a year and a half; greyhounds at the same time; pointers and setters from a year and a quarter to a year and a half; while terriers and small toy-dogs reach maturity at a year old, or even earlier.

IN-AND-IN BREEDING.

The questions relating to in-and-in breeding and crossing are of the greatest importance, each plan being strongly advocated by some people, and by others as strenuously opposed. Like many other practices essentially good, in-breeding has been grossly abused, owners of a good kennel having become bigoted to their own strain, and, from keeping to it exclusively, having at length reduced their dogs to a state of idiocy and delicacy of constitution which has rendered him quite useless. Thus I have seen in the course of twenty years a most valuable breed of pointers, by a persistence in avoiding any cross, become so full of excitability that they were perpetually at "a false point," and backing one another at the same time without game near them; and, what is worse, they could not be stirred from their position. This last was from a want of mental capacity, for it is by their reasoning powers that these dogs find out when they have made a mistake, and without a good knowledge-box the pointer and setter are for this reason quite useless. But the breed I allude to, when once they had become stiff, were like Chinese idols, and must absolutely be kicked or whipped up in order to make them start off beating again. Mr. A. Graham, who has had a long experience in breeding greyhounds, and was at one time so successful as to obtain the name of "The Emperor of Coursers," has laid down the rule that "once in and twice out" is the proper extent to which breeding in the greyhound should be carried, and probably the same will apply to other breeds. Sometimes a sister may be put to a brother even, when there was no previous near relationship in their sire and dam; but though this has answered well two or three times, it is not to be generally recommended. A father may in preference be put to a daughter, because there is only half the same blood in them, when the sire and dam of the latter were not related; or an uncle to a niece; but the best plan is to obtain a dog which has some considerable portion of the same blood as the bitch, but separated by one or two crosses; that is to say, to put two animals together whose grandfathers or great-grandfathers were brothers, but whose mothers and grandmothers were no relation to each other. This relationship will do equally well on the dam's side, and the grandmother may be sister to the grandsire, quite as well as having the two grandsires brothers. The practice of breeding-in to this extent has been extensively adopted of late years, and has answered well with the greyhound, in which breed, as used for public coursing, the names of "Harriet Wilson," "Hourglass," "Screw," "Sparrowhawk," "Vraye Foy," "Motley," "Miss Hannah," and "Rival" speak volumes in its approbation, all being in-bred and all wonderfully successful. The last-named bitch is a remarkable instance, being by a half-brother out of a half-sister, and yet continuing honest up to her sixth season, when she broke a toe in running the last course but one in a large stake at Ashdown. In her case, too, the blood of the dam was somewhat notorious for a tendency to run cunning; and indeed the same might be said of nearly all the strains of which she was composed; nevertheless, throughout her career she was entirely free from this vice, and left off without a stain. She has, however, unfortunately refused to breed; but, as I have never known this peculiarity confined to in-bred bitches, I do not allege the fact as arising from her close in-breeding. Thus I have shown that in practice in-and-in breeding, within certain bounds, is not only not prejudicial, but absolutely advantageous, inasmuch as it does not injure the nervous temperament and mental qualities of the produce; and that the body does not suffer is a well-known fact, easily capable of proof by examining the external forms of the dogs so bred. Theoretically, also, it ought to answer, because we find in nature gregarious wild animals resorting to in-breeding in all cases, the stag adding his daughters to his harem as long as he has strength enough to beat off his younger rivals. In the same way the bull and the stallion fight for supremacy, till at length, from age or accident, they are beaten off, and a younger and more vigorous animal masters them and their female attendants. Yet this seems Nature's mode of insuring a superior stock, and preventing the degeneration which we see take place among human beings, when a feeble pair take upon themselves the task of producing a family. It would appear that man is an exception to the general rule, for there is a special revelation prohibiting inter-marriages, while we find them constantly going on among brutes, and especially, as above remarked, among gregarious animals. Hence it should not lead us to reason by analogy from one to the other; nor because we find that first cousins among our own race are apt to produce defective children, bodily and mentally, should we conclude that the same evil results will occur when we breed from dogs or horses having the same degree of relationship to their mates. At the same time, when all that can be desired is obtainable without in-breeding, I should be inclined to avoid it; always taking care to resort to it when it is desired to recover a particular strain, which is becoming merged in some other predominant blood. Then by obtaining an animal bred as purely as possible to the desired strain, and putting him or her to your own, it may be expected that the produce will " go back" to this particular ancestry, and will resemble them more than any other.

BEST TIME OF YEAR.

The best time of the year for breeding dogs is from April to September, inasmuch as in the cold of winter the puppies are apt to become chilled, whereby their growth is stopped, and some disease very often developed. Among public greyhounds there is a particular reason for selecting an earlier period of the year, because, as their age is reckoned from the 1st of January, and as they are wanted to run as saplings or puppies, which are defined by their age, the earlier they are born the more chance they have in competition with their fellows of the same year. Hounds and game-dogs are wanted to begin work in the autumn, and as they do not come to maturity till after they are a year old, they should be whelped in the spring. This is more especially the case with pointers and setters, which are then old enough to have their education nearly completed at "pairing time" in the spring of the next year, when only their breaking can properly be carried on, as birds then lie like stones and allow the dog to be reached, and properly kept under by his breaker. Toy-dogs and all small dogs, which are reared in the house, *may* be bred almost at any time of the year; but even they are stronger and healthier if born in the summer months, because the puppies may then be supposed to get more air and sun than they could do in the winter, when the warmth of the fire is essential to their well-doing.

DURATION OF HEAT.

The duration of the period of heat in the bitch is about three weeks, during the middle week of which she will generally take the dog; but about the eleventh or twelfth day from the first commencement is, on the average, the best time to put her to him. During the first three or four days of the middle week the bitch "bleeds" considerably from the *vulva*, and while this is going on she should not be allowed access to the male, nor will she generally if left to herself; but as soon as it subsides no time should be lost, as it often happens that very shortly afterwards she will refuse him altogether, and thus a whole year may be lost. Most bitches are "in heat" twice a year, at equal periods, some every five, or even every four months; others every seven, eight, nine, ten, eleven, or twelve months; but the far greater proportion of bitches of all breeds are "in season" twice a year pretty regularly. There is, therefore, a necessity for ascertaining the rule in each bitch, as it varies so considerably; for, when it is known, the calculation can better be made as to the probability of the heat returning at the desired time. The period between the first and second "heats" will generally indicate the length of the succeeding ones, but this is not invariable, as the "putting by" of the animal will sometimes throw her out of her regular course.

MANAGEMENT OF THE BITCH IN SEASON.

When bitches are not intended to breed, they are carefully "put by," that is to say, they are secluded from the dog, and during that time they are in great measure deprived of their usual exercise. From this circumstance they are very apt to get out of health, and some injury is thereby done to their offspring as well as themselves. At this time they ought, from their general feverishness, as well as from their deprivation of exercise, to be kept rather lower than usual, and very little meat should be given. Slops and vegetables, mixed with biscuit or oatmeal, form the most suitable diet; but if the bitch has been accustomed to a great deal of flesh, it will not do to deprive her of it altogether. Bearing in mind, then, this caution, it is only necessary to remember that she must be lowered in condition, but not so starved as to do harm by the sudden change. After the end of the period, a little cooling medicine will often be required, consisting of a dose of oil or salts. (See Aperients.)

MANAGEMENT OF THE BITCH IN WHELP.

When it is clearly ascertained that the bitch is in whelp, the exercise should be increased and carried on freely till the sixth week, after which it should be daily given, but with care to avoid strains either in galloping or jumping. A valuable bitch is often led during the last week, but somehow or other she ought to have walking exercise to the last, by which, in great measure, all necessity for opening medicine will be avoided. During the last few weeks her food should be regulated by her condition, which must be raised if she is too low, or the reverse if she is too fat, the desired medium being such a state as is compatible with high health, and neither tending towards exhaustion nor inflammation. Excessive fat in a bitch not only interferes with the birth of the pups, but also is very liable to interfere with the secretion of milk, and if this last does happen, aggravates the attendant or "milk" fever. To know by the eye and hand how to fix upon this proper standard, it is only necessary to feel the ribs, when they should at once be apparent to

the hand, rolling loosely under it, but not evident to the eye so as
to count them.   It is better to separate the bitch from other dogs
during the last week or ten days, as she then becomes restless, and
is instinctively and constantly looking for a place to whelp in,
whereas, if she is prevented from occupying any desirable corner
she is uneasy.   At this time the food should be of a very sloppy
nature, chiefly composed of broth or milk and bread, adding oatmeal according to the state of the bowels.

PREPARATION FOR WHELPING.

The best mode of preparing a place for the bitch to whelp in is
to nail a piece of old carpet over a smooth boarded floor, to a
regular "bench," if in a sporting kennel; or on a door or other
flat piece of board raised a few inches from the ground, if for any
other breed.   When a regular wooden box or kennel, as these are
called in ordinary language, is used for the bitch, she may as well
continue to occupy it, as she will be more contented than in a
fresh place; but it is not so easy to get at her there if anything
goes wrong with either mother or whelps, and on that account it
is not a desirable place.   A board, large or small, according to the
size of the bitch, with a raised edge to prevent the puppies rolling
off, and supported by bricks a few inches from the ground, is all
that is required for the most valuable animal; and if a piece of
carpet, as before mentioned, is tacked upon this, and some straw
placed upon all, the height of comfort is afforded to both mother
and offspring.   The use of the carpet is to allow the puppies to
catch their claws in it as they are working at the mother's teats;
for without it they slip over the board, and they are restless, and
unable to fill themselves well; while, at the same time, they
scratch all the straw away, and are left bare and cold.

HEALTHY PARTURITION.

During whelping the only management required is in regard to
food and quiet, which last should as far as possible be enjoined,
as at this time all bitches are watchful and suspicious, and will

destroy their young if they are at all interfered with, especially by strangers. While the process of labour is going on no food is required, unless it is delayed in an unnatural manner, when the necessary steps will be found described in the Third Book. After it is completed some lukewarm gruel, made with half milk and half water, should be given, and repeated at intervals of two or three hours. Nothing cold is to be allowed for the first two or three days, unless it is in the height of summer, when these precautions are unnecessary, as the ordinary temperature is generally between 60° and 70° of Fahrenheit. If milk is not easily had, broth will do nearly as well, thickening it with oatmeal, which should be well boiled in it. This food is continued till the secretion of milk is fully established, when a more generous diet is gradually to be allowed, consisting of sloppy food, together with an allowance of meat somewhat greater than that to which she has been accustomed. This last is the best rule, for it will be found that no other useful one can be given; those bitches which have been previously accustomed to a flesh diet sinking away if they have not got it at this time, when the demands of the puppies for milk drain the system considerably; and those which have not been used to it being rendered feverish and dyspeptic if they have an inordinate allowance of it. A bitch in good health, and neither over-reduced by starvation nor made too fat by excessive feeding, will rarely give any trouble at this time; but, in either of these conditions, it may happen that the secretion fails to be established. (For the proper remedies, see Parturition, in Book III.) From the first day the bitch should be encouraged to leave her puppies twice or thrice daily to empty herself, which some, in their excessive fondness for their new charge, are apt to neglect. When the milk is thoroughly established, they should be regularly exercised for an hour a day, which increases the secretion of milk, and indeed will often bring it on. After the second week bitches will always be delighted to leave their puppies for an hour or two at a time, and will exercise themselves if allowed to escape from them. The best food for a suckling bitch is strong broth, with a fair proportion of bread and flesh, or bread and milk, according to previous habits.

DESTRUCTION OR CHOICE OF WHELPS AT BIRTH.

Sometimes it is desirable to destroy all the whelps as soon as possible after birth, but this ought very seldom to be done, as in all cases it is better to keep one or two sucking for a short time, to prevent milk fever, and from motives of humanity also. If, however, it is decided to destroy all at once, take them away as fast as they are born, leaving only one with the mother to engage her attention; and when all are born, remove the last before she has become used to it, by which plan less cruelty is practised than if she is permitted to attach herself to her offspring. Low diet and a dose or two of mild aperient medicine, with moderate exercise, will be required to guard against fever; but at best it is a bad business, and can only be justified under extraordinary circumstances.

CHAPTER II.

Management in the Nest—Choosing—The Foster-Nurse—Feeding before
Weaning—Choice of Place for Whelping—Removal of Dew-Claws, &c.—
Weaning—Lodging—Feeding—Exercise—Home-Rearing *v.* Walking—
Food—General Treatment—Choice of Puppies after Weaning—Cropping,
Branding, and Rounding.

THE MANAGEMENT OF WHELPS IN THE NEST.

THIS, till they are weaned, does not require much knowledge or
experience beyond the feeding of the mother, and the necessity for
removing a part when the numbers are too great for her strength
to support. For the first fortnight at least, puppies are entirely
dependent upon the milk of their dam or a foster-nurse, unless they
are brought up by hand, which is a most troublesome office, and
attended also with considerable risk. Sometimes, however, the
bitch produces twelve, fourteen, or even sixteen whelps, and these
being far beyond her powers to suckle properly, either the weak
ones die off or the whole are impoverished and rendered small and
puny. It is better, therefore, especially when size and strength
are objects to the breeder, to destroy a part of the litter, when they
are more than five or six in the greyhound, or seven or eight in the
hound or other dog of that size. In toy-dogs a small size is sometimes a desideratum, and with them, if the strength of the dam is
equal to the drain, which it seldom is, almost any number may be
kept on her. For the first three or four days the bitch will be able
to suckle her whole litter; but if there are more puppies than she
has *good* teats, that is, teats with milk in them, the weak ones are
starved, unless the strong ones are kept away in order to allow them
access, so as to fill themselves in their turn. To manage this a
covered basket, lined with wool if the weather is at all cold, should

be provided; and in this one-third or one-half of the puppies should
be kept, close to the mother, to prevent either from being uneasy,
but the lid fastened down, or she will take them out in her mouth.
Every two or three hours a fresh lot should be exchanged for those
in the basket, first letting them fill themselves, when they will go
to sleep and remain contented for the time fixed above, thus allowing each lot in its turn to fill itself regularly. At the end of ten
days, by introducing a little sweetened cow's milk on the end of
the finger into their mouths, and dipping their noses in a saucer
containing it, they learn to lap; and after this there will be little
difficulty in rearing even a dozen; but they will not, however carefully they may be fed in aid of the mother, be as large as if only a
small number were left on her, and therefore greyhound breeders
limit their litters to five, six, or at most seven; destroying the
remainder, or rearing them with a foster-nurse.

CHOICE OF WHELPS.

To choose the whelps in the nest which are to be kept, most people
select on different principles, each having some peculiar crotchet
to guide himself. Some take the heaviest, some the last-born;
others the longest of the litter; while others again are entirely
guided by colour. In toy-dogs, and those whose appearance is an
important element, colour ought to be allowed all the weight it
deserves, and among certain toy-dogs the value is often affected a
hundred per cent. by a slight variation in the markings. So also
among pointers and setters a dog with a good deal of white should
be preferred, on the score of greater utility in the field, to another
self-coloured puppy which might otherwise be superior in all
respects. Hounds and greyhounds are, however, chosen for shape
and make; and though this is not the same at birth as in after life,
still there are certain indications which are not to be despised.
Among these, the shoulders are more visible than any others, and
if on lifting up a puppy by the tail he puts his fore-legs back beyond
his ears, it may be surmised that there will be no fault in his shape
in reference to his fore-quarter, supposing that his legs are well
formed and his feet of the proper shape, which last point can hardly
be ascertained at this time. The width of the hips and shape of

the chest, with the formation of the loin, may also be conjectured, and the length of the neck is in like measure shadowed forth, though not with the same certainty as the shoulders and ribs. A very fat puppy will look pudgy to an inexperienced eye, so that it is necessary to take this into consideration in making the selection; but fat is a sign of strength, both actual and constitutional, when it is remarkably permanent in one or two among a litter, for it can only be obtained either by depriving the others of their share of milk by main force, or through such constitutional vigour as to thrive better on the same share of aliment. The navel should be examined to ascertain if there is any rupture, and this alone is a reason for deferring the choice till nearly the end of the first week, up to which time there is no means of judging as to its existence. Indeed, if possible, it is always better to rear nearly all till after weaning, either on the dam herself or on a foster-nurse, as at that time the future shape is very manifest, and the consequences of weaning are shown, either in a wasting away of the whole body or in a recovery from its effects in a short time. Sometimes, however, there are not conveniences for either, and then recourse must be had to an early choice on the principles indicated above.

THE FOSTER-NURSE

Need not be of the same breed as the puppies which she is to suckle, and at all times a smooth-skinned bitch is superior for the purpose to one with a rough coat, which is apt to harbour fleas, and in other ways conduce to the increase of dirt. For all large breeds the bull-terrier (which is the most commonly kept among the class who alone are likely to sell the services of a nurse) answers as well as any other, and her milk is generally plentiful and good. For small breeds any little house dog will suffice, taking care that the skin is healthy, and that the constitution is not impaired by confinement or gross feeding. Greyhound puppies are very commonly reared by bull-bitches without any disadvantage, clearly proving the propriety of the plan. It may generally be reckoned, in fixing the number which a bitch can suckle with advantage, that, of greyhound or pointer puppies, for every seven pounds in her own weight the bitch can do one well; so that an average bull-terrier will rear three, her weight being about twenty-one pounds, and smaller dogs in proportion. When the substitution is to be made, the plan is to proceed as follows :—Get a warm basket, put in it some of the litter in which the bitch and her whelps have been lying, then take away all her own progeny, and, together with the whelps to be fostered, put all in the basket, mixing them so that the skins of the fresh ones shall be in contact with the bitch's own pups and also with the litter. Let them remain in this way for three hours, during which time the bitch should be taken out for an hour's walk, and her teats will have become painfully distended with milk. Then put all the pups in her nest, and, carefully watching her, let her go back to them. In ninety-nine cases out of a hundred, she will at once allow them all to suck quietly, and *if she licks all alike* she may be left with them safely enough ; but if she passes the fresh ones over, pushing them on one side, she should be muzzled for twelve hours, leaving all with her, and keeping the muzzle on excepting while she is fed, or watched till she is observed to lick all alike. On the next day, all but one of her own puppies may be withdrawn, with an interval of one hour or two between each two, and taking care that she does not see what is done. After two days the last may also be taken away, and then she acts to her foster-puppies in every way the same as to her own. Some people squeeze a little of the bitch's milk out of her teats, and rub this over the puppies, but I have never seen any advantage in the plan; and, as I have never had any difficulty in getting puppies adopted, I do not recommend any other than that I have described. In most cases the foster-bitch is strange to those about her, having been brought from her own home, and in that case a muzzle is often required for the safety of the servants watching her as well as for the whelps ; but if she seems quiet and good-tempered, it may be dispensed with even here.

FEEDING BEFORE WEANING.

The food of whelps before weaning should be confined at first to cow's milk, or, if this is very rich, reduced with a little water. It is better to boil it, and it should be sweetened with fine sugar, as for the human palate. As much of this as the whelps will take may be given them three times a day, or every four hours if they are a large litter. In the fourth week get a sheep's head, boil it in a quart of water till the meat comes completely to pieces, then carefully take away every particle of bone, and break up the meat into fragments no larger than a small horse-bean; mix all up with the broth, thicken this to the consistence of cream with *fine* wheat-flour, boil for a quarter of an hour, then cool and give alternately with the milk. At this time the milk may also be thickened with flour, and as the puppies grow, and the milk of the bitch decreases in quantity, the amount of milk and thickened broth must be increased each day, as well as more frequently given. Some art, founded on experience, is required not to satiate the puppies; but, by carefully increasing the quantity whenever the puppies have finished it greedily the last time or two, they will not be overdone. In no case should the pan containing the food be left in the intervals with the puppies, if they have not cleared it out, as they only become disgusted with it, and next time refuse to feed. A sheep's head will serve a litter of large-sized puppies two days up to weaning, more or less according to numbers and age.

CHOICE OF PLACE FOR WHELPING.

The whelping-place, up to the third week, may be confined to a square yard or two, floored with board as already described. After the third week, when the puppies begin to run about, access should be given them to a larger run, and an inclined plane should be arranged for them to get up and down from their boarded stage. If the weather is cold, the best place for a bitch to whelp is in a saddle-room warmed by a stove; or an empty stall, with a two-foot board placed across the bottom, opposite the stall-post, so as to prevent the puppies getting among the horses. In either case there is an amount of artificial heat, which conduces to the growth of the puppies, and allows them to be reared sufficiently strong to bear any cold afterwards with impunity. If the weather is not cold, an ordinary horse-box is the best place which can be chosen, fixing the boarded stage at a distance from the door, and either sanding or slightly littering the brick floor, according to the weather; but the latter is to be preferred, excepting in a very hot summer. In these boxes puppies take a vast amount of exercise, which they require for health, and to give that appetite without which sufficient food for growth is not taken.

REMOVAL OF DEW-CLAWS, &c.

Before weaning, any cropping which is intended, whether of the dew-claw or tail, should be practised, but the ears should be left alone till the third or fourth month, as they are not sufficiently developed before. If, however, the operator does not understand his business thoroughly, it is better to leave the latter organs alone till a later period, as otherwise the proper quantity may not be cropped or rounded, as the case may be. Indeed, even the most skilful hand will hardly ever manage either the one or the other well before the fifth month; and in hounds it is usual to defer it till they are nearly full-grown, as they often lose a considerable quantity of blood, which interferes with their growth. But the tail and dew-claws may always be best done, and with least pain, while with the dam; besides which, her tongue serves to heal the wound better than that of the young puppy, who has hardly learnt to use it. Regular dog-fanciers bite off the tail, but a pair of scissors answers equally well; and the same may be said of the dew-claw. If, however, the nail only is to be removed, which it always ought to be, the teeth serve the purposes of a pair of nippers perfectly, and by their aid it may be drawn out, leaving the claw itself attached, but rendered less liable to injury, from having lost the part likely to catch hold of any projecting body.

WEANING.

When weaning is to be commenced, which is usually about the fifth or sixth week, it is better to remove the puppies altogether than to let the bitch go on suckling them at long intervals. By this time their claws and teeth have become so sharp and so long that they punish the bitch terribly, and therefore she does not let them fill their bellies. Her milk generally accumulates in her teats, and becomes stale, in which state it is not fit for the whelps, and by many is supposed to engender worms. The puppies have always learned to lap, and will eat meat or take broth or thickened milk, as described in the last chapter; besides which, when they have no chance of sucking presented to them, they take other food better, whereas, if they are allowed to suck away at empty teats, they only fill themselves with wind, and then lose their appetites for food of any kind. But, having determined to wean them, there are several important particulars which must be attended to, or the result will be a failure, at all events for some time; that is to say, the puppies will fall away in flesh, and will cease to grow at the same rate as before. In almost all cases what is called the "milk-fat" disappears after weaning; but still it is desirable to keep some flesh on their bones, and this can only be done by attending to the following directions, which apply to dogs of all kinds, but are seldom rigidly carried out, except with the greyhound, whose size and strength are so important as to call for every care to procure them in a high degree. In hounds, as well as pointers and setters, a check in the growth is of just as much consequence; but as they are not tested together as to their speed and stoutness so closely as greyhounds are, the slight defects produced in puppyhood are not detected, and, as a consequence, the same attention is not paid. Nevertheless, as most of these points require only care, and cost little beyond it, they ought to be carried out almost as strictly in the kennels of the foxhound and pointer as in those devoted to the longtails. These chief and cardinal elements of success are—1st, a warm, clean, and dry lodging; 2dly, suitable food; 3dly, regularity in feeding; and 4thly, a provision for sufficient exercise.

NECESSITY FOR WARM AND DRY LODGING.

All puppies require a dry lodging, and in the winter season it should also be a warm one. Greyhound whelps, up to their third or fourth month, are sometimes reared in an artificial temperature, either by means of a stove or by using the heat of a stable, the temperature chosen being 60° of Fahrenheit. Beyond this age it can never be necessary to adopt artificial heat in rearing puppies, because for public coursing they are required to be whelped after the last day of the year, and four months from that time takes us on to May, when the weather is seldom cold enough to require a stove; and then during the summer months they are gradually hardened to the vicissitudes of the weather, and as they become older their growth is established, and they are no longer in danger of its being checked. It is true that some few coursers always keep their kennels at 60°; but, on the whole, as we shall hereafter find, the plan is not a good one, and need not be considered here. But far beyond the warmth is dryness essential to success. Dogs will bear almost any amount of cold if unaccompanied by damp, provided they have plenty of straw to lie on; but a damp kennel, even if warm, is sure to lead to rickets or rheumatism, if the puppies escape inflammation of some one or more of the internal organs. Take care, therefore, to give a dry bedstead of boards, lined with the same material towards the wall (the cold of which strikes inwards and gives cold), and raised somewhat from the floor, which will otherwise keep it damp. Puppies soon learn to lie on this, and avoid the cold stones or bricks, except in the heat of summer, when these do no harm. The stone or brick floor should be so made as to avoid absorption of the urine, &c., which can only be effected by employing glazed tiles or bricks that are not porous, or by *covering the whole with a layer of London or Portland cement*, or with *asphalt*, which answers nearly as well. Care should be taken that there are no interstices between the boards, if the kennel is made of them; and in every way, while ventilation is provided, cold draughts must be prevented. Cleanliness must also be attended to rigidly by sweeping out the floor daily, and washing it down at short intervals, and by changing the litter once a week at the least. In the summer-time straw is not desirable, as it harbours fleas; and if the boarded floor is not considered sufficient, a thick layer of deal sawdust will be the best material, as it is soft enough, without harbouring vermin of any kind; the only objection to it being that the puppies are apt to wet it often, after which it becomes offensive.

FEEDING.

The *feeding* of puppies is all important, and unless they have plenty of food sufficiently nourishing to allow of a proper growth, it is impossible that they should become what they might be if fed with the best materials for the purpose. From the time of weaning to the end of the third month, when a decision must be arrived at as to their subsequent mauagement, very little deviation is required from the plans described at pp. 256–7; that is, the puppies should be fed every four hours upon the thickened broth made from sheep's head and thickened milk alternately. After that time, however, their food must be given them rather stronger and of a somewhat different nature, as we shall find in its proper place. This food will be required for any kind of dog, but a single puppy may very well be reared upon thickened milk, with the scraps of the house in addition, including bones, which it will greedily pick, and any odds and ends which are left on the plates.

Regularity of feeding in puppies, as in adult animals, is of the utmost importance; and it will always be found that if two puppies are equally well reared in other respects, and one fed at regular hours, while the other is only supplied at the caprice of servants, the former will greatly excel the latter in size and health, as well as in the symmetrical development of the body. It is also very necessary to avoid leaving any part of one meal in the pans or feeding-troughs till the next, as nothing disgusts the dog more than seeing food left in this way. The moment the puppies fill themselves, take away the surplus; and, indeed, it is better still to anticipate them by stopping them before they have quite done. All this requires considerable tact and experience, and there are very few servants who are able and willing to carry out these directions fully.

EXERCISE.

Exercise is necessary at all ages, but the fully developed dog may be confined for some little time without permanent injury, the formation of his feet and the texture of his bones and muscles being then finally settled. On the other hand, the puppy will grow according to the demands made upon his mechanism, and if the muscles are left idle they do not enlarge, while the feet remain thin and weak, with the tendons and ligaments relaxed, so that they spread out like a human hand. Growing puppies should be provided with an area sufficiently large for them to play in, according to their size, and under cover up to the end of the third month; after which, if they have a sheltered sleeping-place to run into, they will generally avoid heavy rain. Young puppies play sufficiently in a loose box or similar enclosure; but, after the time specified above, they must either have their entire liberty, or be allowed the run of a large space, the alternative being bad feet, defective development, and weak joints.

HOME REARING *VERSUS* WALKING.

When one or two puppies only are to be reared, they may be readily brought up at home, excepting in towns or other confined situations where due liberty and a proper amount of sun and air cannot be obtained. But where a larger number are to be reared, as in the case of hounds, greyhounds, pointers and setters, &c., there is a difficulty attending upon numbers, as a dozen or two of puppies about a house are not conducive to the neatness and beauty of the garden; besides which, the collection together in masses of young dogs is prejudicial to their health. To avoid this evil, therefore, it is customary to send puppies out at three or four months of age to be kept by cottagers, butchers, small farmers, &c., at a weekly sum for each, which is called "walking" them. Young greyhounds may be reared in a large enclosure, which should be not less than thirty or forty feet long, with a lodging-house at one end; but hounds do not take exercise enough in a confined space, and should invariably be sent out. It is only, therefore, in reference to the rearing of greyhounds that the two plans can be compared, or perhaps also with pointers and setters, if they are taken out to exercise after they are four or five months old.

The two plans have been extensively tried with the longtails, and in my own opinion the preference should be given to the home-rearing *if properly carried out*, because it has all the advantages of the " walk " without those disadvantages attending upon it in the shape of bad habits acquired in chasing poultry, rabbits, and often hares, during whith the puppy learns to run cunning. One of the first symptoms of this vice is the waiting to cut off a corner, which is soon learnt if there is the necessity for it, and even in mutual play the puppy will often develop it. Hence I have seen a " walked " greyhound, with his very first hare, show as much waiting as any old worn-out runner, evidently acquired in his farm-yard education, or possibly from having been tempted after a hare or two by the sheep-dog belonging to the farm. Moreover, the home-reared puppy, being confined in a limited space during the greater part of his time, is inclined to gallop when first let out, and takes in this way more exercise than those brought up on the other plan; so that, after considering both methods, I have come to the conclusion that the home-rearing is preferable on the whole, though there is no doubt that good dogs may be reared in either way.

The best plan is to fence off a long slip of turf; or, if a small walled enclosure can be procured, fence off about a yard or two all round, by which last plan an excellent gallop is secured, without the possibility of cutting corners, and with a very slight loss of ground. An admirable plan is to build four large sleeping-rooms in a square block, and then all round this let there be a run two yards wide, which may be separated into four divisions or thrown into one at will. If the latter, the puppies will exercise themselves well round and round the building, which is a practice they are very fond of; and even if two or more lots are wanted to occupy the compartments, the whole can be thrown open to each lot in turn. When this plan is adopted the run should be paved, so that the expense is much greater than in the other mode, in which the natural soil is allowable, because the puppies are not kept on it long enough to stain it. (See page 272.)

THE FOOD OF PUPPIES AT HOME OR "AT WALK," AND ITS PROPER PREPARATION.

Whether at home or out, puppies require the same kind of food, and the more regularly this is given as to quantity and quality, as well as the times of feeding, the more healthy the puppy will be, and the faster he will grow. Many people consider milk to be by far the best article of food for growing puppies, and undoubtedly it is a good one; but it is not superior to a mixed diet of meal and animal food in proper proportions, and occasionally varied by the addition of green vegetables. Indeed, after three months, or at most four, puppies may be fed like grown dogs as to the quality of their food, requiring it, however, to be given them more frequently the younger they are. Up to six months they require it three times a day, at equal intervals, and after that age twice; for although there is a difference of opinion as to the propriety of feeding the adult once or twice a day, there is none about the puppy demanding a supply morning and evening. In all cases they should be encouraged to empty themselves (by allowing a run, if they are confined to kennel) just before feeding, and for an hour or two afterwards they are best at rest. If milk is given, it may be thickened by boiling in it oatmeal or wheat-flour, or both together, or biscuits may be scalded and added to it; but no flesh is needed in addition, bones only being required to amuse the dog and to clean his teeth by gnawing them. With these any dog may be very well reared, but the plan is an expensive one, if the milk has anything like the ordinary value attached to it, and if it has to be purchased the cost is generally quite prohibitory of its employment.

Besides milk, the following articles are employed in feeding dogs, each of which will be separately considered, as to price and value. Of these, Indian meal is by far the best in proportion to its price (being quite equal to anything but the very best wheat-flour, which is perhaps slightly more nourishing), and, being so much cheaper, is, on that account, to be preferred. It requires to be mixed with oatmeal, in about equal proportions, or less of the latter if the bowels are at all relaxed. The usual price of Indian meal is about £10 or £12 per ton, half that of wheat and the same as that of barley, to which it is greatly to be preferred, being far less heating, and producing muscle in larger proportion. Oatmeal is considerably dearer, though the grain itself is cheaper; but the quantity of meal obtained, owing to the amount of chaff, is so small, that when this is got rid of the meal is necessarily sold at a higher price, being from £12 to £18 per ton, according to the season. But a much larger *bulk* of thick stuff, commonly called " puddings," is produced by oatmeal than can be obtained from any other meal in proportion to weight, the absorption of water being greater, and also varying in different qualities of oatmeal itself; so that, after all, this meal is not so expensive as it looks to be, when comparing an equal weight of it with barley or Indian meal. The real coarse Scotch oatmeal yields the greatest bulk of puddings, and is to be preferred on that account; besides which, it appears to agree best with dogs, and altogether is a very superior article ; but in any case it ought to be nearly a year old. It may, therefore, be considered that Indian meal or Scotch oatmeal, both of which may always be procured from the corn-dealers, will be the best meal, unless the price of wheat-flour can be afforded, when the best red wheat should be coarsely ground and not dressed, and in this state made into biscuits or dumplings, or used to thicken the broth.

If *Indian meal* is employed, it must be mixed with water or broth while cold, and then boiled for at least an hour, stirring it occasionally to prevent burning. If it is intended to mix oatmeal with the Indian meal, the former may be first mixed with cold water to a paste, and then stirred in after boiling the latter for three quarters of an hour ; then boil another quarter, reckoning from the time that the contents of the copper came to the boiling-point a second time.

Wheat-flour should be boiled from fifteen to twenty minutes, and may be mixed with the oatmeal in the same way as the Indian meal.

Oatmeal pudding and *porridge* or *stirabout* are made as follows ; the first name being given to it when so thick as to bear the weight of the body after it is cold, and the last two to a somewhat thinner composition. In any case the meal is stirred up with *cold* water to a thick paste, and, when quite smooth, some of the broth should be ladled out and added to it, still stirring it steadily. Then return the whole to the copper, and stir till it thickens, ladle out into coolers, and let it " set," when it will cut with a spade and is quite solid. The directions as to length of time for the boiling of oatmeal vary a good deal, some preferring at least half an hour's boil, while others are content with ten or fifteen minutes ; but for most purposes from a quarter to half an hour is the proper time, remembering that this is to be reckoned *from the moment that the water boils.*

The *animal food* used should be carefully selected to avoid infectious diseases, and the flesh of those creatures which have been loaded with drugs should also be avoided.   Horseflesh, if death has been caused by accident, is as good as anything, and in many cases of rapid disease the flesh is little the worse ; but though in foxhound kennels there is little choice, yet for greyhounds those horses which have been much drugged for lingering diseases, and those also which are much emaciated, are likely to do more harm than good.   Slipped calves and lambs, as well as beef and mutton, the result of death from natural causes, make an excellent change, but are seldom better than *bad* horseflesh.   Still, as variety is essentia to success in rearing, they should not be rejected.   Flesh may be kept for a long time, even in summer, by brushing it over with a quicklime wash, or dusting it with the powder, and then hanging it up in trees with thick foliage, carefully watching the attacks of the flies, which will not blow in the lime.   In this way I have kept the shank ends of legs and shoulders good for six weeks in the height of summer, and in winter for three months.   Whatever this kind of food is composed of, it should be boiled, with the exception of paunches, which may be given raw ; but even they are better boiled, and I think an occasional meal of well-kept horseflesh is rather a good change.   The flesh with the bones should be boiled for hours, till the meat is thoroughly done ; then take it out and let it hang till cold, cut or strip it from the bones and mix with the puddings or stirabout according to the quantity required.   The broth should always be used, as there are important elements of nutrition dissolved in it which are absent in the boiled flesh.   It is, therefore, necessary to make the puddings or stirabout with it or to soak in it the biscuit, when this is the food selected.   The bones should be given for the dogs to gnaw, together with any others from the house which can be obtained, but taking care to remove all fragments small enough for them to swallow whole.   Bones should be given on grass or clean flags.

The *comparative value* of the various articles of diet enumerated above, according to the authority of Liebig, is as follows :—

The proportions in		Materials used for making muscle, bone, &c.	Materials used in respiration, or in forming fat.
		Parts,	Parts,
Cow's milk	are	as 10	to 30
Fat mutton	,,	10	27 to 45
Lean mutton	,,	10	19
Lean beef	,,	10	17
Lean horseflesh	,,	10	15
Hare and rabbit	,,	10	2 to 5
Wheat-flour	,,	10	46
Oatmeal	,,	10	50
Barley-meal	,,	10	57
Potatoes	,,	10	86 to 115
Rice	,,	10	153

From this high authority it appears that barley-meal is superior both to wheat-flour and oatmeal in fat-making materials, but it is greatly inferior in muscle-making power, and hence, in dogs where fat is not required, it is of inferior value. Science and practical experiment here go hand in hand, as they always do when the former is based upon true premises. In cow's milk, which is the natural food of the young of the Mammalia, the proportion is 30 to 10, and this seems to be about what is required in mixing the animal and vegetable food. Now, by adding equal weights of wheat-meal and lean horseflesh, we obtain exactly the same proportions within the merest trifle ; thus—

Wheat-flour	.	.	.	.	10	46
Horseflesh	.	.	.	.	10	15
					20	61

—being equal to 10 of muscle-making to $30\frac{1}{2}$ of fat-making matter ; and this is practically the proportion of animal food to meal which best suits the dog's stomach and general system. The reader is not to suppose that a dog is to be fed on equal parts of *cooked* meat and *puddings*, but of *raw* meat and dry meal, which when both are boiled would, by the loss of juice in the flesh and the absorption of water in the meal, become converted into about two quantities by weight of pudding to one of cooked meat. Even this proportion of flesh is a large one for growing dogs which have not much exercise, but those which are "at walk" or which have their liberty in any situation will bear it. Most people prefer a much smaller proportion of meat, especially for hounds, pointers, setters, and spaniels, which depend on their nose, this organ being supposed to be rendered less delicate by high feeding. From long experience in this matter, however, I am satisfied that, while the health is maintained in a perfect state, there is no occasion to fear the loss of nose, and that such may be avoided with the above diet I am confident from actual practice. At the same time, it must not be forgotten that all dogs so fed require a great supply of green vegetables, which should be given once or twice a week during the summer, without which they become heated, and throw out an eruption as a proof of it, the nose also being hot and dry. Green cabbage, turnip-tops, turnips, nettle-tops, or carrots, as well as potatoes, may all be given with advantage boiled and mixed with the meal and broth, in which way they are much relished.

Greaves, bought at the chandler's, and consisting of the refuse of the fat melted to make tallow, make a very common article for flavouring the meal of sporting dogs of all kinds. Beyond this they have little value, but they certainly afford some degree of nourishment, and are not altogether to be despised. They are boiled in water first till soft, and then mixed with the meal to form the stirabout or pudding. With oatmeal they form a good food enough for pointers and setters, as they are not so heating as flesh.

The *quantity by weight* which is required by the growing puppy daily of such food as the above is from a twelfth to one-twentieth of the weight of its body, varying with the rapidity of growth, and a good deal with the breed also. Thus a 12-lb. dog will take from five-eighths of a pound to a pound, and a 36-lb. dog from two pounds to three pounds. When they arrive at full growth, more than the smaller of these weights is very seldom wanted, and it may be taken as the average weight of food of this kind for all dogs in tolerably active exercise.

Spratt's or other meat biscuits are now in very general use for puppies above four or five months old as well as for adult dogs. For shooting dogs those made with 25 per cent. of meat are far too strong; 10 per cent. is quite enough.*

GENERAL TREATMENT.

During the whole time of growth the only general management required is, firstly, a habit of obedience, the dog being taught his kennel name, to follow at heel, and to lead. Some breeds require more than this; as, for instance, the pointer and setter, which will be mentioned under the head of breaking. Secondly, great cleanliness in all respects, the kennel being kept scrupulously clean by washing the floor, and at least once a year lime-washing the walls, while the skins are freed from any vermin which may be found by the means described in the Third Book. In the summer a straw bed is seldom required, but in the winter it must be given for the sake of warmth, and changed once or twice a week. Physic is not needed as a regular practice, if feeding is conducted on the above plan and the exercise is sufficient; but if the puppies are dull a dose of castor-oil occasionally will do good.

CHOICE OF PUPPIES AFTER WEANING THEM.

Puppies of all kinds vary in form so much between the weaning-time and the period of full growth that there is great difficulty in making a choice which shall be proved by subsequent events to be on reliable grounds. All young animals grow by fits and starts, the proportions varying with the stage of development in which any part is at the time of examination. Thus at the fourth month a puppy may look too long, but during the next month he may have grown so much in the legs that he no longer looks so. Again, another may be all legs and wings in the middle of his growth, but he may finally grow down to a strong, low, and muscular dog. So also with the fore and hind quarters, they may grow alternately, and one month the fore quarter may be low, and the next the hind. None but an experienced eye, therefore, can

* Spratt's Patent Company also make biscuits and food specially intended for puppies, but I prefer the articles before mentioned.

pretend to foresee, after the period of weaning, what will be the final shape; but either soon after that time or a day or two after birth a pretty good guess may be given, subject to the continuation of health and to proper rearing in all respects. Bad feet can soon be detected; but the limbs grow into a good shape after most extraordinary deviations from the line of beauty, particularly in the greyhound, which is often apparently deformed in his joints when half-grown. The most unwieldy-looking animals often fine down into the best shapes, and should not be carelessly rejected without the *fiat* being pronounced by a breeder of experience.

CROPPING, BRANDING, AND ROUNDING.

If terriers are to be cropped, the beginning or end of the fourth month is the best time to choose; and, before sending out to walk, hounds are branded with the initials of the master or of the hunt, a hot iron shaped like the letter itself being used. This practice is, however, now abandoned in some kennels, notably the Fitz-william. Both cropping and rounding require practice to perform them well, a large sharp pair of scissors being used, and care being necessary to hold the two layers of skin in the ear in their natural position, to prevent the one rolling on the other, and thus leaving one larger than the other. Foxhounds have so much work in covert that rounding is imperatively called for to prevent the ears from being torn, and it always has been adopted as a universal practice, different huntsmen varying in the quantity removed. Some people after cutting one ear lay the piece removed on the other, and so mark exactly the amount which is to be removed from it; but this is a clumsy expedient, and, if the eye is not good enough to direct the hand without this measurement, the operation will seldom be effected to the satisfaction of the owner of the dog. It is usual to round foxhound puppies *after* they come in from their walks; but it would be far better to perform the operation *before* their return, as it only makes them more sulky and unhappy than they otherwise would be, and is a poor introduction to their new masters. The men could easily go round to the different walks during the summer, and it would ensure a supervision which is often required.

CHAPTER III.

Greyhound Kennels—Foxhound Kennels—Pointer Kennels—Kennels
for Single Dogs—House-Dogs.

BETWEEN the kennels intended for the various kinds of dogs and
the methods of management therein some considerable difference
exists, though the same principles are adopted throughout. Thus,
packs of foxhounds are often kept to the number of 80 or even
100 couples, and these must be managed rather differently to the
three or four brace of greyhounds or pointers which usually constitute the extent of each of these kinds in one man's possession,
or at all events in one building. Besides this, foxhounds are much
more exposed to the weather than greyhounds, which are usually
clothed out of doors, and otherwise protected by dog-carts, &c.
The former, therefore, must be hardened to the duties they have
to perform, while the latter may be brought out in more vigorous
health and with their speed very highly developed, but at the
same time in so delicate a condition as to be liable to take cold if
allowed to remain in the rain for any length of time. Hence it
will be necessary to describe the kennels for greyhounds, hounds,
pointers, &c., separately.

GREYHOUND KENNELS.

Every kennel intended for greyhounds should be thoroughly
protected from the weather, and should have the yard covered in
as well as the lodging-house. The plan which has been indicated
at page 263, as useful for the kennel intended to rear puppies,
is also best adapted for their future keeping, and this it will be
desirable to describe more fully here.

The central square, comprised between the four angles *a b c d*, is divided into four lodging-houses, having a ventilating shaft in the middle, with which they all communicate. These are filled up with benches separated by low partitions, as shown in the diagram, and raised about a foot from the ground. Each opens into a yard, with a door of communication so arranged as to be left partly open without allowing the slightest draught to blow upon the beds. These yards, *ab, bc, cd, da*, are all roofed in, and bounded on the outer side by open pales guarded by coarse wire net, to prevent the teeth of the inmates gnawing them. They are separated by narrow

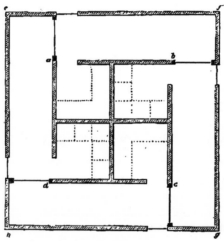

Ground Plan of Greyhound Kennel.

partitions, which slide up to allow of the dogs having the whole run; or they may be left down, and the upper part open, so as to encourage the puppies to fence, by the necessity for jumping over them in pursuing one another. The floors should be of *glazed* tiles, adamantine clinkers, Dutch clinkers, Broseley bricks, or cement, the last being the most clean and free from absorption, which ought always to be entirely prevented. Each sleeping-place and yard should have a trapped drain, so as to carry off any wet directly it falls, and the former should be built exteriorly of brick cemented at least a foot from the ground, with board partitions between them. A window should be in each, which is capable of being opened, and the ventilation should be secured by the plan introduced by Mr. Muir, whose address is 11 Ducie Street, Exchange, Manchester. This always secures a down-current as well as an up-current, so that there is little or no necessity for having the door open except for cleanliness; but in very windy weather the ventilation on the side of the wind should be closed, or the down-draught will be enough to chill the greyhounds. As these kennels are to be paved with a non-porous material, the soil is not of much consequence, but the situation should be dry and healthy, and the shade of a large tree is to be obtained if possible.

Elevation of Greyhound Kennel.

The kennel management of the greyhound consists in little more than the adoption of cleanliness, which should be of the most scrupulous kind, together with regular feeding. Water is by some people constantly left for them to get at, but others object to it for dogs in training, and they then only give it with the food. My own opinion is decidedly in favour of the constant supply, as it is impossible to prevent these animals from getting to it when at exercise; and I am sure that, when they are kept from it in-doors, they take too much while they are out. On the contrary, if it is regularly supplied to them, they take very little, and are quite careless about it at all times. The dressing and management of the feet form a part of the training of the greyhound, and will be treated of under the head of Coursing.

s

FOXHOUND AND HARRIER KENNELS, &c.

Unlike the greyhound kennel in many respects, that which we are now considering must be adapted for from thirty to a hundred couples of hounds, and the accommodation should therefore be more extensive, while a less degree of protection from the weather is desirable, because these hounds must be constantly exposed to long-continued wind and wet, and should therefore be hardened to them. The annexed description of the most desirable plan for kennels is chiefly derived from " Scrutator," who is, I believe, the most trust-worthy as well as the most recent writer on the subject.

The kennel should be placed upon some high and dry situation; the building should face the south, and there should be no large trees near it. To hunt three or four days a week, you will require about forty couples of hounds, according to the country. The lodging-rooms should be four in number, by which you will have a dry floor for the hounds to go on to every morning (the pack in the hunting season being in two divisions), instead of its being washed down whilst the hounds are left shivering in the cold on a bleak winter's day, which I have seen done when the huntsman has been too busy to walk them out during this process.

Nothing is more prejudicial to hounds than damp lodging-rooms —a sure cause of rheumatism and mange, to which dogs are pecu-liarly liable. I have seen them affected by rheumatism in various ways, and totally incapacitated from working; sometimes they are attacked in the loins, but more often in the shoulders, both pro-ceeding either from a damp situation, damp lodging-room, or damp straw, often combined with the abuse of mercury in the shape of physic. In building kennels, therefore, the earth should be re-moved from the lodging-room floor to the depth of a foot at least, and in its place broken stones, sifted gravel, or cinders should be substituted, with a layer of fine coal-ashes, upon which the brick floor is to be laid, in cement or hot coal-ash mortar, taking care to use bricks which are not porous, or to cover them with a layer of cement, which last is an admirable plan. Outside the walls and close to them an air-drain about three feet deep should be con-structed, with a draining pipe of two inches bore at the bottom, and filled up with broken stones to within six inches of the surface. This drain is to be carried quite round the building, and should fall into the main sewer. For a roof to the building I prefer thatch to tiles, as affording more warmth in winter and coolness in summer; but as slate or tiles are more agreeable to the eye, a thin layer of reed placed under the tiles will answer the purpose.

Over the centre of the lodging-rooms should be a sleeping apartment for the feeder, which being raised above the level of the other roof will break the monotony of its appearance. At the rear of the kennel should be the boiling-house, feeding-court, straw-house, and separate lodgings for bitches. In front of the kennels, and extending round to the back-door of the feeding-house, should be a good large green yard, enclosed by a wall or palings. The former I prefer, although more expensive, because hounds, being able to see through the latter, will be excited by passing objects; and young hounds, for whose service the green yard is more particularly intended, are inclined to become noisy, barking and running round the palings when any strange dog makes his appearance.

In the boiling-house will be required two cast-iron boilers, one for the meal, the other for flesh. Pure water must be in some way conducted to the kennels, both for cleanliness and for the preparation of food, and this should be laid on at the service of the kennel-man at all parts, so that there may be no excuse on the score of trouble in carrying it. There must also be coolers fixed in proportion to the number of hounds, each couple requiring from half a foot to a foot superficial, according as it is intended to make the puddings daily or every other day. Stone or iron feeding and water troughs are the best; the latter should be fixed high enough to keep them clean.

To each lodging-room there should be two doors—one at the back with a small sliding panel and high up, through which the huntsman may observe the hounds without their seeing him; and another in the front with a large opening cut at the bottom, high enough and wide enough for a hound to pass through easily, and which should always be left open at night to allow free egress to the court. In addition, there must also be another between each of the rooms, so as to throw two into one in the summer for the purpose of making them more airy. The benches should be made of pine or oak spars, and if they are made to turn up according to the following plan several advantages result, being described by a correspondent signing himself "Lepus," in the columns of *The Field*, as follows:—

"KENNEL BENCHES.

"My benches are made of inch deal, cut into widths of three

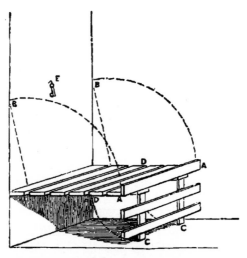

Plan of Kennel Bench for Hounds. A A folds to B B ; C C folds to D D ; E, hook to fasten bench back.

inches, and nailed half an inch apart to two transverse pieces, to which hinges are fixed to connect the bench with a board six inches wide, fastened firmly to the wall about a foot from the ground.   In front is a piece of board about three inches in width, to keep the straw from drawing off with the hounds.   To prevent the hounds from creeping under, I nail two long laths the length of the bench across in front of the legs, which are hung with hinges in front of the bench, so that when the bench is hooked back they fall down and hang flat.   By having the six-inch board between the hinges and the wall, it prevents the former from being strained when the bench is hooked back with straw upon it."

In some establishments there is a separate kennel for the

young hounds, with a grass yard attached, for their own use, and it is certainly very advantageous; but with a little management the buildings above recommended will be sufficient, and with a saving of considerable expense. The hounds during the hunting season will not require it at all, as they should be walked out several times a day into a paddock or field, and should not be allowed to lie about anywhere but on their benches.

In the rear of the kennels should be a covered passage into which the doors of the middle kennel should open, and leading to the feeding-house, which stands under the same roof as the boiling-house, only separated from it by a partition. This passage should be so constructed as to make a foot-bath for the hounds as they pass through after hunting, the bricks being gradually sloped from each end to the centre, where it should be a foot deep, with a plugged drain in the lowest part, to let the hot liquor or water off into a drain. On each side of this passage should be a paved court with a small lodging-house at each end; one for lame hounds, and the other for those which are sick.

The *ventilation* of the rooms composing the lodgings of the hounds must be carefully attended to, and for this purpose the shaft alluded to at page 272 is by far the best adapted. It resembles in external appearance that usually placed above well-constructed stables, &c.; but there is this important internal alteration, that the square is divided perpendicularly into four triangular tubes, one of which is sure to be presented to the wind, from whatever quarter of the compass it is blowing, while the opposite one allows the foul air to escape, to make room for that descending through the first-named tube. When this is once constructed, it only remains to lead a metal tube from each of these four compartments to every one of the lodging-rooms, which will thus be as effectually ventilated as if each had an apparatus to itself. To carry this out well the lodging-rooms should be in a block, and then there will be a corner of each meeting in a common centre, above which the ventilator should be placed with the arrangement of tubes above described.

The *kennel management* of hounds is a much more difficult and important affair than is generally supposed, as upon its proper performance, in great measure, depends the obedience of the pack

in the field. Sometimes it is entirely committed to the care of
the feeder, but every huntsman who knows his business will take
as much pains with his hounds in kennel as out ; and though he
will not, of course, prepare the food, yet he will take care to super-
intend it, and will always "draw" his hounds himself, for no one
else can possibly know how to feed them. During the season
this duty must of necessity devolve on the feeder or kennel-man

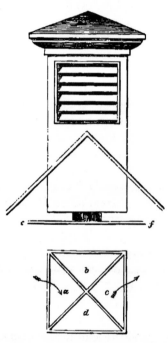

Muir's Ventilating Apparatus. a, b, c, d, the four divisions of shaft ; e, f, board
for distributing down-current.

on the hunting days, but the huntsman should always carry it out
himself whenever he can. Hounds cannot be too fond of their
huntsman, and though "cupboard love" is not to be encouraged
in man, yet it is at the bottom of most of that which is exhibited
by the dog, however much it may appear to take a higher range
when once it has been properly developed.

The *regular daily kennel discipline* is as follows :—With the four lodging-rooms described there should always be two dry and clean in the early morning, having been washed the day before. Into these the general pack should be turned as soon as the doors are opened, or, if the morning is not wet, directly after a short airing in the paddock. The feeder then sweeps out the room in which they have slept, and afterwards mops it clean, drying the floor as much as possible, so that by ten or eleven o'clock it is fit for the hounds to re-enter. The men then get their breakfast, and directly afterwards the hounds are taken out to exercise, or the hunting hounds to their regular day's work. If the former, they are brought back to kennel at eleven o'clock, fed, and returned to their regular lodging-room, or in some kennels they are still kept in a separate room during the day and night, always taking care that they are not turned into a room while the floor is damp, and that strict cleanliness is practised nevertheless. The hour of feeding is generally fixed for eleven o'clock, but for the day before hunting it should be an hour or two later, varying with the distance they have to travel. Water should be constantly provided, taking care that the troughs are raised above the height at which dogs can pass their urine into it, which they will otherwise be constantly doing. As before remarked, iron troughs are the best. After feeding, the hounds should remain quiet for the rest of the day, only stirring them in removing them from their day-room to their night-room, if two are allowed, which, I think, is an excellent practice.

The *food* of hounds is composed of meal flavoured with broth, to which more or less flesh is added, or with greaves as a substitute when flesh cannot be obtained. The relative value of the various meals is described at page 262, but I may here remark that old oatmeal is the recognised food of hounds, though Indian meal is an excellent substitute. After boiling the flesh till the meat leaves the bones readily, take all out with a pitchfork and put it to cool, skim all the fat off the broth, and fill up with water to the proper quantity; next mix the meal carefully with cold water, and then pour this into the hot broth, keeping it constantly stirred till it thickens; after which it should be boiled *very gently* till it has been on the fire for half an hour, continuing the stirring to prevent its burning. Lastly, draw the fire and ladle out the stuff into the coolers, where it remains till it has set, when it acquires the name with the solidity of "puddings." There should always be two qualities made, one better than the other for the more delicate hounds, which must be apportioned by the huntsman properly among them. This may be reduced with cold broth, when wanted, to any degree of thinness; and the meat, being cut or torn up, is mixed with it.

In *feeding the hounds*, the huntsman, having the troughs supplied with the different qualities of food, orders the door to be thrown open which communicates with the lodging-room; then, having the hounds under proper control, they all wait till each is called by name, the huntsman pronouncing each name in a decided tone, and generally summoning two or three couples at a time, one after the other. When these have had what he considers sufficient, they are dismissed, and others called in their turn; the gross feeders being kept to the last, when the best and most nourishing part has been eaten. By thus accustoming hounds in kennel to wait their proper turn and to come when called, a control is obtained out of doors which could never be accomplished in any other way. Once a week, on a non-hunting day in the winter, and every three or four days in the summer, some green food, or potatoes or turnips, should be boiled up with the puddings, which serves to cool the hounds very considerably. If this is attended to very little physic is required, except from accidental causes.

A regular dressing and physicking is practised in some kennels, the former to keep the skin free from vermin and eruptions, and the latter with the same view, but also to cool the blood. This is by no means necessary, if great care is taken with regard to cleanliness, feeding, and exercise; and in the royal kennels neither one nor the other is practised, excepting when disease actually appears, and not as a preventive measure. When it is considered desirable to adopt either or both, directions for their use will be found given in the next Book.

POINTERS AND SETTERS.

These dogs do not require a covered yard, and may be treated in all respects like hounds, the only difference being in regard to numbers. More than three or four brace should not be kept together if it can be avoided, as they are apt to quarrel when not thoroughly exercised or worked, and then a whole lot will fall upon one and tear him almost to pieces. The rules of cleanliness, feeding, &c., are the same as for hounds.

SINGLE DOGS KENNELLED OUT OF DOORS.

Where a single dog is kept chained up to what is called a kennel, care should be taken to pave the ground on which he lies, unless he can be moved every month, or still more frequently, as in course of time his urine stains the ground so much as to produce disease. It should always be borne in mind that the dog requires more exercise than he can take when chained up, and he should therefore be set at liberty for an hour or two daily, or at all events every other day.

HOUSE-DOGS.

The great bane of dogs which are at liberty to run through the house is, that they are constantly receiving bits from their kitchen as well as from their parlour friends. The dog's stomach is peculiarly unfitted for this increasing demand upon it, and if the practice is adopted it is sure to end in disease before many years are passed. The rule should be strictly enforced to avoid feeding more than once or twice daily, at regular hours, and then the quantity and quality should be proportioned to the size of the dog and to the amount of exercise which he takes. About one-twentieth to one-twelfth of the weight of the dog is the proper amount of food, and all beyond this is improper in most cases, though, of course, there are some exceptions. Dogs are very cleanly animals, and often refuse to dirty a carpet or even a clean floor; they should therefore be turned out at proper times to relieve themselves, the neglect of which is cruel, as well as injurious to the health. I have known dogs retain their excretions for days together rather than expose themselves to the anger which they think they should incur, and I believe some high-couraged animals would almost die before they would make a mess. Long-haired dogs, when confined to the house, are apt to smell disagreeably if they have much flesh, and they should therefore be chiefly fed upon oatmeal porridge, with very little flavouring of broth or meat mixed up with it, and with the addition of boiled greens every other day.

CHAPTER IV.

BREAKING AND ENTERING.

The Entering of the Greyhound and Deerhound—Of Foxhounds and Harriers —Breaking the Pointer and Setter—The Retriever (Land and Water)— The Spaniel—The Vermin Dog.

WITH the exception of the greyhound, sporting dogs require some considerable education to the sport in which they are to be engaged. Unlike the hound and the dogs intended for the gun, greyhounds have only their instinctive desires to be developed, and as no restraint is at any time placed upon these, except that depending upon mechanical means which they cannot get rid of, nature has uncontrolled sway. Hence their entering is a very easy process; nevertheless, there are some precautions to be taken which it is necessary to describe. The deerhound as well as the greyhound is held in slips, a single one being used for him, and a double slip, or pair of slips as it is called, for the two greyhounds which form the complement for coursing the hare, a greater number being considered unfair, and therefore unsportsmanlike. These slips are so made that by pulling a string the neck-strap is loosed, and the two dogs are let go exactly at the same moment. They are always used in public coursing, but in private the greyhounds are sometimes suffered to run loose, waiting for the moment when the hare is put up by the beaters or by the spaniels, which are occasionally employed. Hounds also are coupled under certain circumstances, but they are never slipped at the moment when game is on foot, and they must therefore be made steady from " riot."

THE ENTERING OF THE GREYHOUND AND DEERHOUND.

Whether for public or private coursing, the greyhound should not be suffered to course a hare until he is nearly at maturity;

but as the bitches come to their growth before the dogs, they may be entered earlier than the latter. About the tenth month is the best time for forward bitches, and the twelfth or fourteenth for dogs. If, therefore, a greyhound is to be allowed to see a hare or two at this age, he or she must be bred early in the year, in order to have a brace late in the spring, so as to be ready for the next season. Some people invariably prefer keeping them on to the autumn, and for private coursing there is no reason whatever for beginning so early; but public coursers begin to run their dogs in puppy stakes in the month of October, prior to which there is so little time after the summer is passed that they prefer beginning in the spring if their dogs are old enough, and if they are not they will not be fit to bring out in October.

Before being entered the dogs must be taught to lead quietly, as they cannot be brought on to the ground loose, and if not previously accustomed to it, they knock about and tear themselves dreadfully, and, moreover, will not go quietly in slips. As soon, therefore, as the ground is soft, after they are six or eight months old, they should have a neck-strap put on, and should be led about for a short time daily, till they follow quietly. Some puppies are very violent, and will fight against the strap for a long time, but by a little tact they soon give in, and follow their leader without resistance. The coursing-field is the best school for this purpose, as the puppies have something to engage their attention, and until they will bear their straps without pulling against them their education in this respect is not complete. A dog pulling in slips will do himself so much harm as often to cause the loss of a course, and therefore every precaution should be taken to avoid this fault. The leader should never pull against the puppy steadily, but the moment he finds him beginning to hang forward, give him a severe check with the strap, and repeat it as often as necessary. It is a very common defect, but never ought to occur with proper management; though when once established it is very difficult to get rid of. Two or three days' leading on the coursing-field will serve to make any puppies handy to lead if properly managed, and they may then be put in slips with perfect safety.

The *condition* of the puppy at the time of entering is too

often neglected, but it should be known that a fat over-fed puppy without previous exercise may be seriously injured even by a short course, which, moreover, can never be assured under any circumstances, as the hare will sometimes run in a different direction to that which is expected.

A *sapling*, as the young greyhound is called to the end of the first season after he is whelped, should never be trained like an old one, as the work is too severe, and his frame is not calculated to bear it; but he may be reduced in flesh by light feeding, and allowed to gallop at liberty for two or three hours a day, giving him that amount of walking exercise and as much galloping as he likes to take. With these precautions, he will be fit to encounter any hare in a short course, which is all that should ever be allowed, as far as it is possible to foresee what will happen.

Whether an old assistant or a young one shall be put down with a sapling is a subject which admits of some discussion. If the former, the young dog has small chance of getting to work at all, and if the latter, he may have so little assistance as to be greatly distressed. Few people like to put down an honest old dog with a sapling, and a cunning one soon teaches the tricks which he himself displays. Sometimes young dogs have great difficulty in killing, and want the encouragement afforded by blood; in such a case a good killer may be desirable, but with no other object could I ever put down an old dog with a sapling. Before they are going to run in a stake, an old dog of known speed should be put in slips with the puppy, in order to arrive at a knowledge of the powers of the latter; but this is with a view to a *trial*, and not as part of the entering of the greyhound. When a sapling has run enough hares to know his work, and has killed a hare, or been present at the death of one, he may be put by as properly entered; and the number required will average about five or six—more or less according to the cleverness of the particular animal, which will generally depend upon his breed.

The deerhound is entered at his game on the same principles as the greyhound; but as red deer are more scarce than hares, it requires more time. It is always better to slip him with an older companion, but beyond this precaution everything must be left to his natural sagacity. As his nose is to be brought into play, and as he may possibly cross the scent of hares or other game, he must be made steady from all "riot," and, if possible, should be taken up, in couples, to the death of a deer once or twice and "blooded," so as to make him understand the nature of the scent. His instinctive fondness for it will, however, generally serve him without this; but the precaution is a good one, and may save some trouble and risk. He will not do much in aid of his older companion in *hunting* the animal he is slipped at, but when "at bay" he is soon encouraged by example to go in and afford his help, and this is the time when a second deerhound is chiefly wanted.

THE ENTERING OF FOXHOUNDS AND HARRIERS.

The first thing to be done with hound puppies, when they come into kennel, is to get them used to their new masters and to their names, which ought to have been given them "at walk." For some little time the puppy often refuses to be reconciled to his confinement in his new home, and sulks by himself in a corner, refusing to eat and to follow his feeder or huntsman. This, however, soon goes off; but till it does there is no use in attempting to do anything with the dog. When the puppies are quite at home they may be taken out by the feeder, at first in couples, and then by degrees removing these and allowing them to run free. For some time it will be prudent to take only six or seven couples at a time, as when any "riot" makes its appearance, there is enough to do even with this number, and more would be quite unmanageable. Indeed, the huntsman will do well to take out only a couple or two at a time into the paddock with him, till they are thoroughly accustomed to his voice and have found out that he must be obeyed. As soon as they are tractable on the road they may be walked among sheep and deer, where they should at first all be in couples, and then only one or two should be loosed at a time; but before long the whole pack should be accustomed to resist the temptation, till which time they are unfit to be entered. It is also highly necessary that foxhounds should in the same way be broken from hare and rabbit; but too much must not be attempted with them until they are entered to fox, as their spirit and dash would be discouraged if the whip or rate were always being used without the counter-cheer in favour of some kind of game.

All hounds require daily exercise, without which they cannot be preserved in health, nor can their high spirits be controlled, as if they are not exercised they will be always requiring the whip. If, however, the huntsman takes them out daily in the morning on the road, which hardens their feet, and in the evening in the paddock, they are so orderly that anything may be done with them. For this purpose the men should be mounted in the morning, but in the evening they may be on foot.

Cub-hunting, which is the name given to the process by which young hounds are entered, begins in August as soon as the corn is cut, and the time will therefore vary with the season and the country. In some places, as in the New Forest, for instance, it may be carried on at any time, but this month is early enough. It is better to take out the old hounds once or twice till they have recovered their summer idleness, as a good example is everything to the young hound. When the young entry are to be brought out, it is very desirable to find as quickly as possible, and some cautious huntsmen go so far as to keep them coupled till the old hounds have found their fox; but if they have been made steady from "riot" there is no occasion for this. If, however, they have never been rated for "riot," there is no great harm in their hunting hare or anything else at first, till they know what they ought to do; after which they must be rigidly kept to their game. But cub-hunting is not solely intended to break in and "enter" the hound, it has also for its object to disperse the foxes from the large woodlands which form their chief holds in all countries; and as these cannot show good sport during the season, they are well routed before it commences, to drive the foxes into smaller coverts, while at the same time the hounds may be rendered steady, and by practice enabled to work their fox. Very often the master will take advantage of an opportunity to have a nice little burst to himself; and if the hounds are not made to hustle the foxes through the large woodlands, good after-sport cannot be expected. Independently of the above object, cub-hunting is practised in August, September, and October, firstly, in order to give the young hounds blood, which they can obtain easily from a litter of fat cubs; secondly, to break them from " riot," while they are encouraged to hunt their own game; and thirdly, to endeavour to break them off sundry faults, such as skirting, &c., or, if apparently incurable, to draft them at once. These objects are generally attained by the end of October, when the regular season begins.

Harriers and beagles are entered to hare on the same principle, the scent of the fox and deer, as well as that of the rabbit, being " riot " to them, and strictly prohibited. *Otterhounds* also have exactly the same kind of entry, although the element they work in is of a different character.

THE BREAKING OF THE POINTER AND SETTER.

The following observations on the breaking of these dogs appeared in *The Field* during the spring of 1858, and are believed to embody the general practice of good breakers :—

As the method is the same for each kind, whenever the word pointer is used it is to be understood as applying equally to the setter.

It is scarcely necessary for me to remark that no single life would suffice to bring the art of breaking dogs to all the perfection of which it is capable, when the various improvements of succeeding generations are handed down from one to the other ; and therefore I neither pretend to be the inventor of any method here detailed, nor do I claim any peculiarity as my own. All the plans of teaching the young dog that will be found described by me are practised by most good breakers; so that there will be nothing to be met with in my remarks but what is well known to them. Nevertheless, they are not generally known ; and there are many good shots who are now entirely dependent upon dog-dealers for the supply of their kennels, and who yet would infinitely prefer to break their own dogs, if they only knew how to set about it. Others, again, cannot afford the large sum which a highly accomplished brace of pointers or setters are worth in the market; and these gentlemen would far rather obtain two or three good puppies and break them with their own hands, with expenditure of little more than time, than put up with the wretchedly broken animals which are offered for sale by the dozen at the commencement of every shooting season. To make the utmost of any dog requires great experience and tact, and therefore the ordinary sportsman, however ardent he may be, can scarcely expect his dogs to attain this amount of perfection; but by attending to the following instructions, which will be given in plain language, he may fairly hope to turn out a brace of dogs far above the average of those belonging to his neighbours. One advantage he will assuredly have when he begins the actual war against the birds in September, namely, that his dogs will cheerfully work for him, and will be obedient to his orders; but, at the same time, he must not expect that they will behave as well *then* as they did when he considered their education complete in the previous April or May. No one who values "the bag" above the performance of his dogs will take a young pointer into the field at all till he has been shot over for some time by a man who makes it his business to break dogs, and who is not himself over-excited by the sport. It is astonishing what a difference is seen in the behaviour of the young dog when he begins to see game falling to the gun. He *may* go out with all the steadiness which he had acquired by two months' drilling in the spring, but more frequently he will have forgotten all about it, unless he is well hunted in the week previous to the opening of the campaign. But no sooner has he found his birds or backed his fellow-pointer, and this good behaviour has been followed by the report of the gun, heard now almost for the first time, and by the fall of a bird or two within a short distance, than he becomes wild with excitement, and, trying to rival the gun in destructiveness, he runs into his birds, or plays some other trick almost equally worthy of punishment. For this there is no remedy but patience and plenty of hard work, as we shall presently find; and I only mention it here in order that my readers may not undertake the task without knowing all its disagreeables as well as the advantages attending upon it.

Supposing, therefore, that a gentleman has determined to break a brace of pointers for his own use, without assistance from a keeper, let us now consider how he should set about it.

In the first place, let him procure his puppies of a breed in which he can have confidence. He will do well to secure a brace and a half, to guard against accidents or defects in growth. Let these be well reared up to the end of January, or, in fact, until the birds *are paired and will lie well*, whatever that time may be. They should be fed as directed in the last chapter. A few bones should be given daily, but little flesh, as the nose is certainly injuriously affected by this kind of food; and without attention to his health, so as to give the dog every chance of finding his game, it is useless to attempt to break him. The puppies should either be reared at full liberty at a good walk, or they should have an airy yard, and should then be walked out daily, taking care to make them know their names at a very early age, and teaching them instant obedience to every order, without breaking their spirit. Here great patience and tact are required; but, by the owner walking them out himself two or three times a week and making them fond of him, a little severity has no injurious effect. In crossing fields the puppies should never be allowed to " break fence," even if the gates are open, but should be called back the moment they attempt to do so. These points are of great import- ance, and by attending to them half the difficulty of breaking is got over; for if the puppy is early taught obedience, you have only to let him know what he is required to do, and he does it as a matter of course. So also the master should accustom his puppies from the earliest age to place a restraint upon their appetites when ordered to do so; and if he will provide himself with pieces of biscuit, and will place them within reach of the dog, whilst he prevents his taking them by the voice only, he will greatly aid the object he has in view. Many breakers carry this practice so far as to place a dainty morsel on the ground before the dog when hungry, and use the word " Toho " to restrain him; but this, though perhaps hereafter useful when inclined to run in upon game, is by no means an unmixed good, as the desire for game in a well-bred dog is much greater than the appetite for food, unless the stomach has long been deprived of it.

Besides these lessons prior to breaking, it will be well to teach the dog to come to heel, and to keep there; also to run forward at the word of command, to lie down when ordered, and to remain down. All these several orders should be accompanied by the appropriate words afterwards used in the field, viz. :—

T

WORDS OF COMMAND USED TO THE POINTER AND SETTER.

1. To avoid breaking fence—"Ware fence."
2. To come back from chasing cats, poultry, hares, &c.—"Ware chase."
3. To come to heel and remain there—"To heel," or "Heel."
4. To gallop forward—"Hold up."
5. To lie down—"Down," or "Down charge."
6. To abstain from taking food placed near, equally applied to running in to birds—"Toho."

When these orders are cheerfully and instantly complied with by the puppy, it will be time to take him into the field, but not till then. Many breakers during this period accustom their dogs to the report of the gun by firing a pistol off occasionally while they are a short distance off, and in a way so as not to alarm them. This is all very well, and may prevent all danger of a dog becoming "shy of the gun;" but with a well-bred puppy, properly reared, and not confined too much so as to make him shy in other respects, such a fault will seldom occur. Nevertheless, as it does sometimes show itself, from some cause or other, the above precaution, as it costs little trouble or expense, is not to be objected to. It is also advantageous to accustom the dog to drop when the pistol is discharged, and if he is of high courage, he may be drilled to this so effectually that he never forgets it. By the aid of a "check-cord," wherever the dog is when the pistol is discharged, he is suddenly brought up and made to drop with the command, "Down charge;" and in process of time he associates one with the other, so that whenever he hears a gun he drops in an instant. Timid dogs may, however, be made shy in this way, and unless the puppy is evidently of high courage, it is a dangerous expedient to resort to, as, instead of making the dog, it may mar him for ever.

Next comes the teaching to "range," which is about the most difficult part of breaking. Many sportsmen who have shot all their lives are not aware of the extent to which this may be, and indeed ought to be, carried, and are quite content if their dogs "potter" about where they like and find game anyhow.

But the real lover of the dog, who understands his capabilities, knows that for perfect ranging the whole field ought to be beaten systematically, and in such a way as to reach all parts in succession, the dog being always as near to the gun as is consistent with the nature of the ground, the walking powers of the man, and the degree of wildness of the game. All these varying points of detail in the management of the dog while beating his ground will, however, be better considered at a future stage of the inquiry; so that at present, taking it for granted that what I have assumed is the real *desideratum*, we will proceed to inquire how this mode of ranging is best taught. It must be understood that what we want is—first, that the puppy should hunt freely, which soon comes if he is well-bred; secondly, that he should range only where he is ordered, and that he should always be on the look-out for his master's hand or whistle to direct him. This also is greatly dependent on breed, some dogs being naturally wilful, while others from their birth are dependent upon their master, and readily do what they are desired. Thirdly, great pains must be taken to keep the puppy from depending upon any other dog and following him in his line, and also from "pottering" or dwelling on the "foot-scent," which, again, is a great deal owing to defective blood. Now, then, how are these points to be attained? By a reference to the annexed diagram, the principle upon which two dogs should beat their ground is laid down; the dotted line *a a a a* representing the beat of one, and the plain line *b b b b* that of the other dog. But, with a raw puppy, it is useless to expect him to go off to the right while his fellow proceeds to the left, as they afterwards must do if they perform their duty properly; but, taking an old dog into a field with the puppy, the former is started off with the ordinary words "Hold up" in either line laid down, which, being properly broken, he proceeds to follow out, accompanied by the puppy, who does not at all understand what he is about. Presently the old dog "finds," and very probably the young one goes on and puts up the birds, to the intense disgust of his elder companion, but to his own great delight, as shown by his appreciation of the scent, and by chasing his game till out of sight. At the present stage of breaking the puppy should by no means be checked for this, as he knows no better, and the great object is to give him zest for the work, not to make him dislike it; so that, even if he runs in to half a dozen pairs of birds, it will do him no harm, however jealous it may make the old dog. As soon, however, as the young one seems decidedly inclined to go to work by himself, take up the old dog, and hunt the young one till he is thoroughly tired or till he begins to point,

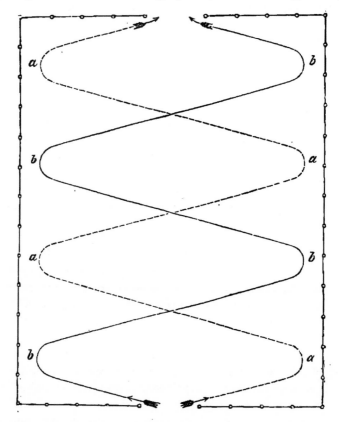

which he will often do before that time arrives if he is well enough bred. At first, when he comes upon a scent, he will stop in a hesitating way, then draw rapidly up and flush his birds, chasing them as before; but gradually, as he tires, he gains steadiness; and after a time he assumes the firm attitude of the true pointer or setter, though this is seldom shown in perfection for the first two or three days. Let it be clearly understood that the present lesson is solely with a view to teach the range, steadiness in the point being at first quite subordinate to this quality, though in well-bred dogs it may often be taught at the same time. Hundreds of puppies are irretrievably spoiled by attempting to begin with teaching them to stand, when, by undue hardship and severity, their relish for hunting or beating the ground is destroyed; and they are never made to do this part of the work well, although their noses are good enough when they come upon game, and they stand for a week if allowed to do so. Keep to the one object till the puppy will beat his ground as shown in the diagram, at first single-handed, and then crossing it with another dog; but it seldom answers to use two together until steadiness at "the point" is attained, as there are few old dogs which will beat their ground properly long together when they find that they are worked with a young one which is constantly flushing his birds or committing some other *faux pas*. For these reasons it is better to work the young ones at first singly, that is, as soon as they *will* work; and then, after they range freely and work to the hand and whistle, turning to the right or left, forwards or backwards, at the slightest wave of the hand, and when they also begin to point, it is time enough to "hunt them double."

In order to complete the education of the pointer in *ranging or beating his ground*, it is not only necessary that he should "quarter" it, as it is called, according to the method inculcated at page 291, *et seq.*, but that he should do it with every advantage of the wind, and also without losing time by dwelling on a false scent, and, above all, avoiding such careless work as to put up game without standing to a point at all. I have before explained the principle upon which a field is to be "quartered," and described the way in which the dog is to be set to do his work, by the hand and voice, aided by the whistle. As a general rule, pointers find their game by the scent being blown to them from *the body*, constituting what is called a "body-scent," and not from that left by the *foot* on the ground, which is called a "foot-scent." Hence it is desirable in all cases to give the dog the wind, that is to say, to beat up towards the wind's eye; and therefore the breaker will put his dogs to work in that direction; and then, though they do not always

beat directly towards the wind, yet they have it blowing from the
game towards them in each of their crossings. (See diagram on
page 292.) But suppose, as it sometimes happens, that the sportsman cannot well do this, as when birds are likely to be on the edge
of a manor, with the wind blowing on to it from that over which
he has no right of shooting ;—here, if he gave his dog the wind in
the usual way, he would drive all the birds off his own beat; and,
to avoid this, he begins at the edge of it, and makes his pointers
(if they are well enough broken) leave him and go up the other
side to the far end of the field (if not too long), and then beat
towards him in the usual way. It is true that the necessity for
this kind of beating does not often occur; but sometimes a considerable number of shots are lost for want of teaching it, and the
perfect dog should understand it thoroughly. When, therefore,
the puppy has learnt to range in the ordinary way, and will work
to the hand well, as before described, give him a lesson in this
kind of beating; and, if any difficulty occurs, send a boy to lead
him until he is far enough away, and then let the biped loose his
charge, first catching the dog's eye yourself, so as to make him
aware that you are the person he is to range to. In a few lessons
he soon begins to find out the object of this departure from the
usual plan, and by a little perseverance he will, of his own accord,
when he finds he has not got the wind, work so as to make a cir-
cuit and get it for himself. Nevertheless, a good dog, *who has a
master as good as himself*, should always wait for orders, and there
is always some excuse for very clever ones becoming headstrong
when they are constantly misdirected. Let me again repeat what
I have observed on the importance of teaching, *at first*, the correct
mode of quartering the ground, and of persevering (without regard
to standing or pointing) in the lessons on this subject alone, until
the puppy is tolerably perfect in them. At the same time, it is
true that some little attention may be paid to the "point;" but
this is of far less consequence at the early stage which we are now
considering. Indeed, in most well-bred dogs it comes naturally;
but none beat to the hand without an education in that particular
department.

But at this stage it will be frequently needful to correct *various
faults* which are apt to show themselves in young dogs, such

as (1) "hunting too low," leading to "pottering or dwelling on the foot-scent;" (2) hunting too wide from the breaker; and (3) "blinking," or leaving the game as soon as found, which last is a fault depending on undue previous severity. With regard to the first of them, there is, unfortunately, no certain remedy for it; and the puppy which shows it to any great extent after a week or ten days' breaking will seldom be good for much, in spite of all the skill and trouble which an experienced breaker can apply. The method of cure most commonly adopted is that called hunting with a "puzzle-peg" on, which is shown applied in the annexed cut. It consists of a piece of strong wood, such as ash or oak, attached to the neck by a leather collar, and to the jaw by a string tied just behind the tusks or canine teeth, so as to constitute a firm projection in continuation of the lower jaw; and as it extends from six to nine inches beyond it, the dog cannot put his nose nearer to the ground than that amount of projection will allow of. The young dog should be well accustomed to it in kennel and in the field, before he is hunted in it; for when it is put on for the first time it inevitably "cows" him so much as to stop all disposition to range; but by putting it on him for an hour or two daily while he is at liberty and not expected to hunt, he soon becomes tolerably reconciled to it, and will set off on his range when ordered or allowed. With it on a foot-scent can seldom be made out, unless pretty strong; but, at all events, the dog does not stoop to make it out in that spaniel-like style which occasions its adoption. Nevertheless, when it is left off the old tendency to stoop most frequently reappears, more or less, and the sportsman finds that all his care has been thrown away. Still, 1 have known it cure this fault, and if it fails I have no other suggestion to offer but sixpennyworth of cord or "a hole in the water." If used at all, it must be kept on for many days together, that is to say, while at work; and when left off it should be occasionally reapplied if the dog shows the slightest tendency to put his nose down or dwell on the scent where birds have been rising or have "gone away." I may here remark that "false pointing" is altogether different from this low hunting, though often coupled with it; but this we shall come to after describing the nature of, and mode of teaching, that part of the pointer's education. There is a wonderful faculty in some breeds of feeling a body-scent at long distances, while they have no perception of the foot-scent, and this is the quality which ought to be most highly prized in the pointer or setter, unless he is also wanted to retrieve, in which latter case such a nose will be found to be defective. But of this also we shall come to a more close understanding in a future part of this inquiry. In addition to the use of the "puzzle-peg"—which should only be resorted to in extreme cases, and even in them is, as I before remarked, of doubtful utility—the voice should be used to cheer the dog when he dwells on the scent too long or carries his nose too low. "Hold up!" may be cried in a

cheering way, and the dog encouraged with the hand waved forward as well. Colonel Hutchinson recommends the previous inculcation of the perception of *height*,—in fact, to make the dog understand that you mean, when you use the word "Up," that he should raise his head. But this is a refinement in dog-breaking which possibly *may* be carried out, yet which, I confess, I think practically inoperative. Few of us would like to teach our hacks to lift their knees by giving them to understand the nature of height, and then telling them to lift them. We should certainly find it much more simple to select hacks with good action, or to breed them even, rather than to convert our colt-breakers into circus-men. If there were no other method of attaining the object, by all means adopt it ; but when a far easier one is at hand, I should certainly select it in preference. Nevertheless, it may serve to prove the teachableness of the dog ; and, knowing the extent to which his education may be carried by patience and perseverance, I have no doubt that Colonel Hutchinson's plan is capable of execution, if the time and trouble necessary for it were properly remunerated. But we must now proceed to the second fault, which consists in ranging too far from the breaker. This may readily be cured, either by compelling attention to the hand and voice, with the aid of the whip in bad cases, or by attaching to the dog's collar a long cord, which is then suffered to trail on the ground, or is held in the hand of the breaker when the dog is very wild. Twenty, thirty, or at most forty, yards of a small box-cord will suffice for this purpose, and will soon tire down the strongest and most unruly dog. Indeed, an application of it for a short time will make many dogs give in entirely ; but some high-couraged ones, and setters especially, will persevere with it on till they are fairly exhausted. This "check-cord," as it is called, is also necessary in some dogs, to perfect their education in other respects, and, indeed, is chiefly wanted at a later period of breaking, not being often required at this stage.

Having described the mode of teaching pointers and setters to beat their ground, I have now to consider the best modes of teaching them (1) to point, set, or stand (which are different names for the same act), (2) to back, (3) to down charge, (4) to retrieve, if considered desirable, and (5) how to remedy certain faults, such as blinking, &c.

Pointing, setting, or *standing* is taught as follows. It will, of course, be discovered in practice that, in teaching the range, most dogs begin to point, and nineteen out of twenty, if well-bred, become steady enough, *without the gun,* before they are perfect in the proper mode of beating their ground. For these, then, it is unnecessary to describe any other means of teaching their trade ; but there are some few exceptions, in which, even after a fortnight's work, the dog is still deficient in this essential ; and though he beats his ground in ever so perfect a manner, and finds his birds well enough, yet he invariably runs them up, sometimes with

great zest and impudent disregard of his breaker, and at others
with evident fear of the consequences. Here, then, something more
must be done, and it is effected by taking the young dog out with
a steady companion and hunting them together; then, keeping
the old dog within forty yards, let him, if possible, be the one to
find, and take care to walk up to him before the young one comes
up, which he is sure to do as soon as he catches his eye on the
point. Now use your voice in a severe but low tone to stop him;
and as he has been accustomed to halt with the word " Toho ! " he
will at once do so, generally standing in a cautious attitude, at a
distance varying with his fear of his breaker and the amount of
courage which he possesses. If the birds lie close, let him draw
up and get the scent; and the excitement will then be so great,
that if he is under sufficient command to be held in check by
the " Toho ! " he will be sure to assume the rigid condition characteristic of his breed. Now go quietly up to him, pat him, and
encourage him, but in such a tone as to prevent his running in
—still using the " Toho ! good dog; toho !"—and keeping him
for a few minutes where he is, so long as he can scent his birds,
which he shows by champing and frothing at the mouth. After
the lapse of this time walk quietly forward, keeping your eye on
him, and still restraining him with the " Toho," put up the birds,
and then, if possible, make him drop with the words " Down
charge ! " the meaning of which he has already been taught. But
if he is very wild and of high courage, do not attempt this at first,
as it is better to proceed step by step, and to teach each department thoroughly before another is commenced. In this way, by
perseverance and hard work (which last is the keystone of the
breaker's arch), any dog, whether of the special breeds used for the
purpose or not, may be made to point when he finds game ; but
none but the pointer and setter become rigid or cataleptic, a
peculiarity which is confined to them. In very high-couraged
dogs a check-cord, thirty or forty yards in length, is sometimes
suffered to trail on the ground, or is held by the breaker, so as to
assist the voice in stopping the dog when he is wanted to make
his stand; but the cases where this is wanted are so rare as
scarcely to require any allusion to it, if the breaker is sufficiently
industrious to give work enough to his charge. This part of the

education is generally effected in a couple of lessons, without trouble, and indeed the young dog often points steadily enough at the first or second scenting of game.

Backing.—When a dog has acquired the merely instinctive property already described, he is said to be "steady before," and may be used *alone* or *single-handed* without any further education; but when he is to be hunted with other dogs he requires to be made "steady behind," that is to say, he must be taught to "back" another dog as the latter stands. In very high-bred dogs this property, like the former, is developed very early; but the more hardy and courageous the breed, the longer they generally are in acquiring it, and therefore the young breaker should not be discouraged if he finds that his puppies give him some trouble after they have learnt to stand perfectly steady. Backing is usually taught in the same way as described for standing, that is to say, by hunting with an old steady dog, *taking care that he is one whose find is to be depended on,* and then stopping the young one with the voice and hand, or with the aid of a check-cord if necessary. The great art consists here in managing to get between the two dogs at the moment when the old one stands, and thus to be able to face the puppy as he rushes up to share the scent with his rival, which he at first considers his companion to be. Jealousy is a natural feeling in all dogs, from their desire to obtain approbation; but it must be eradicated in the pointer and setter, or they never become steady together, and whichever finds first, the other tries to run up and take the point from him. To avoid this failing, leave the dog which first finds alone, and walk up to the one which you have stopped, pat and encourage him with the word "Toho!" in a low but pleased tone; let him not on any account creep forward a step, but keep him exactly where he is for some minutes, if the birds lie well. Then walk forward to the old dog, take no notice of him, and, with your eyes still on the puppy, put up the birds, having stopped him with voice and hand if he moves a limb. Supposing the old dog has pointed falsely, the young one is materially injured, inasmuch as he has lost confidence in him, and next time he is with more difficulty restrained from running in to judge for himself; hence the necessity for a good nose in the old dog, who ought to be very steady and perfect in all respects.

It will thus be seen that very little art is required in carrying out this part of the education, which really demands only hard walking, patience, and perseverance to complete it, in the most satisfactory manner. It should be pursued day after day, till the young dog not only finds game for himself and stands quite steadily, but also backs his fellows at any distance, and without drawing towards them a single step after he sees them at point. When this desirable consummation is effected to such an extent that the puppy will back even a strange dog, and has already learnt to beat his ground properly, as explained in my previous remarks, he is as steady and well broken as he can be without the gun, and may be thrown by until a fortnight before the shooting season, when he ought to be taken out again for two or three days, as in the interval he will generally have lost some of his steadiness. Still, he will only require *work* to restore it, as he knows what he ought to do; and with patience, joined if necessary with a little punishment, he soon reacquires all that he had forgotten. Many masters now fancy that all is done towards "making the pointer;" but, on the contrary, they find that after birds are killed the puppy, which was previously steady, becomes wild and ungovernable, and spoils the day's shooting by all sorts of bad behaviour. Hence it is that breakers so often are blamed without cause; but when it is found by experience that such conduct is the rule, and not the exception, young dogs are left by their owners to be shot over by a keeper for a few days, or even longer, before they are taken into the field. Another reason for this wildness may be assigned, namely, the dogs are often hunted in the commencement of the season by almost perfect strangers, two or three guns together; whereas, if their breaker had the management, they would be under much more control, and especially if he went out quietly by himself. Here again is another reason for gentlemen breaking their own dogs, or, at all events, finishing their education by giving their dogs and *themselves* a few lessons together.

Down charge, as already described, ought to be taught from a very early period, the dog being made to drop at the word or elevation of the hand of his master, without the slightest hesitation. It is not, therefore, necessary to dwell upon this part of his education, further than to remark that after each point, or, indeed, directly after birds rise under any circumstances, the dog should be made to drop by the voice, using the order, " Down charge!" or by raising the hand if the eye of the dog can be caught. When this practice is made habitual there is little trouble in carrying out the order until the gun is added; but then it will be found that great patience and forbearance are required to prevent the dog from running to his birds as they drop; for if this is allowed, it is sure to make him unsteady in every case as soon as his eye catches sight of game, whether after the point or not. It is now that the advantage of having made the dog drop to the gun is manifested, for the first thing he thinks of when the gun is fired is the necessity for dropping, and if this is encouraged all goes on well. Too often the shooter himself produces unsteadiness by disregarding his dog at the moment when he ought to attend to him most particularly, and by running in himself to take care of his " bag," considering that more important than the steadiness of his dog. It is true that a runner is sometimes lost by the delay of a few seconds while the discharged barrel is reloaded; but, in the long run, the shooter who keeps his dog down till he has loaded will bag the most game.

The *faults* which chiefly require correction *at this stage* are— *blinking, shying the gun, pottering* at the hedges, *hunting too wide,* and *chasing fur.* The vice of *blinking* has been caused by over-severity in punishment for chasing poultry, &c., and takes a great deal of time to remove. Indeed, until the dog sees game killed he seldom loses the fear which has produced it. It is, therefore, frequently useless to continue the breaking in the spring, although such a dog sometimes becomes very useful by careful management in the shooting season. Generally speaking, it is occasioned by undue severity, either applied for chasing cats or poultry, or for chasing game when first hunted. The former kind of castigation should be very cautiously applied, as the puppy is very apt to associate the punishment given for the chasing of game with that due to the destruction of poultry or cats; and as he has been compelled to leave the latter by the use of the whip, and has been afterwards kept "at heel," so he thinks he must do so now, and in fear he comes there, and consequently "blinks his birds."

This defect is only to be remedied by instilling confidence and by avoiding punishment; but it is often one which gives great trouble before it is got over. It is not so bad as the obstinately refusing to work at all, but is only next to it. Both occur in dogs which are deficient in courage, and both require the most delicate and encouraging treatment to remove them. Let such dogs run "riot," and commit any fault they like, without fear for a time; then afterwards (that is, when they begin to be quite bold and are full of the zest for game) begin very cautiously to steady them, and something may yet be done. In very bad cases all attempts at breaking must be given up at "pairing time," and the gun must be relied on as a last resource, the killing of game having sometimes a wonderful effect in giving courage to a dog which has been depressed by undue correction. Punishment is not to be condemned altogether, for in some breeds and individuals without the whip nothing could be done; but it should be very cautiously applied, and the temper of each dog should be well studied in every case before it is adopted. Kindness will effect wonders, especially where united with firmness, and with a persevering determination to compel obedience somehow; but if that "how" can be effected without the whip, so much the better; still, if it cannot, the rod must not be spared, and if used at all, it should be used sufficiently.

Shyness of the gun will generally also go off in time; but as it seldom occurs except in very timid and nervous dogs, they do not often become very useful even when they have lost it. The best plan is to lead a shy dog quietly behind the shooters, and not to give him an opportunity of running off, which he generally does on the first discharge. When game falls, lead him up and let him mouth it; and thus, in course of time, he connects cause with effect, and loses that fear of the report, which he finds is followed by a result that gives him the pleasure of scenting fresh blood.

Pottering at the hedges in partridge-shooting is the result of using dogs to find rabbits, or of allowing them to look for them, which they always are ready to do, especially if permitted to chase or even to retrieve hares. There is no remedy for it, and a potterer of this kind is utterly worthless and irreclaimable.

Hunting too wide for close partridge-shooting may be easily remedied by constantly keeping in the dog by the whistle and hand; and if he has been properly taught to range at command, little trouble is required in making him change from the wide beat, necessary in countries where game is scarce, to the confined and limited range of sixty yards, which is best where it is thick on the ground.

Chasing fur and also *running in to dead birds* are often most unmanageable vices; but either can generally be cured by patience and severe treatment, aided if necessary by the check-cord, or in very bad cases by the spike-collar in addition. When these are used it is only necessary to work the dog with them on, the cord either trailing loosely on the ground or held in an assistant's hand. Then, the moment the dog runs in, check him severely, and if he is not very bold, the plain collar will suffice, as it may be made by a sharp jerk to throw him back, to his great annoyance; but the spike-collar punishes far more, and if it is used will soon give the dog cause to leave off his malpractices.

BREAKING TO RETRIEVE.

Retrieving, in my opinion, should be invariably committed to a dog specially kept for that purpose; but as this is not the universal practice, it will be necessary to say a few words on this subject. When pointers or setters are broken to retrieve, in addition to those qualities peculiar to them they should always be so much under command as to wait "down charge," until they are ordered on by the words "Seek dead," when they at once go up to the place where they saw their game drop, and taking up the scent, foot it till they find it. Some breeds have no nose for a foot-scent, and if ordered to "Seek dead," will beat for the body-scent as they would for a single bird; and when they come upon the lost bird, they "peg" it with a steady point in the same way. This does not injure the dog nearly so much as the working out a runner by the foot-scent; but a retrieving pointer of this kind is of little use for any but a badly wounded bird which has not run far. Few pointers and setters will carry game far, nor indeed is it worth while to spend much time in teaching them to do so; and when they are set to retrieve, it is better to follow them, and help them in their search, so as to avoid all necessity for developing the "fetch-and-carry" quality which in the genuine retriever is so valuable. But it is chiefly for wounded hares or running pheasants that such a retriever is required; and as the former spoil a pointer or setter, and are sure to make him unsteady if he is allowed to hunt them, it is desirable to keep clear of the position altogether, while pheasants are so rarely killed to these dogs that their retrieval by them need not be considered.

The *regular land retriever* requires a much more careful education, inasmuch as he is wanted to abstain from hunting, and from his own especial duties, excepting when ordered to commence. The breed generally used is the cross of the Newfoundland with the setter or water-spaniel, but, as I have described at page 220, other breeds are equally useful. In educating these dogs they should be undertaken at a very early age, as it is almost impossible to ensure perfect obedience at a later period. The disposition to "fetch and carry," which is the essence of retrieving, is very early developed in these dogs, and without it there is little chance of making a puppy perfect in his vocation. Young dogs of this breed will be seen carrying sticks about, and watching for their master to throw them, that they may fetch them to him. This fondness for the amusement should be encouraged to a certain extent, almost daily, but not so far as to tire and disgust the dog, and care should always be taken that he does not tear or bite the object which he has in charge. On no account should it be dragged from his mouth, but he should be ordered to drop it on the ground at the feet of his master, or to release it directly it is laid hold of. The consequence of pulling anything out of the young retriever's mouth is that he becomes "hard bitten," as it is called; and when he retrieves a wounded bird he makes his teeth meet, and mangles it so much that it is utterly useless. A dog which is not naturally inclined to retrieve may be made so by encouraging him to pull at a handkerchief or a stick; but such animals very seldom turn out well in this line, and it is far better to put them to some other task. As soon as the puppy has learnt to bring everything to his master when ordered, he may be taught to seek for trifling articles in long grass or other covert, such as bushes, &c.; and when he succeeds in this, get some young rabbits which are hardly old enough to run, and hide one at a time at a little distance, after trailing it through the grass so as to imitate the natural progress of the animal when wounded. When putting the young retriever on the scent at the commencement of the " run," let him puzzle it out till he finds the rabbit, and then make him bring it to his master without injuring it in the least. Encouragement should be given for success, and during the search the dog should have the notice of his master, by the words " Seek! seek! seek dead! " &c. A perseverance in this kind of practice will soon make the dog very clever in tracing out the concealed rabbits, and in process of time he may be entrusted with the task of retrieving a wounded partridge or pheasant in actual shooting. But it is always a long time before the retriever becomes perfect, practice being all important to him.

Most shooters now use a slip for the retriever, at battues and other shooting parties, the keeper leading him in it till he is wanted, which is a good plan when a keeper is always in attendance. In any case, however, these dogs should be made to drop "down charge," as the gun may be used while they are at work, and if they are not broken to drop they become excited, and often flush other game before it is reloaded.

The breaking of the water-spaniel or retriever is also a complicated task, and as he has to hunt in the water and on the banks, his duties are twofold. These dogs are used in the punt as well as on the edge of the water, but when the education is finished in the river, the pupil will generally do what is wanted from the punt. As in the land retriever, so in this variety, the first thing to be done is to get the puppy to "fetch and carry" well; after which he may be introduced to " flappers " in July and August, when the water is warm, and he does not feel the ill effects and disagreeables attendant on a cold winter's day with a wet coat. The young birds are also slow and awkward in swimming and diving, so that every encouragement is afforded to the dog, and he may readily be induced to continue the sport, to which he is naturally inclined, for hours together. The chief difficulty at first is in breaking the water-spaniel from rats, which infest the banks of most streams, and which are apt to engage the attention of most dogs. The dog should be taught to beat to the hand, and whenever a flapper is

U

shot and falls in the water, then he must be encouraged to bring it to land without delay. No art must be neglected to induce him to do this, and, failing every other plan, the breaker must himself enter the water; for if the dog is once allowed to leave a duck behind him, he is much more difficult afterwards to break. Indeed, perseverance in the breaker is necessary at all times, to insure the same quality in the pupil. The object in teaching the range to hand to the spaniel is, because without this there will often be a difficulty in showing him where a bird lies in the water, the eye of the dog being so little above its level, and the bird very often so much immersed, that when there is the slightest ruffle he can scarcely see it a yard from his nose. As in all other cases, the water-retriever must be strictly " down charge," and he must be thoroughly steady and quiet at heel, or he will be sure to disturb the water-fowl when the shooter is in ambush waiting for them. The slightest whine is fatal, and the dog should, therefore, be taught to be as quiet as a mouse until ordered to move.

THE ENTERING AND BREAKING OF THE COVERT SPANIEL.

The breaking of all spaniels should be commenced as early as possible, as they are naturally impetuous, and require considerable restraint to keep them near enough to the shooter while they are at work. After teaching them the ordinary rules of obedience, such as to "come to heel," to "hold up," to drop "down charge," &c., which may all be done with the pistol and check-cord, aided if necessary by the spiked collar, the next thing is to enter them to the game which they are intended to hunt. Generally it is the practice to use spaniels for pheasants, cocks, and hares, disregarding rabbits, which take their chance with the shooter. The spaniel, therefore, is not expected to "speak" to them, and if he can be induced to give a different note at each of the three varieties above mentioned, he is all the more highly prized. These dogs are better taken out first into small coverts or hedgerows (provided there are not too many rabbits in the latter), as they are more under command here than in large woodlands; self-hunting should be strictly discouraged, that is the say, the dog should neither be allowed to hunt *by* himself nor *for* himself, but should be made to understand that he is always in aid of the gun, and that he must keep within shot. For this purpose spaniels must be taught not to press their game till the shooter is within range, which is one of the most difficult things to teach them. When they are to be kept exclusively for "feather," they must be stopped and rated as soon as it is discovered that they are speaking to "fur." This requires a long time, and therefore few spaniels are worth much till they have had one or two seasons' practice, from which circumstance it should not occasion surprise that a thoroughly broken Clumber spaniel fetches from thirty to forty guineas. When they are too riotous and hunt too freely, these methods of sobering them are adopted :— first, to put on a collar, and slip one of the fore-legs into it, which compels the dog to run on three only; secondly, to buckle a small strap or tie a piece of tape tightly round the hind-leg above the hock, by which that limb is rendered useless, and the dog has to go upon three also; and, thirdly, to put on a collar loaded with shot. If either of the legs is fastened up, it must be occasionally changed, especially if the strap is adopted, as it cramps the muscles after a certain time, and if persisted in too long, renders the dog lame for days afterwards. On the other hand, when the puppy is slack in hunting, put him on the scent of pheasants as they are going off their feed, when they generally run back into covert, and at that time the scent is very strong, especially in the evening. The birds soon rise into the trees, and after that are no longer disturbed by the dog. In hunting hedgerows, the young dog should at first be kept on the same side as the shooter, so that his movements may be watched; but as soon as he can be trusted, he should be sent through to the other side, and made to drive his game towards the gun, always taking care that the dog does not get out of shot. In first introducing a young dog to a large covert, he must be put down with a couple of old ones which are very steady; and, at the same time, he should have a shot-collar on, or one of his legs up. Without this precaution he will be sure to range too wide, and if he gets on the scent of a hare, he will probably follow her all over the covert, to the entire destruction of the day's sport; but by the above precautions he is prevented doing this, and by imitating his fellows, he soon learns to keep within the proper distance. Here, as in all dogs intended for the gun, the great principle is to make them understand that *it* is the instrument of destruction, not *themselves*, and that it is only by paying proper attention to the gun that they can be expected to succeed in obtaining game. In working spaniels in covert great quiet is desirable, as game will never come within distance of the shooter if they hear a noise proceeding from him, and hence the constant encouragement to the dogs, which some sportsmen indulge in, is by no means necessary. If the spaniel is properly broken, he can hear his master as he passes through the underwood, and he will take care to drive the game towards him, while if he is slack and idle the voice does him little good, and prevents the only chance of getting a shot which might otherwise occur. In *battue* shooting, spaniels, if employed, are in aid of the beaters, not of the shooters, most of whom do not even know the dogs' names, and the latter cannot, therefore, be expected to work to them; but as they go forward with the beaters in line, they must be kept from getting on too far, or they will often drive game back. For this work, however, they do not require to be nearly so thoroughly broken as for hunting to the single shooter, for which purpose they must know him, and should, in fact, be broken by him.

THE ENTERING AND BREAKING OF VERMIN DOGS.

Terriers are entered to vermin with great facility, and require very little breaking, unless they are intended to be used with ferrets, when they must be broken to let these animals alone, as they are apt to make their appearance occasionally in passing from one hole to another. It is only necessary to let the ferret and the terrier be together in a yard or stable, cautioning the latter not to touch the former, for a few times, and the young dog soon learns to distinguish his friends from his foes. Some terriers are not hardy enough to brave the bites which they are liable to in ratting, &c., and indeed the true terrier without any cross of the bulldog is a great coward, so that he is quite useless for the purpose. In such a case he must be encouraged by letting him kill young rats first, and as he gains confidence he will perhaps also increase in courage. If, however, the terrier is well-bred, he will seldom want anything but practice.

CHAPTER V.

THE EMPLOYMENT OF THE DOG IN COURSING, HUNTING, SHOOTING, &c.

Coursing—Deerstalking—Hunting—Partridge and Grouse Shooting—Snipe-Shooting—Covert-Shooting—Wildfowl-Shooting—Ferreting.

PRIVATE COURSING.

BETWEEN private and public coursing there is a considerable difference, not only in the methods adopted, but also in the kind of greyhound most useful for each. In the first place, the private courser will not like the expense of rearing a fresh set of greyhounds each year, but will expect them to last several seasons; and hence speed and cleverness must to some extent be sacrificed to honesty, which is the *sine quâ non* of the private greyhound, excepting for those who course for currant jelly purposes only. It is true that a cunning old dog, if fast and clever, will kill more hares than any other, but he will do it in a way to disgust every sportsman, and such an animal is not to be recommended on any account. If, therefore, the private courser regards the sport independently of the obtaining hares, he will see that his greyhounds combine as many good qualities as possible, with an amount of honesty which will carry them through three or four seasons without lurching. These, however, are only now to be obtained from private sources, for every strain of public greyhounds with which I am acquainted will show a tendency to lurch after a couple of seasons, if used as much and as freely as the greyhounds of most private coursers are expected to be.

The *feeding* of these greyhounds should be on oatmeal porridge, with more or less wheat-flour or Indian meal, as described at page 261, and flavoured with greaves, or with broth made from flesh of some kind. If half a pound a day, or rather more, of flesh can be

given in addition, they will be so much the better; but in that case
they ought to have a couple of hours' exercise every day, without
which they become fat and unwieldy.   Vegetables should be carefully given, as in all cases with dogs, and due attention should be
paid to cleanliness.   In fact, there is no reason why the system
adopted in the feeding of the public greyhound should not be fully
carried out.   *The sport of private coursing* may be conducted exactly
on the same principles as public coursing, excepting that stakes
are not usually run for, but in almost all cases the dogs are matched
together, without which the sport is tame and uninteresting.
The essence of coursing is the competition between the two dogs
engaged, that being the number which is considered fair to the
hare, and coursing with more than two being by general consent
stamped as poaching ever since the days of Arrian, A.D. 150.   When,
therefore, greyhounds are kept with this purpose, it promotes the
object of sport if two or more gentlemen will meet together to
run their dogs in competition with one another; and when this is
done there is often quite as much excitement produced as in the
most important public meeting.   But then there must be a person
appointed to act as judge, for without this functionary there must
be endless disputes as to the respective qualifications of the greyhounds engaged.   With him, if he understands the points of the
course, it is only necessary to conduct the beating of the ground
properly, and to appoint a proper person to slip the greyhounds,
and then everything is *en règle.*

In beating the ground, when there are no gentlemen present on
horseback, five or six beaters must be provided, whose task is somewhat onerous if there is much ploughed land, especially in clay
districts when wet.   In any case a line should be formed, with
one person at every twenty yards, and then walking abreast from
one extremity of the field to theother, so as either to find the hare
sitting or to put her up from her form.   The proper direction of this
line of beaters, so as to drive the hare in the best direction, requires
some considerable experience and tact.   Thus, when there is a
covert near, the beat should be *from* it, so as to compel the hare
to go in the opposite direction, by which a sufficiently long course
is often ensured, whereas otherwise she would be safe before she
was well reached.   At the end of this beat the men should return

over the beaten ground, taking what is called a "dead beat," and then again beating from covert. When the part of a field is beaten near the hedge, the line on that side should be extended forwards; and if there is a horseman present, he should walk up close to the hedge, thirty yards in front of the others, so as to prevent the hare at once running through it. Hares may often be driven out of turnips, clover, or small coverts by a line of beaters driving them towards the dogs, which are held at a particular spot, and kept as much as possible out of sight. The *slipper* uses the same kind of slips as are adopted in public coursing, and slips his dogs in the same way, adapting the length of the slip allowed to the nature of the ground. It is a very bad plan to let the greyhounds run loose while the hare is looked for, as the two rarely start on even terms, and consequently they cannot be compared together. Unless, therefore, coursing is pursued solely to get the hare, slips are indispensable.

When private coursing is conducted in the above way, it is quite as good a sport as the public kind; but too often it degenerates into a series of mobbings of the hare, followed by perpetual squabblings of the owners of the dogs engaged, as to their respective merits or demerits.

PUBLIC COURSING.

This amusement has now become very general since the last alteration of the Game Laws, which permitted any person to course a hare without a certificate. It differs from private coursing, firstly, in requiring rather a different greyhound, and secondly, in being governed strictly by rules which settle all the preliminaries.

The *public greyhound,* to be successful, must be a dog which can beat his competitors in the stake in which he is engaged, even if he never runs afterwards respectably. Hence, unlike the dog which we have been just considering, everything is sacrificed to this point, and it has at last come to pass that the animal has been bred to such a degree of cleverness combined with speed that he very soon runs cunning, and is then no longer useful, because he will not exert his powers. The consequence is, that a great many dogs begin by running with extraordinary pace and working powers, but after winning one or two stakes they are not to be depended on. This is so common, that, as a rule, most coursers do not think it worth their while to keep their dogs for more than one season, and bring up a succession of puppies one year after another, reserving only one or two old ones to their second season. It must be remembered that this animal is kept for a specific purpose, namely, to compete with his fellows *in killing the hare under certain conditions, which are defined by general consent and laid down in certain specified rules.* Hence it is not the greyhound which will most certainly pull down his hare that is always to be prized, but he that will comply with these rules most fully in the act of running her, and will, in other words, score most points ; and, in effecting this, four cardinal virtues must be combined as far as possible, consisting in speed, working power, bottom, and courage. It is almost impossible to obtain the fullest development of these several qualities in one individual, and therefore all that can be done is to sacrifice those which are of the least importance. Thus, excessive speed, as shown from the slips, is hardly consistent with a high degree of working power, or with a capability of lasting throughout a long course ; and for this reason extremely fast dogs are not adapted to down countries, where the hares are not only stout, but short in their turns. In some localities, however, where there is no room for a long course, or where the hares are weak, a fast dog, even if he is not stout, and probably even if he is a bad worker, will be able to win a stake ; but wherever the hares are good, and there is scope for them to display their powers, there must be both bottom and working power displayed in order to ensure success. The best plan in breeding greyhounds is to obtain a brood bitch of stout blood and good working powers, combined with as much speed as possible, but still laying the most stress on the first two qualities, and then put her to a dog essentially fast, but in him also looking to bottom and working power, though secondary to speed. Courage is essential in all greyhounds, and may be obtained equally well whether the breed is fast or slow, clever in working or the reverse. It must exist with bottom, but may also be developed without it, some very soft greyhounds being high-couraged, and going till they drop from exhaustion of their delicate frames. In looking for these several qualities it is necessary to observe that speed depends upon the formation of the body and limbs, which must be of the most perfect make, as described under the head of *the points of the greyhound* at page 19 ; but with the most perfect shape there is often a want of speed, apparently owing to the absence of that nervous *stimulus* which sets the frame in motion. Such dogs want quickness and elasticity in using their organs, and though they often move elegantly, there is a deficiency in the rapidity of repetition in the muscular contractions which constitute high speed. Hence the necessity for attending to breed, and to its purity, which is the only guarantee (short of an actual trial) that the perfect frame will give perfect action. The same remarks apply to working power : a dog may look to be exceedingly cleverly made, with good shoulders, and all the other parts essential to this faculty, and yet there may be a want of cleverness and tact, as well as a deficiency in courage, which will render him absolutely useless. But when the breed is known to be almost invariably good in these respects, and the formation of the individual is good, there is a reasonable ground for expecting that he will exhibit them in more or less perfection. Nothing is more provoking than to find a splendidly formed dog beaten in his trial by a wretched-looking brute, the sole advantage attending the latter being that he is descended from good blood, while the former perhaps owns a sire and dam of well-known and ascertained imperfect nervous organisation.

When the young courser determines upon getting together a kennel of greyhounds, he must, therefore, carefully attend to all these points ; but, with all his care, he will be disappointed unless he knows how to manage them, or can entrust them to some one who does. Public greyhounds, as I have already explained, are easily spoiled by using them too frequently ; and yet they must have some amount of practice before they run in a stake, or they will inevitably be beaten from awkwardness. Some breeds are naturally more clever than others, and take less time in coming to their best ; so that, if they have as many courses as would barely suffice in many cases, they would be past their prime. All this, therefore, requires considerable practice, and theoretical knowledge as well ; and, for this reason, the young courser should not fancy that he can at once compete on even terms with the experienced hand. Let him, therefore, content himself with creeping before he runs, and let him undertake a brace or two at the most for a season before he rushes into the thick of the contest. No one can hope for much success who keeps a very large kennel under the management of one man, because he cannot do justice to more than eight or ten running dogs; but at first he had better content himself with half that number, and he will find afterwards that he has made many mistakes about these. It is also very difficult to purchase good dogs, though occasionally they may be met with; but when a young courser begins, he wants the experience which is required to know how to select them. On all these accounts, therefore, he had better begin by sporting a brace, and in the meantime he can be bringing forward a moderate number of puppies bred by himself, which will be ready for work in a year or two.

The kennel management of greyhounds has been described at page 260, and it only remains to describe the method of *training* which is adopted for the purpose of enabling them to bear the severe work often experienced in going through a stake. Many a greyhound will run one course quite as well without training as with, that is, if it is not a long one; but there are few untrained dogs that will go on through a series of courses as well as if they had had the pains bestowed upon them which a man of experience would be able to give. It is often said that certain dogs have run better untrained than trained, but this only shows that the training in their particular case was mismanaged; for if they had been treated properly, they would not have been worked to the extent which produced the change for the worse. Scarcely any two dogs require the same treatment, and the chief art in training is to discover the exact amount which each will bear and require in order to bring him out to the best advantage. It must, therefore, be understood that by training is here meant the act of preparing a dog for certain public performances in the way best fitted for each individual; and that it does not by any means consist in putting him through a specified course of physic, diet, and work, which, in his case, may be altogether unsuited to him.

Before commencing to train a greyhound it is necessary to consider what condition he is in at the time, and what amount of work he

is likely to bear, judging from his breed, and also from his bodily
formation. The first thing to be done is to see that his health is
good, and that his liver and kidneys are doing their work properly,
without which it is useless to attempt to train him. If he is
known to be descended from a stock which has been accustomed to
severe preparatory work, and if he also has a stout frame and *good
feet*, it may reasonably be expected that he will bear as much
training as his progenitors, and he may be treated accordingly.
If, on the other hand, he comes of a soft strain, that has never
been used to road-work, and of which the dogs composing it have
always trained themselves in their play to the highest pitch of
which their frames are capable, then it will be safer to follow suit,
and to take the descendant of these latter animals out for two or
three hours a day on the greensward, simply keeping him moving,
and encouraging him to play with his fellows till he is tired.
Less than three hours' exercise can never be sufficient, as the dog
is only compelled to walk, and any faster pace is voluntary, and
will not be attempted if he is at all exhausted. From this it will
appear that the trainer's art greatly consists in apportioning the
proper quantity of work, which he can only do by studying the
constitutions and breeding of the dogs under his charge; after
which he will determine in his own mind the probable amount
of work which each will bear, and will proceed to put his theory
into practice, always carefully watching the progress which is
made, and altering his plans as he goes on, according as he finds
that he has calculated erroneously. One great guide which he has
is the weight which is gained or lost; for if he finds the dog is
putting on flesh when he wants some off, or if he is losing it when
he is already too light, there must be some alteration made, or the
dog will not come out fit for his duties. Thus, then, the trainer
first fixes in his mind the weight to which he wishes to bring his
dog on a certain day, and then, by apportioning the work, physic,
and food according to his ideas of the dog's constitution, he
endeavours to attain that standard of proportion; altering his
plans as he goes on if necessary. It must, however, always be
remembered that training should not attempt to produce an unnatural condition, but rather the highest state of health consistent
with that free play of the lungs and heart which will enable the

dog to continue his highest speed for the longest time, and guarantees the retention of his spirit and courage, so as to induce him to exert it.

Work for training purposes is effected in two ways : the object being to get rid of the superfluous fat, which interferes with muscular action, and with the free play of the lungs; and also to accustom the muscles, ligaments, and tendons to severe and long-continued exertions. These two methods are often combined; and indeed, though the one by means of slipping is effectual by itself, yet the other, or horse-exercise alone, will not develop the wind sufficiently, and if it is adopted, it must be aided by slipping the dogs as well. Horse-exercise is chiefly confined to countries where the courses are very long and severe, and where, also, much of the work can be given on turf, so that it is only in down countries that it is very available, but there it is almost essential to full success in training the greyhound. The amount of this kind of exercise which a greyhound of stout blood will take with advantage is very great, and it is sometimes more than one horse will be able to lead; but this is not often the case. Few greyhounds will be the better for more than fifteen miles every other day, and this is quite within the compass of a horse's powers, especially when it is considered that not more than two or three miles of this distance should be at the gallop. But the great object of horse-exercise is not to produce a fast pace so much as to ensure a sufficiency of slow work; for there are few trainers who will walk fifteen or sixteen miles a day on foot, and yet in order to keep the dogs out for four hours they ought to do so. A certain amount of road-work is essential to the hardening of the feet, but this should be commenced two or three months prior to the time of training, as it cannot be done without time to cause the growth of the thick horny matter which covers the sole of the foot. If, therefore, horse-exercise is to be adopted, it is better to commence it two or three months before the meeting for which the dog is to be trained; and after giving him two or three days a week, up to within a fortnight of the time, discontinue it, and proceed to develop the highest degree of wind, by slipping the dog to its trainer's call. A short gallop of a couple of miles *on turf* will be nearly as beneficial, but the long dragging road-work, which will serve to prepare the dog earlier in his training, is now to be discontinued, because it interferes with the spirit, and will render him disinclined to exert himself with that fiery courage which is requisite for success. The slipping-work is effected by the aid of an assistant, who leads the greyhounds off in one direction, while the trainer walks to another point; and when half a mile apart or thereabouts the dogs are let loose, one after another, the trainer whistling and shouting to them, so as to excite them to their highest speed. The assistant should be a stranger to them, and it is better to buckle a stirrup-leather round his waist with the noose at the end of each leading-strap inserted, so that he may have both his hands at liberty to unbuckle the collars in succession. If there is a gently sloping valley composed of ground similar to that over which the public coursing is to take place, it is better to select it, as the dog then sees his trainer plainly, and also finishes up-hill, which is of great service in "opening the pipes." By means of these two kinds of work properly proportioned, and taking care not to overdo them, the dog is at last rendered equal to any ordinary amount of exertion; but in hardy animals which are allowed to eat as much as they like, the work which would reduce them sufficiently would make them stale in their joints and dull in spirit, so that it is found necessary to call in the aid of physic and a reduction of food.

Since the introduction of enclosed coursing, the necessity for severe training has not been so great as before, but still training cannot be entirely dispensed with even before these particular meetings. If a dog, however, is moderately fit in point of flesh, a very few slips of half a mile or a little more are considered sufficient.

The physic proper for a dog in training should be of such a nature as simply to cause an increase of his secretions, without rendering him liable to catch cold. Hence mercury should be carefully avoided; and jalap, salts, or aloes will be found to be the best. Some people use emetics, but these do not reduce the weight of the dog, and they are solely useful in giving tone to the stomach, which they certainly appear to do. Even within two or three days of running they are often given, and will then render the dog lively and full of spirits, when he would otherwise be dull and disinclined to exert himself. The trainer, throughout, should watch the secretions, and if he finds that they are deficient he may give a dose of aloes or jalap; but if in good order it is better to avoid medicine, if the weight can be kept down by other means.

The diet is of the greatest importance, and indeed it is in this point that more mistakes are made than in any other. If a hardy dog is fed as heavily as his inclination prompts him, no kind of work will reduce him without also destroying his elasticity and fire, and hence it is found necessary to limit his food. For this reason reduction of food is indispensable in most cases, and in very few will the dog in training require the same *quantity* as before, though the *quality* can hardly be too good, provided it does not upset his stomach. These animals are extremely liable to become bilious, and suffer from disorder of the stomach and liver, just as man does. Hence it follows that any concentrated food like eggs or strong soup, although in theory it may be better than meat and bread, is inadmissible, because, being so prone to dyspepsia, just at the time when the greyhound is wanted to run he is off his feed, sick and sorry. The dog naturally requires variety in his feeding, but the change should be always gradual in the proportions of the elements of which it is composed. The changes may be rung on beef, mutton, and horseflesh as often as may be convenient, but the proportion of flesh to meal must be very carefully kept at the same ratio. For the dog in high training lean mutton is the best of all flesh, as it is milder than either of the others, and though quite as nourishing, yet it is less heating; so that careful trainers prefer it to all others, especially when from home, as it can always be procured at the butcher's, while good horseflesh must be carried about, and is on that account troublesome to get. But if a good leg of well-hung horseflesh from a tolerably healthy horse can be procured, it is very nearly as good as mutton, and far better than beef, being more tender, and, I think, not so heating. No one, however, who wishes to take advantage of every chance in his favour should use bad meat; and the difference between the one and the other cannot exceed 6d. per day per dog, which at a meeting lasting a week amounts to 3s. 6d. per head. About three-quarters of a pound of dressed meat and the same quantity of biscuit or bread soaked in jelly will be sufficient, *on the average*, for most dogs in training; but some take more and some less, so that this can only be taken as an approximation to what each animal requires. The water which is given should be boiled, by which it deposits its lime, when over-abundant, and unless this precaution is taken the change of water often upsets the dog's kidneys. Many people do not leave water in the dog's kennel while in training, but I prefer the plan, taking care to remove it on the morning of running, after the kennel is first entered.

The amount of friction on the skin which is of service during the course of training is very considerable, and each dog ought to have half an hour a day after his exercise, first washing the feet, and if necessary touching their pads with a little tar-ointment; then, taking the dog between the knees, and putting on a pair of hair-gloves, rub him well in the direction of the hair, applying the pressure over the large muscles, especially those of the shoulders, loins, and haunches, and avoiding the bones as much as possible. The spine or backbone should be left between the two hands in rubbing the loin, but the ribs, as a matter of course, must be included. After this friction has been continued, rub all over gently with a linen rubber and again put on the clothing.

Dogs in training are clothed, because they are more liable to cold than at other times, and also because their strange lodgings are seldom so free from draughts as their regular kennels. The clothing is made in one sheet which covers them from the head to the tail, but when in kennel the head and neck part is turned back over the shoulders. The clothing is necessary to put on when the dogs are carried out to the coursing-field, as they are often kept standing about in the cold for hours. A waterproof cloth is of great service in wet weather. This clothing can be obtained at almost any saddler's throughout the country. The *following summary* will be useful in giving *general directions* for training the greyhound :—

1. Give no more physic than just enough to freshen the stomach, unless it is wanted as a means of reduction.

2. When used in this way, try mild physic before giving stronger.

3. Give about three-quarters of a pound of mutton or horseflesh daily, mixed with as little bread as will suffice for health. The

quantity of bread necessary may be known by the colour of the faeces, which ought to continue of a good gingerbread colour, and which become black, or nearly so, when the flesh is overdone.

4. Reduce the dog more by increase of work and reduction of food than by physic.

5. Give as much horse or other exercise as the stoutness of the dog will enable him to bear, without overdoing him.

6. Use plenty of friction.

7. Feed from one to three o'clock on the day before running.

8. Do not give more than walking exercise on the day before running, or on the morning prior to the course.

Greyhounds require very careful management at the meeting when they are to run, inasmuch as there are many strange circumstances which often affect their health. In the first place, the travelling is apt to upset them, especially if by railway, the excitement of which is too much for irritable dogs, and therefore they should be moved to their new quarters several days before they are wanted. It is customary to feed rather more lightly than usual on the day before running, but this plan is often carried to extremes, and the dog runs weak in consequence. After running very little is needed, except to get the dog home, and feed him for next day if he is required. If, however, there is much distress, and the dog has to run again, a cordial must be given, which is sometimes egg and sherry. The egg I do not believe to be useful, as it has a tendency to make the dog bilious, but a little sherry or spirit and water may be employed. What is far better is some kind of spice mixed with a little mutton or by itself, and given about half an hour before the dog will be wanted; using plenty of friction just before he is put in the slips. Cold tea, with or without the addition of a little spirit, is also an excellent restorative.

SPICED-MEAT BALL.

Take of Caraway seeds, 10 grains.
., Cardamoms, 10 grains.
., Grains of paradise, 5 grains.
„ Ginger, 5 grains.
„ Lean boiled knuckle of mutton, ½ oz.

Bruise the seeds in a mortar, and then mix with the mutton, and form it into a ball.

Common Cordial Ball.

Take of Cumin seeds, 10 grains.

,,   Coriander seeds, 10 grains.

,,   Caraway seeds, 10 grains.

,,   Grains of paradise, 10 grains.

,,   Saffron, 1 drachm.

,,   Syrup, enough to form a ball.

Bruise in a mortar, and mix well together, then make up into a ball.

THE NATIONAL COURSING CLUB.

Public coursing is conducted under certain rules which have repeatedly been revised by a committee appointed at the Great Waterloo Meeting held at Liverpool. These supersede all previous rules, and also those drawn up by Mr. Thacker for the decision of courses. Rules for the guidance of judges are now appended to those for the regulation of meetings, and are supposed to be acted on, but it is often difficult to reconcile the actual awards with the theory laid down.

To the National Coursing Club are now referred all complaints, of whatever description, connected with coursing, or any matters in dispute.

The National Club consists of members selected by the various Coursing Clubs of the three kingdoms on the elective principle, the Clubs electing members in rotation, and eight retiring every year.

Two General Meetings of the Club are held in each year— viz., one in London during the summer, and one at Liverpool during the Waterloo Coursing Meeting—for the despatch of business and for the revision and alteration of rules; but the Secretary shall be authorised, upon a requisition addressed to him in writing by any three of the secretary and stewards of a meeting, or upon a remonstrance signed by six public coursers who may happen to be present, to summon such special meetings as may be necessary from time to time, at the earliest convenient opportunity, for adjudication upon such questions as may be referred to the Club.

x

The National Coursing Club recommends that the following code of laws shall be adopted universally for the guidance both of open and club meetings, clubs merely adding such special or local regulations as may be required to adapt the national code to their own peculiar use ; in fact, it is generally used throughout the kingdom :—

CODE OF RULES.

A COMMITTEE OF MANAGEMENT should be formed in any case, who should meet and decide upon the election of the judge and slipper, the stakes to be run for, and their appointment, and the rules which shall guide the meeting. All disputed questions to be decided by vote, and the chairman, in case of an even number, to have the casting-vote.

THE ELECTION OF JUDGE either to rest with the committee, in which case it should be published with the advertisements giving notice of the meeting, or else it should be vested in the general subscribers to the stakes, each of whom should have one vote.

The secretary to draw up, with the approbation of the committee, a programme of the meeting, which should be advertised, and should specify—

1st—The date of the meeting.
2d—The names of the stakes.
3d—The qualification for ditto.
4th—The entries for ditto and the money added, if any.
5th—The apportionment of ditto.
6th—The expenses to be deducted.
7th—To whom applications are to be made for entries.
8th—The time and place of entry and drawing.
9th—The rules to regulate the meeting.
10th—The judge, if named, or, if not, the mode of election to be stated.
11th—The names of the stewards or committee, or both.
12th—The secretary's signature.

THE DRAW should be conducted on the following plan : first, the money for each stake should be paid to the secretary by the subscribers; secondly, after this is completed, small squares of paper, exactly like each other, should be handed round, and each subscriber should, either himself or by his deputy, write the name of his dog, with the pedigree, colour, and age, upon one of them; after which they are folded up. The secretary then collects these for each stake in succession, placing them at once in a hat, from which they should be drawn in regular order, and entered as they are drawn. Nothing can be more simple than this plan, and it does away with all necessity for numbered cards, &c., which are the source of constant confusion and mistakes. It also facilitates guarding, and prevents all hanging back to see what dogs are entered, which is not conducive to fair and large entries.

STEWARDS should be appointed by the subscribers present, according to Law I.

THE DUTIES OF THE FLAG-STEWARD are to receive the fiat of the judge and see that the flagman hoists the right flag (red or white for the left or right side of the card respectively, and *both* for undecided courses).

THE SLIP-STEWARD, if there is one, regulates the proceedings of the dogs at the slips and sees that the next brace is ready.

THE FIELD-STEWARDS regulate the beating and the general proceedings of the field. They should have one or two flagmen, with blue flags, who should always be in sight of the beaters, and should restrain the progress of the crowd beyond their own boundary. The field-stewards should also see to the beaters, with the assistance of the secretary, who is usually one of their number.

THE RULES FOR THE GUIDANCE of meetings are of great importance to their success, and are now under the control of the National Coursing Club, which is elected by the various coursing clubs. They may be, and are, altered from time to time, and are now as follows :—

SECT. II.—THE NATIONAL COURSING CLUB. CONSTITUTION AND BYE-LAWS.

(*a.*) The National Coursing Club shall be composed of members elected by the coursing clubs of the United Kingdom of more than one year's standing, having not less than twenty-four members each, and of members elected as hereinafter provided.

(*b.*) No coursing club shall elect more than two representatives ; and should any club fail to hold a coursing meeting for two consecutive seasons, that club shall cease to send representative members.*

(*c.*) The National Coursing Club may elect as members of the club (the number of members so elected not to exceed twenty-five) any well-known supporters of public coursing who have been proposed and seconded by two members of the National Coursing Club at either of the club meetings held in London or Liverpool. Members are elected by the National Coursing Club for five years, and are eligible for re-election. A month's notice must be given to the secretary of the names of candidates for election to the National Coursing Club, with their addresses, and the names of their proposers and seconders, before they can come up for ballot. The election shall be by ballot, in which one black ball in seven will exclude. If a quorum of members be not present, then the election shall stand over till the next meeting of the National Coursing Club. The secretary shall insert in the notice of business to be transacted at the ordinary meetings of the National Coursing Club the name of any candidate for election to the National Coursing Club, with his address, and the names of his proposer and seconder.

(*d.*) The National Coursing Club shall annually, on the day of entry for the Waterloo Cup, elect two of its members as president and secretary. At all its meetings seven shall be a quorum.

(*e.*) Ten members, elected by the coursing clubs, shall retire annually, in the regular rotation of their clubs ; and the secretary shall, on or before the 1st of September in each year, give notice to the clubs whose turn it is to elect representatives. Returns of the various representatives, so elected, shall be sent to the secretary on or before the 1st of January in each year. Vacancies in the representation of coursing clubs shall be filled up by those clubs respectively.

---

* By a season is meant from September 1st to April 1st inclusive.

(*f.*) Coursing clubs desirous of joining the National Coursing Club must send evidence of their qualification to the secretary. All clubs having joined must contribute their *quota* towards the expenses, and any club failing to do so will be disqualified from returning members to the National Coursing Club. At the Summer Meeting, in each year, a statement of expenses shall be submitted to the secretary, and the contribution required from each club shall be fixed.

(*g.*) Every coursing meeting shall, unless the contrary be declared by the programme of an open meeting or by club rules, be subject to all the rules and regulations of the National Coursing Club. Every question or matter in dispute connected with coursing can be brought before the National Coursing Club for its decision.

(*h.*) The National Coursing Club may, if it thinks fit, refer the examination of any case brought before the club to a committee consisting of not less than three members. Every such committee shall make a written report to the secretary, to be laid before the National Coursing Club for its approval.

(*i.*) Every decision of the National Coursing Club shall be final, unless either party within six months shall apply for a re-hearing, on the ground that evidence will be adduced which was not procurable at the previous hearing: and the National Coursing Club may order that the expenses attending any case or matter in dispute brought before it shall be borne by the parties interested as the National Coursing Club may direct.

(*j.*) The secretary shall place on record in the minutes of the business of the National Coursing Club, and shall send to the keeper of the Stud-Book, and make public, every case brought before the National Coursing Club, with the decision arrived at.

(*k.*) Meetings for the despatch of business, for the revision or alteration of rules, and for the election of members shall be held in London on the last Wednesday in June, and in Liverpool on the day of entry for the Waterloo Cup. The secretary, upon a requisition addressed to him in writing by any three stewards of a meeting held under the National Coursing Club rules, or by six public coursers, members of an established coursing club, may call a special meeting of the National Coursing Club at such time and place as the president may appoint.

(*l.*) All cases arising in Ireland or Scotland, where evidence is required to be taken, shall be heard by the National Coursing Club at its meetings in Liverpool.

(*m.*) A month's notice must be given to the secretary of any business or proposed alteration of rules before it can be discussed at an ordinary meeting of the National Coursing Club; and at a special meeting nothing but the special business for which the meeting was called can be brought before it.

SECT. III.—CODE OF RULES OF THE NATIONAL COURSING CLUB.

1. THE SECRETARY AND STEWARDS.—For any proposed open meeting a committee of not less than three shall be formed, who, with the secretary, shall settle preliminaries. The management of the meeting shall be entrusted to this committee, in conjunction with stewards who shall be elected by the subscribers present on the first evening of a meeting. The stewards alone shall decide any disputed question, by a majority of those present, subject to an appeal to the National Coursing Club. The secretary, if honorary, shall be a member of

committee and a steward *ex officio.* No steward shall have a right to vote in any case relating to his own dogs. The secretary shall declare, on or before the evening preceding the last day's running, how the prizes are to be divided, and shall give a statement of expenses if called upon to do so by any six of the subscribers within fourteen days after the meeting.

2. ELECTION OF JUDGE.—The judge may either be appointed by the secretary and committee acting under Rule 1, in which case his name shall be announced simultaneously with the meeting, or elected by the votes of the subscribers taking nominations; but each subscriber shall have only one vote, whatever the number of his nominations. Not less than ten days' notice of the day of election shall be given to the subscribers, and the appointment shall be published at least a fortnight before the meeting. The names of the subscribers voting, with the votes given by them, shall be recorded in a book open to the inspection of the stewards, who shall declare the number of votes for each judge, if called upon to do so by any of the subscribers. When a judge is prevented from attending or finishing a meeting, the committee and the stewards (if appointed) shall have the power of deciding what is to be done.

3. DESCRIPTION OF ENTRY.—Every subscriber to a stake must name his dog before the time fixed for closing the entry, giving the names (the running names, if they had any) of the sire and dam of the dog entered. The secretary shall publish on the cards the names of those who are subscribers but do not comply with these conditions. These nominations shall not be drawn, but must be paid for. For Produce Stakes the names, pedigrees, ages, and colours, and distinguishing marks of puppies, shall be detailed in writing to the secretary of a meeting at the time of the original entry. Every subscriber must also, if required, state in writing to the secretary, before or during the meeting for which such entry is made, the names and addresses of the parties who reared his puppies; and any puppy whose marks and pedigree shall be proved not to correspond with the entry given shall be disqualified, and the whole of its stakes or winnings forfeited. No greyhound is to be considered a puppy which was whelped before the 1st of January of the year preceding the commencement of the season of running. A sapling is a greyhound whelped on or after the 1st of January of the year in which the season of running commenced.

4. The colours, sex, names, pedigrees, and ages of all greyhounds, with the names of their owners and the owners of their sires and dams, shall be registered in a Greyhound Stud-Book. The registration fee shall be one shilling for each dog registered on or before the 1st of July, and a double fee shall be charged for registration of all greyhounds (other than saplings) after that date to the end of the coursing season immediately following. Any owner may, by payment of £1 annually, compound for the registration of any number of greyhounds *bonâ fide* his own property. The keeper of the Stud-Book shall give a receipt for the registration fee of every greyhound, which shall be called a certificate of registration.

5. The Greyhound Stud-Book shall be published, under the authority of the National Coursing Club, on the first day of September, or as soon after as possible.

6. Applications for registration of greyhounds shall be made on or before the first day of July, and registrations applied for subsequent to that date that do not appear in the Stud-Book of that year will appear in that of the following year.

7. If the same name has been given to more than one greyhound, the keeper of the Stud-Book shall give priority to the dog first registered, and shall add to every other such name, except the one first registered, a numeral, commencing with II.

8. All greyhounds whose names do not appear in the Stud-Book, or whose owners cannot produce a certificate of registration from the keeper of the Stud-Book on being required to do so by a steward or the secretary of any coursing meeting, shall be disqualified, and shall forfeit all entry moneys which may have been paid, and any stake or prize or share of any stake or prize won at such meeting, and such entry moneys, stake, or prize, or share thereof, won by any dog so disqualified shall be disposed of as provided by Rule 37 applicable to disqualification.

9. PAYMENT OF ENTRY MONEY.—All moneys due for nominations taken must be paid at or before the time fixed for closing the entry, whether the stakes fill or not, and although, from insufficient description or any other cause, the dogs named may be disqualified. No entry shall be valid unless the amount due for it has been paid in full. For all Produce and other stakes where a forfeit is payable no declaration is necessary; the non-payment of the remainder of the entry money at the time fixed for that purpose is to be considered a declaration of forfeit. The secretary is to be responsible for the entry money of all dogs whose names appear upon the card.

10. ALTERATION OF NAME.—If any subscriber should enter a greyhound by a different name from that in which it shall have last been entered to run in public, or shall have been registered in the Stud-Book, he shall give notice of the alteration to the secretary at the time of entry, and the secretary shall place on the card both the late and the present names of the dog, and this must be done at all meetings at which the dog runs throughout the coursing season in which the alteration has been made. If notice of the alteration be not given, the dog shall be disqualified. The new name must be registered before the dog can run under it.

11. PREFIX OF "Ns."—Any subscriber taking an entry in a stake must prove to the satisfaction of the stewards, if called upon by them to do so, that any greyhound entered by him without the prefix of the word "Names" is *bonâ fide* his own property. If a subscriber enters a dog, not his own property, without putting "Ns" after his own name, the dog so entered shall be disqualified. Every subscriber shall, if requested, deliver in writing to the secretary of the meeting the name of the *bonâ fide* owner of the greyhound named by him, and this communication is to be produced should any dispute arise. No dog purchased or procured for a less time than the entire period still remaining of its public running, or belonging to two or more persons, unless they are declared confederates, shall be held as *bonâ fide* the property of a subscriber. The names of confederates must be registered with the keeper of the Stud-Book—fee, 1s. for each name. Assumed names must also be registered with the keeper of the Stud-Book—fee, five guineas.

12. DEATH OF A SUBSCRIBER.—The death of a subscriber shall only affect his nominations if it occur before the draw, in which case, subject to the exceptions stated below, they shall be void, whether the entries have been made or not; and any money received for forfeits or stakes shall be returned, less the proportion of expenses when the amount has been advertised, and when the

nominations rendered vacant are not filled by other subscribers. If he has parted with all interest in the nominations, and dogs not his property are entered and paid for, such entries shall not subsequently be disturbed. When dogs that have been entered in Produce Stakes change owners, with their engagements and with their forfeits paid, the then owner, if entitled to run them in those stakes, shall not be prevented from doing so by reason of the death of the former owner.

13. DRAW.—Immediately before the greyhounds are drawn at any meeting, and before nine o'clock on every subsequent evening during the continuance of such meeting, the time and place of putting the first brace of dogs into the slips on the following morning shall be declared. A card or counter bearing a corresponding number shall be assigned to each entry. These numbered cards or counters shall then be placed together and drawn indiscriminately. This classification, once made, shall not be disturbed throughout the meeting, except for the purpose of guarding or on account of byes.

14. GUARDING.—When two or more nominations in a stake are taken in one name, the greyhounds, if bonâ fide the property of the same owner, shall be guarded throughout. This is always to be arranged, as far as possible, by bringing up dogs from below to meet those which are to be guarded. This guarding is not, however, to deprive any dog of a natural bye to which he may be entitled, either in the draw or in running through the stake. Dogs whose position has been altered in consequence of guarding or of byes must return to their original position in the next round, if guarding does not prevent it.

15. BYES.—A natural bye shall be given to the lowest available dog in each round. No dog shall run a second such bye in any stake, unless it is unavoidable. When a dog is entitled to a bye, either natural or accidental, his owner or nominator may run any greyhound he pleases to assist in the course, provided always that in Sapling Stakes only a sapling may be used, and in Puppy Stakes none older than a puppy. But if it is proved to the satisfaction of the stewards that no sapling or puppy respectively can be found to run an accidental bye, an older dog may be used. No dog shall run any bye earlier than his position on the card entitles him to do. The slip and the course in a bye shall be the same as in a course in which a decision is required, and the judge shall decide whether enough has been done to constitute a course or whether it must be run again, and in the latter case the judge shall give the order. If at the commencement of any round in a stake one dog in each course of that round has a bye, those byes shall not be run, but the dogs shall take their places for the next round as if the byes had been run. A bye must be run before a dog can claim the advantage of it.

16. SLIP-STEWARD.—The committee of an open meeting and the members of a club meeting shall appoint, on the first evening of a meeting, a slip-steward, whose duty shall be to see that every greyhound is brought to slips in its proper turn, to report to the stewards without delay any greyhound that does not come to the slips in time, and any act on the part of the slipper, nominators, or their representatives which he may consider should be brought to their knowledge. If a nominator or his representative should refuse to comply with the directions of the slip-steward, or should use abusive and insulting language towards him, the stewards may inflict a penalty not exceeding £2 on the person so offending.

17. POSTPONEMENT OF MEETING.—A meeting appointed to take place on a certain day may, if a majority of the committee and the stewards (if appointed) consider the weather unfit for coursing, be postponed from day to day ; but if the running does not commence within the current week all nominations shall be void, and the expenses shall be paid by the subscribers, in proportion to the value of nominations taken by each. In the case of Produce Stakes, however, the original entries shall continue binding, if the meeting is held at a later period of the season

18. TAKING DOGS TO THE SLIPS.—Every dog must be brought to the slips in its proper turn, without delay, under a penalty of £1. If absent for more than ten minutes (according to the report of the slip steward or of one of the stewards), its opponent shall be entitled to claim the course, subject to the discretion of the stewards, and shall in that case run a bye. If both dogs be absent at the expiration of ten minutes, the stewards shall have power to disqualify both dogs, or to fine their owners any sum not exceeding £5 each. The nominator is answerable for his dog being put into the slips at the right time, on the right side, and against the right dog. No allowance shall be made for mistakes. No dog shall be put into the slips for a deciding course until thirty minutes after its course in the previous round without the consent of its owner. (*See* Rule 31.)

19. CONTROL OF DOGS IN SLIPS.—The control of all matters connected with slipping the greyhounds shall rest with the stewards of a meeting. Owners or servants, after delivering their dogs into the hands of the slipper, may follow close after them, but not so as to inconvenience the slipper, or in any way interfere with the dogs, under a penalty of £1. Neither must they holloa them on while running, under the same penalty. Any greyhound found to be beyond control in slips may, by order of the stewards, be taken out of the slips and disqualified.

20. GREYHOUNDS OF SAME COLOUR TO WEAR COLLARS.—When two greyhounds drawn together are of the same colour they shall each wear a collar, and the owners shall be subject to a penalty of 10s. for non-observance of this rule. The colour of the collar shall be red for the left-hand side and white for the right-hand side of the slips. The upper dog on the card must be placed on the left hand, and the lower dog on the right hand of the slips.

21. The order to slip may be given by the judge or the slip-steward, or the stewards of a meeting may leave the slip to the sole discretion of the slipper. The length of slip must necessarily vary with the nature of the ground, but should never be less than from three to four score yards, and must be maintained of one uniform length, as far as possible, throughout each stake.

22. THE SLIPPER.—If one greyhound gets out of the slips the slipper shall not let the other go. In any case of slips breaking, and either or both dogs getting away in consequence, the slipper may be fined not exceeding £1, at the discretion of the stewards.

23. The judge shall be subject to the general rules which may be established by the National Coursing Club for his guidance. He shall, on the termination of each course, immediately deliver his decision aloud, and shall not recall or reverse his decision, on any pretext whatever, after it has been declared ; but no decision shall be delivered until the judge is perfectly satisfied that the course is absolutely terminated.

24. The judge shall decide all courses upon the one uniform principle that the

greyhound which does most towards killing the hare during the continuance of the course is to be declared the winner. The principle is to be carried out by estimating the value of the work done by each greyhound, as seen by the judge, upon a balance of points according to the scale hereafter laid down, from which also are to be deducted certain specified allowances and penalties.

25.—The points of the course are—

(a.) *Speed*—which shall be estimated as one, two, or three points, according to the degree of superiority shown. [See definition below (a).]

(b.) *The Go-bye.*—Two points, or if gained on the outer circle, three points.

(c.) *The Turn.*—One point.

(d.) *The Wrench.*—Half a point.

(e.) *The Kill.*—Two points, or, in a descending scale, in proportion to the degree of merit displayed in that kill, which may be of no value.

(f.) *The Trip.*—One point.

DEFINITION OF POINTS.

(a.) In estimating the value of speed to the hare the judge must take into account the several forms in which it may be displayed, viz. :—

1. Where in the run up a clear lead is gained by one of the dogs, in which case one, two, or three points may be given, according to the length of lead, apart from the score for a turn or wrench. In awarding these points the judge shall take into consideration the merit of a lead obtained by a dog which has lost ground at the start, either from being unsighted or from a bad slip, or which has had to run the outer circle.

2. Where one greyhound leads the other so long as the hare runs straight, but loses the lead from her bending round decidedly in favour of the slower dog of her own accord, in which case the one greyhound shall score one point for the speed shown, and the other dog score one point for the first turn.

3. Under no circumstances is speed without subsequent work to be allowed to decide a course, except where great superiority is shown by one greyhound over another in a long lead to covert.

If a dog, after gaining the first six points, still keeps possession of the hare by superior speed, he shall have double the prescribed allowance for the subsequent points made before his opponent begins to score.

(b.) *The Go-Bye* is where a greyhound starts a clear length behind his opponent, and yet passes him in a straight run, and gets a clear length before him.

(c.) *The Turn* is where the hare is brought round at not less than a right angle from her previous line.

(d.) *The Wrench* is where the hare is bent from her line at less than a right angle; but where she only leaves her line to suit herself, and not from the greyhound pressing her, nothing is to be allowed.

(e.) *The Merit of a Kill* must be estimated according to whether a greyhound, by his own superior dash and skill, bears the hare; whether he picks her up through any little accidental circumstances favouring him; or whether she is turned into his mouth, as it were, by the other greyhound.

(f.) *The Trip*, or unsuccessful effort to kill, is where the hare is thrown off her legs, or where a greyhound flecks her, but cannot hold her.

26. The following allowances shall be made for accidents to a greyhound

during a course; but in every case they shall only be deducted from the other dog's score :—

(*a.*) For losing ground at the start, either from being unsighted, or from a bad slip, in which case the judge is to decide what amount of allowance is to be made, on the principle that the score of the foremost dog is not to begin until the second has had an opportunity of joining in the course, and the judge may decide the course or declare the course to be an undecided or no course, as he may think fit.

(*b.*) Where a hare bears very decidedly in favour of one of the greyhounds, after the first or subsequent turns, in which case the next point shall not be scored by the dog unduly favoured, or only half his points allowed, according to circumstances. No greyhound shall receive any allowance for a fall or an accident, with the exception of being ridden over by the owner of the competing greyhound or his servant, provided for by Rule 30, or when pressing his hare, in which case his opponent shall not count the next point made.

27. Penalties are as follow :—

(*a.*) Where a greyhound, from his own defect, refuses to follow the hare at which he is slipped, he shall lose the course.

(*b.*) Where a dog wilfully stands still in a course, or departs from directly pursuing the hare, no points subsequently made by him shall be scored; and if the points made by him up to that time be just equal to those made by his antagonist in the whole course, he shall thereby lose the course; but where one or both dogs stop with the hare in view, through inability to continue the course, it shall be decided according to the number of points gained by each dog during the whole course.

(*c.*) If a dog refuses to fence where the other fences, any points subsequently made by him are not to be scored; but if he does his best to fence, and is foiled by sticking in a meuse, the course shall end there. When the points are equal, the superior fencer shall win the course.

28. If a second hare be started during a course, and one of the dogs follow her, the course shall end there.

29. GREYHOUND GETTING LOOSE.—Any person allowing a greyhound to get loose and join in a course which is being run shall be fined £1. If the loose greyhound belong to either of the owners of the dogs engaged in the particular course, such owner shall forfeit his chance of the stake with the dog then running, unless he can prove, to the satisfaction of the stewards, that he had not been able to get the loose greyhound taken up after running its own course. The course is not to be considered as necessarily ended when a third dog joins in.

30. RIDING OVER A GREYHOUND.—If any subscriber, or his servant, shall ride over his opponent's greyhound while running a course, the owner of the dog so ridden over shall (although the course be given against him) be deemed the winner of it, or shall have the option of allowing the other dog to remain and run out the stake, and in such case shall be entitled to half its winnings.

31. A "no course" is when by accident or by the shortness of the course the dogs are not tried together, and if one be then drawn the other must run a bye, unless the judge on being appealed to shall decide that he has done work enough to be exempted from it. An undecided course is where the judge considers the merits of the dogs equal; and if either is then drawn, the other cannot be required to run a bye; but the owners must at the time declare which dog remains in. (*See* Rule 33.) The judge shall signify the distinction between a

"no course" and an "undecided" by taking off his hat in the latter case only. After an "undecided" or "no course," if the dogs before being taken up get on another or the same hare, the judge must follow, and shall decide in favour of one if he considers that there has been a sufficient trial to justify his doing so. A "no course" or an "undecided" may be run off immediately, if claimed on behalf of both dogs before the next brace are put into the slips, or in case of "no course," if so ordered by the judge ; otherwise it shall be run again after the two next courses, unless it stand over till the next morning, when it shall be the first course run ; if it is the last course of the day, fifteen minutes shall be allowed after both dogs are taken up.

32. The judge shall render an explanation of any decision only to the stewards of the meeting if required, through them, before the third succeeding course, by the owner, or nominator, or representative of the owner or nominator, of either of the greyhounds engaged in the course. The stewards shall, if requested to do so, express their opinion whether the explanation is satisfactory or not, and their opinion in writing may be asked for and published afterwards ; but the decision of the judge, once given, shall not be reversed for any cause.

33. WITHDRAWAL OF A DOG.—If a dog be withdrawn from any stake on the field, its owner, or some one having his authority, must at once give notice to the secretary or flag or slip steward. If the dog belongs to either of these officials, the notice must be given to the other. When after a "no course" or an "undecided" one of the greyhounds has been officially drawn, and the dogs are again, by mistake, put into slips and run a course, the arrangement come to shall stand, whatever the judge's decision may be, and all bets on the course shall be void.

34. IMPUGNING JUDGE.—If any subscriber, owner, or any other person proved to be interested, openly impugns the decision of the judge on the ground except by a complaint to the stewards, according to Rule 32, he shall forfeit not more than £5, nor less than £2, at the discretion of the stewards.

35. STAKES NOT RUN OUT.—When two greyhounds remain in for the deciding course, the stakes shall be considered divided if they belong to the same owner, or to confederates, and also if the owner of one of the two dogs induces the owner of the other to draw him for any payment or consideration ; but if one of the two be drawn without payment or consideration, from lameness, or from any cause clearly affecting his chance of winning, the other may be declared the winner, the facts of the case being clearly proved to the satisfaction of the stewards. The same rule shall apply when more than two dogs remain in at the end of a stake which is not run out ; and in case of a division between three or more dogs, of which two or more belong to the same owner, these latter shall be held to take equal shares of the total amount received by their owner in a division. When there is a compulsory division all greyhounds remaining in the class that is being run, even where one is entitled to a bye, shall take equal shares. The terms of any arrangement to divide winnings, and the amount of any money given to induce the owner of a dog to draw him, must be declared to the secretary.

36. WINNERS OF STAKES RUNNING TOGETHER.—If two or more greyhounds shall each win a stake, and have to run together for a final prize or challenge cup, should they not have run an equal number of ties in their respective stakes, the greyhound which has run the smaller number of courses must run a bye, or byes, to put itself upon an equality in this respect with its opponent.

37. OBJECTIONS.—An objection to a greyhound may be made to any one of the stewards of a meeting at any time before the stakes are paid over, upon the objector lodging in the hands of such steward, or the secretary, the sum of £5, which shall be forfeited if the objection proves frivolous, or if he shall not bring the case before the next meeting of the National Coursing Club, or give notice to the stewards previous thereto of his intention to withdraw the objection. The owner of the greyhound objected to must deposit equally the sum of £5 and prove the correctness of his entry. Expenses in consequence of an objection shall be borne as the National Coursing Club may direct. Should an objection be made which cannot at the time be substantiated or disproved, the greyhound may be allowed to run under protest, the stewards retaining the winnings until the objection has been withdrawn, or heard and decided. If the greyhound objected to be disqualified, the amount to which he would otherwise have been entitled shall be divided equally among the dogs beaten by him; and if a piece of plate or prize has been added, and won by him, only the dogs which he beat in the several rounds shall have a right to contend for it.

38. DEFAULTERS.—No person shall be allowed to enter or run a greyhound, in his own or any other person's name, who is a defaulter for either stakes, forfeits, or bets, or for money due under an arrangement for a division of winnings, or for penalties regularly imposed for the infraction of rules by the stewards of any meeting, or for any payment required by a decision of the National Coursing Club, or for subscriptions due to any club entitled to have representatives in the National Coursing Club. As regards bets, however, this rule shall only apply when a complaint is lodged with the secretary of the National Coursing Club within six months after the bet becomes due. On receipt of such complaint the secretary shall give notice of the claim to the person against whom it is made, with a copy of this rule; and if he shall not pay the bet, or appear before the next meeting of the National Coursing Club and resist the claim successfully, he shall be considered a defaulter.

39. JUDGE OR SLIPPER INTERESTED.—If a judge or slipper be in any way interested in the winnings of a greyhound or greyhounds, the owner and nominator in each case, unless they can prove satisfactorily that such interest was without their cognisance, shall forfeit all claim to the winnings, and the dog shall be disqualified; and if any nominator or owner of greyhounds shall give, offer, or lend money, or anything of value, to any judge or slipper, such owner or nominator shall not be allowed to run dogs in his own or any other person's name during any subsequent period that the National Coursing Club may decide upon.

40. Any person who is proved to the satisfaction of the National Coursing Club to have been guilty of any fraudulent or discreditable conduct in connection with coursing may, in addition to any pecuniary penalty to which he may be liable, be declared incapable of running or entering a greyhound in his own or any other person's name during any subsequent period that the National Coursing Club may decide upon; and any dogs under his care, training, management, or superintendence shall be disqualified during such subsequent period.

41. BETS.—All bets upon an undecided course shall stand, unless one of the greyhounds be drawn. All bets upon a dog running farther than another in the stake shall be p.p., whatever accident may happen. Bets upon a deciding, as upon every other, course are off if the course is not run. Long odds bets shall

be void unless the greyhound the bet refers to shall run one course in the stake, other than a bye, after the bet is made. Long odds bets, with this exception, shall be p.p.

42. BETS ON STAKES DIVIDED.—Where money has been laid against a dog winning a stake, and he divides it, the two sums must be put together and divided in the same proportion as the value of the stakes.

DEER-STALKING.

It is needless to dilate upon the employment of the dog in deer-stalking, as his perfection depends entirely upon his amount of experience and the degree of nose and sagacity which he naturally possesses, and, moreover, he is seldom used.

HUNTING.

Fox-hunting has now become a science in itself, and it would be useless to attempt any minute detail here of all the features which attend upon it. I have already alluded at some length to the duties and peculiarities of the foxhound, in the description of the hound himself at page 48, and of the mode of entering him at page 48, beyond which I must refer my readers to the pages of Beckford and Somerville, among the old authorities, and to "Nimrod," Colonel Cooke, the Hon. Grantley Berkeley, Mr. Delmé Radcliffe, and lastly "Scrutator," among the modern writers on this subject. A treatise on Hunting must comprise at least as large a volume as the present, and, therefore, I may well be excused from going into it. For the same reason hare-hunting, both with harriers and beagles, must be passed over, as well as otter-hunting, beyond the notices which are given of the hounds used in these sports.

THE USE OF THE DOG IN SHOOTING.

The dogs used in aid of the gun are—the pointer, and the setter in grouse and partridge shooting; the spaniel, beagle and terrier in covert-shooting; either of the above in snipe-shooting; and water-spaniel or retriever in wildfowl-shooting.

GROUSE AND PARTRIDGE SHOOTING.

In open shooting, whether of the grouse or partridge, there is a great difference of opinion respecting the choice of a dog, that is, whether the pointer or setter shall be selected, and, if either, the particular breed. In order to arrive at any conclusion on this *quæstio vexata*, it is desirable to consider what are the chief differences between the two kinds of shooting, and also between the two kinds of dog which have to beat the respective grounds on which partridge and grouse are found. Every sportsman knows that the former are chiefly met with in cultivated cornlands, and especially on a light sandy soil suited to barley, such as that of Norfolk and part of Suffolk. Here these birds are preserved in immense numbers; and there is no heather, or other rough undergrowth of any kind, to scratch the skin or to wear away the hair on the legs, the only parts which suffer at all being the pads of the feet. Indeed in too many cases, according to my opinion, the dog is dispensed with altogether in actual shooting; and the birds being driven into the turnips by spaniels assisted by a man on horseback, are afterwards walked up by the shooters, who require only a retriever to find the wounded birds. In wilder districts, where the birds are more scarce the pointer or the setter is used, but he is always worked within fifty or sixty yards of his master, and is never on any account suffered to "break fence." Hence the amount of ground beaten is comparatively small, but it is of such a nature, being composed almost entirely of stubble, fallow, or turnips, that it requires a good nose to find game, while at the same time the scent of the partridge is very mild as compared with that of the grouse; on the other hand, this latter bird is found where they are scattered indiscriminately over the heath-covered slopes, and where dogs are essential to success, because there are no turnips or other cover to drive them into, and they are as likely to be on one spot as another. Hence every inch of ground must be beaten, and often a day's sport covers two or three thousand acres, or even more. The scent of the grouse is also stronger than that of the partridge, and from the nature of the heather he is disposed to lie closely, unless made wild by constant disturbance, so that with good dogs he is seldom put up out of shot. The heather is very rough and irritating, and as it works up between the toes it makes the interspaces extremely sore if they are not well covered with hair.

From these varying circumstances it results that a careful dog, not ranging too wide, but going steadily to work, and keeping at it at such a pace as to make sure of not flushing a bird, perfectly steady "before and behind" and "down charge," is the dog for partridge-shooting; while a wider ranger, with perhaps a trifle less delicacy of nose, will be preferred for grouse-shooting, especially if he will last for a longer time at his work, and will bear the constant friction of the heather. Now, it is clear to every one who has had much experience of the two kinds of dog, that the pointer has the more delicate nose; for though some setters may compete with any pointer in this particular, yet, on the whole, the average of setters are inferior to the average of pointers in powers of scent. The pointer is also more easily broken, and when perfect, remains so with more certainty; but he has the disadvantage of more readily tiring, and his toes sooner become sore if used in heather. On the whole, therefore, though there are numerous exceptions, the pointer is more suited to partridge-shooting, and the setter to grouse. If, however, the sportsman has a fancy for or against either, and selects the smooth dog for the moors, he should fix upon a strong coarse-haired dog, and those with a cross of the foxhound seem to be generally preferred; but they have some of the disadvantages of the setter, being much more difficult to break than the genuine pointer, but are far more hardy and enduring. Indeed some of this breed will beat the setter in pace and endurance; while the nose of the hound, being as good as that of the pointer, or nearly so, does not lower the power of scent, but it has a tendency to make the dog lose that fine handsome range which the true breed possess, as displayed in the high carriage of the head when at work, which is so beautiful to the eye of the sportsman. With regard to the peculiar breed of each which is to be selected, I should advise the modern pointer without the foxhound cross (or if any, very remote), taking care that there is endurance enough to carry the dog through a good day's shooting. On the average, few pointers will beat as they should do for more than four or six hours, and even this amount of work cannot be maintained for many days together. I have had one or two dogs which no one man could tire, but these were light greyhound-like animals; and though they could do wonders on a good scenting day, they were useless on a dry September afternoon, without any wind stirring. It is true that few dogs will find game on such a day; but there are some which will reduce their pace accordingly, and these are generally to be found among the true pointers, bred with as large heads as possible consistently with the possession of frames suited to go through their work. They need not be very fast, but they should keep at their work steadily, and in that way will cover a vast deal of ground in a short time, never flushing even a single bird, and rarely leaving one behind them. Such a dog, if well matched with another, is the one to kill game to; and if the sportsman will only give the brace time to try their ground, and will avoid spoiling them by running into wounded birds and other indiscretions, he will find that for all kinds of open shooting they are invaluable. Irish setters are thought very highly of by some people; but those which I have used have been headstrong and unruly, while I never found any superiority in their noses; nor is their endurance, as far as I have seen, greater than that of our best English breeds. With a dog formed like the animal from which the engraving of the Irish setter was taken, great endurance may be expected, and his nose was equal to any emergency. The Russian setter I know very little of, so can give no reliable opinion on his merits.

In conducting the beat, whether for partridge or grouse, it is always desirable to give these dogs the wind, inasmuch as they generally find their game by the scent wafted to them in the air, and not by the foot-scent. Sometimes they are obliged to "road" a running bird, especially with grouse, which will often take the pointer or setter a long way, and a stupidly stiff old-fashioned pointer which refuses to stir is an abomination. Nothing is more annoying than to see birds get up far out of shot, while the pointer is "steady as a crutch" at his first point, where he caught the scent and where they started from. A sensible dog would either have drawn up to his birds after waiting till his master was close up, or he would have left his point and gone round to head them if he was unusually clever in his vocation. Such a feat is by no means unattainable, if dogs are broken to beat *towards* the shooter as explained at page 294; but some stupid brutes will never learn to do it of their own accord, and must be sent round by their master, which causes delay and takes away half the advantage of the plan. Beyond a repetition of the cautions as to making the dog work to hand and keeping him steady " down charge," there is little more to be said on the use of the pointer and setter. In driving, whether of the partridge or grouse, two dogs are used, as far as the gun is concerned.

SNIPE-SHOOTING.

The following observations on snipe-shooting in Ireland, by an Irish sportsman, recently appeared in the columns of *The Field*; and as the writer has had far more experience in this department of sport than I can lay claim to, I prefer introducing these extracts to inserting the results of my own experience, which, however, are strictly in accordance with his :—

" In Ireland the best sportsmen do not commence snipe-shooting until the November frosts set in. This is sometimes considered an old-fashioned prejudice ; but there are good reasons why it should be postponed until that season ; for, although the birds bred here are in good condition in September, or even earlier, they do not, except to the mere tyro, afford anything like the same sport. Instead of the ringing scream and rapid eccentric flight with which they dart away from the shooter through the thin frosty air of a winter's day, they flutter up with a faint cry from his feet, fly straight forward, and pitch almost immediately ; while, to the gourmand, the difference in flavour between a bird placed on the table in September and December is almost as great as between a spent salmon and one fresh run from the sea. On the other hand, those birds which arrive here in October, during the equinoctial gales, are so thin and worn out with their long flight as scarcely to be worth powder and shot.

" In shooting these birds, with or without a dog, it is always better to hunt down the wind, as, unless it is blowing a hurricane, they always fly against it. By this means the sportsman will get two shots for one he would otherwise obtain. The popular idea that the slightest graze will bring down a snipe is, like many popular ideas, a fallacy ; no bird requires more careful marking. After being fired at, I have known them fly nearly out of sight when shot clean through the body, and then drop suddenly dead. This happens most frequently when very light shot has been used ; and for that reason I would always recommend the shooter to load the second barrel with No. 6 shot. It has another advantage. He will often meet hares, teal, and duck at distances where his light shot would be thrown away ; and it is well to be prepared for them. If a snipe stops screaming and stoops in his flight after being fired at, it is a pretty good sign that he is hit hard. If his legs drop he is mortally wounded, and will never fly far.

" In some marshes snipe are very wild, rising in wisps, before you can come within range. This generally occurs when the ground is wet, and the birds are sitting upon the little hillocks above the water. In such cases the dog should be tied up, and the sportsman ought to walk them up alone. If this does not succeed, the only chance left is to stand (under cover if possible)

Y

at the windward end of the bog, and send the attendant in to leeward, with directions to make as little noise as possible ; by this means a few shots may be obtained, and you will have an opportunity of, perhaps, marking some of the birds down in more favourable ground. At all events, there is the chance of meeting them when scattered through the country.

"Many an old Irish sportsman will smile at the idea of any person giving directions for finding snipe. Until the last few seasons they have been so numerous that all he had to do was to walk into the first marsh and blaze away until the light failed or his ammunition was expended. What with severe and long-continued frosts, however, drainage and other 'dreadful inventions of science,' as one of your correspondents terms agricultural improvements, we are not (except in a few happily situated Alsatias) so sure of a good bag as we were ; it may, therefore, be worth the shooter's while to study the habits of these birds. Indeed, every sportsman ought to be something of a 'field naturalist,' as it gives him an additional enjoyment in his favourite sport.

"The state of the weather is, I believe, the great clue to the haunts of the snipe, their delicate organisation making them peculiarly sensitive to atmospheric influences. At the first breath of the autumn frosts those birds which have been bred upon the mountains leave their summer quarters, and come down to the vast bogs which still abound in some parts of our island. Here they are soon joined by their comrades from Scotland and the North of Europe, who rapidly recover from the effects of their long flight ; and from that time forward, until the arrival of spring scatters them again, their life is one constant succession of changes from one part of the country to another, moving towards the sea-shore, the mountains, or inland, according as the season is mild or severe.

"In very mild wet weather snipe leave the bogs and return to the mountains, where it is scarcely worth the sportsman's while to follow them. With a good dog, however, fair sport can be had at such times by beating rushy, coarse pastures and heathery uplands, where he will be sure to find a considerable number of outlying birds. In this description of ground they lie well to a dog, and are much easier to shoot than in the bogs, where the unsteadiness of footing makes it difficult to take accurate aim.

"I have always found northerly winds with hail-showers the best weather for the marshes. The hail drives the birds down from the mountains, collects them together, and makes them unwilling to rise. In white frosts they are generally wild, though numerous ; in hard black frosts they assemble in wisps about the margin of unfrozen springs, along the borders of streams, or in marshes near the shore. Bent grass is also a favourite haunt at such times, as frost has seldom any effect upon it. Should the severe weather continue, they take to the plantations like woodcocks, to furze-covers on southern slopes, and to the rocks on the shore.

"Snipe are very restless at night, but, unless disturbed, seldom move in the daytime. During bright moonlight nights they travel a great deal, and are fond of feeding on the sea-shore. Walking along the coast at such times, I have put them up in dozens, and even in daylight have shot them on a strand. In beating a marsh near the sea I have always been least successful when the tide was out, which I could only account for by the supposition that the birds were then feeding upon the strand.

"In some districts in Ireland there are what are called black and red bogs. The sportsman will sometimes find them in one and sometimes in the other, *never* in both together. I cannot account for this, as the weather does not appear to be the cause ; at least, I could not observe any marked change.

"Almost any dog can be trained to set snipe. Water-spaniels and New-foundlands have been known to do it ; and I once shot for part of a season over a little Dinmont terrier. But the dog of all dogs for that sport—or indeed any sport—is the old Irish setter, when he can be got pure. Handsome, courageous, hardy, and delighting in water, he is (as an old gamekeeper remarked to me once) 'a companion for any gentleman.' The dropper is also a capital dog for general purposes in a wet country. One of the finest animals I ever saw of this kind was the produce of a cross between a Russian and a smooth pointer. They are, however, difficult to train and curiously ugly. The smooth pointer should never be used in snipe-shooting. They have a natural dislike to the water, and although their high breeding and courage make them disregard it when in pursuit of game, any one who has seen them cowering at their master's heels after a hard day's work on a cold wintry day cannot but feel compassion for these noble animals.

"In training dogs for snipe-shooting they should be broken as much as possible to 'hand.' Shouting or talking in a bog ought always to be avoided ; more birds will be sprung in that way than by the report of the gun. No dog that splashes through the water, or with bad feet, should be used for snipe. It is in his peculiar style of going that the old Irish setter shows his supe-riority to all other dogs for this sport ; not pottering or plowtering among the reeds, like a tame drake, but moving through the marsh with a long, light, stealthy pace, like a panther in search of prey.

"The system of training dogs in Ireland is, generally speaking, very bad—in fact, cannot well be worse. Three guineas and a hundredweight of meal is the usual charge ; and for this you will get plenty of so-called gamekeepers and trainers willing to undertake the duty. I do not object to the price, which is moderate enough, if the duty was properly performed ; but do object, and very strongly, to the fact that not one grain of the meal ever finds its way to the stomach of the unfortunate animal for whose benefit it was ostensibly bought. This would not suit the trainer's purpose, whose object is to return him 'broken' in the shortest possible time (and broken he certainly is, with a vengeance). This can only be accomplished by fasting and flagellation, and accordingly both are put liberally in requisition ; the former by leaving the dog entirely to his own resources, when the chances are he takes to killing his own mutton ; and the latter, by the unsparing use of the whip or the butt-end of the gun, according as his master is drunk or out of temper. The conse-quences may easily be anticipated. Should he survive this treatment, he is returned at the end of three months, thoroughly cowed and heart-broken, and in such a state of starvation that his owner will have some difficulty in recog-nising his favourite. Should he succeed in getting once more into condition, it will be found that he has forgotten all he ever learned under the former system, and will require to be trained over again.

"I would therefore recommend the sportsman, if he can spare time, by all means to break his own dogs. If he succeeds—and a little patience and temper are all that is required to make success certain—he will be amply repaid, for a dog works far better for the man who trains him than for any one else. A sort of mutual understanding springs up between them ; the dog gets into his master's ways, and a look or a gesture is sufficient to make him comprehend his meaning. Better this, surely, than the constant rating and flagellations, which make it positively painful to go out with some men, who are everlastingly using the whip upon their unhappy slaves.

"If the snipe-shooter wishes to keep his dogs in health and condition, free from coughs and colds, and always fit for work, he must not be above looking after them himself when their day's work is done, instead of handing them over to ignorant or careless servants. Their legs and feet should be well washed in warm water before consigning them to the kennel, which ought to be comfortable and dry, and provided with a liberal allowance of straw. —HENRY CLIVE."

COVERT-SHOOTING.

This kind of shooting is generally carried out by the aid of human beaters, who, either with or without dogs, enter the covert and drive the game to the shooter. Sometimes, however, the sportsman has a train of thoroughly broken spaniels, beagles, or terriers, and with these he goes quietly to work, either making them drive the game to him, or else keeping them at work so close to him, as he walks through the covert, that any game which is disturbed comes within shot. In either case the dogs should be thoroughly under command, as has been explained in the chapter treating of the breaking of them to the gun, and, beyond the remarks there introduced, there is little to be said. A practical acquaintance with each animal is more requisite here than in any other kind of shooting, because the sportsman always is being called upon to judge of the proximity of the dog to his game, and of the kind of game also by his note at the time. Hence practice is all important, and directions are of little avail. The shooter must, however, be quick in his movements in getting to his dogs when they give tongue in a way to lead him to expect that they are close upon their game, or he will get few shots; and in this one of the chief arts of covert-shooting consists. It is, however, useless to attempt any further explanation of its details.

Whether spaniels, beagles, or terriers make the best covert dogs is a point which is sometimes discussed; but I think there is a general feeling in favour of the first, and at present the Clumber spaniel is certainly the fashion. He is more suited to *battues*, which are now the only kinds of covert-shooting much in vogue, for the reason that pheasants will not bear disturbing many times in the season, and so the proprietor of a large preserve likes to give the greatest happiness to the greatest number of his friends on the small number of days which his gamekeeper advises him that he can afford. These spaniels, however, are too heavy for wild woodlands or for cock-shooting, for which the light corky cocker must be employed. But between these two there is little room for the too noisy beagle or the too silent terrier, and they are therefore seldom used, though the last is very useful to the single sportsman who goes quietly poking about in search of a shot.

WILDFOWL-SHOOTING.

As far as the dog is concerned, this kind of sport requires a steady water-spaniel or retriever, with a good nose, and thoroughly accustomed to his work. In river and pond shooting, he will have to find as well as to retrieve the ducks or other kinds of water-fowl which are sought for; but in the marine variety his sole use is to retrieve the dead and crippled birds, which would otherwise be beyond the reach of the shooter. For each kind, however, the power of retrieving is most important, and no one would think of embarking in this sport without a dog thoroughly broken in this respect, or likely to become so. Those who wish to become expert in it, and have no friend or servant able to teach them the various details necessary for its successful prosecution, will do well to consult the pages of Colonel Hawker, who has written most minute instructions for the construction and management of punts, punt guns, &c., in his celebrated work on shooting.

THE USE OF TERRIERS IN FERRETING, RATTING, ETC.

Beyond the necessity for entering these dogs to their game, and breaking them from destroying the ferrets, little can be said on the mode of using them. Some practice is, of course, required to do these things well and successfully, but the oral instructions of a good keeper or ratcatcher are of far more value than all the written directions which can be given.

BOOK III.

THE DISEASES OF THE DOG AND THEIR TREATMENT.

CHAPTER I.

The Skeleton, including the Teeth—The Muscular System—The Brain and Nervous System—The Digestive System—The Heart and Lungs—The Skin.

THE SKELETON,* INCLUDING THE TEETH.

IN the skeleton of the dog, and in that of the horse, as well as of all other animals remarkable for their speed, there is a peculiar formation of the chest which deserves to be noticed. The principle of construction in every *thorax*, as this part is called scientifically, is that of dilatation and contraction, by which its entire contents are lessened or increased, and thereby air is made to pass in and out. In man this is chiefly caused by the front of the chest rising and falling, and in this way increasing the diameter from before backwards, but in the dog, horse, deer, &c., the increase is from side to side, the ribs being sickle-shaped, and acting laterally like the gill-covers of a fish. From this it often arises that a narrow-chested horse or dog may have better wind than another with a round barrel, because he is able to alter the cubic contents of his chest more rapidly, and thus inspire and expire a larger volume of air. A round barrel is nearly at its greatest expansion, and though it can contract it cannot dilate its volume, while the chest that is too flat can expand rapidly, but then it has not the power of contraction beyond its natural limits. A medium transverse diameter is therefore to be desired, and is practically found to de advantageous, in allowing a better action of the shoulder-blades rolling upon the surface on each side. On the other hand, man requires great depth of chest from before

* See next page.

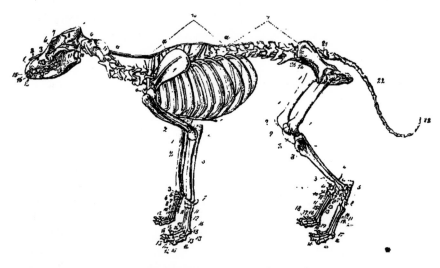

The Skeleton of the Dog.   (Youatt.)

THE HEAD.

1. The intermaxillary bone.
2. Nasal bone.
3. Maxilla superior.
4. Lachrymal bone.
5. Zygomatic bone.
6. Orbit.
7. Frontal bone.
8. Parietal bone.
9, 9. Occipital bone.
10, 10, 10. Temporal bone.

11, 11, 11. Inferior maxillary or jaw bone.
12, 12. Seven inferior maxillary molar teeth.
13, 13. Six molar teeth of the superior jaw.
14. Canine teeth of the superior and inferior jaws.
15. Three incisor teeth of the superior maxillary bone.
16. The three inferior ditto.

THE TRUNK.

a, u, a. The ligamentum nuchæ.
I. II. III. IV. V. VI. VII. The seven vertebræ of the neck.
13. The thirteen dorsal vertebræ.
17. The seven lumbar vertebræ.
21. Os sacrum, or rump-bone.

22, 22. Twenty caudal vertebræ—vertebræ of the tail.
23. The left os innominatum.
24. Right ditto.
The nine true ribs, with their cartilages.
The four false ribs, with their cartilages.

o o. The sternum.

THE LEFT ANTERIOR EXTREMITY.

1. The scapula, or shoulder-blade.
2. Os humeri, or arm-bone.
3. Radius—the lesser bone of the arm.
4. The elbow, or olecranon process of the ulna.
7. Os pisiforme, or pisiform bone.
10. Os metacarpi digiti tertii—the third metacarpal bone.

11. Os metacarpi digiti quarti—fourth metacarpal.
12. Os metacarpi digiti quinti.
13, 13, 13, 13. The first phalanges of the fore-feet.
14, 14, 14, 14. The second ditto.
15. The third ditto.
16. The sesamoid bone.

THE RIGHT ANTERIOR EXTREMITY.

1. Radius.
2. Ulna.
3. Os triquetrum—the triangular bone.
5. Os semilunare—the semilunar bone.
6. Os multangulum majus—the larger multangular bone.
7. Os multangulum minus — the small multangular bone.
8. Os metacarpi pollicis—the thumb.

9. Ossa metacarpi digitorum quatuor —the four bones of the meta-carpus.
10. Phalanx prima pollicis—first phalange of the thumb.
11. Phalanx tertia pollicis—third phalange of ditto.
12. Digiti quatuor—phalanges of the four toes.

THE LEFT POSTERIOR EXTREMITY.

1, 1. Os femoris—thigh-bone.
2. Patella—the knee-pan.
3, 3. Tibia—the shank of the leg.
4, 4. Fibula—the small bone of ditto.
5. Os calcis—the heel.
6. Astragalus—one of the seven bones of the tarsus.
7. Os naviculare—the navicular bone.
8. Os cuboideum—or cubic bone.

9. Os cuneiforme tertium et maximum.
10. Os metatarsi digiti quarti.
11. Os metatarsi digiti tertii.
12. Os metatarsi digiti secundi.
13. Os metatarsi digiti primi.
14. Phalanges primæ digitorum pedis.
15. Phalanges secundæ digitorum pedis.
16. Phalanges tertiæ digitorum pedis.
17. Os sesamoideum—the sesamoid.

THE RIGHT POSTERIOR EXTREMITY.

1. Os femoris—the thigh-bone.
2. Patella—the knee-pan.
3. Tibia—the shank of the leg.
4. Os calcis—the heel-bone.
5. Astragalus—one of the seven bones of the tarsus.
7. Os naviculare—the navicular bone.
8. Os cuneiforme primum et medium.
9. Os cuboideum, or cubic bone.
10. Os cuneiforme tertium et maximum

11. Os cuneiforme secundum et minimum.
12. Rudimentum ossis metatarsi hallucis.
13. Os metatarsi digiti primi.
14. Os metatarsi digiti secundi.
15. Os metatarsi digiti tertii.
16. Phalanges primæ digitorum.
17. Phalanges secundæ digitorum pedis.
18. Phalanges tertiæ digitorum pedis.
19. Os sesamoideum—the sesamoid.

backwards if he is to have good wind, and the lateral diameter
is of less importance. These facts ought to be taken into consideration in selecting the best kind of frame for the purposes
of speed and endurance.

Large size of bone contributes to the strength of the limbs, and
foxhounds especially, which have continual blows and strains in
their scrambling over or through fences of all kinds, require big
limbs and joints. When, however, extreme speed is desired, as
in the greyhound, there may be an excess of bone, which then
acts as so much lumber and impedes the activity. Still, even in
this dog the bones and joints must be strong enough to resist the
shocks of the course, without which we constantly find them liable
to fracture or dislocation. If, however, a dog is brought up at
liberty, and from his earliest years is encouraged in his play, the
bones, though small, are strong, and the joints are united by firm
ligaments which will seldom give way.

The dog has no collar-bone, so that his fore-quarter is only
attached to the body by muscular tissue. This is effected chiefly
by a broad sling of muscle, which is attached above to the edge
of the shoulder-blade, and below to the ribs near their lower ends.
It is also moved backwards by muscles attached to the spine, and
forwards by others connected in front to the neck and head, so
that at the will of the animal it plays freely in all directions.

The teeth are 42 in number, arranged as follows :—

$$\text{Incisors } \tfrac{3-3}{3-3}: \quad \text{Canines } \tfrac{1-1}{1-1}: \quad \text{Molars } \tfrac{6-6}{7-7}:$$

TEETH OF THE DOG AT VARIOUS AGES.

The *incisors* are somewhat remarkable in shape, having three
little lobules at their edges resembling a *fleur-de-lis* (Fig. 1). Next
to these come the canine teeth or tusks, and then the molars,
which vary in form considerably. In the upper jaw, in front, are
three sharp and cutting teeth, which Cuvier calls *false* molars ;
then a tooth with two cutting lobes ; and lastly, two flat teeth,
or *true* molars. In the under jaw the first four molars on each
side are *false,* or cutters ; then an intermediate one, with the
posterior part flat ; and lastly, two tubercular teeth, or true molars.
As the incisors are worn away and the dog becomes old, the

lobules on the edges wear away and are flattened (see Figs. 3 and 4). The teeth are developed in two sets; the first, called *milk-teeth*, showing themselves through the gums about a fortnight or three weeks after birth, and lasting till the fifth or sixth month, when they are displaced by the *permanent set*, the growth of which is accompanied by a degree of feverishness which is often mis-

Fig. 1.   Fig. 2.

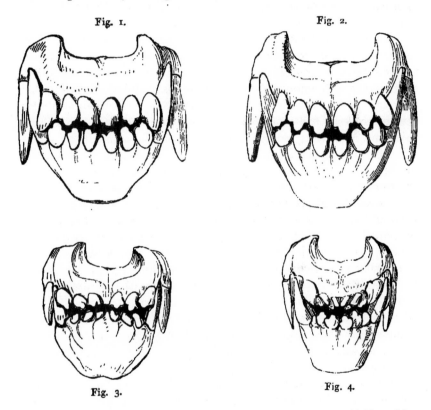

Fig. 3.   Fig. 4.

taken for distemper. The dog's teeth should be beautifully white, if he is healthy and well reared, and until the third year there should be no deposit of tartar upon them; but after that time they are always coated with this substance at the roots, more or less, according to the feeding and state of health. The dentition of the dog varies so much that his teeth form no reliable guide to his age.

The *fore-feet* are generally provided with five toes, and the *hind* with four, all furnished with strong nails that are not retractile. he inner toe on the fore-feet is more or less rudimental, and is called the dew-claw; while there is also sometimes present in the hind-foot a claw in the same situation still more rudimental, inasmuch as there is often no bony connection with the metatarsal bone. This also is called the dew-claw, when present.

THE MUSCULAR SYSTEM.

The *muscles* of the dog have nothing remarkable about them, excepting that they are renewed and wasted faster than in most animals. This has passed into a proverb, and should be known as influencing the time which dogs take to recruit their strength.

THE BRAIN AND NERVOUS SYSTEM.

The *nervous system* is highly developed in those breeds which have been carefully attended to, that is, where individuals of high nervous sensibility have been selected to breed from. This is therefore remarkable in the bulldog, selected for generations for courage; in the pointer, where steadiness in pointing has been the prominent cause of choice; and in the greyhound, whose characteristic is speed; all requiring a high development of the nervous system, and all particularly liable to nervous diseases, such as fits, chorea, &c. On the other hand, the cur, the common sheep-dog, &c., seldom suffer from any disease whatever.

THE DIGESTIVE SYSTEM.

The *stomach* of this animal is extremely powerful in dissolving bones, but it is also very liable to sickness, and on the slightest disturbance rejects its contents. This appears to be almost a natural effect, and not a diseased or disordered condition, as there is scarcely a dog which does not wilfully produce vomiting occasionally by swallowing grass. Few medicines which are at all irritating will remain down, and a vast number which are supposed to be given are not retained on the stomach, while others are only partially so. The bowels are extremely liable to become costive, which is in great measure owing to the want of proper exercise, and this also is very apt to produce torpidity of the liver. It may, however, be observed that in almost all particulars, except the tendency to vomit, the digestive organs of the dog resemble those of man.

THE HEART AND LUNGS.

There is nothing whatever remarkable in the heart and lungs; but the blood-vessels, like those of most of the lower animals, are so elastic in their coats that they quickly contract when divided, and a fatal bleeding rarely results.

THE SKIN.

The skin of the dog is said to be quite free from perspiration, but this is a mistake, as I have often seen the short hairs of a smooth-coated dog glistening with fine beads of liquid, poured out on a hot day, when strong exercise was taken. The tongue, however, is the grand means of carrying off heat by evaporation, and its extensive surface, when hanging out of the mouth, is sufficient for the purpose, as the fluid is carried off more rapidly from the air passing over it in expiration. I am persuaded that a considerable amount of insensible perspiration is constantly going on from the surface of the skin, and that nothing ought to be done which is likely to check it. This, however, is contrary to the generally received opinion, which is, that nothing of the kind takes place in this animal.

CHAPTER II.

Alteratives—Anodynes — Anti-spasmodics — Aperients — Astringents — Blisters — Caustics — Charges — Cordials — Diuretics — Embrocations—Emetics — Expectorants — Fever Medicines — Clysters — Lotions — Ointments —Stomachics — Styptics—Tonics—Worm Medicines—Administration of Remedies.

ALTERATIVES.

THESE are medicines which are given with a view of changing an unhealthy into a healthy action. We know nothing of the mode in which the change is produced, and we can only judge of them by the results. The most powerful are mercury, iodine, hemlock, hellebore, and cod-liver oil, which are given in the following formulas :—

> 1.—Æthiop's mineral, 1½ to 5 grains.
> Powdered rhubarb, 1 to 4 grains.
> „ ginger, ½ to 1½ grain.
> Mix, and make into a pill, to be given every evening.

> 2.—Hemlock extract, or fresh-bruised leaves, 2 to 4 grains.
> Plummer's pill, 1½ to 5 grains.
> Mix, and give every night, or every other night.

> 3.—Iodide of potassium, 2 to 4 grains.
> Liquid extract of sarsaparilla, 1 drachm.
> Mix, and give in a little water once or twice a day.

> 4.—Stinking hellebore, 5 to 10 grains.
> Powdered jalap, 2 to 4 grains.
> Mix into a bolus, and give every other night.

> 5.—Cod-liver oil, from a teaspoonful to a tablespoonful.
> To be given twice a day.

ANODYNES.

Anodynes are required in the dog chiefly to stop diarrhœa, which is a very common disease in him. Sometimes, also, they are used for the purpose of relieving spasm. Opium is so little objectionable in the dog that it is almost the only anodyne used; but the dose must be far larger than for human beings, and less than a teaspoonful of laudanum for an average dog will be found to be wholly inert.

For slight purging:

6.—Prepared chalk, 2 to 3 drachms.
    Aromatic confection, 1 drachm.
    Laudanum, 3 to 8 drachms.
    Powder of gum arabic, 2 drachms.
    Water, 7 ounces.

Mix, and give two tablespoonfuls every time the bowels are relaxed.

Or,

7.—Castor oil, from a dessert to a tablespoonful.
    Laudanum, 1 to 2 drachms.

Mix, and give as a drench, repeating it in a day or two, if necessary.

For long standing and severe purgation :

8.—Creosote, 2 drachms.
    Laudanum, 6 to 8 drachms.
    Prepared chalk, 2 drachms.
    Powdered gum arabic, 2 drachms.
    Tincture of ginger, 2 drachms.
    Pepperment water, 6 ounces.

Mix, and give two tablespoonfuls every time the bowels are relaxed, but not more often than every four hours.

ANTI-SPASMODICS

Are useful in allaying cramp or spasm, but, as in the case of Alteratives, we do not know how they act. The chief are opium, æther, spirit of turpentine, and camphor, prescribed according to the following formulas :—

9.—Laudanum.
    Sulphuric æther, of each ½ to 1 drachm.
    Camphor mixture, 1 ounce.

Mix, and give in any ordinary spasm, as colic, &c.

An anti-spasmodic injection :

10.—Laudanum.
    Sulphuric æther.
    Spirit of turpentine, of each 1 to 2 drachms.
    Gruel, 3 to 8 ounces.

Mix, and inject with a common clyster syringe.

APERIENTS.

Aperients, opening medicines, or purges, by which several names this class of medicines is known, are constantly required by the dog, though it is a great mistake to give them when they are not absolutely demanded by the necessity of the case. All act by quickening the ordinary muscular action of the bowels, but some also stimulate the lining membrane to pour out large quantities of watery fluid, and others either directly or indirectly compel the liver to increase its secretion of bile. Hence they are often classed into corresponding divisions, as laxatives, drastic purgatives, &c. The chief of these drugs used in the dog-kennel are aloes, colocynth, rhubarb, jalap, ipecacuanha, senna, calomel, and blue pill, all of which act more or less on the liver; while Epsom salts, castor oil, and croton oil open the bowels without any such effect. Syrup of buckthorn is commonly given, but has little effect; and, indeed, the syrup of red poppies is generally substituted for it by the druggist, who seldom keeps the genuine article, from the belief that it is inert.

A mild bolus :
> 11.—Barbadoes aloes, 10 to 15 grains.
> Powdered jalap, 5 to 8 grains.
> Ginger, 2 or 3 grains.
> Soap, 10 grains.
> Mix into one bolus for a large dog, or divide into two or three for small ones, and give as required.

Strong bolus :
> 12.—Calomel, 3 to 5 grains.
> Jalap, 10 to 20 grains.
> Mix with syrup, and give as a bolus.'

A good common aperient when the liver is sluggish : .
> 13.—Podophyllin, ½ grain.
> Compound extract of colocynth, 12 to 18 grains.
> Powdered rhubarb, 3 to 5 grains.
> Oil of cloves, 2 drops.
> Mix, and give as a bolus to a large strong dog, or divide into two or three for smaller dogs.

Very strong purgative when there is an obstruction :
> 14.—Croton oil, 1 to 2 drops.
> Purified opium, 1 to 2 grains.
> Linseed meal, 10 grains.
> Mix the meal with boiling water into a thick paste, then add the oil and spices, and give as a bolus.

Ordinary castor oil mixture:

> 15.—Castor oil, 3 ounces.
> Syrup of buckthorn, 2 ounces.
> Syrup of poppies, 1 ounce.
> Mix, and give a tablespoonful to a medium-sized dog.

Very strong purgative mixture:

> 16.—Jalap, 10 grains.
> Epsom salts, 2 drachms.
> Subcarbonate of soda, 10 grains.
> Infusion of senna, 1 ounce.
> Tincture of senna, 2 drachms.
> Tincture of ginger, 15 drops.
> Mix and give as a drench. For a small dog, give one-half, one-third, or one-quarter, according to size.

A purgative clyster:

> 17.—Castor oil, $\frac{1}{2}$ ounce.
> Spirit of turpentine, 2 to 3 drachms.
> Common salt, $\frac{1}{2}$ ounce.
> Gruel, 6 to 8 ounces.
> Mix all together, and inject carefully *per anum*.

ASTRINGENTS

Produce contraction in all living tissues with which they are placed in apposition, either directly or by means of absorption into the circulation. Of these, opium, gallic acid, alum, bark, catechu, sulphate of zinc, nitrate of silver, and chloride of zinc are the most commonly used.

An astringent bolus for diabetes or internal hemorrhage:

> 18.—Gallic acid, 3 to 6 grains.
> Alum, 4 to 7 grains.
> Purified opium, 1 to 2 grains.
> Mix with syrup, and give two or three times a day to a large dog.

Or,

> 19.—Nitrate of silver, $\frac{1}{2}$ grain.
> Crumb of bread, enough to make a small pill.
> To be given twice a day.

Astringent wash for the eyes:

> 20.—Sulphate of zinc, 5 to 8 grains.
> Water, 2 ounces.—Mix.

Or,

> 21.—Extract of goulard, 1 drachm.
> Water, 1 ounce.—Mix.

Or,

    22.—Nitrate of silver, 2 to 6 grains.
         Distilled water, 1 ounce.—Mix.

Wash for the penis:

    23.—Chloride of zinc, ½ to 2 grains.
         Water, 1 ounce.—Mix.

Astringent application for piles:

    24.—Gallic acid, 10 grains.
         Extract of goulard, 15 drops.
         Powdered opium, 15 grains.
         Lard, 1 ounce.
Mix, and apply night and morning.

BLISTERS

Are not often used for the dog, because unless he has a proper muzzle on he will lick them off, and injure himself very materially. Sometimes, however, as in inflammation of the lungs, they are absolutely necessary. Iodine blisters to reduce local swellings may often be applied with a bandage over them, but even then, unless there is a muzzle on, the dog soon gets the bandage off, and uses his tongue. The chief are cantharides, turpentine, sulphuric acid, mustard, ammonia, tincture of iodine, and biniodide of mercury; the last two having some peculiar sect in producing absorption of any diseased substance lying beneath. In all cases the hair ought to be cut off as closely as possible.

A mild blister:

    25.—Powdered cantharides, 5 or 6 drachms.
         Venice turpentine, 1 ounce.
         Lard, 4 ounces.—Mix, and rub in.

Strong blister:

    26.—Strong mercurial ointment, 4 ounces.
         Oil of origanum, ½ ounce.
         Finely powdered euphorbium, 3 drachms.
         Powdered cantharides, ½ ounce.—Mix.

Very quick blister:

    27.—Flour of mustard, 4 ounces.
         Spirit of turpentine, 1 ounce.
         Strong liquid of ammonia, ½ ounce.
Mix the mustard with water into a paste, then add the other ingredients and rub in.

For bony growths or other tumours:

> 28.—Tincture of iodine.
> Painted on every day, by means of a common painter's brush.

Or,

> 29.—Red iodide of mercury, 1 to 1½ drachms.
> Lard, 1 ounce.
> Mix, and rub in a piece the size of a nutmeg every day, keeping the part wet with tincture of arnica, ½ ounce, mixed with half a pint of water.

CAUSTICS.

This name is given to substances which either *actually* or *potentially* destroy the living tissue; the actual cautery is an iron heated in the fire, the potential of some chemical substance, such as corrosive sublimate, lunar caustic, caustic potash, a mineral acid, or the like. The actual cautery, or firing, is not often used for the dog, but in some cases it is of great service. Both kinds are used for two purposes—one to relieve the effects of strains and other injuries of the limbs, by which the ligaments are inflamed; and the other to remove diseased growth, such as warts, fungus, &c.

> 30.—Firing, when adopted for the dog, should be carried out with a very small thin-edged iron, as the dog's skin is thin, and very liable to slough. No one should attempt this without experience or previously watching others.
>
> 31.—Lunar caustic, or nitrate of silver, is constantly required, being very manageable in the hands of any person accustomed to wounds, &c.
>
> 32.—Sulphate of copper, or bluestone, is much milder than the lunar caustic, and may be freely rubbed into the surface of fungus or proud flesh. It is very useful in ulcerations about the toes.
>
> 33.—Fused potass is not fit for any one but the experienced surgeon.
>
> 34.—Corrosive sublimate in powder may be applied, carefully and in very small quantities, to warts, and then washed off. It is apt to extend its effects to the surrounding tissues.
>
> 35.—Yellow orpiment is not so strong as corrosive sublimate, and may be used in the same way.
>
> 36.—Burnt alum and white sugar, in powder, act as mild caustics.

CHARGES.

Charges are plasters which act chiefly by mechanical pressure, being spread on while hot, and then covered with tow. They are not much used among dogs, but in strains they are sometimes useful, as they allow the limb to be used without injury. The best for the dog is composed as follows:—

37.—Canada balsam, 2 ounces.
Powdered arnica leaves, ½ ounce.

Melt the balsam, and mix up with the powder, with the addition of a little turpentine, if necessary. Then smear over the part, and cover with tow, which is to be well matted in with the hand ; or use thin leather.

CORDIALS.

Warm stimulating stomachics are so called. They may be given either as a ball or a drench.

Cordial ball :

38.—Powdered caraway seeds, 10 to 15 grains.
Ginger, 3 to 5 grains.
Oil of cloves, 2 drops.
Linseed meal, enough to make a ball, first mixing it with boiling water.

Cordial drench :

39.—Tincture of cardamoms, ½ to 1 drachm.
Sal volatile, 15 to 30 drops.
Tincture of cascarilla, ½ to 1 drachm.
Camphor mixture, 1 ounce.—Mix.

DIURETICS.

Medicines which act on the secretion of urine are called *diuretics*. They are either employed when the kidneys are sluggish to restore the proper quantity, or to increase it beyond the natural standard, when it is desired to lower the system.

Diuretic bolus :

40.—Nitre, 5 to 8 grains.
Digitalis, ½ grain.
Ginger, 2 or 3 grains.

Mix with linseed meal and water, and give all or part, according to the size of the dog.

Diuretic and alterative bolus :

41.—Iodide of potassium, 2 to 4 grains.
Nitre, 3 to 6 grains.
Digitalis, ½ grain.
Extract of camomile, 5 grains.

Mix, and give all or part.

EMBROCATIONS.

These external applications, otherwise called *liniments*, are extremely useful in the dog, for strains, or sometimes to relieve

muscular inflammation or chronic rheumatism of the joints.
Mustard, ammonia, laudanum, and turpentine are the chief
agents employed.

Mustard embrocation :

> 42.—Best mustard, 3 to 5 ounces.
> Liquor of ammonia, 1 ounce.
> Spirit of turpentine, 1 ounce.
> Mix into a thin paste, and rub into the part affected.

Embrocation for strains or rheumatism :

> 43.—Spirit of turpentine.
> Liquor of ammonia.
> Laudanum. Of each ½ ounce.
> Mix, and shake well before using, then rub in.

EMETICS.

Emetics are very commonly used in the diseases of the dog,
and sometimes act very beneficially ; but they have a tendency to
weaken the stomach, and should therefore be used with caution.
If not frequently resorted to no harm is likely to accrue, as vomiting is almost a natural process in the dog.

Common salt emetic :

> 44.—Dissolve a teaspoonful of salt and half a teaspoonful of
> mustard in half a pint of tepid water, and give it as a
> drench.

Strong emetic :

> 45.—Tartar emetic, 1 to 3 grains.
> Dissolve in a tablespoonful of warm water, and give as a drench ; fol-
> lowing it up in a quarter of an hour by pouring down as much thin
> gruel as the dog can be made to swallow.

EXPECTORANTS, OR COUGH MEDICINES.

The action of these remedies is to promote the flow of mucus, so
as to relieve the congestion of the air-passages.

Common cough bolus :

> 46.—Ipecacuanha in powder, ½ to 1½ grain.
> Powdered rhubarb, 1 to 2 grains,
> Purified opium, ½ to 1½ grain.
> Compound squill pill, 1 to 2 grains.
> Mix, and give night and morning.

Expectorant draught, useful in recent cough :

> 47.—Ipecacuanha wine, 5 to 10 drops.
> Common mucilage, 2 drachms.
> Sweet spirit of nitre, 20 to 30 drops.
> Paregoric, 1 drachm.
> Camphor mixture, ½ ounce.

Mix, and give two or three times a day.

Expectorant draught for chronic cough :

> 48.—Friar's balsam, 8 to 12 drops.
> Syrup of poppies, 1 drachm.
> Diluted sulphuric acid, 3 to 8 drops.
> Mucilage, 2 drachms.
> Paregoric, 1 drachm.
> Camphor mixture, ½ ounce.

Mix, and give twice a day.

FEVER MEDICINES.

These medicines reduce fever by increasing the secretions of urine and perspiration, and by reducing the action of the heart to some extent.

Common fever powder :

> 49.—Nitre in powder, 3 to 5 grains.
> Tartar emetic, ¼ grain.

Mix, and put *dry* on the dog's tongue every night and morning.

More active powder :

> 50.—Calomel, ½ to 1½ grain.
> Nitre, 3 to 5 grains.
> Digitalis, ½ to 1 grain.

Mix, and give once or twice a day, in the same way ; or made into a pill with confection.

Fever mixture :

> 51.—Nitre, 1 drachm.
> Sweet spirit of nitre, 3 drachms.
> Mindererus' spirit, 1 ounce.
> Camphor mixture, 6½ ounces.

Mix, and give two tablespoonfuls every six hours.

CLYSTERS

Are extremely useful in the dog, which is very liable to constipation from want of exercise, and in that case is *mechanically* bound. A pint of warm water in which some yellow soap has been dissolved will generally have the desired effect.

Turpentine clyster in colic:

> 52.—Spirit of turpentine, ½ ounce.
> Castor oil, 1 ounce.
> Laudanum, 2 to 3 drachms.
> Gruel, 1 pint.
> Mix, and throw up, using only half or one-third for a small dog.

LOTIONS,

Otherwise called Washes, are intended either to reduce the temperature in inflammation of the surface to which they are applied, or to brace the vessels of the part.

Cooling lotion for bruises:

> 53.—Extract of lead, 1 drachm.
> Tincture of arnica, ½ to 1 drachm.
> Water, ½ pint.
> Mix, and apply by means of a bandage or sponge.

For severe stiffness from over-exercise:

> 54.—Tincture of arnica, ½ drachm.
> Strong spirit of wine, whisky, or brandy, 7½ drachms.
> Mix, and rub well into the back and limbs, before the fire.

Lotion for the eyes:

> 55.—Sulphate of zinc, 20 to 25 grains.
> Water, ½ pint.
> Mix, and wash the eyes night and morning.

Strong drops for the eyes:

> 56.—Nitrate of silver, 3 to 8 grains.
> Distilled water, 1 ounce.
> Mix, and drop in with a quill.

OINTMENTS.

By means of lard, wax, &c., various substances are mixed up so as to be applied to wounds, chiefly to keep out the air.

A good ointment for old sores:

> 57.—Yellow basilicon.
> Ointment of nitric-oxide of mercury, equal parts.

Digestive ointment:

> 58.—Red precipitate, 2 ounces.
> Venice turpentine, 3 ounces.
> Beeswax, 1½ ounce.
> Lard, 4 ounces.—Mix.

Mange ointment:

> 58a.—Green iodide of mercury, 1 drachm.
> Lard, 8 drachms.
> Mix, and rub in carefully every second or third day.

STIMULANTS—see CORDIALS.

STOMACHICS.

The name describes the use of the remedies, which are intended to give tone to the stomach.

Stomachic bolus:

> 59.—Extract of gentian, 6 to 8 grains.
> Powdered rhubarb, 2 to 3 grains.
> Mix, and give twice a day.

Stomachic draught:

> 60.—Tincture of cardamoms, ½ to 1 drachm.
> Compound infusion of gentian, 1 ounce.
> Carbonate of soda, 3 grains.
> Powdered ginger, 2 grains.
> Mix, and give twice a day.

STYPTICS

Are remedies applied to stop bleeding. In the dog the vessels seldom give way externally, but internally the disease is frequent enough, either in the shape of a bloody flux or bloody urine, or bleeding from the lungs, for which the following may be tried:—

> 61.—Superacetate of lead, 2 to 3 grains.
> Tincture of matico, 30 to 50 drops.
> Vinegar, 10 drops.
> Water, 1 ounce.
> Mix, and give two or three times a day.

TONICS.

Tonics permanently increase the tone or vigour of the system, being particularly useful in the recovery from low fever.

Tonic pill:

> 62.—Sulphate of quinine, 1 to 3 grains.
> Extract of hemlock, 2 grains.
> Ginger, 2 grains.
> Mix, and give twice a day.

Tonic mixture:

> 63.—Compound tincture of bark, 2 ounces.
> Decoction of yellow bark, 14 ounces.
> Mix, and give three tablespoonfuls twice or thrice daily to a large dog.

WORM MEDICINES.

By this term we are to understand such substances as will expel worms from the intestines of the dog, their action being either poisonous to the worm itself, or so irritating as to cause them to evacuate their position. All ought either to be in themselves purgative, or to be followed by a medicine of that class, in order to ensure the removal of the eggs, as well as the worms themselves. The more detailed directions will be found in the chapter on Worms.

Aperient worm bolus:

> 64.—Calomel, 2 to 5 grains.
> Jalap, 10 to 20 grains.
> Mix into a bolus, with treacle.

For general worms. Not aperient, and therefore to be followed by castor oil:

> 65.—Recently powdered areca nut, 1 to 2 drachms.
> Mix up with broth, and give to the dog directly, as there is no taste in it till it has been soaked some time, when the broth becomes bitter. If the dog refuses it he must be drenched. Four hours after give a dose of castor oil. N.B.—The exact dose is 2 grains for each pound the dog weighs.

For round worms:

> 66.—Indian pink, ½ ounce.
> Boiling water, 8 ounces.
> Let it stand for an hour, then strain, and give half to a large dog, a quarter to a middle-sized dog, or an eighth to a very small one. This, however, is a severe remedy, and is not unattended with danger. It should be followed by castor oil in six hours.

Mild remedy, unattended with any danger:

> 67.—Powdered glass, as much as will lie on a shilling, heaped up.
> To be mixed with butter, and given as a bolus, following it up with castor oil after six hours.

For tape-worm or maw-worm:

> 68.—Kousso, ¼ to ½ ounce.
> Lemon juice, 1 tablespoonful.
> Boiling water, ¼ pint.
> Pour the water on the kousso, and when nearly cold add the lemon

juice. Stir all up together, and give as a drench. It should be followed up in six or eight hours by a dose of oil.

Another remedy for tape-worm :

> 69.—Spirit of turpentine, 1 to 4 drachms.

Tie this up firmly in a piece of bladder, then give as a bolus, taking care not to burst the bladder. This also requires a dose of oil to follow. Or mix the turpentine with suet into a bolus.

Another :

> 70.—Fresh root of male fern, 1 to 4 drachms.
> Powdered jalap, 15 grains.
> Liquorice powder and water, enough to make a bolus.

N.B.—The oil of male fern is better than the dry root, the dose being ten to thirty drops.

ADMINISTRATION OF REMEDIES.

Some considerable tact and knowledge of the animal are required in order to give medicines to the dog to the best advantage. In the first place, his stomach is peculiarly irritable, and so much under the control of the will that most dogs can vomit whenever they like. Hence it is not only necessary to give the medicine, but also to ensure its being kept down. For this purpose, however, it is generally only necessary to keep up the dog's head, as he will not readily vomit without bringing his nose to the ground ; and so it is the regular practice in large kennels, in giving a dose of physic, to put the couples on, and fasten them up to a hook, at such a height that the dog cannot lower his head, maintaining this position for two or three hours. A single dog may be watched, if such is preferred, but a lot of hounds in physic must be treated with less ceremony.

THE DOG'S SYSTEM RESEMBLES THAT OF MAN.

The effects of remedies on the dog are nearly the same as on man, so that any one who understands how to manage himself may readily extend his sphere of usefulness to the dog. On the other hand, horses require a very different treatment, which accounts for the ignorance of the diseases of the dog so often displayed by otherwise clever veterinary surgeons who have confined their attention to the more valuable animal. Some remedies affect the dog differently, however ; thus laudanum, which is a very dangerous drug in human medicine, rarely does harm to the canine species, and treble the dose which is enough for a man will be required for the dog. On the other hand, calomel is quite the reverse, being extremely liable to produce great irritation on the lining membrane of the dog's stomach and bowels.

MODE OF GIVING A BOLUS OR PILL.

If the dog is small, take him on the lap, without harshness, and if inclined to use his claws tie a coarse towel round his neck, letting it fall down in front, which will muffle them effectually; then with the finger and thumb of the left hand press open the mouth by insinuating them between the teeth, far enough back to take in the cheeks, and so to compel the mouth to open from the pain given by the pressure against the teeth, while it also prevents the dog from biting the fingers. Then raising the nose, drop the pill as far back as possible, and push it well down the throat with the forefinger of the right hand. Let go with the left, still hold the nose up, keeping the mouth shut, and the pill is sure to go down. A large dog requires two persons to give a pill if he is at all inclined to resist. First, back him into a corner, then stride over him, and putting a thick cloth into his mouth, bring it together over the nose, where it is held by the left hand; the right can then generally lay hold of the lower jaw. But if the dog is very obstinate and inclined to resist, another cloth must also be placed over that, and then drawing them apart, an assistant can push the pill down. Very often a piece of meat may be used to wrap the pill up in, and the dog will readily bolt it; but sometimes it is desirable to avoid this, as it may be necessary to give the medicine by itself. Even large dogs, however, are seldom so troublesome as to require the above precautions in giving pills, though they almost always obstinately refuse liquid medicine when they have tasted it once or twice.

MODE OF DRENCHING THE DOG.

If a small quantity only is to be given, the dog's head being held, the liquid may be poured through the closed teeth, by making a little pouch of the cheek; but this is a tedious process, as the animal often refuses to swallow it for a long time, and then struggles till half is wasted. A spoon answers for small quantities, but for larger a soda-water bottle is the best instrument. Then, having the dog held on either of the plans recommended in the last paragraph, pour a little down, and shut the mouth, which is necessary, because the act of swallowing cannot be performed with it open. Repeat this till all is swallowed. Then watch the dog, or tie his head up, till it is clear that the medicine will be retained on the stomach.

CLYSTERS, OR INJECTIONS.

When the bowels are very much confined, a pint or two of warm gruel will often be of great service, if thrown up into the rectum. The dog should be placed on his side, and held in this position on a table by an assistant, while the operator passes the pipe carefully up into the rectum, and then pumps the fluid up.

THE APPLICATION OF THE MUZZLE.

When any operation is to be performed which is likely to make the dog use his teeth, he must be muzzled, either with an instrument made on purpose, or with a piece of tape, which is to be first wound round the nose of the dog, as close to the eyes as possible without touching them, then tied in a knot between them, and both ends brought back over the forehead to the collar, where they are to be made fast. When a muzzle is required to be worn by a savage dog, either indoors or out, it must be so made as to allow of his readily putting his tongue out. For this purpose either a cone of leather pierced with holes, or of wire, is strapped on by a neck-strap and two or three short side-straps.

CHAPTER III.

FEVERS, AND THEIR TREATMENT.

Simple Ephemeral Fever, or Cold—Epidemic Fever, or Influenza—Typhus
Fever, or Distemper—Rheumatic Fever—Small-pox—Sympathetic Fever.

THE dog is peculiarly liable to febrile attacks, which have always
a tendency to put on a low form, very similar in its nature to that
known as typhus in human medicine. This is so generally the
case, that every dog is said to have the distemper at some time of
his life, that name being given to this low form of fever. Hence,
an attack may commence with a common cold, or any inflammatory
affection of the lungs, bowels, &c.; but, this going on to assume
the low form, it becomes a case of genuine typhus fever, or distemper. Nevertheless, it does not follow that the one must
necessarily end in the other; and so the dog may have simple
fever, known as "a cold," or various other complaints, without
being subjected to the true distemper. The fevers occurring in the
dog are—first, simple ephemeral fever, commonly called "a cold;"
second, simple epidemic fever, or influenza; third, typhus fever,
known as distemper; fourth, rheumatic fever, attacking the muscular
and fibrous systems; and fifthly, small-pox.

SIMPLE EPHEMERAL FEVER.

Symptoms.—This slight disease, known as "a common cold," is
ushered in by chilliness, with increased heat of surface, a quick
pulse, and slightly hurried breathing. The appetite is not as good
as usual, eyes look dull, bowels costive, urine scanty and high-
coloured. There are often cough and slight running at the nose
and eyes, and sometimes the other internal organs are attacked;
or the disease goes on till a different form of fever is established,

known as typhus, and this is particularly the case when many dogs are collected together, or when one or two are kept in a close kennel, and are neither properly ventilated nor cleaned.

Cause.—Exposure to wet or cold.

Treatment.—Complete rest. A gentle dose of opening medicine; (12) or (13) if the liver is torpid, (15) if acting. After this has acted, give slops, and if there is still much fever, one of the remedies (45) or (51). If there is much cough, give the draught (47) or the bolus (46).

INFLUENZA.

The symptoms of influenza at first closely resemble those of the last-described attack, but as they depend upon some peculiar condition of the air which prevails at the time, and as they are more persistent, the name influenza is given. After the first few days, the running at the eyes and nose increases, and a cough is almost always present, which symptoms often persist for two or three weeks, leaving great prostration of strength at the end of that time, and often a chronic cough, which requires careful treatment.

The *cause* is to be looked for in some peculiar state of the air, of the nature of which nothing is known at present.

Treatment.—In the early stage the remedies should be the same as for ordinary or simple "cold." Towards the second week a cough-bolus (46) or draught (47) will generally be required. When the strength is much reduced after the second week, and the cough is nearly gone, give a tonic pill (62) or mixture (63). Great care should be taken not to bring on a relapse by improper food or by too early an allowance of exercise. Fresh air is of the utmost importance, but it must be taken at a slow pace, as a gallop will often undo all that has been effected in the way of a cure.

TYPHUS FEVER, OR DISTEMPER.

Having in previously published works proved the similarity of this disease to the typhus fever of man, and the identity of the two methods of treatment, I shall take this for granted, more especially as it is now generally admitted.

The essence of the disease is some poison admitted from without, or developed within the blood, by which the various secretions are either totally checked or so altered as no longer to purify the system. The exact nature of this poison is beyond our present state of knowledge, but from analogy there is little doubt that it resides in the blood. As in all cases of poison absorbed into the system, there is a most rapidly depressing effect upon the muscular powers, which is to be expected, inasmuch as their action requires a constant formation of new material from the blood; and as this is retarded in common with all other functions, the muscles waste away rapidly, and their contractions are not performed with any strength. The disease is sometimes contracted by infection, and at others developed within the body; just as in the case of fermentation in vegetable substances there may be a ferment added to a saccharine solution, by which the process is hastened, although if left to itself it will come on in due course.

The *symptoms* are very various, but they may be divided into two sets, one of which comprises a set always attending upon distemper, while the other may or may not be present in any individual attack. The *invariable* symptoms are—a low insidious fever, with prostration of strength to a remarkable degree, in proportion to the duration and strength of the attack, and rapid emaciation, so that a thick muscular dog is often made quite thin and lanky in three days. As a part of the fever there is shivering, attended by quick pulse, hurried respiration, loss of appetite, and impaired secretions; but, beyond these, there are no signs which can be called positively invariable; though the running at the eyes and nose and the short husky cough, especially after exercise, are very nearly always present. The *accidental* symptoms depend upon the particular complication which may exist; for one of the most remarkable features in distemper is that, coupled with the above invariable symptoms, there may be congestion, or inflammation of the head, chest, bowels, or skin. So that in one case the disease may appear to be entirely confined to the head, in another to the chest, and in a third to the bowels; yet all are strictly from the same cause, and require the same general plan of treatment, modified according to the seat of the complication.

The ordinary course of an attack of distemper is as follows; that is, when contracted by contagion or clearly epidemic. (On the other hand, when it is developed in consequence of neglect, it comes on at the end of some other attack of disease, which may have existed for an indefinite time.) Almost always the first thing noticed is a general dulness or lassitude, together with loss of appetite. In a day or two there is generally a peculiar husky cough, which sounds as if the dog were trying to get a piece of straw out of his throat, and always comes on at exercise after a gallop. With this there is also a tendency to sneeze, but not so marked as the " husk " or " tissuck " which *may* occur in common " cold " or influenza, but is then usually more severe, and also more variable in its severity, soon going on to inflammation, or else entirely ceasing in a few days. In distemper the strength and flesh rapidly fail and waste, while in common " cold " the cough may continue for days without much alteration in either; and this is one of the chief characteristics of the true disease. There is, also, generally a black pitchy condition of the *fæces*, and the urine is scanty and high-coloured. The white of the eyes is always more or less reddened, the colour being of a bluish red cast, and the vessels being evidently gorged with blood. When the brain is attacked, the eyes are more injected than when the bowels or lungs are the seats of complication. The corners of the eyes have a small drop of mucus, and the nose runs more or less, which symptoms, as the disease goes on, are much aggravated, both being glued up by brownish matter, while the teeth also are covered with a blackish brown fur. Such are the regular symptoms of a severe attack of distemper, gradually increasing in severity to the third, fourth, or fifth week, when the dog dies from exhaustion, or from disease of the brain, lungs, or bowels, marked by peculiar signs in each case. In this course the disease may be described as passing through four *stages* or *periods*—first, that in which the poison is spreading through the system, called *the period of incubation;* second, that in which nature rouses her powers to expel it, called *the period of reaction;* third, *the period of prostration*, during which the powers of nature are exhausted, or nearly so, by the efforts which have been made; and fourth, *the period of convalescence.* On the average, each of these will occupy a week or ten days, varying with the mildness or severity of the attack.

When the head is attacked there may or may not be a running from the nose and eyes; but more usually there is some evidence of congestion in these organs, the eyes being weak and glued up with the mucus, and the nose running more or less. A fit is, however, the clearest evidence of brain affection, and, to a common observer, the only reliable one. Sometimes there is stupor without a fit, gradually increasing till the dog becomes insensible and dies ; at others a raving delirium comes on, easily mistaken for hydrophobia, but distinguished from it by the presence of the premonitory symptoms peculiar to distemper. This is the most fatal complication of all, and if the dog recovers he is often a victim to palsy or chorea for the rest of his life.

If the lungs are attacked there is very rapid breathing, with cough, and almost always a considerable running from the eyes and nose, and expectoration of thick frothy mucus. If inflammation of the lungs is established, the danger is as great as when the head is the seat of the seizure.

The bowels may be known to be seized when there is a violent purging of black offensive matter, often tinged with blood, and sometimes mixed with patches or shreds of a white leathery substance, which is coagulable lymph. The discharge of blood is in some cases excessive, and rapidly carries off the dog.

If the skin is attacked, which is a favourable sign, there is a breaking out of pustules on the inside of the thighs and belly, which fill with matter often tinged with dark blood, and sometimes with blood itself of a dark purple colour.

To distinguish distemper from similar affections is not always easy to an inexperienced observer, but the practised eye at once detects the difference. The chief diseases which are likely to be confounded with it are, the true canine madness, common " cold," or influenza, inflammation of the lungs, and diarrhœa. The first of these runs a more rapid course, and is ushered in by peculiar changes in the temper, which will be described under the head of HYDROPHOBIA. "Cold" and influenza cause no great prostration of strength; and the former comes on after exposure to the weather, while the latter is sure to be prevalent at the time. Inflammation of the lungs must be studied to be known, and simple diarrhœa has no fever attending upon it.

The *treatment of distemper* is twofold ; firstly, being directed to the safe conduct through the lowering effects of the complaint ; and secondly, to ward off the fatal results which are likely to be occasioned by the local complications in the brain, lungs, or bowels. It must be remembered that the disease is an effort of nature to get rid of a poison ; and, therefore, the powers of the system must be aided throughout, or they will be incompetent to their task. One great means of carrying off this poison is to be looked for in the bowels and kidneys ; and, as far as possible, these organs must be restored to their natural state, taking care that, in trying to effect these desirable objects, they are not injured by the remedies used. Thus it is well known that aperients, and especially calomel, have the property of restoring the suspended action of the liver ; but they also have an injurious effect upon the strength of the general system, and therefore must be used with great caution ; the best formulæ being (13) or (15,) given only once or twice, at intervals of two or three days. After the secretions are restored, the next thing to be done is to look out for the complications in the brain, lungs, and bowels which are to be expected ; and if present, to counteract them by appropriate remedies. Thus a seton put into the back of the neck, covering the tape with blister ointment, will be likely to relieve the *head*, together with cold applications of vinegar and water by means of a sponge. At the same time, the fever mixture (51) may be regularly administered. For any trifling complication in the *lungs* the fever powder (49) will generally suffice ; but if severe, blood must be taken from the neck vein ; though this, if possible, should be avoided, and the cough bolus or draught (46) or (47) administered. *Diarrhœa* must be at once checked by one of the mixtures (6) or (8), or if very severe, by the pill (19). At the same time, rice-water should be given as the only drink ; and beef-tea, thickened with arrowroot or rice, as the sole article of diet, changing it occasionally for port wine and arrowroot. When the stage of exhaustion has commenced, the tonic mixture (63) will almost always be required ; and it is astonishing what may be done by a perseverance in its use. Dogs which appear to be dying will often recover ; and no case should be given up as long as there is any life remaining.

The *diet* should be carefully attended to, little or no food being required on the first four or six days beyond weak broth or gruel, no solid food from the first being permitted, and this restriction being maintained till the dog is quite recovered. When the state of exhaustion or prostration comes on, good strong beef-tea should be given every three or four hours, and if the dog will not swallow it, force should be used; a spoonful at a time being given in the way ordered for drenching at page 365. At this time, also, port wine is often of service, thickened with arrowroot, and given alternately with the beef-tea. For a dog of average size the plan is to give a teacupful of beef-tea, then, after two hours, the same quantity of arrowroot and wine; then, again after two hours, a dose of the tonic mixture; and so on through the twenty-four hours. Perseverance in this troublesome plan will generally be rewarded with success; but, of course, it is only a valuable dog which will reward it properly. In less important animals the beef-tea may be provided, and if it is not voluntarily swallowed the poor patient often dies for want of the compulsion, so that humanity as well as self-interest counsels the adoption of what often appears a harsh proceeding.

No exercise, even of the most gentle kind, should be allowed, it being found invariably to bring on a return of the disease whenever it is indulged in. Many a young dog has been sacrificed to the mistaken kindness of his master, who has thought that a "breath of fresh air" would do him good; and so it would if taken in an easy carriage, at rest; but the muscular exertion necessary to procure it is highly injurious, and should be delayed until the strength is restored. This is one reason why dogs in the country bear distemper so much better than in towns; for, as it is known that they are in the fresh air, no attempt is made to take them to it, and so they are left alone, and are not induced to exert their strength prematurely. Even when the dog appears nearly well, it is better to lead him out to exercise for the first day or two, for otherwise he is almost sure to over-exert himself, and a gallop will often do more harm than can be rectified in many days afterwards.

Ventilation should not be neglected, but moderate warmth is essential to a cure, and a delicate dog like the greyhound should have a cloth on him in cold weather. The greatest cleanliness should be observed, but this should be done as far as possible without making the kennel damp with water. Clean straw must be liberally provided, and all offensive matters removed as often as they are voided.

Summary of treatment.—In the early stage get the bowels into good order by mild doses of aperient medicine—(11), (13), or (15). Attend to any complication which may come on, using a seton for the head, or the appropriate remedies for the chest or mixture for the bowels (6) if there is diarrhœa. For the exhaustion, when the violent symptoms are abated, give the tonic (63), and during the whole period attend to the diet, ventilation, cleanliness, and rest, as previously described.

Vaccination has been recommended as a remedy for distemper, and has been largely tried both in foxhound and greyhound kennels, as well as among pointers and setters. The result has been that some people fancy it to be a sure preventive, and there is evidence that, for years after it has been adopted in certain kennels, distemper, which was previously rife in them, has been kept at bay. On the other hand, a still more numerous party have found no change produced in the mortality among their dogs, and they have come, as a natural consequence, to the opposite conclusion. Reasoning from analogy, there is no ground for supposing that the matter of small-pox or cow-pox should prevent the access of a disease totally dissimilar to these complaints; but as experience is here the best guide, the appeal must be made to it in order to settle the question. Judging from this test, I can see no reason whatever for the faith which is placed in vaccination, because there are at least as many recorded failures as successes; and as we know that after any remedy there will always be a certain number of assumed cures held out by sanguine individuals, so we must allow for a great many in this particular case. Distemper is well known to be most irregular in its attacks, and to hit or miss particular kennels, as the case may be, for years together; after which it reverses its tactics; and as vaccination is used at any of these various periods of change, so it gains credit or discredit which it does not deserve. My own belief is, after trying it myself and seeing it tried, and after also comparing the experience of others, that vaccination is wholly inoperative; but as others may like to test it for themselves, I here append directions for the operation.

To vaccinate the dog.—Select the thin skin on the inside of the ear, then with a lancet charged with vaccine lymph (which should be as fresh as possible) make three or four oblique punctures in the skin, to such a depth as barely to draw blood, charging the lancet afresh each time. If the lymph cannot be procured fresh, the punctures must be made as above described, and then the points charged with dry lymph must be introduced, one in each puncture, and well rubbed into the cut surface, so as to ensure the removal of the lymph from the points. In four or five days an imperfect vesicle is formed, which, if not rubbed, goes on to maturity and scabs at the end of ten days or thereabout. There are various other methods suggested, such as introducing a piece of thread dipped in the virus, &c.; but the above is the proper plan, if any is likely to be effectual.

The *treatment* of the various sequels of distemper, including fits, palsy, &c., will be given under those heads respectively.

RHEUMATIC FEVER.

One of the most common diseases in the dog is rheumatism in some form, generally showing itself with very little fever, but sometimes being accompanied with a high degree of that attendant evil. The frequency of this disease is owing to the constant exposure of the dog to cold and wet, and very often to his kennel being damp, which is the fertile source of kennel lameness, or chest-founder, which is nothing more than rheumatism of the muscles of the shoulders. Again, those which spend half their time before a roasting fire, and the other half in the wet and cold, are extremely apt to contract this kind of fever, but not in so intractable a form as the denizen of the damp kennel. By some writers this affection is classed among the inflammations; and it is a debatable point to which of these divisions it should be assigned; but this is of little consequence so that it is properly known and easily recognised by the symptoms. I shall therefore include here rheumatic fever, which is a general affection, and also the partial attacks known as kennel lameness, or chest-founder, and rheumatism of the loins, commonly called palsy of the back.

Rheumatic fever is known by the following signs:—There is

considerable evidence of fever, but not of a very high character, the pulse being full but not very quick, with shivering and dulness, except when touched or threatened, the slightest approach causing a shriek, evidently from the fear of pain. The dog almost always retires into a corner, and is very reluctant to come out of it. On being forcibly brought out he snarls at the hand even of his best friend, and stands with his back up, evidently prepared to defend himself from the pat of the hand, which to him is anguish. The bowels are confined, and the urine high-coloured and scanty.

The *treatment* consists in bleeding from the neck, to a moderate extent, if the dog is very gross and full of condition, then giving a smart dose of opening physic, (12) or (13). After this has acted give the following pills :—

> Calomel.
> Purified opium, of each 1 grain.
> Powdered root of colchicum, 2 to 3 grains.
> Syrup, enough to make a pill.

This is the dose for an average-sized dog. A hot bath will often be of service, taking care to dry the skin afterwards before the fire. Then follow up with a liberal friction by the aid of the liniment (43).

Kennel lameness, or *chest-founder*, shows itself in a stiffness or soreness of the shoulders, so that the dog is unable to gallop freely downhill, and is often reluctant to jump off his bench to the ground, the shock giving pain to the muscles suspending the body to the shoulder-blades, which are affected with rheumatism. It is peculiarly prominent in the kennels of foxhounds, for these dogs, being exposed to wet and cold for hours together, and then being sometimes brought home to a damp lodging-room, contract the disease with great frequency. Pampered house pets are also very liable to chest-founder, over-feeding being quite as likely to produce rheumatism as exposure to cold; and when both are united this state is almost sure to be established. When it becomes chronic there is little or no fever attendant on it, nor is there much in the recent state. After it has existed for some months it is generally considered to be incurable, but instances are known in which the stiffness has entirely disappeared. *Chest-founder* also arises from a sprain of the muscles suspending the chest between the shoulders.

The *remedies* for kennel lameness are nearly the same as for general rheumatism, taking care to remove the cause if it has existed in the shape of a damp cold lodging-room. The food should be light, and composed chiefly of vegetable materials, strong animal food being inclined to increase the rheumatic affection. The liniment (43) is very likely to be of service, especially if used after the hot bath, as previously described. It has been asserted by persons of experience that a red herring given two or three times a week will cure this disease. I have no personal experience of the merits of this remedy, but, according to Colonel Whyte, it has recently been discovered that there is an active principle in the herring that is a complete specific in human rheumatism, and therefore his apparently inert remedy may really be a very powerful one. At all events, it is worth a trial. It is ordered to be given with two drachms of nitre and one of camphor, most dogs readily eating the herring and camphor, and the nitre being added in a little water as a drench. Cod-liver oil is also said to be of great service (5). Iodine with sarsaparilla (3) is a combination which I have known of more service than any internal medicines.

A dragging of the hind limbs is common enough in the dog, and though often called palsy, it really is almost always of a rheumatic nature. It exactly resembles chest-founder in all its symptoms, excepting that the muscles affected are situated in the loins and hips, corresponding with human lumbago in all particulars, excepting that it is far more permanent. The *causes* and *treatment* are the same as those of kennel lameness.

Nimethy lamine, extracted from the herring in doses of four drops for a full-sized dog, given in milk twice a day, is now used with success instead of the herring.

SMALL-POX.

Never having seen a case of this disease in the dog, I must be content with extracting entire Mr. Youatt's description of it:—

" In 1809 there was observed, at the Royal Veterinary School at Lyons, an eruptive malady among the dogs, to which they gave the name of *small-pox*. It appeared to be propagated from dog to dog by contagion. It was not difficult of cure ; and it quickly disappeared when no other remedies were employed than mild aperients and diaphoretics. A sheep was inoculated from one of these dogs. There was a slight eruption of pustules formed on the place of inoculation, but nowhere else ; nor was there the least fever.

"At another time, also at the school at Lyons, a sheep died of the regular sheep-pox. A part of the skin was fastened, during four and twenty hours, on a healthy sheep, and the other part of it on a dog, both of them being in apparent good health. No effect was produced on the dog, but the sheep died of confluent sheep-pox.

"The essential symptoms of small-pox in dogs succeed each other in the following order :—The skin of the belly, the groin, and the inside of the forearm becomes of a redder colour than in its natural state, and sprinkled with small red spots irregularly rounded. They are sometimes isolated, sometimes clustered together. The near approach of this eruption is announced by an increase of fever.

"On the second day the spots are larger, and the integument is slightly tumefied at the centre of each.

"On the third day the spots are generally enlarged, and the skin is still more prominent at the centre.

"On the fourth day the summit of the tumour is yet more prominent. Towards the end of that day the redness of the centre begins to assume a somewhat grey colour. On the following days the pustules take on their peculiar characteristic appearance, and cannot be confounded with any other eruption. On the summit is a white circular point, corresponding with a certain quantity of nearly transparent fluid which it contains, and covered by a thin and transparent pellicle. This fluid becomes less and less transparent, until it acquires the colour and consistence of pus. The pustule, during its serous state, is of a rounded form. It is flattened when the fluid acquires a purulent character, and even slightly depressed towards the close of the period of suppuration and when that of desiccation is about to commence, which ordinarily happens towards the ninth or tenth day of the eruption. The desiccation and the desquamation occupy an exceedingly variable length of time ; and so, indeed, do all the different periods of the disease. What is the least inconstant is the duration of the serous eruption, which is about four days, if it has been distinctly produced and guarded from all friction. If the general character of the pustules is considered, it will be observed that, while some of them are in a state of serous secretion, others will only have begun to appear.

"The eruption terminates when desiccation commences in the first pustules and if some red spots show themselves at that period of the malady, they disappear without being followed by the development of pustules. They are a species of abortive pustules. After the desiccation the skin remains covered by brown spots, which by degrees die away. There remains no trace of the disease, except a few superficial cicatrices on which the hair does not grow.

"The causes which produce the greatest variation in the periods of the eruption are, the age of the dog, and the temperature of the situation and of the season. The eruption runs through its different stages with much more rapidity in dogs from one to five months old than in those of greater age. I have never seen it in dogs more than eighteen months old. An elevated temperature singularly favours the eruption, and also renders it confluent and of a serous character. A cold atmosphere is unfavourable to the eruption, or even prevents it altogether. Death is almost constantly the result of the exposure of dogs having small-pox to any considerable degree of cold. A moderate temperature is most favourable to the recovery of the animal. A frequent renewal or change of air, the temperature remaining nearly the same, is highly favourable to the patient; consequently close boxes or kennels should be altogether avoided.

"I have often observed that the perspiration or breath of dogs labouring under variola em is a very unpleasant odour. This smell is particularly observed at the commencement of the desiccation of the pustules and when the animals are lying upon dry straw; for the friction of the bed against the pustules destroys their pellicles, and permits the purulent matter to escape; and the influence of this purulent matter is most pernicious. The fever is increased and also the unpleasant smell from the mouth, and that of the *fœces*. In this state there is a disposition, which is rapidly developed in the lungs, to assume the character of pneumonia. This last complication is a most serious one, and almost always terminates fatally. It has a peculiar character. It shows itself suddenly, and with all its alarming symptoms. It is almost immediately accompanied by a purulent secretion from the bronchi, and the second day does not pass without the characters of pneumonia being completely developed. The respiration is accompanied by a mucous *râle*, which often becomes sibilant. The nasal cavities are filled with a purulent fluid. The dog that coughs violently at the commencement of the disease employs himself, probably, on the following day in ejecting, by a forcible expulsion from the nostrils, the purulent secretion which is soon and plentifully developed. When he is lying quiet, and even when he seems to be asleep, there is a loud, stertorous guttural breathing."

SYMPATHETIC FEVER.

This term is applied to the fever which comes on either before or after some severe local affection, and being, as it were, eclipsed by it. Thus in all severe inflammations there is an accompanying fever which generally shows itself before the exact nature of the attack is made manifest; and though it runs high, yet it has no tendency in itself to produce fatal results, subsiding, as a matter of course, with the inflammation which attends it. The same happens in severe injuries; but here also, if there is no inflammation, there is no fever; so that the same rule applies as where there is an external cause.

The *treatment* of this kind of fever is always merged in that which is necessary for the attendant inflammation, and this being removed the fever subsides; it therefore requires no special notice to be taken of it, or any remedy to be directed to it.

CHAPTER IV.

INFLAMMATIONS.

Definition of Inflammation—Symptoms and Treatment of Rabies, Tetanus, and Turnside—Of Inflammation of the Eye, Ear (canker), Mouth, and Nose—Of the Lungs—Of the Stomach—Of the Bowels—Of the Liver—Of the Kidneys and Bladder—Of the Skin.

DEFINITION OF INFLAMMATION.

INFLAMMATION consists in a retardation of the flow of blood in the small vessels, which requires an increased action of the large ones to overcome it. When external and visible, it is characterised by increased heat, swelling, pain, and redness, and internally by the first three, the last not being discoverable, though existing. It may be *acute* when coming on rapidly, or *chronic* when slow, and without very active symptoms. In the acute form there is always an increased rapidity of the pulse, with a greater reaction on the heart's pulsations, known as hardness of the pulse. In the dog the healthy pulsations are from 90 to 100 in the minute, which may be taken as the standard of health; the arterial pulse may be felt on the inside of the arm above the knee; or by putting the hand against the lower part of the chest the contractions of the heart may be readily felt. In different breeds, however, there is considerable variation in the pulsations of the heart.

HYDROPHOBIA, RABIES, OR MADNESS.

This disease has been classed among the inflammations, although it has not been proved to arise from that cause; but as it is generally supposed to be connected with an inflammation or congestion of the spinal column and brain, there is every reason for placing it at the head of this division; and as it is of the utmost importance to understand its symptoms, the sooner it is studied the better. At present there appears to be little or no control over this horrible complaint, so that it is solely with a view to recognise the attack and prevent its transmission by inoculation that it is interesting to the owner of the dog.

The *symptoms* are chiefly as follows:—The first is a marked change of temper; the naturally cheerful dog becoming waspish and morose, and the bold fondling pet retreating from his master's hand as if it was that of a stranger. On the other hand, the shy dog sometimes becomes bold; but in almost every case there is a total change of manner for several days before the absolute outbreak of the attack, which is indicated by a kind of delirious watching of imaginary objects, the dog snapping at the wall, or if anything comes in his way, tearing it to pieces with savage fury. With this there is constant watchfulness, and sometimes a peculiarly hollow howl, while at others no sound whatever is given, the case being then described as "dumb madness." Fever is always present, but it is difficult to ascertain its extent on account of the danger of approaching the patient, and with this (in contradiction to the name hydrophobia) there is invariably an urgent thirst, which the dog is in such a hurry to gratify that he generally upsets the vessel containing his water. Mr. Grantley Berkeley maintains very strongly that no dog really attacked with rabies will touch water, and that the presence of thirst is a clear sign of the absence of this disease; but this opinion is so entirely in opposition to the careful accounts given by all those who have witnessed the disease when it had unquestionably been communicated either to man or to some of the lower animals that no reliance ought to be placed upon it, especially where so important a stake is involved. Mr. Youatt witnessed more cases of rabies than perhaps any equally good observer ever did, and he strongly insists upon the presence of thirst, as may be gathered from the concluding portion of the following extract:—

"Some very important conclusions may be drawn from the appearance and character of the urine. The dog, and at particular times when he is more than usually salacious, may, and does, diligently search the uriningplaces; he may even at those periods be seen to lick the spot which another has just wetted; but if a peculiar eagerness accompanies this strange employment, if in the parlour, which is rarely disgraced by this evacuation, every corner is perseveringly examined, and licked with unwearied and unceasing industry, that dog cannot be too carefully watched; there is great danger about him; he may, without any other symptom, be pronounced to be decidedly rabid. I never knew a single mistake about this.

"Much has been said of the profuse discharge of saliva from the mouth of the rabid dog. It is an undoubted fact that in this disease all the glands concerned in the secretion of saliva become increased in bulk and vascularity. The sublingual glands wear an evident character of inflammation; but it never equals the increased discharge that accompanies epilepsy or nausea. The frothy spume at the corners of the mouth is not for a moment to be compared with that which is evident enough in both of these affections. It is a symptom of short duration, and seldom lasts longer than twelve hours. The stories that are told of the mad dog covered with froth are altogether fabulous. The dog recovering from or attacked by a fit may be seen in this state, but not the rabid dog. Fits are often mistaken for rabies, and hence the delusion.

"The increased secretion of saliva soon passes away. It lessens in quantity; it becomes thicker, viscid, adhesive, and glutinous. It clings to the corners of the mouth, and probably more annoyingly so to the membrane of the fauces. The human being is sadly distressed by it; he forces it out with the greatest violence, or utters the falsely supposed bark of a dog in his attempts to force it from his mouth. This symptom occurs in the human being when the disease is fully established, or at a late period of it. The dog furiously attempts to detach it with his paws.

"It is an early symptom in the dog, and it can scarcely be mistaken in him. When he is fighting with his paws at the corners of his mouth, let no one suppose that a bone is sticking between the poor fellow's teeth; nor should any useless and dangerous effort be made to relieve him. If all this uneasiness arose from a bone in the mouth, the mouth would continue permanently open, instead of closing when the animal for a moment discontinues his efforts. If after a while he loses his balance and tumbles over, there can be no longer any mistake. It is the saliva becoming more and more glutinous, irritating the fauces, and threatening suffocation.

To this naturally and rapidly succeeds an insatiable thirst. The dog that still has full power over the muscles of his jaws continues to lap; he knows not when to cease; while the poor fellow labouring under the dumb madness, presently to be described, and whose jaw and tongue are paralysed, plunges his muzzle into the water-dish to his very eyes, in order that he may get one drop of water into the back part of his mouth to moisten and to cool his dry and parched fauces. Hence, instead of this disease being always characterised by the dread of water in the dog, it is marked by a thirst often perfectly unquenchable. Twenty years ago this assertion would have been peremptorily denied. Even at the present day we occasionally meet with those who ought to know better, and who will not believe that the dog which fairly, or perhaps eagerly, drinks can be rabid."—YOUATT, pp. 135, 136.

From my own experience I can fully confirm the above account, having seen seven cases of genuine rabies, in all of which thirst was present in a greater or less degree, and in five of which the disease was communicated to other dogs.

If the rabid dog is not molested, he will seldom attack any living object; but the slightest obstruction in his path is sufficient to rouse his fury, and he then bites savagely, and in the most unreasoning manner, so as to be wholly uncontrollable by fear of the consequences. The gait, when at liberty, is a long trot, without any deviation from the straight line, except what is compulsory from the nature of the surrounding objects.

The average time of the occurrence of rabies after the bite is, in the dog, from three weeks to six months, or possibly even longer; so that a suspected case requires careful watching for at least that time; but after three months the animal suspected to have been bitten may be considered tolerably safe.

The duration of the disease is about four or five days, but I have myself known a case fatal in forty-eight hours.

There is reason to hope that *a cure* for rabies has at length been discovered by M. Pasteur, in the dog as well as in man. It consists in inoculating the bitten patient ten or twelve times with rabic virus, diluted in strength by passing through the rabbit. This acts on the same principle as vaccination on small-pox, and it may be used on dogs in the same way to prevent as well as cure the disease. At present it is not generally introduced into this country, but very shortly I expect it to be so.

TETANUS.

Resembling rabies in some degree, tetanus differs from it in the absence of any affection of the brain, the senses remaining perfect to the last. It is not common with the dog, and when it does manifest itself, is generally produced by a severe injury, and shows itself in the form known as "lock-jaw." Hence in France it is known as *mal de cerf*, from its supervening upon wounds from the horns of that animal. It consists in spasmodic rigidity of certain muscles, alternately with relaxation, but the stiffness continuing for some length of time, and not appearing and disappearing as quickly as in cramp. If the tetanic spasm affects the muscles of the jaw, the state is called "lock-jaw." When it seizes on all the muscles of the back the body is drawn into a bow, the head being brought nearly close to the tail. Sometimes the contraction is of one side only, and at others of the muscles of the belly, producing a bow in the opposite direction to that alluded to above. These various conditions exactly resemble the contractions produced by the poison of strychnine; so that when they occur, as the disease is extremely rare, it is fair to suspect that poison has been used. Nevertheless, it should be known that they were witnessed long before this poison was in use; and, therefore, they may arise independently of it.

The successful treatment of tetanus is a hopeless affair if the case is clearly established. Purgatives and bleeding may be tried, followed by chloroform, which will always relieve the spasm for the time; but as it returns soon after the withdrawal of the remedy, no good is likely to accrue from its use. Excepting in the case of very valuable or highly valued dogs, I should never advise any remedies being tried, and the most humane course is at once to put the poor animal out of his misery, the spasms being evidently of a most painful nature.

TURNSIDE

Is more frequently seen in the dog than tetanus, but nevertheless is by no means common. It consists in some obscure affection of the brain, resembling the "gid" of sheep, and most probably produced from the same cause, namely, from the presence of a hydatid. (*See* WORMS, Chap. V.) The dog has no fit, but keeps continually turning round and round, and at last dies worn out. It is most commonly met with in high-bred puppies, whose constitutions are of great delicacy; and I have known a whole litter carried off, one after the other, in this way. As far as I know, no *remedy* is of any avail; but bleeding, blistering, and purgatives are said to have restored some few cases. The seton, also, has been recommended, and is, in my opinion, more likely than any other remedy to produce a cure, taking care to keep the strength supported against the lowering effects of this remedy.

INFLAMMATION OF THE EYE.

Ophthalmia, or simple inflammation of the eyes, is very common in the dog, especially in the latter stages of distemper, when the condition of this organ is often apparently hopeless; though a little patience will show that no mischief eventually occurs. On more than one occasion I have saved puppies from a watery grave whose eyes were said to be hopelessly gone; but without any remedy being applied locally, and simply by attending to the general health, the organ has recovered its transparency, and the sight has become as good as ever. The appearance of this form, as seen in distemper, consists in an unnatural bluish redness of the "white" of the eye, together with a film over the transparent part, which may or may not show red vessels spreading over it. There is great intolerance of light, with a constant watering; and if the eye is opened by force the dog resists most strenuously, giving evidence of pain from exposure to the rays of the sun. This state resembles the "strumous ophthalmia" of children, and may be *treated* in the same way, by the internal use of tonics, the pills (62) being especially serviceable. In the *ordinary ophthalmia* the "white" of the eye is of a brighter red, and the lids are more swollen, while the discharge is thicker, and the intolerance of light is not so great. The *treatment* here which is most likely to be of service is of the ordinary lowering kind, exactly the reverse of that indicated above. Purgatives, low diet, and sometimes bleeding will be required, together with local washes, such as (55) or (56). If the eyes still remain covered with a film, a seton may be inserted in the back of the neck with advantage, and kept open for two or three months.

2 B

Cataract may be known by a whiteness, more or less marked, in the pupil, and evidently beneath the surface of the eye, the disease consisting in an opacity of the lens, which is situated *behind* the pupil. It may occur from a blow, or as the result of inflammation, or from hereditary tendency. No *treatment* is of any use.

In *amaurosis* the eye looks clear, and there is no inflammation ; but the nerve is destroyed, and there is partial or total blindness. It may be known by the great size of the pupil.

CANKER, OR INFLAMMATION OF THE EAR.

From high feeding generally and exposure to the weather many dogs (especially of a sporting kind) contract an inflammation of the membrane or skin lining the ear. This produces irritation, and the dog shakes his head continually, which, together with the tendency to spread externally, causes an ulceration of the tips of the ears of those dogs, such as the hound, pointer, setter, spaniel, &c., which have these organs long and pendulous. Hence the superficial observer is apt to confine his observation to this external ulceration, and I have even known the tips of the ears cut off in the hope of getting rid of the mischief, whereas it was only aggravated, because the incessant shaking caused the wound to extend, while the internal mischief was not in the slightest degree relieved. The pointer is particularly liable to " canker," as shown on the tips of the ears, because he has little hair on this part to take off the acuteness of the " smack " which is given in the shaking of the head. Long-haired dogs, on the other hand, are quite as liable to the real disease, as evidenced on an examination of the internal surface, but from the protection afforded by the hair, the pendulous ear is not so much ulcerated or inflamed. Whenever, therefore, a dog is seen to be continually shaking his head and abortively trying to rub or scratch his ear, not being able to succeed because he cannot reach the interior, an examination should be made of the passage leading into the head ; and if the lining is red and inflamed, there is clear evidence of the disease, even if the external ear is altogether free from it. On the other hand, the mere existence of an ulceration on the tips of the ears is no absolute proof of " canker," because it may have been caused by the briars and thorns which a spaniel or hound has to pass through in hunting for his game.   Still, it should lead to a careful inspection, and if it continues for any length of time it may be generally concluded that there is an internal cause for it.

The *treatment* should in every case be chiefly directed to the internal passage, but the cap which is sometimes ordered to be applied to the head, with a view of keeping the ears quiet, having a tendency to increase the internal inflammation, is, therefore, rather prejudicial than otherwise.   The first thing to be done is to lower the system by purgatives (11), (12), (15), or (16), with low diet, including no animal food.   As soon as this has produced a decided effect, the nitrate of silver wash (22), the ointment (58*a*), melted, or the sulphate of zinc (20) should be dropped into the ear-passage, changing the one for the other every second or third day.   Or the powder of the green iodide of mercury should be brushed in.   At the same time the sores on the edges of the ears may be touched with bluestone daily, which will dry them up.   In slight cases this treatment will suffice for a cure, if carried on for three weeks or a month, but in long-standing attacks a seton must be put into the back of the neck, and this seldom fails to afford relief.   If the inflammation in the external ear has been so great as to produce abscesses, they must be slit open with the knife to the very lowest point, as wherever matter is confined in a pouch there can be no tendency to heal.   Whenever anything is to be done to the ear the dog must be muzzled, as the head cannot otherwise be held sufficiently still, and in pouring in the lotion the head must be placed on a table, and held there steadily for some minutes, so that the fluid may have time to penetrate the whole canal.

Deafness may arise from canker, or from rheumatic or other inflammation of the internal ear; but as no treatment is likely to be beneficial, there is no use in enlarging on the subject.   The only remedy at all to be relied on in recent cases is the seton in the back of the neck.

INFLAMMATION OF THE MOUTH AND TEETH.

Dogs which are fed on strongly stimulating food are very apt to lose their teeth by decay, and also to suffer from a spongy state of the gums, attended with a collection of tartar about the roots of the teeth. Decayed teeth are better extracted, but the tartar, when it produces inflammation, may be removed by instruments if it is considered worth the trouble. By carefully scraping the teeth there is little or no difficulty in removing it if the dog's head is held steadily, but few people are handy enough with the necessary tools to effect this, excepting those who make a business of the art; and if the dog is so highly valued as to make it desirable to incur the expense, he should be taken to a veterinary surgeon. A lotion composed of 1 part of a solution of chlorinated soda, 1 part of tincture of myrrh, and 6 parts of water will be afterwards of service if the teeth are occasionally brushed with it. When puppies are shedding their milk teeth it often happens that these are not easily got rid of, producing a good deal of soreness in the mouth, which prevents the puppy eating. In such a case the old tooth is better removed with a pair of forceps.

Blain is a watery swelling beneath the tongue, showing itself in several large vesicles containing straw-coloured lymph, which is sometimes stained with blood. When discovered, the *treatment* consists in pricking them with a lancet or penknife, after which the sores may be washed with the lotion given above.

INFLAMMATIONS.

Ozœna is an inflamed state of the lining membrane of the nose, producing a stinking discharge from the nostrils. This is very common in the pug-dog, and also more or less in toy-spaniels. There is little to be done in the way of treatment, but a solution of chloride of zinc (2 grains to the ounce of water) may be thrown up into the nostrils with a syringe.

LARYNGITIS AND BRONCHOCELE.

Laryngitis consists in inflammation of the top of the windpipe, where there is a very narrow passage for the air, and consequently where a slight extra contraction caused by swelling is necessarily

fatal. When *acute* it is a very dangerous disease, and is characterised by quick and laborious breathing, accompanied by a snoring
kind of noise. There is also a hoarse and evidently painful cough.
Pulse quick and sharp, and some degree of fever. The *treatment*
must be active, or it will be of no use. Large bleedings, followed
by a calomel purge (12) and the fever powder (50), will be necessary; but no time should be lost in calling in skilful aid, if the
life of the dog is of any consequence.

Chronic laryngitis attacks the same part, but comes on insidi-
ously, and is shown chiefly in a hoarse cough and stridulous bark.
It is best treated by a seton in the throat, together with low diet
and the alterative pill (1).

Bronchocele is known by an enlargement (often to the size of
the fist) of the thyroid body placed just on each side of the windpipe. If this does not press upon the air-passage there is no
inconvenience; but in course of time it has that ill effect, and the
dog becomes wheezy and short-winded. It is chiefly seen in house-
pets, and may be relieved by the internal use of iodine (3), given
for weeks together.

INFLAMMATION OF THE LUNGS.

The organs of respiration consist of an external serous and an
internal mucous membrane, united together by a cellular tissue,
and each of these is the seat of a peculiar inflammation (*pleurisy,
pneumonia,* and *bronchitis*), attended by different symptoms and
requiring a variation in the treatment. There is also, as in all
other inflammations, an *acute* and a *chronic* kind, so that here we
have six different inflammatory disorders of the contents of the
chest, besides heart disease and phthisis or consumption, which
last requires a separate notice. All the acute forms are attended
with severe sympathetic fever, and with a quick pulse; but the
character of the latter varies a good deal. The chronic forms
have also some slight febrile symptoms, but generally in proportion to the acuteness is the amount of this attendant on sympathetic
fever. As these three forms are liable to be easily mistaken for
each other, I shall place the symptoms of each in juxtaposition in
the following Table :—

COMPARATIVE TABLE OF SYMPTOMS.

	Acute Pleurisy.	Acute Pneumonia.	Acute Bronchitis.
Early symptoms.	Shivering, with slight spasms of the muscles of the chest; inspiration short and unequal in its depth, expiration full, air expired not hotter than usual; cough slight and dry; pulse quick, small, and wiry.	Strong shivering, but no spasms; inspiration tolerably full, expiration short, air expired perceptibly hotter than natural; nostrils red inside; cough violent and sonorous, with expectoration of rusty-colored mucus; pulse quick, full, and soft.	Shivering, soon followed by continual hard cough; inspiration and expiration equally full; air expired warm, but not so hot as in pneumonia; cough soon becomes moist, the mucus expectorated being frothy, scanty at first, but afterwards profuse; pulse full and hard.
Stethoscopic sounds.	No very readily distinguishable sound. A practised ear discovers a friction sound or rubbing.	A crackling sound, audible in the early stage, followed by crepitating wheezing.	The sound in this form varies from that of soap-bubbles to a hissing or wheezing sound.
Percussion.	Produces at first no result different from a state of health. After a time, when serum is thrown out, there is increased dulness.	Dulness after the early stage is produced by the thickening of the tissue, approaching to the substance of liver, hence called "hepatisation."	No change.
Termination.	The symptoms either gradually disappear or lymph is thrown out, or there is an effusion of serum or matter, with a frequently fatal result.	If the symptoms do not disappear there is a solidification of the lung, by which it is rendered impervious to air, and in bad cases suffocation takes place, or matter is formed, producing abscess.	The inflammation generally subsides by a discharge of mucus, which relieves the inflammation; or it may go on to the extent of causing suffocation, by the swelling of the lining membrane filling up the area of the tubes.
Treatment.	Bleeding in the early stage, in degree according to the severity of the attack. Relieve the bowels by (12) or (13). No blistering, which is actually prejudicial.	Bleeding in the early stage, in amount according to the severity of the attack. Give an aperient (12) or (13). Blisters to the chest of service, or the mustard	No bleeding is required. In the early stage give an emetic (44). Follow this up with a mild aperient, (11) or (15). Apply the embrocation (42) to the

COMPARATIVE TABLE OF SYMPTOMS—(*Continued*).

	Acute Pleurisy.	Acute Pneumonia.	Acute Bronchitis.
Treatment.	Try the fever powder (49) or (50), and if not active enough give calomel and opium, of each 1 grain, in a pill, three times a day. Low diet of slops only.	embrocation (42). Give the cough bolus (46) or the draught (47). If the inflammation is very high, give calomel and opium, of each 1 grain, digitalis ½ grain, tartar emetic ¼ grain, in a pill, three times daily. Low diet of slops.	chest, and give the cough bolus (46) or the draught (47). Low diet in the early stages; afterwards a little solid food, not meat, may be given.

COMPARATIVE TABLE OF CHRONIC SYMPTOMS.

	Chronic Pleurisy.	Chronic Pneumonia.	Chronic Bronchitis.
Early symptoms.	Inspiration slower than expiration; cough dry; pulse quicker than natural, small and wiry.	Respiration quick and painful; cough troublesome but restrained; expectoration trifling; pulse quick and full.	Respiration quick but free; cough constant and severe, but without pain; pulse scarcely affected.
Termination.	Either in a cure, or else there is an effusion of serum into the chest, and generally also into the belly and limbs, causing suffocation by pressure.	If not ending in a cure there is great difficulty of breathing, often ending in suffocation. The animal does not lie down, but sits upon his hind-legs, supporting himself on his fore-legs.	Ends in a cure, or in a permanently chronic state of inflammation. Or, if fatal, there is suffocation from effusion, but this is very rare in chronic bronchitis.
Treatment.	The same as for acute pleurisy, but milder in degree, and the diet is not required to be so strictly confined to slops.	Bleeding will seldom be required. Give the calomel, opium, and tartar emetic, without the digitalis, in the doses ordered for acute pneumonia. After a few days have recourse to the bolus (46). Diet nourishing, but strictly confined to farinaceous articles. The embrocation is of great service.	Dispense with the emetic, and at once try the cough bolus (46). In very mild cases give ipecacuanha ½ grain, rhubarb 2 grains, opium 1 grain, in a pill, three times a day. Apply the mustard embrocation (43). Milk diet with nourishing slops.

These various forms constantly run into one another, so that we seldom see pleurisy without some degree of pneumonia, or the latter without bronchitis. Still, one generally predominates over the other, and, as far as treatment is concerned, that one may be considered as distinct. So also there is every shade between the very acute form, the acute, the subacute, the chronic, and the permanently chronic ; but for practical purposes the two divisions are sufficient.

SPASMODIC ASTHMA.

What is often called asthma in the dog is nothing more than a permanently chronic form of bronchitis, which is very common among petted toy-dogs or house-dogs, which are not allowed much exercise. The symptoms and treatment are detailed under the head of Chronic Bronchitis, at p. 389. But there is a form of true asthma with spasm, which is also met with among the same kind of dogs, the *symptoms* of which are much more urgent, comprising a sudden accession of difficulty in breathing, so severe that the dog evidently gasps for breath, and yet there is no evidence of inflammation. It may be known by the suddenness of the attack, inflammation being comparatively slow in its approach. The *treatment* consists in the administration of an emetic (45), followed by the cough bolus (46), or the draught (47) ; but if the spasms are very severe, a full dose of laudanum and ether must be given, viz., 1 drachm of laudanum and 30 drops of the ether, in a little water, every three hours, till relief is afforded. The mustard embrocation (42) or the turpentine liniment (43) may be rubbed into the chest with great advantage.

PHTHISIS, OR CONSUMPTION.

This disease, though very commonly fatal among highly-bred animals, has not been noticed by the writers on the diseases of the dog in this country, neither Blain, Youatt, nor Mayhew making the slightest allusion to it. I have, however, seen so many cases of tubercular disease in the dog that I cannot doubt its existence as an ordinary affection, and since I know that hundreds die every year from it I cannot pass it over without notice. I have seen the tubercules in almost every stage of softening, and have known scores of cases in which a blood-vessel has given way, producing the condition known in the human being as "spitting of blood," without any other attendant symptoms than those which are seen in man.

The *symptoms* of consumption are, a slow insidious cough, without fever in the early stage, followed by emaciation, and ending after some months in diarrhœa, or exhaustion from the amount of expectoration, or in the bursting of a blood-vessel, which last is generally the termination in those dogs that are kept for use, the work to which they are subjected leading to excessive action of the heart, which is likely to burst the vessel. In the latter stages there is a good deal of constitutional fever, but it is seldom that the dog lives long enough to show this condition, being either destroyed as incurable or dying rapidly from loss of blood or diarrhœa. *Treatment* is of little use, as, though the attack may be postponed, the disease cannot be cured, and no phthisical animal should be bred from. Cod-liver oil is of just as much service as in the human subject, but, as before remarked, it can only put off the fatal result. Except, therefore, in the case of house-pets, it is not desirable to use it. The dose is from a teaspoonful to a tablespoonful three times a day.

GASTRITIS, OR INFLAMMATION OF THE STOMACH.

This affection is, like all others of the same kind, either *acute* or *chronic*. The former very rarely accurs except from poison or highly improper food, which has the same effect. The *symptoms* are a constant and evidently painful straining to vomit, with an intense thirst, dry hot nose, quick breathing, and an attitude which is peculiar, the animal lying extended on the floor, with his belly in contact with the ground, and in the intervals of the retching licking anything cold within reach. The *treatment* consists in bleeding, if the attack is very violent; calomel and opium, of each a grain, in a pill every four hours; and two drops of the diluted hydrocyanic acid in a little distilled water following each. Thin gruel or arrowroot may be given occasionally in very small quantities, but until the vomiting ceases they are of little service. If poison has clearly been swallowed, the appropriate treatment must be adopted.

Chronic gastritis is only another name for one of the forms of dyspepsia, for the symptoms and treatment of which see p. 421.

INFLAMMATION OF THE LIVER (Hepatitis, or Yellows).

This is one of the most common of the diseases to which sporting dogs are subject, in consequence of the exposure to cold and wet which they are subjected to, producing congestion of the liver, and this going on to inflammation. Dogs deprived of exercise also contract it, because their livers first becoming torpid the bile accumulates, and then, in order to get rid of it, nature establishes an action which ends in inflammation. The *symptoms* are a yellow state of the white of the eye and skin generally, from which the disease is commonly called "the yellows."

Acute hepatitis comes on rapidly, and with a good deal of fever, generally showing itself on the day after a long exposure to wet and cold, as in shooting or hunting. The dog shivers, his nose is hot, his breathing is slightly quicker than usual, and his pulse quick, *small* and *wiry*. The bowels are confined, and when moved the motions are clay-coloured or slaty. If these symptoms are not soon relieved the case ends fatally, sickness coming on and the strength being rapidly exhausted. The *treatment* should be, first, a considerable abstraction of blood; then give the bolus (13); and as soon as it has acted rub on to the right side, over the liver, the embrocation (42) or (43); and at the same time give calomel and opium, of each a grain in a pill, every four hours, taking care to keep the bowels open by the bolus (13), or by castor oil (15). As soon as the proper colour returns to the motions the calomel may be entirely or partially discontinued, substituting small doses of rhubarb and ipecacuanha. An emetic in the early stage (45) will sometimes act like a charm, unloading the liver, and thus at once cutting short the congestion, but when inflammation has set in actively it is worse than useless, inasmuch as it aggravates the disease tenfold.

Chronic hepatitis is more frequently caused by improper food than exposure, and is very different in its *symptoms* from the acute form. Whenever the *fæces* are pale, or dark, or slate-coloured, the approach of this disease may be suspected, and appropriate treatment should be commenced; but it is not until the liver is perceptibly enlarged and the dog is evidently out of condition that it is generally considered to be established, and then scarcely any remedies will be of much service. At this time there is often not only a hard enlarged state of the liver, easily felt through and below the ribs on the right side, but also a yielding watery enlargement of the belly, from a collection of serous fluid, which is thrown out in consequence of the pressure on the veins as they return through the liver itself. The skin is "hidebound," and the hair dull and awry; while, altogether, the dog looks thin and wretched. The *treatment* consists in the use of small doses of mercury, or podophyllin, according to the state of the liver (1) or (13); or sometimes ipecacuanha may be given instead of the mercury, in half-grain doses; but it requires a long time to act, and will only suffice in very mild cases. The red iodide of mercury may be rubbed into the side, mixed with lard (one drachm to one ounce of the lard), or the embrocation (42) or (43) may be used instead. Gentle exercise may be given at the same time, and mild farinaceous food, with a small quantity of weak broth. After a time, as the liver begins to act (shown by the yellow colour of the *fæccs*), the disease relaxes, and the mercury may be dispensed with; but it is usually some considerable time before the stomach recovers its tone. A strong decoction of dandelion roots (made by boiling them for an hour in as little water as will serve to cover them, and then straining) may be given for this purpose, the dose being half a teacupful every morning.

INFLAMMATION OF THE BOWELS.

Four varieties of this condition are met with, viz.—(1) acute inflammation of the peritonæal coat; (2) spasms of the muscular coat, attended with congestion or inflammation, and known as *colic;* (3) inflammation of the mucous coat, attended by *diarrhœa;* and (4) chronic inflammation, almost always followed by constipation.

Acute inflammation of the peritonæal coat is known as *pcritonitis* and *enteritis,* according as its attacks are confined to the membrane lining the general cavity (*peritoneum*), or to that covering the intestines (*enteron*); but as there is seldom one without more or less of the other, there is little practical use in the distinction.

The *symptoms* are very severe, and are shown by shivering, feverishness, cold dry nose, ears, and legs, breath hot, and the expression anxious, showing evidence of pain, which is increased on pressing the bowels with the hand. The tail is kept closely pressed against the body, and the attitude is peculiar to the disease, the back being arched and the legs all drawn together. The bowels are costive, the urine scanty and high-coloured; there is thirst, and the appetite is absent altogether. Sometimes there is a slight vomiting after food, but at others it is retained; though in the later stages the former condition generally prevails. The disease soon runs on, and if not relieved is fatal in a few days. To *treat it*, take a large quantity of blood; give calomel and opium in grain doses of each, every three or four hours; put the dog in a warm bath for half an hour, and, after drying him, rub in the embrocation (43), avoiding pressure, and applying it rapidly but lightly. After twelve hours the bowels may be moved by means of the castor oil (15); or, if necessary, the strong mixture (16), repeating the calomel pills till the tenderness ceases. Great skill is required in adapting the remedies to the disease, and a veterinary surgeon should be called in whenever the dog is worth the expense.

Colic is also a frequent complaint among the dog tribe, the *signs* being intense pain, aggravated at intervals to such a degree as to cause the patient to howl most loudly, the back being at the same time arched as far as possible, and the legs drawn together. If this shows itself suddenly after a full meal, the colic may at once be surmised to exist; but the howl at first is not very loud, the dog starting up with a sharp moan, and then lying down again, to repeat the start and moan in a few minutes with increased intensity, until it becomes a howl continued for many seconds together. The nose is of a natural appearance, and there is little or no fever, the evidence of pain being all that directs the attention to the bowels, where there is no tenderness, and, on the contrary, pressure gradually made with the hand seems to afford relief. The *treatment* should be by means of laudanum (1 drachm) and ether (30 drops) in a little water every two or three hours; or, in very bad cases, croton oil (1 drop) may be given in a pill with three grains of solid opium every four hours till the pain ceases. The embrocation (45) may also be rubbed into the bowels, either at once or after a *very hot* bath continued for at least half an hour, which last remedy is of the greatest service. The clyster (17) may also be tried with advantage, and sometimes a very large quantity of warm water thrown up into the bowels while the dog is in the warm bath will afford instant relief. Colic sometimes ends in *intussusception*, which is a drawing of one portion of the bowel into the other ; but of this there is no evidence during life, nor if there was would any remedy be of service, short of opening the belly with the knife and drawing out the inverted portion with the hand.

Diarrhœa, or inflammation of the mucous membrane of the bowels, is a constant visitor to the kennel. Sometimes it is produced by chronic inflammation of the mucous membrane ; at others by improper food irritating it, but not to that extent ; and at others again by an epidemic influence, the nature of which it is difficult to understand. The *symptoms* are too plain to need description, further than to remark that the motions may be merely loose, marking slight irritation, or there may be a good deal of mucus (slime), which is an evidence of great irritation of the membrane ; or, again, there may be shreds or lumps of a white substance resembling boiled white of egg, in which case the inflammation has run very high. Lastly, blood may be poured out, marking either ulceration of the bowel, when the blood is bright in colour, or an oozing from the small intestines, when it is of a pitchy consistence and chocolate colour ; or a similar oozing from the large intestines, when the blood is similar to that drawn from a vein. It may also be poured out from piles, which are not uncommon in the dog, though they seldom bleed as they do in the human being, the horizontal position of the dog accounting for this immunity. The *treatment* for these several conditions will vary considerably. If there is reason to believe that there is irritation from improper food, a dose of oil (15) will clear all away, and nothing more is needed. In slight cases of mucous diarrhœa laudanum may be added to a small dose of oil (7), and if this does not have the desired effect try (6), (8), or (9). Bleeding from an ulcerated surface or from the small intestines seldom occurs except in distemper, and can rarely be restrained when severe. Relief may be attempted by the bolus (18) or the pill (19), but the shock to the system is generally too great to allow of perfect health being restored. In case of bleeding from the large intestines, the chalk mixture (6), together with the bolus (18), will often avail. Rice-water should be given as the only drink, and well-boiled rice flavoured with milk as the only solid food.

Chronic inflammation with constipation is very apt to occur in dogs which are not exercised, and are fed with biscuit or meal without vegetables. The consequence is, that the bowels after a time become inflamed, and diarrhœa is set up ; but, this soon ceasing, the mucous membrane is impaired in tone, and there is a want of the proper secretion, so that the *fœces* become hard and the muscular coat refuses to act as it should do. In such a case the belly becomes distended, and there is excessive pain, with more or less spasm. In some instances the *fœces* have become so impacted that no means could be used which would overcome the mechanical difficulty, and the dogs have died "undelivered." It is easy to distinguish these collections, because they may be readily felt through the flank, and nothing but a case of pregnancy can be mistaken for them. The *treatment* of habitual constipation should be by giving regular exercise and green vegetables with the food. Coarse oatmeal will almost always act gently on the bowels of the dog, and a costive animal may be fed upon porridge with great advantage, mixing wheat flour with it or Indian meal, so as to correct any over-activity. It is better to avoid opening medicine as a rule, though there is no objection to an occasional dose of a mild drug like castor oil. (*See* Aperients, page 354.) If the *fœces* are impacted, throw up warm water or gruel repeatedly, till they are softened, and at the same time give the aperient (12), (15), or (16). If there are piles, which may be seen as dark nut-like tumours round the anus, give as much brimstone as will lie on a shilling to a dog of average size every morning mixed up in his food.

INFLAMMATION OF THE KIDNEYS AND BLADDER.

The former of these affections, which may be known by a great scantiness of urine and evident pain in the loins, is not very common in the dog, but it does occasionally occur. The only *treatment* likely to be of service is the administration of carbonate of soda (5 grains), with 30 drops of sweet spirit of nitre, in a little water twice a day.

The *bladder* and the *urethra* leading from it for the passage of the urine are often subject to a mucous inflammation characterised by pain and constant irritation in passing water, and by a gradual dropping of a yellowish discharge from the penis. This is generally the result of cold, and may be treated by giving full doses of nitre (10 grains) with Epsom salts (half an ounce) in some water twice a week. If the discharge and pain are very severe, balsam of copaiba may be administered, the best form being the "capsules" now sold, of which two form a dose for an average-sized dog. If the discharge has spread to the exterior of the penis, the wash (20) will be of service.

SKIN DISEASES.

Almost all skin diseases depend on neglect in some form ; and in the dog they arise either from improper management, as in the case of "blotch," or "surfeit," or from the presence of parasites, as in mange. These three names are all that are applied to skin diseases in the dog, though there can be no doubt that they vary greatly, and mange itself is subdivided by different writers so as to comprehend several varieties. Fleas, ticks, &c., also irritate the skin greatly, and all will therefore be included here, the inflammation produced by them being entitled to be considered a skin disease as much as mange itself.

Blotch, or *surfeit*, shows itself in the shape of scabby lumps of matted hair on the back, sides, head, and quarters, as well as occasionally on the inside of the thighs. They vary from the size of a sixpence to that of half a crown, are irregularly round in shape, and after about three or four days the scab and hair fall off, leaving the skin bare, red, and slightly inclined to discharge a thin serum. The disease is not contagious, and evidently arises from gross feeding joined very frequently with want of exercise, and often brought out by a gallop after long confinement to the kennel. The appropriate treatment is to remove the cause by giving mild aperients (11), (13), or (14), with low diet and regular exercise, by the aid of which, continued for some little time, there is seldom any difficulty in effecting a cure.

An eruption between the toes, similar in its nature and cause to

".blotch," is also very common, showing itself chiefly at the roots of the nails, where there are considerable redness and swelling, and so much tenderness as to make the dog quite lame. In bad cases, when the constitution is impaired by defective kennel arrangements, the sores become very foul, and are then very difficult to heal. In order to remove this state of things, the general health must first be attended to, using the same means as in " blotch " if the cause is the same, and touching the sores themselves with bluestone, which should be well rubbed into the roots of the nails, first scraping it to a fine point. When. the health is much impaired and the sores are in the foul state described above, give from five to eight drops of *liquor arsenicalis* with each meal, which for this condition should be of good nourishing food. This remedy must be continued for weeks, or even months in some obstinate cases. Here, after applying the bluestone, it is often of service to rub in a *very* little tar-ointment, and then dust all over with powdered brimstone, dipping the foot into a box of it being the best mode of applying it.

. *Foul mange* (resembling the *psoriasis* of man in its nature) is a most unmanageable disease, inasmuch as it has become quite constitutional before it can be so designated, and because, being a disease of the blood, it requires a complete change in the composition of this fluid before it can be eradicated. It is doubtful whether mange is contagious, but that it is hereditary I have no doubt whatever, the proofs within my own knowledge being amply sufficient to convince me of the fact. Thus I have seen a bitch apparently cured of it, and with a perfectly healthy skin, produce a litter of whelps all of which broke out with mange at four or five months old, though scattered in various parts of the country at their walks; the bitch afterwards showing the impurity of her blood by again and again becoming the subject of mange. I should, therefore, never breed from either a dog or bitch who was attacked by this form of eruption. There is considerable thickening of the skin, with an offensive discharge from the surface, chiefly flowing from the cracks and ulcerations under the scabs on it. This dries and falls off in scales, taking with them a good deal of the hair, which is further removed by the constant scratching of the poor dog, who is tormented with incessant itching. Almost always there is a fat unwieldy state of the system from want of exercise, but the appetite is often deficient. The *treatment* is founded upon the constitutional nature of the disease, which is not caused by any parasite or vegetable growth, and is solely the result of what is commonly called foulness of the blood. The first thing to be done is to clear out the bowels by a brisk aperient, such as (12) or (13). Then give low diet without flesh, starving the dog till he is ready to eat potatoes and green vegetables, alternately with oatmeal porridge—and then only in moderate quantities. As soon as the stomach is brought down to this kind of food, but not before, begin to give the *liquor arsenicalis* with the food, the dose being a drop to each four pounds in weight of the animal, and thus a dog of eight pounds weight will require two drops three times daily ; taking care to divide the food into three equal portions, and not to give more of this altogether than is required for the purpose of health. The arsenic must be administered for weeks, or even months, and as soon as the itching seems abating and the health is improved the mangy parts of the skin may be slightly dressed with small quantities of sulphur and pitch ointments mixed in equal proportions. By a perseverance in these remedies for two or three months the blood becomes purified and the eruption disappears, after which, if the health seems impaired, a stomachic or tonic (59) or (62) will often be required. Sometimes the ointment (58a) will be required.

Virulent mange (which may be compared to *psora* and *porrigo* in the human subject) is of two kinds, one attributable to a parasitic insect, and the other of vegetable origin. In the former case, which is its most common form, it appears in large kennels where cleanliness is not sufficiently attended to, and when the floors become loaded with the excretions. There is no doubt that this is highly contagious, but there is also little difference of opinion as to its being capable of being bred or developed among a lot of previously healthy dogs if mismanaged in the above way. The skin shows itself bare of hair in large patches of irregular form, and the hair being, as it were, gradually worn away at the edges, as if by scratching. The skin is dry and rough, with cracks and creases in various directions, from some of which a thin ichorous

2 C

discharge may be seen to flow on removing the scabs which fill them. The dog feeds well, but from want of sleep is languid and listless; there is considerable thirst and some slight feverishness, but very often the flesh is maintained for months at a high rate. The *treatment* of this form of mange is founded upon the belief that it is caused by an insect, *Sarcoptes canis*, which has been detected by the microscope in many cases, but which by some people is maintained to be an accidental effect, and not a cause of mange. However this may be, it is found that remedies which are destructive to insect life are by far the most efficacious, such as hellebore, sulphur, corrosive sublimate, tobacco, &c. The *second kind* of virulent mange is more rare than that described above, and still more difficult of cure, the vegetable parasite being less easily destroyed than the insect. This parasite is supposed to be of the nature of mould or fungus, which we all know is most obstinately tenacious of life, and is reproduced again and again in any liquid where it has once developed its germs. In outward appearance this variety of mange differs very little from the insect-produced form, but it may be known by its generally attacking young puppies; while the other appears at all ages, but chiefly in the adult animal. The hair falls off in both, but there is more scab in the insect mange, probably from the fact that it does not produce such violent itching, and therefore the scratching is not so incessant. The *treatment* is nearly the same in both cases, being chiefly by external remedies, though alteratives, stomachics, and tonics are often required from the loss of health which generally accompanies the disease. In all cases, therefore, it is necessary to attend to this, giving generally a mild aperient first, such as (12) or (13) and subsequently (2) and (3) combined together, or (1) and (59), according to circumstances. At the same time one of the following applications may be tried externally, with the greatest care that the dog does not lick them off, as they are highly poisonous when taken into the stomach. To the wash some aloes is added, with the view of preventing this by the bitter taste of the drug; but though it has this good effect partially, there is nothing like a wire or leathern muzzle kept constantly on, except when feeding, at which time, of course, the tongue is otherwise engaged. All applications must be rubbed well into the *roots* of the hair.

Ointment (or dressing) for virulent mange :

> Green iodide of mercury, 2 drachms.
> Lard, 2 ounces.

Mix, and rub as much as can be got rid of in this way into the diseased skin, every other day, for a week ; then wait a week, and dress again. Take care to leave no superfluous ointment.

A milder ointment :

> Compound sulphur ointment, 4 ounces.
> Spirit of turpentine, 1 ounce.

Mix, and rub in every other day.

Red mange, resembling *eczœma* in man, is quite of a different nature to either of the above forms, being evidently a disease of the bulb which produces the hair, inasmuch as the colouring matter of the hair itself is altered, and, if white, the hair looks like a pale brick-dust colour, almost as if the dog had been sprinkled over with this material. It first shows itself almost invariably at the elbows and inside the arms, then on the front and inside of the thighs, next on the buttocks, and finally on the back, which is only attacked when the disease has existed for some weeks or months. The health does not seem to suffer, and the skin, though rough and dry, is not at all scabbed, except from the effects of the scratching, which is very frequent, but not so severe as in the virulent or foul mange. It appears most probable that red mange is contagious, but it is by no means a settled question, as it will often be seen in single dogs which are in the same kennel with others free from it entirely. Of its exact nature I know nothing beyond the belief that the disease is in the blood, and is not caused by any parasite. Dogs which are highly fed, and which are allowed to lie before the fire, are the most subject to it, while the poor half-starved cur becomes affected with the foul or virulent forms. The *treatment* consists in lowering the diet, giving aperients (12) or (13) ; following these up with the addition of green vegetables to the food, and at the same time using one or other of the following applications every other day. In obstinate cases arsenic may be given internally (see page 401) :—

Dressing for red mange :

> Green iodide of mercury, 1½ drachm.
> Spirit of turpentine, 2 drachms.
> Lard, 1½ ounce.

Mix, rub a very little of this well into the roots of the hair every other day; or,

Bishop's mange lotion, sold by Barclay & Sons, Farringdon Street. Use as a wash.

Canker of the ear has been alluded to under the disease of that organ at page 386.

Irritative inflammation of the skin is produced by fleas, lice, and ticks, which are readily discovered by examining the roots of the hair. Dog-fleas resemble in appearance those of the human subject. The lice infesting him are, however, much larger, but otherwise similar in appearance. Dog-ticks may easily be recognised by their spider-like form and bloated bodies, the claws adhering firmly to the skin, so that they are with some difficulty removed from it. These last are of all sizes, from that of an average pin's head to the dimensions of a ladybird, beyond which they seldom grow in the dog. They suck a great quantity of blood when they are numerous, and impoverish the animal to a terrible extent, partly by the drain on the system, and partly by the constant irritation which they produce. The remedies are as follows :—

To remove fleas and lice :

Mix soft soap with as much carbonate of soda as will make it into a thick paste, then rub this well into the roots of the hair all over the dog's body, adding a little hot water so as to enable the operator to completely saturate the skin with it. Let it remain on for half an hour, then put the dog into a warm bath for ten minutes, letting him quietly soak, and now and then ducking his head under. Lastly, wash the soap completely out, and dry before the fire, or at exercise, if the weather is not too cold. This, after two or three repetitions, will completely cleanse the foulest skin.

Dry remedies for lice and ticks :

Break up the lumps of some white precipitate, then with a hard brush rub it well into the roots of the hair over the whole body. Get rid of the superfluous powder from the external surface of the coat by means of light brushing or rubbing with a cloth. Put a muzzle on, and leave the dog with the powder in the coat for five or six hours. Then brush all well out, reversing the hair for this purpose, and the ticks and lice will all be found dead. A repetition at the expiration of a week will be necessary, or even perhaps a third time.

Or, use the Persian Insect Destroying Powder, sold by Keating, of St. Paul's Churchyard, and other druggists, which seems to answer well.

Or the following wash may be tried :

Acetic acid (Pharm. Lond.), 3½ ounces.
Borax, ½ drachm.
Distilled water, 4½ ounces.
Mix, and wash into the roots of the hair.

CHAPTER V.

DISEASES ACCOMPANIED BY WANT OF POWER.

Chorea—Shaking Palsy—Fits—Worms—General Dropsy or Anasarca.

As inflammation is attended by increased action of the heart and arteries, so this class of diseases is, on the contrary, accompanied by a want of tone (atony) in these organs, as well as by an irritability of the nervous system, which arises from the same cause. None of them require lowering measures, but, on the contrary, tonics and generous living will almost always be demanded. I have included worms among them, because these parasites produce a lowering effect, and seldom infest to any extent a strong healthy subject, preferring the delicate and half-starved puppy to the full-grown and hardy dog.

CHOREA.

Chorea, or *St. Vitus' Dance*, may be known by the spasmodic twitches which accompany it, and by their ceasing during sleep. In slight cases the spasm is a mere drop of the head and shoulder, or sometimes of the hind-quarter only, the nods in the former case, or the backward drop in the latter, giving a very silly and weak expression to the animal. Chorea is almost always a consequence of distemper, so that it is unnecessary to describe its early stages, and the disease itself cannot be further defined than by the above description. It seldom goes on to destroy life, though occasionally it is accompanied by fits, the disease in the brain and spine then being of such a severe nature as to end fatally in the course of time, the dog apparently dying from exhaustion. Of the exact nature of the disease we know nothing, the most careful examination of the brain and spinal cord leading to no useful result. But

it often happens that there is present at the same time a degree
of mischief in the stomach, caused apparently by the presence of
worms, and then the chorea is said to be sympathetic with this.
In the *treatment*, therefore, it is desirable to ascertain the existence
of worms, and if they are found, no remedy will be likely to be
beneficial so long as they are allowed to continue their attacks.
If they are only suspected, it is prudent to give a dose of the most
simple worm-medicine, such as the areca-nut (65); and if this
brings away only one or two, the presence of others may be pre-
dicated, and a persistence in the proper remedies (see p. 416) will
be necessary, till the dog is supposed to be be cleansed from them.
Beyond this, the remedies must be directed to improve the general
health, and at the same time to relieve any possible congestion of
the brain or spine by the insertion of a seton in the neck.   Fresh
country air is the best giver of strength, and it alone will often
suffice; but if not, after trying good nourishing animal food, mixed
with a proper proportion of vegetables, recourse may be had to the
following tonic, which is often of the greatest service :—

> Sulphate of zinc, 2 to 5 grains.
> Extract of gentian, 3 grains.
> Mix, and form a bolus.   To be given three times a day.

Attention must be carefully paid to the state of the bowels, both
constipation and looseness being prejudicial to the health, and
each requiring the appropriate treatment laid down at pages 394
and 395. Sometimes the tonic pill (62) will do wonders, and often
the change from it to the sulphate of zinc and back again will be
of more service than either of them continued by itself. A perseverance in these methods, with the aid of the shower-bath, used
by means of a watering-pot, applied to the head and spine, and
followed by moderate exercise, will sometimes entirely remove the
disease, though in the majority of cases a slight drop will be ever
afterwards noticed, and in sporting-dogs the strength is seldom
restored to the same extent as before.

SHAKING PALSY.

This resembles chorea in its nature, but it is incessant, except
during sleep, and attacks the whole body. The *same remedies*

may be applied, but it is an incurable disease, though not always destroying life.

FITS.

Fits are of three kinds—first, those arising from irritation, especially in the puppy, and known as convulsive fits; second, those connected with pressure on the brain, and being of the nature of apoplexy; and third, epileptic fits, which may occur at all ages, and even at intervals throughout the whole life of the animal.

Convulsive fits are generally produced by the irritation of dentition, and occur chiefly at the two periods when the teeth are cut, that is, in the first month, and from the fifth to the seventh. They come on suddenly, the puppy lying on its side, and being more or less convulsed, the extent and severity of the struggling being no indication of the amount of the disease. There is no foaming at the mouth, and the recovery from them is gradual, in both these points differing from epilepsy. The only *treatment* at all likely to be of service is the use of the hot bath, which in young and delicate puppies may sometimes give relief. Fits arising in distemper are caused by absolute mischief in the brain, unless they occur as a consequence of worms, which will also produce them at other times, and are nearly as often the cause as teething. In such cases, these parasites being removed, the fits cease.

In *apoplectic fits* the dog lies insensible, or nearly so, without foaming at the mouth, but snoring and breathing heavily. Here the *treatment* must be conducted by taking away blood from the neck-vein, afterwards purging by means of croton oil, and inserting a seton in the back of the neck. The attack, however, is generally fatal, in spite of the most scientific treatment.

Epilepsy may be distinguished by the blueness of the lips and gums, and by the constant champing of the jaws and frothing at the mouth, which constantly accompany its attacks. The fit comes on without any notice, frequently in sporting-dogs while they are at work, a hot day being specially provocative of it. In the pointer and setter the fit almost always occurs just after a " point," the excitement of which seems to act upon the brain in producing it. The dog falls directly the birds are sprung, and after lying struggling for a few minutes, or perhaps a quarter of an hour, rises, looking wildly about him; and then sitting or lying down again for a few minutes, he is ready to go to work again, appa-rently unconscious of anything having been the matter. As in chorea so in epilepsy, nothing is known of the *cause*, and the *treat-ment* is therefore guided by the most empirical principles. Within the last few years bromide of potassium has been used with great success in the human subject; but although I have recommended its use in many cases on the dog, I have not heard the result. The dose for a moderate-sized animal is 3 grains twice a day in a pill, continued for a month at least.

WORMS.

Worms are a fertile source of disease in the dog, destroying every year more puppies than distemper itself, and, in spite of every precaution, appearing in the kennelled hound or shooting-dog, as well as the pampered house-pet and the half-starved cur. In old and constantly used kennels they are particularly rife, and I believe that, in some way, their *ova* remain from year to year, attached either to the walls or to the benches. All of the varieties met with are propagated by *ova*, though some, as the *Ascaris lum-bricoides*, are also viviparous, so that the destruction of the worms actually existing at the time the vermifuge is given does not neces-sarily imply the after clearance of the animal, who may be infested with them as badly as before, from the hatching of the eggs left behind. The natural history of these parasites is, however, very imperfectly understood, in spite of the carefully recorded and ex-tended labours of Rudolphi, Schmalz, Cloquet, Creplin, and our own Owen; indeed, as it is not till after the death of the animal infested by them that they can be reached, it is only wonderful that so much is known. Besides the intestinal worms, there are also others met with in the dog, including the large kidney worm (*Strongylus gigas*), which shall presently be described, and the hydatid, which is in all probability the cause of turnside; but though found in the dog's brain, its presence has not, I believe, been clearly associated with that disease. I shall, therefore, first describe the appearance of each kind of worm; then the symptoms of worms in general; and lastly, the best means for their expulsion.

The *Maw-worm* in the dog is about an inch in length (*fig.* 1), of a milky white colour, with one end cut off obtusely and slightly puckered (the mouth), and the other pointed (the tail). Maw-worms exist in great numbers in the dog, chiefly occupying the large intestines, and have been usually considered not to injure the

Fig. 1.

health to any great degree, unless they exist in very large numbers; but Dr. Cobbold is of opinion that they are merely sections of the tape-worm, and if so, the above opinion must be erroneous. The subject is one which requires a special study, and I must therefore accept Dr. Cobbold's statement without dispute.

The *Round-worm* (*Ascaris lumbricoïdes*) is from four to seven inches long, round, firm, and of a pale pink colour. The two extremities are exactly alike, and are slightly flattened in one direction at the point (see *fig.* 2), in which *a* shows the worm extended,

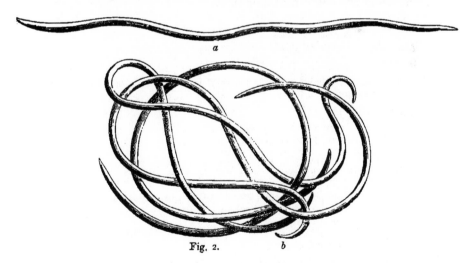

Fig. 2.   *b*

and *b* a group of three as actually discharged from the intestine of a dog in which they were thus knotted. I have often seen from six to a dozen round-worms thus collected together, so as when discharged to form a solid mass as large as an egg. Like the last species, they are propagated by *ova*, but sometimes these are hatched in the body of the parent, so that a large worm may be

Fig. 4.

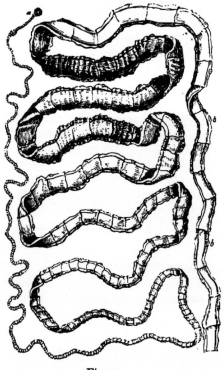

Fig. 3.

seen full of small ones. This species occasions much more inconvenience than the maw-worm, but still far less than the tape-worm, supposing the two be distinct.

Tape-worms in the dog are described by foreign writers as of five kinds, of which the *Tænia solium* and *Bothriocephalus latus* are common to man and the dog. The others are not readily distinguished from these two, and all are now said to be developed from the hydatid forms found in the livers of sheep, rabbits, &c. The peculiarity in the bothriocephalus consists in the shape of the head (see *fig.* 4), which has two lateral longitudinal grooves (*bothria*), while that of the true tænia is hemispherical. The following is a description according to Professor Owen :—" The *Tænia solium* attains the length of several feet, extending sometimes from the mouth to the anus. The breadth varies from one-fourth of a line at its anterior part to three or four lines towards the posterior part of the body, which then again diminishes. The head (*fig.* 3, *a*) is small, and generally hemispherical, broader than long, and often as if truncated anteriorly ; the four mouths, or oscula, are situated on the anterior surface, and surround the central rostellum, which is very short, terminated by a minute apical papilla, and surrounded by a double circle of small recurved hooks. The segments of the neck, or anterior part of the body, are represented by transverse rugæ, the marginal angles of which scarcely project beyond the lateral line ; the succeeding segments are subquadrate, their length scarcely exceeding their breadth ; they then become sensibly longer, narrower anteriorly, thicker and broader at the posterior margin, which slightly overlaps the succeeding joint. The last series of segments are sometimes twice or three times as long as they are broad. The generative orifices (*b b*) are placed near the middle of one of the margins of each joint, and are generally alternate (*fig.* 5, *c d*). The *Tænia solium* is androgynous ; that is to say, it produces its *ova* without the necessity for the contact of two individuals, the male and female organs being contained in each." Professor Owen thus describes them—" In each joint of this worm there is a large branched ovarium (*fig.* 5, *i*), from which a duct (*h*) is continued to the lateral opening ; the *ova* are crowded in the ovary, and in those situated on the posterior segments of the body they generally present a brownish colour, which renders the form of their receptacle sufficiently conspicuous. In segments which have been expelled separately we have observed the ovary to be nearly empty ; and it is in these that the male duct and gland are most easily perceived. For this purpose, it is only necessary to place the segment between two slips of glass, and view it by means of a simple lens magnifying from 20 to 30 diameters. A well-defined line (*g*), more slender and opaque than the oviduct, may then be traced, extending from the termination of the oviduct, at the lateral opening, to the middle of the joint, and inclined in a curved or slightly wavy line to near the middle of the posterior margin of the segment, where it terminates in a small oval vesicle. This, as seen by transmitted light, is subtransparent in the centre and opaque at the circumference, indicating its hollow or vesicular structure. The duct, or *vas deferens*, contains a grumous secretion; it is slightly dilated just before its termination. In this species, therefore, the ova are impregnated on their passage outward."— (*Cyclopædia of Anatomy*, art. *Entozoa*.) From this minute description it may be gathered that the ova are in enormous numbers, each section of the worm being capable of producing them to an almost indefinite extent; and as they are passed out of the body with the *fæces*, it is not surprising that they are readily communicated from one dog to another, as is almost proved to be the case from the fact of their prevalence in certain kennels and absence from others. The injury caused by these worms is twofold, depending partly upon the abstraction of nourishment which is absorbed by the worm, and partly by the irritation produced by its presence in the intestines; and hence it is of the utmost importance to get rid of so troublesome a customer.

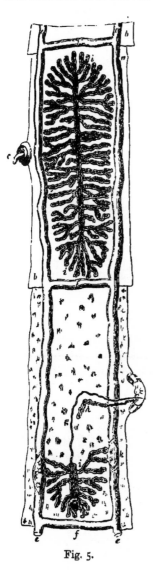

Fig. 5.

The *Kidney-worm* (*Strongylus gigas*) "inhabits the kidney of the dog, as well as that of the wolf, otter, raccoon, glutton, horse, and bull (see *fig. 6*). It is generally of a dark blood-colour, which seems to be owing to the nature of its food, which is derived from the vessels of the kidney, as when suppuration has taken place round it the worm has been found of a whitish hue." In the human kidney it has been known to attain the length of three feet, with a diameter of half an inch. "The head (*a*) is obtuse, the mouth orbicular and surrounded by six hemispherical papillæ (A); the body is slightly impressed with circular striæ, and with two longitudinal impressions; the tail is incurved in the male, and terminated by a dilated point or *bursa* (B), from the base of which the single intromittent spiculum (*b*) projects. In the female the caudal extremity is less attenuated and straighter, with the anus (C) a little below the apex." (*Cyclopædia of Anatomy*, art. *Entozoa*.) I have been thus particular in inserting descriptions of these worms, because I find that the study of their natural history is becoming more general; and as there is a large field for the microscopic inquirer, it is well to have a good ground to start from. The generation of parasites is at all times of great interest, but, with reference to the *Entozoa*, there is so much still unknown, that the natural historian who would be able to throw light on this branch of his favourite study would deserve the thanks of those who, while they take an equal interest in it with himself, have not the opportunity, or perhaps the industry, which he possesses.

Fig. 6.

The *symptoms* of the presence of worms in the dog should be carefully noted and anxiously looked

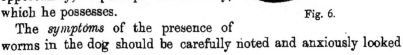

for, if the health of the animal is of any importance. They are, an unhealthy appearance of the coat, the hair looking dead and not lying smoothly and evenly; appetite ravenous in proportion to the condition, which is generally low, though worms may exist for months without interfering much with the presence of fat. After a time, however, the fat of the body is absorbed, and the muscles, without being firm and prominent, are marked with intervening lines from its absence. The *fœces* are passed frequently and in small quantities, the separate passage of a small quantity of mucus each time being particularly indicative of worms, especially if there is first a solid lump, and then a small portion of frothy mucus. The spirits also are dull, the nose hot and dry, and the breath offensive. These signs are only present to the full extent when the dog is troubled with tape-worm, or with the round-worm in large quantities; the maw-worm being only slightly injurious in comparison with the others, and seldom producing the whole of the above train of symptoms. The kidney-worm, of course, has no effect upon the intestinal secretions, but it produces bloody urine, more or less mixed with *pus*. Still, as these are often present without this worm, it is impossible to predict its existence during life with any degree of certainty. When worms are suspected, in order to distinguish the species, it is better to give a dose of calomel and jalap (16), unless the dog is very weakly, when the areca nut may be substituted (65); and then, by watching the *fœces*, the particular worm may be detected and the treatment altered accordingly.

The *expulsion of the worms* is the proper method of *treatment* in all cases, taking care afterwards to prevent their regeneration, by strengthening the system, and by occasional doses of the medicine suited to remove the worm in question. All vermifuges act as poisons to the worms themselves, or as mechanical irritants; the former including the bulk of these medicines, and the latter powdered glass and tin as well as cowhage. These poisons are all more or less injurious to the dog, and in spite of every precaution fatal results will occur after most of them, even the areca nut, innocent as it is said to be, having occasionally nearly destroyed the life of valuable dogs under careful superintendence. There is a wonderful difference in the power of resisting the action of remedies in certain individuals of the dog tribe, as well as in the worms themselves; so that whereas, in some instances, a remedy may clear a dog easily without the slightest ill effect upon him, in another, apparently under the very same circumstances of health and strength, remedy and dose, a fatal result, or nearly so, shall be produced, and even without bringing away the worms. Hence there is always some little risk in conducting the removal of these troublesome parasites, which directly and indirectly cause more deaths than all other diseases put together; the former by their own prejudicial effects, and the latter from the abuse of the power-ful drugs which are employed.

The following *list of remedies* against the various worms is inserted :—

For round-worms :

      Betel nut (*Nux areca*).
      Stinking hellebore (*Helleborus fœtidus*).
      Indian pink (*Spigelia Marylandica*).
      Calomel (*Hydrargyri chloridum*).
      Wormwood (*Artemisia absinthium*).
      Santonine, the active principle of wormseed (*Artemisia contra*).
      Cowhage (*Mucuna pruriens*).
      Powdered tin and glass.

For tape-worm :

      Spirit of turpentine (*Spiritus terebinthinæ*).
      Kousso (*Brayera anthelmintica*).
      Pomegranate bark (*Punica Granatum*).
      Leaves and oil of male fern (*Filix mas*).

The *areca nut* was first recommended in this country as a vermi-fuge about 35 years ago by Major Besant, who had seen it used in India for that purpose. Since that time it has been very gene-rally adopted, and appears to answer the purpose remarkably well, if it is frequently used, and dependence is not placed on a single dose. It should be given every week or ten days, for six or seven times, if the round-worm is present; but two or three doses occa-sionally given will suffice for the maw-worm. Six or eight hours afterwards a dose of castor oil should be given. The dose of the freshly powdered areca nut is about two grains to every lb. of the dog's weight. Thus a dog of 30 lbs. will take one drachm, or half an average nut. The powder should be merely the nut roughly grated with a coarse "grater;" and it should be quickly mixed with some good broth, thickened with oatmeal, and given before the bitter taste is extracted by soaking; after which the dog will not voluntarily take it.

Stinking hellebore is very innocent, and even useful in other ways. The dose for a 30-lbs. dog is five or six grains mixed up with eight or ten of jalap, and formed into a bolus, to be given every five or six days.

Indian pink is a very powerful vermifuge; but it also occasionally acts very prejudicially on the dog; and it must never be given without knowing the risk which is incurred. I have myself used it in numberless instances without injury; but its employment has so frequently been followed by fatal results in other hands that I cannot do otherwise than caution my readers against it. How, or why, this has been I have never been able to ascertain; but that it is so I have no doubt whatever. If it is determined to use it, half an ounce of the drug, as purchased, should be infused in half a pint of boiling water; and of this infusion, after straining it, from a tablespoonful to two tablespoonsful should be given to the dogs, according to size, followed by a dose of oil.

Calomel is a powerful expellent, but it also is attended with danger. The dose is from three to five grains, mixed with jalap. (See (12), page 354.)

Wormwood may be given with advantage to young puppies, being mild in its operation; but I do not believe it to be as generally useful as the areca nut. The dose is from ten to thirty grains in syrup or honey.

Santonine is an admirable remedy, when it can be procured in a pure state. The brown is the best, of which from one-half to three grains is the dose, mixed with from five to fifteen grains of jalap, and given at intervals of a week.

Cowhage, powdered tin, and *glass* all act by their mechanical irritation, and may be given without the slightest fear at any time. The first should be mixed with treacle, and a teaspoonful or two given occasionally. The second and third are better mixed with butter, the dose being as much as can be heaped upon a shilling.

Spirit of turpentine is without doubt the most efficacious of all worm medicines; but if not given with care it is apt to upset the health of the dog, by irritating the mucous membrane of the alimentary canal, and of the kidneys also. I am satisfied, however, that it is not necessary to give it in its undiluted form, and that by mixing it with oil its dangerous qualities are altogether suppressed. I have known young puppies, under two months of age, cleared of worms without the slightest injury by giving them from three to ten drops, according to their size, in a teaspoonful of oil. The old plan was to tie up the turpentine in a piece of bladder, which is then to be given as a bolus; but this is either broken in the throat, causing suffocation by getting into the windpipe, or it is dissolved in the stomach, which is then irritated by the almost caustic nature of the turpentine. The ordinary dose given in this way is from half a drachm to half an ounce, the latter being only adapted to very strong and full-sized dogs. Certainly it is very useful given in this way, if it does not irritate; but I should prefer the mixture with oil, though it is sometimes rejected from the stomach.

Kousso, when employed, should be given entire, first pouring boiling water upon it, and, when cool, adding the juice of half a lemon, which seems to increase its power. Like Indian pink and turpentine, it sometimes acts prejudicially, or even fatally, though it is generally quite innocent. The dose is from two drachms to four, in half a pint of boiling water, which should be repeated two or three times at intervals of a week.

Pomegranate bark is an admirable remedy, but it is not often to be obtained genuine, it being little used in this country. The dose is from half an ounce to an ounce of the bark, which, after standing for twenty-four hours in a pint and a half of water, is to be boiled down to one-half and filtered. This quantity is then to be divided into three portions, one of which is to be given every half-hour, till the whole is taken.

The *leaves* and *oil of the male fern* are both very efficacious remedies, when obtained in a state of purity, in which there is some difficulty, though the plant is common enough. It should be dug up in the summer, and the top powdered and carefully preserved in stoppered bottles. The dose is from twenty grains to two drachms, made into a bolus, and followed by a jalap purge,

2 D

or castor oil, in two or three hours. Of the oil, from ten to twenty drops are the dose, mixed up with linseed meal and water, and one-half given at night, the remainder next morning, followed in an hour by a dose of castor oil.

GENERAL DROPSY (ANASARCA).

General Dropsy consists in serum infiltrated into the cellular membrane, beneath the skin of the whole body, as shown by swelling without redness, and "pitting" on the pressure of the finger being removed. The *immediate cause* is to be looked for either in general debility, by which the serum is not absorbed in due course, or from defective action of the kidneys, by which the blood is overcharged with it. More *remotely*, improper stimulants or gross food will produce it, especially in foul and dirty kennels, and in old and worn-out dogs when the liver is deficient in activity. The *treatment* must vary with the *cause*, and it is therefore important that this should be ascertained at once. Thus, in case there is merely general debility, tonics (62) or (63) will be the proper remedies. If the kidneys are in fault, but merely torpid, the diuretic bolus (40) or (41) may be relied on; while if they have been inflamed, the treatment proper to that disease (see page 398) must be resorted to. Sometimes, in a broken-down constitution, when the urine is mixed with blood, small doses of cantharides may be found beneficial, as advised by Mayhew; but these cases are so difficult to distinguish, that it is only when veterinary aid cannot be obtained that I should advise the use of this drug. The dose is two to three drops in water twice a day.

> Tincture of cantharides, 2 drops.
> Spirit of nitric ether, 15 drops.
> Water, 1 oz.
> Mix and give as a drench twice a day.

CHAPTER VI.

DISEASES ARISING FROM MISMANAGEMENT OR NEGLECT.

Anæmia—Rickets—Indigestion.

POVERTY OF BLOOD (Anæmia).

WHEN puppies are reared in the densely populated parts of our cities, or even in the country where they are crowded together in large numbers, they are weakly in constitution, and their blood is pale, from being deprived of the red particles which fresh air and good food with *sunlight* will alone produce. The feeding has a good deal to do with this, but not so much as the other causes. The *signs* are clear enough, the young dog looking emaciated and delicate and his coat staring, while his lips and tongue are of a pale pink, as if washed out. Worms are almost always present, and if so they aggravate the disease tenfold. (See page 408.) The *treatment* should consist in plenty of fresh air, in the country if possible, admitting the sun on all occasions; together with good nourishing food, composed of the proper proportions of animal and vegetable ingredients. (See page 363.) Generally a total change in these respects will be the best remedy, but sometimes this cannot be had, and then a combination of quinine and steel may be used as an internal medicine. Thus:

> Sulphate of quinine,
> Sulphate of iron, of each 1 grain.
> Extract of dandelion, 3 grains.
> Mix, and give three times a day, with a spoonful of cod-liver oil.

If worms are present they must, of course, be got rid of. (See page 407.)

RICKETS AND ENLARGED JOINTS.

By *Rickets* is understood a soft and weak condition of the bones, in which the lime is deficient; and, the gelatine comprising their framework having no proper support, they bend in any direction which the superincumbent weight may give them. Hence we so often see puppies which are confined to their kennels with bandy-legs, which is usually the first sign of rickets. Sometimes the shins bend forward, producing what is called the "buck-shin," but whether the legs bow outwards or forwards, the cause is the same. The *remedy* for this is to be looked for in country air, exercise, and good food; but the quinine and steel pills, ordered for poverty of blood, will also be of service here, and notably when supported by cod-liver oil.

Enlarged Joints may be merely a sign of excessive vigour in the formation of bone, as is sometimes seen in the early puppyhood of the greyhound, the mastiff, and other large dogs, between three and nine months old, when the knees and hocks will strike the eye as out of all character with the rest of the frame. Here, so long as the legs are not bent out of shape and there is no lameness, the breeder need feel no anxiety, as in course of time the enlargement of the joints subsides, leaving only what is particularly desired, namely, large bony and strong joints, without any malformation. It is extraordinary to what an extent this bony development sometimes goes, especially in young dogs, bitches seldom showing the same amount of it. Inexperienced breeders are often sadly puzzled to know whether such puppies are worth rearing, and I have often saved the lives of valuable animals, which had been condemned as diseased, but which ultimately turned out to be all that could be wished. When, therefore, such a state of things exists, let the patience of the owner be exercised till the ninth or tenth month, or sometimes still longer, and if about this time the limbs do not grow into shape, it will be quite early enough to consider what is to be done. But, again, there is to be met with a scrofulous enlargement of the joints which is seldom got rid of; but this occurs in delicate puppies, and not in the large overgrown animals which are the subjects of the mere "big joints" above described. There is a puffy and soft feeling communicated to the hand on examining the leg, and usually there is a tenderness on pressure, together with more or less lameness in walking or running. This scrofulous enlargement may occur in the knees, hocks, or stifles, but the last-named joints are most usually the seats of the disease. Sometimes nature rallies and throws off this tendency to scrofula, but more frequently the joints become larger and larger, the lameness increases, and, in most cases, some one joint, being worse than the others, inflames and forms matter within it, when nothing is to be done but to consign the poor animal to the halter or the river.

INDIGESTION (DYSPEPSIA).

Among the most common consequences of improper feeding and neglect of exercise is indigestion, attended by its usual concomitant, constipation. (See pp. 394, 395.) It shows itself in flatulence, loss of appetite, alternations of constipation and diarrhœa, low spirits, and want of muscular vigour; although often the animal is fat enough, or, indeed, sometimes loaded with fat (adipose matter). Such a state of things never occurs to a dog properly reared and afterwards well managed, being confined to those which are either fed on improper food or allowed too much of it, or which are not allowed exercise enough; or, as is too frequently the case, which are submitted to all three of these causes. The *treatment* is simple enough, it being only necessary, except in very old-standing cases, to adopt the proper rules for feeding, exercise, &c., which are laid down at page 360 *et seq.*, and nature asserts her supremacy, rapidly getting the victory over disease. In no animal are the ups and downs so rapid as in the dog, which gets fat and lean in a week; and certainly there are few which will bear with impunity the liberties which are taken with him. If moderate starvation (sometimes, at first, entire, in order to make the pampered dog take food which is fit for him) does not soon restore the stomach, care must be taken that the liver is acting properly, the *fœces* being watched to see if they are of a proper colour; and if not, small doses of calomel or blue bill will be required—(1), (2), or (13). If, on the contrary, the liver acts properly, yet the stomach is out of order, recourse may be had to the stomachic bolus (59), or the draught (60), which will very seldom fail, if aided by proper management. It should, however, never be forgotten that medicine is of no use unless, at the same time, the diet is attended to and sufficient exercise given. In cases of indigestion it is particularly necessary to change the food every third or fourth day, for the stomach is often so fitful that what will agree with it once or twice will afterwards be almost sure to disagree.

CHAPTER VII.

DISEASES AND ACCIDENTS REQUIRING SURGICAL AID.

Tumours—Cancer—Encysted Tumours—Abscesses—Unnatural Parturition—
Accidents and Operations.

TUMOURS.

BRONCHOCELE, or *Goitre*, is very common among house-pets, showing itself in a large and rather soft swelling in the front of the
throat. It is not attended with danger; and even in extreme cases,
when it affects the breathing so as to cause it to be short and even
attended with noise, it very rarely goes on to produce suffocation.
It is called, scientifically, an *hypertrophy* of the thyroid body, being
an excessive and unnatural growth of the part, and not a new or
diseased production. The *treatment* consists in rubbing in iodine
outwardly; and, if this fails, giving it internally also. The internal remedy may be according to the formula (3); but if the
expense is objected to, the sarsaparilla may be omitted. The
ointment is as follows:

Iodide of potassium, 1 drachm.
Lard, 1 ounce.
Mix, and rub in the size of a filbert night and morning.

Or,

Paint over the surface some tincture of iodine twice a week.

CANCER.

Cancer is a malignant disease; that is, it is incapable of a cure by
the natural powers, and must be eradicated either by the knife or
by caustic. It is, however, very doubtful whether by their means
the disease is checked for any length of time, generally returning
afterwards in the course of a few months. The disease may be

known in the early stage by the appearance of a hard lump, varying in size from that of a filbert to a large walnut or common egg,
with an irregular "knotty" feel and a strange hardness.   In process of time this enlarges and the skin adheres to it, by-and-by
ulcerating and a red fungus growth making its appearance.   There
are various forms in which the open cancer shows itself, sometimes
red and smooth, at others very "knotty" and purple, while a
third variety resembles curdy matter mixed with streaks of blood.
The most common seats of cancer in the dog are, the teats or womb
in the bitch, and the penis in the dog.   I have several times seen
a cancerous condition of the womb and vagina cause such constant
irritation that the bitch always appeared to be at heat, and would
take the dog at any time, but without breeding, to the great
astonishment and annoyance of the owner, who is unable to
account for this repeated "heat," as he considers it.   A cancer is
incurable ; the knife is the only remedy, but it should be used by
hands accustomed to operations, and practice with previous demon-
strations is all-important.   When, therefore, a cancer is to be
removed, a veterinary surgeon should at once be called in.

ENCYSTED TUMOURS.

Encysted tumours are sacs or bags of various sizes, which occur just
beneath the skin, and contain a thick, glairy, and transparent fluid
resembling white of egg.   They are readily known by their soft
yielding feel, and by their evident want of connection with the surrounding parts.   Nothing but the knife is of the slightest use,
and by cutting through them the sac may readily be torn out,
each half at a time, taking care not to leave a particle behind, as it
is sure to grow again into another sac of the same size as before.

ABSCESSES.

Abscesses, the result of inflammation, are very common in the
dog, and show themselves in the early stage as hard, painful
swellings, more or less deep, but gradually coming to the surface,
when the skin reddens, and they burst of themselves in the
course of time.   Very often, however, the matter forms so slowly,
and has such a tendency to burrow among the muscles, that, if it
is not let out by the knife in the early stage, it produces great

exhaustion from the quantity formed. Matter may be detected, as soon as it is thrown out, by the sensation given to the fingers of each hand called "fluctuation;" that is to say, on pressing one side of the swelling with the left hand the other side rises beneath the fingers of the right, in an elastic way, just as happens with a water-pillow when pressure is made upon it. When, therefore, this fluctuation is clearly made out, a lancet or knife should be inserted and made to cut its way out, so as to leave a considerable opening, which should be so arranged as to let the matter drain out at all times. This is what in surgery is called a "depending" opening, the opposite plan allowing the matter to remain in the abscess, which cannot therefore heal, because its walls are separated, and the consequence is that a *sinus* forms, which gives infinite trouble to get it well. Should this sinus be established, the only plan is, either to lay it open by slitting it up with a narrow knife, or by passing a probe or other similar smooth body to the end, cutting down upon it, and then inserting a few threads or a piece of tape, convert it into a seton, which will either eat its way out, or after a time the threads may be withdrawn and the sides unite.

UNNATURAL PARTURITION.

I have alluded to the management of healthy parturition at page 250, but in this chapter I must say something of the proper conduct to be observed where the process is disturbed by any accidental complication. As, however, these unnatural labours only occur in any number to the veterinary practitioner, I shall take the liberty of inserting here Mr. Youatt's remarks on the subject, which I believe to be truthful throughout :—

"The pupping usually takes place from the sixty-second to the sixty-fourth day ; and, the process having commenced, from a quarter to three-quarters of an hour generally takes place between the production of each puppy.

"Great numbers of bitches are lost every year in the act of parturition ; there seems to be a propensity in the females to associate with dogs larger than themselves, and they pay for it with their lives. The most neglected circumstance during the period of pregnancy is the little exercise which the mother is permitted to take, while, in point of fact, nothing tends more to safe and easy parturition than her being permitted or compelled to take a fair quantity of exercise.

"When the time of parturition has arrived, and there is evident difficulty in producing the fœtus, recourse should be had to the ergot of rye, which should be given every hour or half-hour, according to circumstances. If after a certain time some, although little, progress has been made, the ergot must be continued in smaller doses, or perhaps suspended for a while ; but if all progress is evidently suspended, recourse must be had to the hook or the forceps. By gentle but continued manipulation much may be done, especially when the muzzle of the puppy can be brought into the passage. As little force as possible must be used, and especially the fœtus little broken. Many a valuable animal is destroyed by the undue application of force.

"If the animal seems to be losing strength, a small quantity of laudanum and ether may be administered. 'The patience of bitches in labour is extreme,' says Mr. Blaine ; 'and their distress, if not removed, is most striking and affecting. Their look is at such time particularly expressive and apparently imploring.' When the pupping is protracted, and the young ones are evidently dead, the mother may be saved, if none of the puppies have been broken. In process of time the different puppies may, one after another, be extracted ; but when violence has been used at the commencement, or almost at any part of the process, death will assuredly follow.

"*June* 15, 1832.—A spaniel bitch was brought to my infirmary to-day who has been in great and constant pain since yesterday, making repeated but fruitless efforts to expel her puppies. She is in a very plethoric habit of body ; her bowels are much confined, and she exhibits some general symptoms of febrile derangement, arising, doubtless, from her protracted labour. This is her first litter. Upon examination no young could be distinctly felt.

"Place her in a warm bath, and give her a dose of castor oil morning and evening.

"*June* 16.—The bitch appears in the same state as yesterday, except that the medicine has operated freely upon the bowels, and the febrile symptoms have somewhat decreased. Her strainings are as frequent and distressing as ever. Take two scruples of the ergot of rye, and divide into six doses, of which let one be given every half-hour.

"In about ten minutes after the exhibition of the last dose of this medicine she brought forth with great difficulty one dead puppy, upon taking which away from her she became so uneasy that I was induced to return it to her. In about a quarter of an hour after this I paid her another visit ; the puppy could not now be found ; but a suspicious appearance in the mother's eye betrayed at once that she had devoured it. I immediately administered an emetic ; and in a very short time the whole fœtus was returned in five distinct parts, viz., the four quarters and the head. After this the bitch began to amend very fast ; she produced no other puppy ; and as her supply of milk was small, she was soon convalescent.

"Twelve months afterwards she was again taken in labour, about eleven o'clock in the morning, and after very great difficulty one puppy was produced. After this the bitch appeared in great pain, but did not succeed in expelling another fœtus, in consequence of which I was sent for about three o'clock P.M. I found her very uneasy, breathing laboriously ; the mouth hot, and the bowels costive ; but I could not discover any trace of another fœtus. She was put into a warm bath, and a dose of opening medicine was administered.

"About five o'clock she got rid of one dead and two living puppies.

"*2nd.* She is still very ill ; she evinces great pain when pressed upon the abdomen ; and it is manifest that she has another fœtus within her. I ordered a dose of the ergot, and in about twenty minutes a large puppy was produced, nearly dying. She survived with due care.

"I cannot refrain from inserting the following case at considerable length :—

"*Sept. 4th*, 1820.—A very diminutive terrier, weighing not 5 lbs., was sent to my hospital in order to lie in. She was already restless and panting. About eight o'clock at night the labour pains commenced ; but until eleven scarcely any progress was made. The *os uteri* would not admit my finger, although I frequently attempted it.

"At half-past eleven the membranes began to protrude ; at one the head had descended into the pelvis and the puppy was dead. In a previous labour she had been unable to produce her young, although the ergot of rye had been freely used. I was obliged to use considerable force, and she fought terribly with me throughout the whole process. At half-past one, and after applying considerable force, I brought away a large fœtus, compared with her own size. On passing my finger as high as possible I felt another fœtus living, but the night passed and the whole of the following day, and she ate and drank, and did not appear to be much injured.

"Several times in the day I gave her some strong soup and the ergot. Some slight pains now returned, and by pressing on the belly the nose of the fœtus was brought to the superior edge of the pelvis. The pains again ceased, the pudenda began to swell from frequent examination, the bitch began to stagger, and made frequent attempts to void her urine, with extreme difficulty in accomplishing it. I now resorted to the crotchet ; and after many unsuccessful attempts, in which the superior part of the vagina must have been considerably bruised, I fixed it sufficiently firm to draw the head into the cavity of the pelvis. Here for a while the shoulder resisted every attempt which I could make without the danger of detruncating the fœtus. At length, by working at the side of the head until my nails were soft and my fingers sore, I extracted one fore-leg. The other was soon brought down ; another large puppy was produced, but destroyed by the means necessary for its production. This was the fruit of two hours' hard work.

"She was completely exhausted, and scarcely able to stand. When placed on the ground she staggered and fell at almost every step. Her efforts to void her urine were frequent and ineffectual.

"At four o'clock I again examined her ; the external pudenda were sore and swelled, and beginning to assume a black hue. It was with considerable difficulty that I could introduce my finger. A third fœtus irregularly presented was detected. I could just feel one of the hind-legs. No time was to be lost. I introduced a small pair of forceps by the side of my finger, and succeeded in laying hold of the leg without much difficulty, and with two or three weak efforts from the mother—I could scarcely call them pains—I brought the leg down until it was in the cavity of the pelvis. I solicited it forward with my finger, and, by forcibly pressing back the *labia pudendi*, I could just grasp it with the finger and thumb of the right hand. Holding it there, I introduced the finger of the right hand, and continued to get down the other leg, and then found little difficulty until the head was brought to the superior edge of the pelvis. After a long interval, and with considerable force, this was brought into the pelvis, and another puppy extracted. This fully occupied two hours.

"The bitch now appeared almost lifeless. As she was unable to stand, and seemed unconscious of everything around her, I concluded that she was lost. I gave her one or two drops of warm brandy and water, covered her up closely, and put her to bed.

"To my surprise, on the following morning, she was curled round in her basket ; she licked my hands, and ate a bit of bread and butter ; but when put on her legs she staggered and fell. The pudendum was dreadfully swollen, and literally black. In the afternoon she again took a little food ; she came voluntarily from her basket, wagged her tail when spoken to, and on the following day she was taken in her basket a journey of seventy miles, and afterwards did well. No one could be more rejoiced than was her master, who was present at, and superintended, the greater part of the proceedings.

"*The Beneficial Effect of Ergot of Rye in Difficult Parturition.*—The following case is from the pen of Professor Dick :—

"'On the 10th instant a pointer bitch produced two puppies : and it was thought by the person having her in charge that she had no more. She was put into a comfortable box, and with a little care was expected to do well. On the next morning, however, she was sick and breathed heavily, and continued rather uneasy all the day.

"'On the forenoon of the following day I was requested to see her. I found her with her nose dry, breath hot, respiration frequent, mouth hot and parched, coat staring, back roached, pulse 120, and a black fœtid discharge from the vagina. Pressure on the abdomen gave pain. A pup could be obscurely felt; the secretion of milk was suppressed, and the skin had lost its natural elasticity.

"'Tepid water with a little soap dissolved in it was immediately injected into the uterus, which in a considerable degree excited its action ; and this injection was repeated two or three times with the same effect.

"'After waiting for half an hour the fœtus was not discharged nor brought forward ; therefore a scruple of the ergot of rye was then made into an infusion with two ounces of water, and one-third of it given as a dose ; in half an hour another one-third of it; the injections of warm water and soap being also continued. Soon after the second dose of the infusion a dead puppy was expelled ; the bitch rapidly recovered, and, with the exception of deficiency of milk, is now quite well.

"'This case would seem to prove the great power of the ergot of rye over the uterus ; but, until more experiments are made, it is necessary to be cautious in ascribing powers to medicines which have not been much tried in our practice. It is not improbable that the warm water and soap might have roused the uterus into action without the aid of the ergot ; and it is therefore necessary that those who repeat this experiment should try the effects of the medicine unaided by the auxiliary.'

"The Professor adds, that the great power which this drug is said to have on the human being, and the apparent effect in the case just given, suggest the propriety of instituting a further trial of it, and of our extending our observations to cattle, amongst which difficult cases of calving so frequently occur.

"Mr. Simpson thus concludes some remarks on ergot in difficult parturition :—'This medicine possesses a very great power over the uterus, rousing its dormant or debilitated contractility, and stimulating it to an extra performance of this necessary function after its natural energy has been in some measure destroyed by forcible but useless action. The direct utility of the ergot was manifested in cases where the uterus appeared quite exhausted by its repeated efforts ; and certainly it is but fair to ascribe the decidedly augmented power of the organ to the stimulus of the ergot, for no other means were resorted to in order to procure the desired effect. Its action, too, is prompt. Within ten minutes of the administration of a second or third dose, when nature has been nearly exhausted, the parturition has been safely effected.'

"*Puerperal Fits.*—Nature proportions the power and resources of the mother to the wants of her offspring. In her wild undomesticated state she is able to suckle her progeny to the full time ; but in the artificial state 'in which we have placed her we shorten the interval between each period of parturition, we increase the number of her young ones at each birth, we diminish her natural powers of affording them nutriment, and we give her a degree of irritability which renders her whole system liable to he excited and deranged by causes that would otherwise be harmless ; therefore it happens that when the petted bitch is permitted to suckle the whole of her litter, her supply of nutriment soon becomes exhausted, and the continued drain upon her produces a great degree of irritability. She gets rapidly thin ; she staggers, is half-unconscious, neglects her puppies, and suddenly falls into a fit of a very peculiar character. It begins with, and is sometimes confined to, the respiratory apparatus ; she lies on her side and pants violently, and the sound of her laboured breathing may be heard at a distance of twenty yards. Sometimes spasms steal over her limbs ; at other times the diaphragm and respiratory muscles alone are convulsed. In a few hours she is certainly lost ; or if there are moments of remission, they are speedily succeeded by increased heavings.

"The practitioner unaccustomed to this fearful state of excitation, and forgetful or unaware of its cause, proceeds to bleed her, and he seals her fate. Although one system is thus convulsively labouring, it is because others are suddenly and perfectly exhausted, and by abstraction of the vital current he reduces this last hold of life to the helpless condition of the rest. There is not a more common or fatal error than this.

"The veterinary practitioner is unable to apply the tepid bath to his larger patients, in order to quiet the erethism of certain parts of the system, and produce an equable diffusion of nervous influence and action ; and he often forgets it when he has it in his power to save the smaller ones. Let the bitch in a fit be put into a bath, temperature 96° of Fahrenheit, and covered with the water, her head excepted. It will be surprising to see how soon the simple application of this equable temperament will quiet down the erethism of the excited system. In ten minutes or a quarter of an hour she may be taken out of the bath evidently relieved, and then a hasty and not very accurate drying having taken place, she is wrapped in a blanket and placed in some warm situation, a good dose of physic having been previously administered. She soon breaks out in a profuse perspiration. Everything becomes gradually quiet, and she falls into a deep and long sleep, and at length awakes somewhat weak, but to a certain degree restored.

"If, then, all her puppies except one or two are taken from her, and her food is, for a day or two, somewhat restricted, and after that given again of its usual quantity and kind, she will live and do well : but a bleeding at the time of her fit, or suffering all her puppies to return to her, will inevitably destroy her.

"A bitch that was often brought to my house was suckling a litter of puppies. She was foolishly taken up and thrown into the Serpentine in the month of April. The suppression of milk was immediate and complete. There was also a determination to the head and attacks resembling epilepsy. The puppies that were suffered to remain with the mother were very soon as epileptic as she was, and were destroyed. A seton was inserted on each side of her neck. Ipecacuanha was administered, and, that having sufficiently worked, a small quantity of diluted sulphuric acid was given. A fortnight afterwards she was perfectly well.

"*Inversion of the Uterus in a Bull Bitch after Pupping. Extirpation and Cure.* By M. Cross, M. V., Milan.—'In July 1829 I was desired to attend a small bull bitch six years old, and who had had puppies four times. The uterus was completely inverted, and rested all its weight on the vaginal orifice of the urethra, preventing the discharge of the urine, and thus being the cause of great pain when the animal endeavoured to void it or the fæcal matter. The uterus was become of almost a black colour, swelled, softened, and exhaling an insupportable odour. Judging from this that the preservation of the uterus was impossible, and reckoning much on the good constitution of the patient, I warned the proprietor of the danger of its reduction, even supposing that it was practicable, and proposed to him the complete extirpation of the uterus as the only means that remained of saving the bitch.

" ' Armed with his consent, I passed a ligature round the neck of the uterus, at the bottom of the vagina, and drew it as tight as I possibly could. On the following day I again tightened the ligature, in order to complete the mortification of the part and the separation of the womb. On the third day I extirpated the womb entirely, close to the haunch. There was very slight loss of blood, but there ran from the walls of the vagina a small quantity of ichorous fluid, with a strong fœtid smell. The operation was scarcely completed ere she voided a considerable quantity of urine, and then searched about for something to eat and to drink.

" ' The portion of the uterus that was removed weighed fourteen ounces. The mucous membrane by which it was lined was in a highly disorganised state. From time to time injections of a slight infusion of aromatic plants were introduced into the vagina, and the animal was nourished with liquid food of easy digestion.

" ' The first day passed without the animal being in the slightest degree affected ; but on the following day, in despite of all our care, an ichorous fluid was discharged, which the dog would lick notwithstanding all our efforts to prevent it. The general health of the animal did not seem to be in the slightest degree affected. We continued our aromatic infusion and our regimen.

" ' On the fourth day after the operation the cords that had served as a ligature fell off, and all suppuration from the part gradually ceased.

" ' *October 20th.*—Three months have passed since the operation, and she is perfectly well.' "—*Youatt on the Dog*, pp. 225-230.

ACCIDENTS AND OPERATIONS.

Cuts, tears, and bites, unless they are very extensive, and are therefore likely to occupy a long time in healing, are better left to themselves, the dog's tongue being the best healing remedy. But when a V-shaped flap is torn down, or a very long and straight cut or tear is accidentally made, a few stitches should be put in with a proper curved needle, armed with strong thread or silk. It is only necessary to introduce the needle in two places on exactly opposite sides, and then, an assistant drawing the skin together, the ends are tied in a common knot and cut off closely. When, however, this plan is adopted a muzzle must be worn as long as the stitches are kept in, because the dog never rests satisfied till he has licked the knots open, or in some way with his teeth and tongue has got rid of them. Wounds in the dog do not heal " by the first intention," that is, in three or four days, as in man, but fill up by what is called granulation. Of course in long wounds more than one stitch is required, but as perfect union never can be effected by adhesion, the attempt to bring the edges carefully together is a failure; and, provided that anything like an approach to this is effected, all is done by a few stitches at short distances which can be desired. A bandage may be put on afterwards, and kept on for three days, after which it must be changed daily, still keeping on the muzzle. When the red granulations rise above the level of the skin, called *then* " proud flesh," a piece of blue-stone should be rubbed on them daily, or often enough to keep them down to the proper level. When below the level of the skin they never require caustic of any kind.

In any cuts about the legs or feet, the parts may be protected by collodion painted on rapidly with a camel-hair brush, and allowed to dry; but a very little friction removes it. Canada balsam, spread on white leather and warmed, will keep its place well enough to bear the rubs of a course in the greyhound, and is, I believe, the best application. A leathern boot may be made to fit the pointer's or setter's foot, or indeed that of any dog which requires protection during work. It should be made of two pieces of leather, one considerably larger than the other, and the large one set into the small with a puckered or full edge. This, when firmly tied or stitched round the ankle, just below the knee, will resist all the efforts of the dog to get it off, and may be worn without a muzzle for weeks, taking care to remove it occasionally in order to cleanse the wound. In this way I have obtained the healing of cuts in the ball of the foot in a week or two, without stopping exercise a single day, whereas without a boot the dog would have been lame, and it would take months to heal the wound without resting the dog.

Fractures may occur in any of the bones of the dog, but, excepting in the legs or ribs, little relief can be afforded by art. They are detected by the deformity which is seen in the part, an angle being presented in the interval between two joints, when occurring in the limb, and a *crepitus* or crackling being heard and felt on handling the part. When the ribs have been broken, the injury is easily detected by the depression which is felt, and the grating sound often produced in breathing. In this case a flannel bandage may be bound tightly round the chest, and the dog, after being bled, should be kept quiet and fed on low diet. A horse-girth passed twice or thrice round and buckled answers the purpose pretty well, but is not equal to a well-applied bandage. *Fractures of the limbs* may be set by extending the broken ends, and then carefully applying wooden or gutta-percha splints lined with two or three thicknesses of coarse flannel; they are bound round with tapes and tied, and kept on till the end of three weeks or a month, reapplying them if necessary. This, however, requires some practical experience to perform properly. If there is much local injury it is better to apply the splints very loosely for the first week, keeping the whole wrapped in folds of linen dipped in the lotion (53). In all cases the dog must be strictly kept to his kennel, and the limbs should not be strained by allowing him to jump up and down on a bench, a low bed being provided. In five or six weeks the thigh or hind-leg is united, and the fore-leg in three weeks or a month.

Dislocations occur in the shoulder and elbow very rarely, in the knee and toes commonly, in the hip very often, in the stifle occasionally, and in the hock very seldom, except in connection with fracture. In all cases they are detected by the deformity occurring in any of these joints, which is not capable of restoration by gentle handling, and is not accompanied by the *crepitus* which marks the fracture. *To reduce a dislocation*, two persons must lay firm hold of the two parts of the limb on each side of the injured joint, and then extending them strongly, the head of the bone in slight and recent cases will be felt to slip into the socket. It is only, however, in the knee that any inexperienced operator is likely to succeed, for in the hip, which is the most common seat of dislocation, great tact and knowledge of the anatomy of the part are required to effect a cure. Here the head of the bone may be removed from the socket in three different directions, namely, either forwards, upwards, or backwards, and the pull must be in the direction of the socket, or it will do harm rather than good. At the same time, while an assistant is making the extension, the operator himself, with his hand or a towel, lifts the thigh from the body, with the view of raising the head of the bone over the edge of the cup, into which it is his object to conduct it. Chloroform should always be given during the operation, if the attempt is not immediately successful when made directly after the accident, inasmuch as it relaxes the muscles in a remarkable manner, and enables the operator to proceed without being counteracted by

the struggles of the dog.   Dislocated toes are sometimes reduced
directly after the accident occurs, but they are very apt to return
to their deformed condition immediately, and a small splint should
be bound on at once.   In dislocations of the knee, also, a bandage
should be applied, so as to keep the joint slightly bent and prevent the foot from being put to the ground.

The *operations* which are likely to be practised on the dog are
somewhat numerous, but the only ones fit to be attempted by
any but the professed veterinarian are bleeding, the insertion of
a seton, and the closing of wounds by the ligature.

Bleeding is effected with a common lancet in the neck vein.
The hair is cut off in a small patch close to the windpipe; then,
tying a string tightly round the neck, the vein will be felt to
rise on the side next the head, and then the lancet must be introduced with some little force, cutting out again so as to make
the opening large enough *inside* to allow of the blood escaping.
When enough blood has been taken the string is taken off, a
pin is introduced through and across the lips of the wound, and
some tow or thread wound round the ends; after which the
point is cut off, and the whole is left for three or four days, when
the pin may be safely withdrawn, leaving the tow to fall off.   If
the neck is too fat, a vein on the inside of the fore-arm may be
opened.   *To insert a seton,* all that is necessary is to take any
large needle with an eye (a seton needle is made on purpose),
then, lifting up a fold of skin, a knife or lancet is passed through
it, and on its withdrawal the needle armed with the tape follows,
after which the two ends of the tape are tied with a common
knot, and in that way it is securely kept in.   In bad cases of
brain mischief, when there is a necessity for immediate relief by
counter-irritation, a small red-hot poker is passed through the
opening made by the knife before the introduction of the tape,
which need not then be covered with blistering ointment, as is
required in ordinary cases.   The closing of wonnds and the
application of the muzzle have been already described.